THE ESSENTIAL

Paul Gottfried

1984–2024

THE ESSENTIAL

Paul Gottfried

1984–2024

PASSAGE PUBLISHING

For information, contact support@passage.press.

Hardcover ISBN: 978-1-959403-63-0
eBook ISBN: 978-1-959403-64-7
Audiobook ISBN: 978-1-959403-65-4

Cover design by Wide Dog.

Library of Congress Control Number: 2025937746

Passage Publishing
Los Angeles, CA
www.passage.press

Printed in the United States of America
1 3 5 7 9 10 8 6 4 2

Table of Contents

Preface

THIS COLLECTION of my essays and commentaries is aimed primarily at younger readers. Although older readers are certainly not discouraged from opening this volume, they will not be the ones who will likely shape the future of our civilization now under attack. This work will necessarily come from the rising generation and, more specifically, from the Right broadly understood. Those with both youthful energies and the will for this work of restoration are my intended audience. Although my life's work has had little influence on today's conservative establishment, it should be of greater use to those who will be rebuilding our Right and dedicating themselves to the task of civilizational renewal.

This may be an auspicious time to present such an anthology. Our political culture is in flux, and sooner or later (it might be hoped) the teachings and admonitions in my work will find a much broader resonance than they have in the five decades in which these writings were produced. I see no need to present a justification for what is herein offered. I certainly won't offer excuses for the sharply polemical style in which I respond to critics. Nor will I excuse myself for giving offense to those who may feel offended by my sarcasm. I have paid a high price for upsetting self-designated gatekeepers; and if I continue to vex them, I'm delighted to do so.

Much of what I have written goes against the authorized views of our mainstream establishment, in which the terms "conservative" and "liberal" no longer carry substantive meaning. Those terms once had specific historical reference points, but those older associations have been abandoned by the political culture in which we now live. Once-established ideological reference points have been blurred beyond recognition, but we pretend they still mean what they no longer do.

A new opposition to the globalist Left has now arisen among populist leaders throughout the Western world, and as I write this introduction, incoming President Trump has invited to his inauguration leaders of the nationalist Right in France, Germany, and England. Trump has gone out of his way to send a message to the woke, globalist party coalitions that run Western Europe as fiefdoms by inviting members of the ostracized Right to his inauguration. This sends a signal to the power brokers that the United States no longer stands with them as tightly as it once did.

My work treats not only fascism but Marxism as spent ideologies. Most of those who today describe themselves as Marxists or socialists are advocating woke, not Marxist, politics; and among their most reliable backers are corporate capitalists including CEOs at BlackRock, Goldman Sachs, the Walt Disney Company, and Facebook. Crony capitalists who are bound at the hip with the Deep State and who spout LGBT-BLM slogans are the new face of the Left. It is hard to figure out what these capitalists have in common with past or present communist regimes or with Marx's dialectical materialism.

The woke Left, starting with the dominant political culture in the self-described liberal democracies, is not only awash in funding from capitalists rich beyond the dream of avarice. It is also a major beneficiary of public largess from the usually electorally dominant Democrats, who are the more woke of our two national parties. Green energy money and other forms of government funding go to the plutocratic benefactors of the pseudo-Marxist Left. The Democratic Party, according to the libertarian magazine *Reason*,[1] has recently bestowed on one major donor, Micron, many billions of dollars to produce semiconductors. It turns out the same corporation has more than enough financial resources on hand to fabricate the needed commodity without government funding.

In my corpus I argue that the more conservative side lost the Cold War. By the time the Soviet empire collapsed, the US and other Western countries were becoming culturally radicalized, a trend that would continue until the present time. Today's communist parties in Hungary, Russia, and elsewhere condemn gay marriage and feminism as the excesses of a decadent bourgeois society.

A traditional German Marxist, Holm Leonhardt, has tried to make some sense out of the prodigious transformation undergone by the European Left:

> The class struggle has been replaced by confessions of guilt, rituals of political correctness, and homage being paid to various

disadvantaged groups. The longer this proceeds, the more Marxism collapses, while the new morally driven progressivism gains further ground. This wokeism is becoming increasingly the dominant power factor in society and state. The only resistance is now emanating from opposition on the Right, which the new moralists condemn as Nazi.[2]

Leonhardt's assessment can be found in statements by Frances Widdowson, a Canadian Marxist professor who railed against intersectional politics once too often and who thereafter lost her position at Mount Royal University in Calgary. Capitalist-funded Political Correctness is now claiming victims on the traditional Left as well as on the Right. This doesn't mean that today's cultural Left doesn't include its share of longtime communist sympathizers. But these sympathizers have usually inclined toward whatever is associated, no matter when, with the Left. This leftist disposition, moreover, is typically fueled by a rejection of Western religious and moral norms together with a sense of social insecurity.

There are of course other reasons for this sympathy or predisposition, and I give them in my earlier writings. Communism's sympathizers in the West have often projected onto communist governments their own fantasies about a perfected society, a state of mind that Paul Hollander discusses in detail in *Political Pilgrims* (1981). In France and Italy, moreover, many in the working class following the Second World War voted for communist parties. But as I try to demonstrate in *The Strange Death of Marxism* (2005), that choice was dictated more by the ability of Communist Party leaders to deal effectively with industrial management than by any ideological engagement.

In her celebratory volume *The Romance of American Communism* (1977), Vivian Gornick explains why she and her friends fondly recall a now-defunct American Communist Party. Gornick and her ideological soulmates felt committed to the Left in a general way and therefore advocated for a variety of leftist positions, from radical feminism and intersectional politics to sympathy for the Communist Party USA. Those who share this leftist mindset typically latch on to whatever they believe will weaken or erase a social world that either distresses them or makes them feel threatened in some way.

One finds a similar personal attachment to the generic Left in former President Barack Obama, whose early exposure to communist ideas under the influence of his mentor Frank Marshall Davis may not indicate, as is sometimes believed, an unswerving loyalty to communism as a system of thought or as a historical practice. Despite the efforts of historian Paul Kengor to trace Obama's supposed Marxist engagement back to his adolescent relationship with Davis, a more complex process may have been at work here.

We are dealing in Obama's case with a biracial youth, whose African father deserted his white, hippy mother, and who was trying to confer on his splintered existence a cohesive identity. Obama ended up embracing both intersectional politics and a sense of black victimhood. Aside from his affection for certain communist dictators, like Raúl Castro, it is hard to locate a specifically Marxist core in Obama's political and biographical statements.

Far more decisive for the orientation of such representative cultural leftists has been their sense of social marginality and persistent sense of grievance. In its most self-pitying and least credible form, this attitude pervades a bitter brief by Jason Stanley, a Yale professor of anti-fascist fame. Stanley's writing intermittently descends into a rant against white Christian anti-Semitism, an evil that he finds to be ubiquitous in this country.

The author also notably identifies fascism with the rejection of the present feminist agenda, which is meant to protect us against something as dire as Hitler's Final Solution. One would be hard pressed to locate anything even vaguely Marxist in Stanley's best-selling work, *How Fascism Works: The Politics of Us and Them* (2018). This exemplary anti-fascist work is cited in my book on anti-fascism as evidence of the veritable gulf between Marxism properly understood and what I call "the post-Marxist Left."

Those who feel this revulsion for what most people once considered normal and conventional have been able to convert others to their position and sentiments. This conversionary success, which has depended on controlling "information" and determining the nature of morality, has helped the post-Marxist Left become culturally and politically dominant.

Equally relevant has been the unchanging focus on a fascist enemy that never goes away but becomes increasingly pervasive as the Left consolidates power. The fascist foe takes the form of whatever stands in the way of the further consolidation of leftist control. It is also comparable to the figure of Goldstein in George Orwell's *Nineteen Eighty-Four*, someone who represents an imaginary threat to those in power. The invocation of this supposedly recurrent danger is intended to mobilize one's forces while keeping whatever remains of an opposition fearful and subdued.

Also to be considered here is the insight of German sociobiologist Arnold Gehlen that "hypermorality," by which Gehlen designates an overly righteous state of mind leading to hatred for imagined evildoers, has created a predisposition for the cultural Left. With "hypermorality" the subject loses any sense of proportionality in dealing with what he or she regards as inexpiable injustice. In its latest manifestation, this rage over evildoers that requires immediate remedy has singled out certain blameworthy groups, particularly proudly self-identifying white men, Christians, and defenders of the Western past.

A transferred sense of Christian guilt can also be attached to woke ideology even by those who are destined for degradation. My book *Multiculturalism and the Politics of Guilt* (2002) deals with this masochistic side of the woke Left's cult of victims and victimizers and undertakes to show how a deformation of traditional Christianity has contributed to this situation. Woke ideology has only gained ground in what were once Christian societies; and this connection may not be fortuitous.

The post-Marxist Left stands apart from Marxism, to which it is often misleadingly compared, in two critical respects: One is its lack of interest in the scientific claims made by Marxists about understanding historical laws and forces; the other is the woke Left's widespread resonance in contemporary Western societies. Earlier leftist doctrines never gained the enormous appeal in Western countries that intersectional ideas and policies have now achieved. Why this has happened is a topic that I address in some of the following essays, without ever arriving at a full, and for me satisfactory, answer.

It goes without saying that many who support this state church are not particularly interested in its teachings but find it advantageous to affirm its dogmas. There is no need to imagine that Larry Fink, the CEO of BlackRock, Bob Iger, the head executive of the Walt Disney Company, or Jamie Dimon of JPMorgan Chase and the Business Roundtable agonizes over racial and gender injustices when he and fellow luminaries return to their sumptuous apartments at night or attend dinner parties with other woke capitalists.

Much of what they do to advance the Left—for example, setting up quotas for supposedly victimized minorities—is aimed at short-term financial gain. As Charles Gasparino demonstrates in *Go Woke, Go Broke* (2024), there is a certain business logic, particularly in dealing with the government, in what woke capitalists do to advance wokeness, even though their actions may ultimately drive away clients. And there's no reason to assume that other groups—such as non-Christians, non-whites, or non-heterosexuals—share the woke guilt feelings that I explore in my book *Multiculturalism and the Politics of Guilt*. Their interest lies in making others feel guilty, a situation from which outgroups imagine themselves to be benefiting emotionally and often materially.

We might also consider that humans, being conformist by nature, and, as Hobbes pointed out, fearing above everything else violent death, will be driven to conform their actions and speech to public orthodoxies. Even if they don't believe inwardly what are publicly proclaimed intersectional teachings, they will give lip service to them to avoid personal harm.

This doesn't mean that public orthodoxies have no effect on those who are being hit over the head with them day and night. They can command belief if they are repeated often enough by those in high places. Moreover, the fact that people vote for those who explicitly advance intersectional teachings and favor educational institutions that inculcate them suggests that citizens do not view themselves embracing intersectionality as something alien to their convictions.

About half of American voters seem delighted to vote for candidates who emphatically support wokeness as a government policy. They long ago stopped cringing at such measures as providing sex change operations for illegals and allowing murderers on death row to vote in elections. Efforts to attribute such attitudes to the malign presence of Donald J. Trump on the political scene involve prodigious exaggeration. Most of our blue states support woke politics with or without Trump on the ballot; and surveys on changing American moral positions conducted by Gallup and other reliable pollsters indicate a dramatic turn toward the social and cultural Left in most age categories over the last thirty years.

Additionally, some of my critics have misinterpreted my statements about fascism as belonging to the past. In fact, fascism is not unique in being a time-bound movement. Not only fascism but also liberalism and conservatism may have outlived their relevance for defining today's political identities. A combination of historical ignorance, a penchant for quaint political labeling, and the continuing effectiveness of customary name-calling have all contributed to this continued use of outmoded terms.

Above all, there seems to be an unwillingness to recognize how radically different our present culture and politics have become from those of the past, with which they show less and less continuity. Trying to hide this difference by attaching archaic labels to current movements and persuasions seems to me less and less credible.

Clearly the positions I've taken as a scholar and commentator on current events have deeply upset the conservative establishment, which for many decades has worked to keep me out of their discussions. For at least a decade, I wrote for nonconservative publications and in some cases for magazines associated with the Left. Explicitly conservative presses refused to publish my books, which fortunately came out with leading academic ones. I also had to bear the indignity of establishment conservatives contacting presses and universities that were considering me for publication or positions and speaking ill of my person. The diatribe published against me by Jacob Siegel, editor of *Tablet*, is a relatively recent effort by the same establishment to hurt me professionally. Although perhaps the most detailed invective against me from an authorized conservative source, it is hardly exceptional in its tone.

My labeling practices, however, began decades before I incurred such hostility and was influenced by experiences going back more than sixty years. Already as a graduate student at Yale University in the mid-1960s, I was turned off by progressive professors who habitually denounced what they disliked as "reactionary" or "authoritarian." It seemed entirely possible, or so I already realized, for people in the past to have held views that my professors found unappealing without having been precursors of Hitler.

The same preceptors, nonetheless, attributed all kinds of ominous mischief to those who didn't fit their ideological grid. William M. McGovern's *From Luther to Hitler* (1941) was by no means a caricature of the narrative to which I was exposed by my teachers and classmates in explaining "the German catastrophe." Even then, however, I was annoyed by sweeping historical explanations driven by moral indignation or partisan distortions. Contingencies, unexpected disasters or good fortune, and even Hegel's "cunning of reason," by which private passions result in seemingly providential turning points, all play critical roles in human history. Producing morality plays, which allow the historian to play hanging judge over the past, are no substitute for investigating intricate developmental patterns.

More recently I have criticized representatives of the Catholic Right, who like to imagine that the Protestant Reformation led in some labyrinthine way to the present woke Left. Although those who express such a view are certainly not my personal enemies, I find their *idée fixe* to be every bit as questionable as the pet obsessions of my graduate professors or neoconservative adversaries in the 1980s. It is one thing if the philosopher Martin Heidegger maintained that the teachings of Socrates derailed the future course of Western philosophy. But it's another matter if someone tells me that Luther's questioning of the Doctrine of Purgatory led, however tortuously, to government funding for sex change operations. There is a difference between making a heuristic point as a philosopher and inventing far-fetched historical links.

I certainly won't deny that I've baited my adversaries when I've raised awkward questions about historical causation. For example, why is it impermissible to draw a political or social connection between the American civil rights revolution in the 1960s and what that movement later became? One finds many of the same activists and political demands coming from civil rights spokesmen for decades. Moreover, the activism of this movement extended its focus from blacks to women and then sexual revolutionaries; and the span of years this moral crusade went on coincided with an increasing government commitment to fighting "discrimination" in all aspects of human existence.

Clearly the civil rights movement reveals more internal unity than, say, the relationship between the German Second Empire and Nazi Germany, although droves of Boomer conservatives would dispute that point with varying degrees of ignorance. Those who were raised during the civil rights era are eager to convince us of their anti-racism; at the same time, some of the same people may harbor reservations about where the civil rights movement eventually led. They therefore praise an "original" movement that we are told culminated in the 1960s. Afterward that movement allegedly changed in such a way that it is no longer recognizable as what it once was.

Those who make these distinctions, however, are left with the problem of explaining why one phase of what looks like a process moves into another one, with most of the same players and with most of the same media advocates and administrative agencies participating. Are we really speaking about movements that are unrelated but which occur successively in time?

For example, contrary to what those who accept this thesis would argue, Martin Luther King, who now symbolizes for Republicans the "good" civil rights movement, did support quotas for blacks, and according to his sympathetic but honest biographer, David Garrow, King already took that then controversial position by the 1950s. One can also find speeches and interviews the civil rights leader gave that closely resemble the rhetoric of the radicalized civil rights movement after his death. Further, one finds support for each succeeding initiative of our anti-discrimination regime from those who were involved in earlier stages of this process. The aging militants did not abandon their "struggle" because it took more radical turns.

When it comes to the Germans, however, the search for continuity is treated quite differently. Having absorbed some of the questionable assumptions of the Second World War era, Boomers tend to always see more of the same in the German past. Luther, Bismarck, Kaiser Wilhelm were all the precursors of what happened after 1933. Those who have discussed these matters with me have predictably insisted that Nazism was the inevitable outcome of a multitude of developments that unfolded in German political history up to that point. One "turning point" inescapably led to another, even though Hitler's taking of power was made possible by a number of unhappy accidents that resulted from a particular crisis. Trying to refute those who push this kind of position, I learned, will get you nowhere.

I am always willing (do I have an alternative?) to allow those who think differently from me to express and defend their views. What I do protest is the censoring engaged in by those who claim to be upholding open inquiry. In the last few decades, the conservative establishment has taken over and enforced many of the same taboos as the woke Left. This establishment has engendered a veritable host of gatekeepers who call out others identified with the Right for insensitivity toward one or more of the Left's protected groups. Quite hypocritically the same establishment has attacked the Left for doing exactly what it does.

It is my hope that a younger generation on the intellectual Right will totally reject this practice and defend bold thinking even on the Right. It seems that a younger generation may be up to that task, since from all appearances it has not been suborned by the usual suspects. Our "conservative" gatekeepers remind me of the kept opposition that developed in former Eastern European communist countries. Such "moderate" critics displayed their cooperative spirit by reporting to the regime on the verbal slips of their uncooperative colleagues. Some of our "conservatives" conveniently slip into similar rhetorical tropes as they implausibly tell us that they're just trying to protect their side against "extremists."

Let me confess my irremediable habit of investigating to the discomfort of others the historical context out of which political terminology came. Several of my books, as well as essays included in this anthology, undertake such inquiries. While I treat terms like "conservative" and "liberal" as time-bound and belonging to the nineteenth century, I also stress the continued value of drawing Right/Left distinctions. Contrary to the notion of some French and Spanish traditionalist scholars who maintain that we're living in the "twilight of ideologies," I contend that "Right" and "Left" transcend temporally such now-outdated usages as "conservative" and "liberal." Distinctions between "Right" and "Left" go back at least to the time of the French Revolution and refer to opposed worldviews and political positions that became crystalized by the late eighteenth century.

The point of my exercise is not to furnish talking points for either Republican or Democratic TV networks. It is to underline a longtime polarity that in my view has outlasted other political distinctions. While the Right accentuates particularity and the legitimacy of inherited hierarchy, the Left prioritizes universality and the equalization or homogenization of humanity. A secondary distinction between the two ideological poles is that the Right, unlike the Left, is necessarily reactive. The Right organizes itself after having been challenged by its antagonist; and it becomes increasingly aware of its beliefs while reacting. Unlike the Left, which begins with a project, the Right is pushed into taking up one defensively.

This, mind you, is not a moral judgment but a statement about differences. I arrived at this perspective through both historical observation and the insights of others. My sources for this discovery would include, among many others, Leo Strauss's preface to *Liberalism Ancient and Modern* (1968), Karl Mannheim's writings on conservative thought, and trenchant studies on conservatism, liberalism, and the present Left by the Greek-German political theorist Panajotis Kondylis (with whom I exchanged German notes before his sudden passing in 1998).

While the heavily funded American conservative establishment has been, in my view, little more than a moderate version of the woke Left, a vigorous American Right has taken form with the fading of the Boomer generation. This younger Right holds no brief for governmental efforts to fight discrimination or for anything that reeks of social engineering. Members of this group are also revolting against the campaign being waged by the government, educational institutions, and the mainstream media (MSM) to obliterate what were once accepted social and gender distinctions.

This emerging Right has also not held back in challenging "abstract universals," like democracy and human rights. In such spirited questioning, this Right has gone well beyond what the present, accommodationist conservative movement would consider allowable opposition. The Right to which we're referring obviously differs from the restorationist conservatism of an earlier age. It emerged in the twenty-first century, not the early nineteenth. All the same, it does represent a genuine, unequivocal reaction to the modern Left, and it offers a more decisive reaction to its polar opposite than the movement it's working to replace.

Clearly this challenge has evoked angry responses from the opposite shore. In John Ganz's *When the Clock Broke* (2024) and in Shane Burley's website invectives against my disguised "fascist" message, one finds torrential reactions to an opposition that can no longer be managed.

Such commentators lament the advent of a more uninhibited Right than the one they've grown accustomed to opposing; and it has been gathering steam since the 1990s.

There is undoubtedly some truth in these proliferating diatribes. Defenders of the woke Left are noticing a post-Boomer Right, which looks quite different from its less combative predecessor. Much of this difference may be generational. The more essentialist Right has given up looking for common ground with the Left, and it has noticed how little the previous generation gained through piecemeal capitulation. Patrick Casey, a contributor to *Chronicles* magazine, summed up a common view among this younger generation when he explains:

> The history of conservatism is one of toothless opposition to whatever form of anti-civilizational insanity the Left happens to be promoting at a particular point in time. Established figures on the Right, be they politicians or pundits, are wont to publicly denounce the Left, only to later capitulate to, or adopt outright, the other side's positions.

From this selection of my essays and reviews published over a period of more than fifty years, it should be obvious that I've written on topics other than contextualizing political labels and defining Right and Left. I've also dealt with my favorite biblical verses, Aristotle, Xenophon, Polybius, and Thucydides, and other ancient thinkers whom I spent years reading in Greek, as a leisure activity and for edification. I might be one of the few historians of ideas and political movements generally identified with the Right (Robert Nisbet was another) who can appreciate almost equally the insights of Marx, Gramsci, Burke, Bonald, Maistre, and Donoso Cortés.

What is harder for me to comprehend is what is going on right now. I feel quite at home in the nineteenth century but am puzzled by what I observe in the present age. This profound discomfort has not kept me, however, from trying to understand what admittedly repels me. Looking at it critically brings its own rewards, even if one feels helpless before political and cultural forces that one cannot begin to control.

CHAPTER ONE

Fascism

– ◆ ◆ ◆ –

Fascism and
Anti-Fascism

Chronicles

MARCH 1, 1998

F OR THE last several months, a war crimes trial has been unfolding in Bordeaux in Southwest France. The defendant, Maurice Papon, an octogenarian on the verge of cardiac arrest, was the subprefect of the Gironde during the Vichy regime. At that time Papon and his superior, Maurice Sabatier, oversaw the deportation of thousands of Jews destined for concentration camps and often eventual extermination. The trial of Papon is being used to underscore French complicity in the Holocaust, and, as *L'Express* (November 26, 1997) observes, most of the prosecution's case has consisted of "*discours solennels*" instead of rigorously presented evidence.[3] The trial was originally planned to deal with the misdeeds of Papon's boss, but since Sabatier inconsiderately departed this world before the proceedings began, the prosecution has had to refocus.

But the gloomy sermons are far more central to the trial, as object lesson, than some legal critics recognize. These orations are meant to drive home what the French and American media industry do not want Frenchmen (and other vestigially Christian peoples) to forget, that their societies had eagerly collaborated in Nazi atrocities and that their inher-

3

ited cultures had predisposed them to such behavior. Though this complicity was admittedly more common in France than it should have been, the charges made are all too often questionable. One, featured in the movie *Le Chagrin et la Pitié* (1969), is that religiously indoctrinated Frenchmen ran to welcome the German armies that overran their country in 1940, as a bulwark being offered against Jews and communists. On the basis of highly selective sources, such as the pro-Nazi statements of the rector of the Catholic Institute in Paris, we are led to believe that professing French Christians happily supported Hitler's occupation and the deportation of Jews. But French Calvinists, almost without exception, protected Jews, invariably at the risk of their lives. And though the Catholic record was, on the whole, less impressive, monasteries and convents throughout France took in Jewish refugees. One beneficiary of such kindness is the present French primate, whose parents had been Polish Jewish immigrants.

Another faulty generalization is that most of France's intelligentsia were well-disposed toward Nazism. Here a distinction is appropriate that may also apply to other European intellectuals of the same period, between those who (like Louis-Ferdinand Céline) applauded the Nazi regime in all its grisliness and those who merely went along. It is the latter who were in the vast majority, certainly in France, and who form the subject of Jean-Robert and Gilles Ragache's probing study, *Des écrivains des artistes sous l'occupation 1940–1944* (1988).[4] Unlike such proudly collaborationist authors as Céline, Robert Brasillach, and Pierre Drieu La Rochelle, most intellectuals—for example, Jean-Paul Sartre, Simone de Beauvoir, André Gide, and (throughout most of the Occupation) André Malraux—tried to stay out of harm's way. This also applied to the Russian Jewish artist Marc Chagall, then resident in the French village of Gordes. The Ragaches studiously avoid confusing plainly different actions—such as cheering on the Nazis, keeping a low profile, or expressing generic pro-fascist sentiments—and turning Jews over to the Waffen-SS.

There is, of course, a compelling reason why most Frenchmen no longer ask who did or did not collaborate, and in what way, with the Vichy government. From June 1944 until months after the war ended, French communists (who ironically had been among the most conspicuous Nazi collaborators until Hitler's invasion of the Soviet Union) led the way in meting out rough justice to "collabos" in areas freed of German control. During this "épuration" thousands lost their lives, and many more suffered public humiliation, like being beaten and spat upon or, in the case of women thought to be fraternizing with the enemy, having their heads shaved. Similar ghastly displays occurred in Italy, particularly in liberated Rome in June 1944; a feature story in *Corriere della Sera* in April 1995 describes one such anti-fascist bloodletting.[5] This stage engulfed the innocent and not very guilty as well as those who may have aided the occupying German Army, and it was carried out against hundreds of Italians with the connivance of the Committee of National Liberation, which was in charge of organizing the post-fascist government. Even more ominously, millions of Eastern Europeans were killed, imprisoned, or deported between 1945 and 1948, as Stalin tightened his grip on the region in the name of "anti-fascism." In view of the ugly, bloody history attached to digging up and concocting pro-fascist dossiers, it is understandable that the French were long reluctant to renew the post-liberation witch hunt of 1944–45.

In interwar Europe, fascist and quasi-fascist movements flourished, a situation that has attracted considerable scholarly attention. Historians have debated the differences and overlaps among fascist groups: whether, for example, the German Nazis, who claimed some affinity with European fascism, were representative fascists, or whether the Nazis were more like Stalinist totalitarians, as suggested by George Watson, Robert Conquest, and Stanley Payne. Latin fascists like José Antonio Primo de Rivera and Giuseppe Bottai did not have either the totalitarian agenda or the anti-Semitic fixation of Hitler and his lieutenants. Those fascists spoke for national revolutionary movements that left their mark on non-Latins as well: both black nationalist Marcus Garvey and revisionist Zionist Zev Jabotinsky were strongly drawn to the Italian national revolution, identified with Mussolini. Well into the 1930s (Renzo De Felice has shown in his dissertation), the Zionist Right both expressed admiration for and sought favor with the Duce. He, in turn, granted Jabotinsky's followers the right to build a navy at Genoa for a future Jewish state.

Israeli francophone historian Zeev Sternhell has written copiously on the background of the Latin fascism that came of age in the 1920s. Looking at the "founding generation" of thinkers and activists concerned with bourgeois decadence and the irrational sources of power and social actions, Sternhell traces back to the late nineteenth century a revolutionary force that was "neither Left nor Right" in any traditional sense. It also combined varying degrees of economic collectivism with a belief in hierarchy and a vivid sense of the national past.

Unlike Sternhell, German intellectual historian Ernst Nolte downplays the anti-bourgeois aspect of fascist movements. Rather, he focuses on their role as a bulwark of bourgeois civilization in the face of the social ferment following World War I. For all their invective against the liberal capitalist order, insists Nolte, fascists were essentially bourgeois opponents of the revolutionary Left. The movements they created were "counterrevolutionary imitations of Bolshevism" that drew their ideals from a folkish past.

While Nolte may indeed understate the revolutionary thrust of some interwar fascist movements, he is correct to stress their bourgeois component. Fascist leaders and thinkers were recruited from the business and professional classes, and Italian bourgeois liberals such as Vilfredo Pareto, Luigi Einaudi, and Gino Olivetti generally gave Mussolini the benefit of the doubt, at least in the 1920s. The major proto-fascist movement in early twentieth-century France, Action Française, numbered many professionals, particularly physicians, in its ranks. And faced by a choice between restive socialists and clerical fascists in Austria in the 1930s, classical liberal economist Ludwig von Mises quickly made his peace with the clericalist imitator of Italian fascism, Engelbert Dollfuss.

Despite this bourgeois and occasionally reactionary direction taken by interwar fascism, its reforming image also appealed to some on the Left. Most significantly, American advocates of an expanded welfare state followed English and French socialists in holding up Mussolini's Italy as a political model. In the 1920s, the *New Republic* published essay after essay by, among other contributors, Horace Kallen and Herbert Croly, praising Mussolini's socialist zeal.[6] *Mussolini and Fascism: The View from America* (1972) by John P. Diggins treats this love affair that large parts of the American Left had with fascism, seen as an anti-capitalist, revolutionary force and as a nationalist variation on Marxist-Leninism.[7]

This romance, however, was supplanted by an implacable hate, that has characterized the Left's relation to fascism ever since. While there certainly are explanations for this hate, including the reasons most often given—that all fascism came to be identified, rightly or wrongly, with Nazism, which produced the Holocaust—the standard explanation is not entirely convincing. Mass murder is not a moral problem for much of the Left. When the communists undertook this experiment in Russia and Maoist China, journalists and academics tried to look the other way. Afterward, they urged (and continue to urge) "healing" in dealing with communist killers and their accomplices, in order that we might get on with the unfinished business of atoning for right-wing oppression. Such ideologues here and in Europe do not wish to be diverted by the fact of communist genocide from dealing with the apparently real enemy: anyone thought to have been actively as well as passively implicated in fascist crimes. It is therefore not even worthy of note that at the end of

World War II, Truman, Churchill, and Anthony Eden all collaborated in returning hundreds of thousands of Eastern Europeans to Stalin's rule and certain death, in Operation Keelhaul. Such behavior, which barely amounts to a footnote in most histories of the war, would seem to make the alleged crimes of Subprefect Papon pale by comparison.

It is no longer clear what fascism was or is, save for an extension of Hitlerism into the present. This extended Hitlerism is imagined to be behind every political or religious movement that is guilty of political incorrectness, from anti-immigrationists to homeschoolers and evangelical Christians. Meanwhile, the Holocaust, as depicted in *The New York Times* and *Le Monde*, has been revised to exaggerate the sufferings of homosexuals (fewer than five thousand died directly or indirectly owing to Nazi mistreatment) and to include the entirely fictitious afflictions of lesbians. This is consistent with revised definitions of fascism that make it synonymous with homophobia, sexism, and general insensitivity. As a proclaimed effort to combat such insensitivity and to expiate the national party, the German Bundestag has decided to have two separate monuments erected to homosexual and lesbian victims of the Nazi regime.

In the language of Critical Theory, "fascism" and "anti-fascism" have been instrumentalized. From being a failed model of political management tied to a project of cultural and national regeneration, fascism has evolved into a codeword for genocide associated with insensitive attitudes. The semantic denaturing of the terms in question was already underway by 1950, when volumes of *The Authoritarian Personality*, a study of fascist attitudes and their relation to anti-Semitism, began to appear under the aegis of the American Jewish Committee.[8] All the contributors—among them Seymour Martin Lipset, Max Horkheimer, Else Frenkel-Brunswik, Theodor Adorno, and Paul Lazarsfeld—believed that any departure from their socialist, secularist, and gender-egalitarian outlook betrayed fascist and possibly Nazi sentiments. The "pseudo-democratic" populist danger evoked in this work has now been updated to include such telltale fascist signs as favoring restrictions on immigration and being uncomfortable at the sight of gays fondling each other in public.

"Fascist" is also now exempt from the Aristotelian principle of noncontradiction. As seen in *Le Monde*'s attacks on the National Front, fascism, like liberalism, can be used in ways that contradict a once-settled meaning. While granting the prevalence of Thomas Fleming's mock equation—that European populism equals fascism which equals Hitler which equals Auschwitz—one might still expect some to remember that the Nazis were engaged in far-reaching territorial conquests, not in restricting immigration or in fighting for local democratic autonomy. Are we supposed to believe that *Leghisti* or *lepénistes* are incipient Nazis because they complain about the growth of the welfare state or are unwilling to expand their societies to include culturally alien immigrants?

Although these populists may be provincial or insufficiently cosmopolitan, theirs is not the evil that produced a murderous Nazi empire embracing the European continent. Such decontextualization, encountered daily in journalistic descriptions of "the new fascist threat," makes one wonder whether the slanderers have any idea of the expansionist dynamic embodied by the Third Reich or of the fascist corporatist welfare state vision. Remember the illiterate insolence of Charles Krauthammer, who in March 1992 decried Patrick Buchanan as a Hitlerite? Krauthammer pronounced the "N" word after learning that Buchanan opposed free trade and had a father who admired Francisco Franco. Such malicious pseudo-reasoning abounds in the verbal industries, which makes it unlikely that lying about fascism will soon end.

The Myth of "Red Fascism"

Chronicles

AUGUST 2000

I N A recent discussion with a younger colleague about his book-in-progress on American historian Richard Hofstadter, I learned that, during the student riot at Columbia in 1968, Hofstadter repeatedly likened student radicals to European "fascists." My colleague found this remarkable, given the fact that Hofstadter had spent decades agonizing over the "paranoid style" of the American nativist Right.[9] For Hofstadter and others of like mind, however, the campus radicals were not progressive reformers but haters of "liberal democracy." Some of them, in deference to black nationalists, took a pro-Arab, anti-Israel stand; and this confirmed for Cold War liberals (soon to become neoconservatives) that their enemies—apparently on the Left—were actually throwbacks to the interwar Right.

This political geography went as far back as the "red fascist" images popularized by Truman and other Democrats during the early years of the Cold War. In order to smooth the transition from battling international fascism to resisting international communism, it was useful to blur the distinction between the two. Both were portrayed as faces of the same totalitarian foe; and though Stalinoid European refugees presented the "authoritarian personality" as an exclusively right-wing pathology, it was easily coopted as a Cold War liberal weapon. By the early 1950s, Seymour Martin Lipset was speaking of fascist personality development in Marxist-Leninists. Some historians, most famously A. James Gregor, tried to make the comparison from the opposite direction, though (for obvious reasons) with less acclaim. In an ambitious work on Italian fascism, Gregor, by picking his evidence selectively, made it appear that fascists were on the anti-democratic Left.

Although not everyone who drew such comparisons was on the same wavelength (one thinks especially of the late Erik von Kuehnelt-Leddihn), most exponents of "red fascism" and its thematic permutations belonged to the same club. The postwar center-left found it comforting to believe that everyone opposed to "liberal democracy" (particularly in its New Deal American form) was a "totalitarian" or an "authoritarian" in need of coercive reeducation. This is the recurrent theme of Arthur Schlesinger's *The Vital Center* (1949), Lipset's *Political Man* (1959), and other products of the Cold War liberal imagination that flourished between the late 1940s and mid-1960s. Its supreme illustration, though persistently misrepresented as a "conservative classic," is Allan Bloom's *The Closing of the American Mind* (1987).[10] In this best-selling tirade against Germans, postmodernists, hippies, and popular music, Bloom reprises the *idée fixe* of Cold War liberals: that what appears to be an unkempt, malodorous, and riotous enemy on the Left can be traced back to the anti-American, European, and especially German Right. It was nice for a certified member of the postwar democratic Left to think that he did not have to change his enemies as the Cold War heated up, or as campuses were occupied and littered by self-described Maoists in the late 1960s and by hirsute women burning their bras in the 1970s. Unacceptable leftists could be packed into the far right or introduced as anti-democratic Teutons in drag.

The argument that the New Left had something to do with fascism is absurd. The New Left was far too tame to resemble the Nazis or communist thugs who destroyed the Weimar Republic and routinely murdered people in the process. In terms of violence and anti-Semitism, the New Left fell ridiculously below the standards of savagery of the Nazis, even before they came to power. The comparison of strident hippies to Latin fascists is equally far-fetched, but for opposite reasons. The intellectual fathers of European fascism, in contrast to Angela Davis, Fidel Castro, and Frantz Fanon, were eminently civilized gentlemen, including figures such as Giovanni Gentile, Vilfredo Pareto, Maurice Barrès, and José Antonio Primo de Rivera. The founding generation of this movement had no desire to tear down either civilization or sexual mores. What concerned them was the explosiveness of the Left and the fear that bourgeois society was too decadent to protect the world it had built or inherited. To the extent that fascists began to imitate the opposite side, they did so largely to forestall it. Thus they produced, in the memorable phrase of Ernst Nolte, "a counterrevolutionary imitation" of the revolutionary Left.

It is true that serious thinkers and social critics could be found temporarily connected with the New Left—for example, Eugene Genovese, Paul Piccone, and Christopher Lasch. But these associations proved brittle, and thoughtful fellow travelers fled the movement with varying degrees of disgust. The reasons are clearly put in Stanley Rothman and S. Robert Lichter's *Roots of Radicalism* (1982) and in Genovese's colorful commentaries.[11] Both provide pictures of sexually disordered, often lewd exhibitionists full of uncontrolled rage against authority figures, starting with their parents. Rothman offers further insights into New Left anger by contrasting Jewish and Christian radicals and explaining why the former were more prone to sexual exhibition and the latter to random violence. My own memory attests that we cannot exaggerate the intellectual and social vulgarity of these radicalized louts. Indeed, fairness requires that any comparisons between them and the fascists favor the *squadristi* who marched on Rome in October 1922.

Moreover, the two movements had dramatically different fates. While in the 1920s and early 1930s Western progressives and Catholic corporatists found elements of Italian fascism worth exporting, and labor legislation under Herbert Hoover and FDR looks like it was drafted by the *Confederazione Nazionale Sindacati Fascisti*, by the 1940s the fascist movement had collapsed. It had been vulgarized in Spain by Franco and identified with murderous imperialism through its selective absorption by the Third Reich. Fascism today lives on only as a hate word, invoked by the media against anyone or anything that fails to comply with its ever more stringent standards of political correctness, from Pat Buchanan to European critics of immigration.

The New Left, by contrast, has made out well. While New Leftists had once rapped about the evil of impersonal bureaucratic structures, they were happy to leave that particular concern to others, such as the denizens of right-wing fever swamps, once they became part of the "system." They became the shock troops and cheering gallery of the therapeutic state. Compared to the New Left's policy efforts on behalf of alternative lifestyles and marginalized minorities, the social changes wrought by the Italian fascists were minimal. The *Carta del Lavoro* brought before the Fascist *Gran Consiglio* in 1927 by the "anti-bourgeois" Minister of Labor Giuseppe Bottai did not even begin to create the proclaimed national workers' revolution. The *Carta* was watered down to a pale forerunner of the New Deal, and its fate illustrates the fascist reluctance to tamper with bourgeois society: Don't look to Italian family heads to turn the social order inside out! Only the Nazis could approach the nihilistic mentality of our own political class.

Despite its fire-eating rhetoric, early fascism, which was almost exclusively Latin or Latin-derivative, left the surrounding society largely intact. This was not only due to its counterrevolutionary aspect, but because of where it took root. Latin Catholic cultures were far less open to restructuring than Germanic Protestant ones. The human landscape was too cluttered, especially by a well-organized Church and tight-knit families, to favor a central state or a revolutionary ideology demanding absolute power. Atomized societies that stress individual gratification are more promising terrain for such an enterprise. For these reasons, Latin fascism turned out to be a highly ornate but rudimentary instrument of managerial control. Listening recently to one of the younger neocons, who was up in arms against the "fascist impulse" in literary modernism, I was reminded of Bill Clinton celebrating our victory over "the tyranny of George the Third." Note what Jesus said on the subject of motes and beams!

Who's a Fascist?

The American Conservative

JUNE 6, 2012

HAVING BEEN at work on a book dealing with changing definitions of the "f-word," meaning in this case not the one-time obscenity but the ultimate evil in the world of political correctness, I find my comments on the subject[12] have caused considerable irritation. Although I once assumed that only the conventional Left was fixated on fascist dangers, I now know the fascist specter is scaring libertarians as well. My statements that fascism must be understood in an interwar European context, that it was a reaction from the Right against the threat of communist and other leftist revolutionary upheavals, that garden-variety fascism—for example, as practiced through the first fourteen years of Mussolini's rule in Italy—was neither really socialist nor totalitarian, have all elicited angry comments from libertarian bloggers.

Like the more conventional leftists, these libertarians seem grossly ignorant of twentieth-century history. Right and Left for my critics are what they are thought to be in the US at this moment. The two reference points have always been the same, and for the Right the eternal battle has been about fighting the "state," which has been around since the time the pyramids were built. Those who have advanced state power have always been immutably on the Left; and presumably the Left includes Amenhotep, Henry VIII, Cardinal Richelieu, and Bismarck, just as the Right has always featured such stalwart conservatives as Thomas Paine and John Stuart Mill.

One hostile blogger was concerned that I couldn't see this simple truth because I was "so blinded by [my] hatred for NRO." This obviously referred to my amusement at how the one-time editor of National Review Online had tried to link[13] Hillary Clinton and Barack Obama to the politics of both Italian fascism and German Nazism. Apparently all defenders of the welfare state were or are fascists and somehow implicated in Hitler's crimes. For partisan reasons, Republicans on this telling are spared association with the f-word, even when implicated in the same welfare politics.

I was amused to see an essay on fascism by the Canadian William Gairdner[14] in *The New Criterion* (October 2012) that resuscitates one of Jonah Goldberg's assertions, that the multicultural Left, by supporting minority set asides, is moving along the path of interwar fascism. Like Goldberg and like my hostile bloggers, Gairdner makes "fascism" fit anything he doesn't happen to like. Thus the f-word is stretched to apply to such nuisances as Arab youth rioting in suburban Paris and gender studies at American universities.

Not to dwell overly long on my latest contact with partisan dishonesty and historical ignorance, let me state the following about fascism as a historical phenomenon. Already in 1946 George Orwell, who was definitely a man of the Left, noticed that after the Second World War "everyone in England is calling what he doesn't like fascist."[15] Note Orwell was making this critical observation well before the 1960s, when the rise of the New Left and the emergence of Holocaust studies (which often equates all fascism with Hitler and the Final Solution) turned the f-word into the world's greatest and most insidious evil.

Moreover, the anti–New Deal Right in the United States had added to the semantic and conceptual confusion by equating the New Deal with fascism. In this case, however, there was some justification. FDR and his adviser Rexford Tugwell both expressed admiration for Mussolini's economic reforms in Italy, the extent of which, however, they vastly exaggerated.

Viewed contextually (which according to the historian Herbert Butterfield and Butterfield's biographer Kenneth McIntyre is the way historians should be practicing their craft), fascism was a movement that prospered on the European continent between the two world wars. It was an imitation of the Left that tried to pull along the working class, but it depended mostly on bourgeois support. Its economics were corporatist in theory but in practice usually left most of the economy in private hands. Unlike the Left, fascists believed in hierarchy and in the organization of the nation along organic and vocational lines. But these preferences led only to minimal change in the social structure, and except for their style and fondness for pageantry, it is hard to distinguish some fascist or quasi-fascist regimes from traditional authoritarian ones.

The regime of the Spanish Nationalist leader Francisco Franco was for the most part a military dictatorship that turned into a caretaker government practicing economic modernization. But Franco tried to integrate into his coalition the fascist Falange organization, which had helped him defeat the Left in the Spanish Civil War. And so he adopted some of the trappings and personnel of the Falangists, before unceremoniously dropping both after the Second World War.

In Austria, the anti-Marxist and anti-Nazi regime of the "clerical fascist" Engelbert Dollfuss in the early 1930s glued onto a Catholic–bourgeois ruling coalition some of the rituals and rhetoric of his friend Mussolini, who for several years was Dollfuss's protector against Hitler. The "Austro-fascist" experiment began to unravel when the Nazis killed Dollfuss in 1934, when Mussolini changed sides in 1936, and when Hitler occupied Austria in 1938.

Although the fascists were not "conservative" in any traditional sense, they were probably more so than my libertarian critics. In interwar Europe, being "conservative" did not mean "being for markets," legalizing addictive drugs, or distributing anarcho-capitalist leaflets. It meant favoring a traditional state that accepted a traditional social order and which was usually tied to an established church. In that bygone world my libertarian bloggers would have been considered hopelessly demented leftists. Although fascists were not particularly agreeable to traditional conservatives, philosophical libertarians would have been even less popular in these circles. European liberals may have been closer to the anarcho-capitalist mentality, but only slightly. Unlike our libertarians, old-fashioned liberals held Victorian social and moral views and were highly suspicious of democracy.

Being a broad-minded reactionary, I would allow for a broad understanding of the Right as a counterforce to the Left depending on how the two terms are understood at a particular time and in a particular place. In the present American context, being an advocate of minimal government means opposing leftist public administration and its multicultural and leveling policies. Libertarianism, viewed from this situational perspective, is a reactionary position, just as opposing communist subversives was in Europe after the Bolshevik Revolution. The Right has a functional identity, in the sense that it stands athwart the Left and tries to limit its destructive power. That is what defines the Right operationally, certainly not faith in representative democracy or a belief that each person should be able to do his own thing. Although one may personally like those positions, they are only accidentally right-wing.

Who Isn't Fascist?

The American Conservative

APRIL 14, 2015

H AVING RECENTLY completed a book on fascism, the career of a concept, it seems that all my efforts to lessen the abuse of my key term may go for naught. Fascism will likely live on, not as a resurgent interwar European movement but as a freely bandied about epithet that can be applied to whatever journalists don't like. The unsuspecting reader of our partisan media will go on being made to believe that fascists are one or more of the following villains: anti-American jihadists, outspoken opponents of immigration here and in Western Europe, Democratic presidential candidates, Israeli soldiers, homophobic Christians, foreign-policy isolationists, or the nationalist governments of Viktor Orbán in Hungary and Vladimir Putin in Russia. This "fascist" list continues to grow—a comprehensive one would be at least twice as long.

Almost all attempts to apply "fascist" as a dirty word entail comparisons that have little or no historical basis but evoke all too predictable responses. Put most simply, we are made to think "fascism equals Hitler." By associating what the speaker doesn't like with the f-word or by making this association by indirection, one links the hated object of one's attack to Nazi genocide. In his book *Liberal Fascism* (2008), Jonah Goldberg does not even rely on this implicit equation of bad guys with Nazis.[16] He just plunges ahead and makes the *argumentum ad Hitlerum* when he compares Hillary Clinton's economic planning to the policies of Hitler and the Nazi Minister of Labor Robert Ley. We are thereby made to believe that the Democratic Party has turned Hitlerian, and any fool knows what that means.

Someone who should know better than to abuse the term, the Israeli Francophone historian Zeev Sternhell, is undoubtedly the world's greatest authority on French fascism. In an interview with *Haaretz* last August, Sternhell lashed out against the Israeli bombing of Gaza, which he compared to the behavior of interwar fascists.[17] He asserted that the fascist danger "reached a new peak in Israel during the Gaza operation" and that Israel is now fraught with fascist thinking of the kind that permeated France when Hitler's armies invaded in 1940. These comparisons are inexcusable for two reasons. One, whatever one may think of the Israeli military operation, those carrying it out were not "fascists"—one may disapprove of the violence unleashed by these soldiers without having to reach for the emotive, ill-fitting f-word. Moreover, France fell in 1940 because the Germans outmaneuvered French armies militarily. The country was not overthrown from within by fascists, and the group that collaborated with the enemy most blatantly during the invasion was the French Communists, who were taking orders from Hitler's Soviet allies.

Mentioning these facts in response to Sternhell's abuse of historical parallels seems redundant, given that the writer in question knows the history far better than I. This is what renders his rant all the more remarkable. We are talking about a distinguished historian of fascism who writes brilliantly about his subject when he is not wearing his political hat. Sternhell introduces a sober thought when he reminds us that "there are worse things than fascism." The Italian fascist regime before it was taken over by Nazi Germany killed "no more than a few dozen" opponents, and those were mostly assassinations that occurred outside Italy, probably without Mussolini's knowledge. (One might note that while the partisan use of "fascism" has grown exponentially in recent decades, the scholarship on this topic has not degenerated in the same way.)

Attempts to give fascism a presentist focus range from the serious and scholarly to the crassly opportunistic or abysmally ignorant. The historian A. James Gregor at the University of California, Berkeley, may be the most learned of those who treat fascism as a continuing problem, which Gregor identifies with the revolutionary Left. According to this view, the influence of Italian fascism is still reflected in developing-world dictatorships that feature national solidarity, a socialist economy, and an authoritarian regime. These Third World regimes also exploit resentment against "plutocratic" Western states with corrupt parliamentary systems, a form of rhetoric that made an appearance in Latin fascist oratory of the 1920s.

The problem with this continuity thesis is that it makes too much of chance parallels, without noticing the radical differences in the societies that gave birth to the regimes compared. Gregor also makes too much of the selective borrowing engaged in by Third World developmental dictatorships that adorn their rule with Western ideological regalia. This borrowing does not mean that non-Western governments are becoming the same as the state or society from whence the borrowing comes. One may even challenge the ascription of the specifically Western reference points "Right" and "Left" to Third World political entities.

Once we leave the Ivy Tower, any attempt to demonstrate a continuing fascist threat plummets into the absurd. Thus we find parallels drawn between Obama and Hitler because both did favors for their friends, extended comparisons between the Nazis and the American Democrats because both advanced affirmative-action programs, and a juxtaposing of opponents of gay rights and the amnestying of illegals here and in Europe with the Third Reich.

A few facts about what fascism was may help explain what it wasn't and isn't. Fascist movements developed on the European continent between the two wars and were a reaction primarily to the revolutionary Left but also to the perceived failure of liberal parliamentary governments to respond adequately to a devastating challenge from leftists. Fascist politics seems to have developed most naturally in Latin Catholic countries and drew on corporatist economic concepts that were extracted quite selectively from papal and neo-scholastic documents, as well as from Roman ideas about hierarchy and authority. Not surprisingly, fascist ideas did not resonate well in Protestant individualist societies, a fact that was related not only to the persistence in these places of orderly constitutional governments but also to certain obvious cultural differences. As the British Union of Fascists and its leader, Oswald Mosley, learned in the 1930s, marching around London in Black Shirts singing the Italian fascist anthem with English lyrics while enjoying Mussolini's subsidies created more of a curiosity than a powerful national movement.

Despite attempts by the Italian government to generate a fascist internationalism, their movements did not travel well. The fact that fascists stressed an organic national identity limited the outreach of a movement that aimed at the self-assertion of particular states. Unlike the communists and the current brand of American liberal democracy, fascism was never a truly international force. And its development in nations such as Italy and Spain, which lagged industrially, made it even less appealing outside of places that claimed a great past but revealed a rather modest present. The idea that advanced nations such as the US erected welfare states because fascist Italy did so borders on the hallucinatory. For better or worse, modern Western democracies tend of their own accord to give birth to huge bureaucratic states that dole out social programs. There is no reason to assume that those who built and expanded such enterprises were dependent on a Latin fascist model.

Nor does the organic nationhood preached by the fascists have anything in common with the appeals to American nationhood and an American global mission that now issue from Republican and neoconservative sources. Unlike American hawks, fascists did not appeal to human rights, nor did they associate their sense of solidarity with any kind of propositional nationhood. Mussolini invoked "Latinity" as the essence of Italian national identity, and to whatever extent he hoped to recreate an Italian empire, he saw himself returning to the Roman past. This effort to return to ancient greatness was a recurrent fascist theme, together with the reconstruction of a social hierarchy that would be adapted to present needs. By contrast, our advocates of American outreach justify their politics as helping to liberate backward societies from the shackles of tradition. They wish to make other peoples more like late modern Americans—consumerist, individualist, and free of sexism. This distinction is not an attempt to justify either sense of nationhood or the expansionist foreign policy to which it could lead. It simply calls attention to unlike things.

The historian John Lukacs has observed that any comparison between German Nazism and Latin fascism should prove definitively that there was no generic fascism. Lukacs's statement is half true. There was a veritable gulf between Nazism and the tradition of Latin authoritarianism into which fascism fitted as a counterrevolutionary movement pretending to be a radical revolutionary force. Despite the eventual conversion of some Latin fascists to Hitler's murderous totalitarian ventures, the two were not the same, and most Nazi collaborators in occupied countries were not convinced fascists but opportunistic politicians or military governments that were willing to cooperate with the Third Reich as long as it was winning. Yet there was a generic fascism, and it was Latin, corporatist, and authoritarian and featured a mystical idea of the nation. This fascism was far less radical and less expansive than German Nazism, a movement and regime that borrowed from fascist organizational models but also from the socialist experiment then being tried in Stalin's Russia.

The general view of fascism as retrograde seems correct, and so are comparisons between fascist rule and Latin authoritarian regimes. One is drawn to this conclusion even after reading all the literature—some of it very persuasive—that argues fascism was revolutionary as well as nationalist and authoritarian. The only way one avoids coming to the conclusion that the Italian fascist regime did not look particularly revolutionary is by distinguishing fascism as a movement from fascism as the interwar Italian government. The first is intellectually exciting but the second seems to have been a pretentiously labeled patronage system. It was tied to a class system and a political culture that became obsolete in the course of the last century.

Mussolini went hopelessly astray in his making of allies in the late 1930s, and by 1943 he became a German puppet. But his earlier rule had been a comic opera affair, hidden behind the ornamental hierarchy of offices that Mussolini had constructed under the supposedly supreme authority of the "State." Actually, the Duce ruled with his legions of advisers, while trying to get along with all classes. The attribution to his administration of totalitarian qualities has been much exaggerated. And so was the mistaken judgment made by, among others, FDR and Churchill that Mussolini ran his country efficiently. He managed the Depression by paying off industry to keep the working class employed and the Italian government did so with increasingly devalued money.

Fascism depended on an almost classical Marxist division of classes, with the workers on one side and the owners of productive forces on the other, the lower middle class hovering in between while usually, as Marx predicted, joining the party of order out of a sense of respectability. Marxist analyses of fascism continue to throw light on generic fascism because the revolutionary Left and the fascists faced the same social climate. Significantly, this climate and the stratification on which it rested have vanished since the 1930s, even if our media and political propagandists refuse to notice.

The question finally arises as to why we should care if the meaning of fascism remains in freefall. Three answers come to mind. One, it is bad practice to allow what words mean to be decided by semi-literate journalists and political advocates in accordance with their changing interests. Terms that once had clear meanings are reduced to throwaway labels once the wrong people get hold of them. Herbert Butterfield was right when he insisted that one can only begin to understand the reference points of the past by freeing them from the hold of politicians and party hacks.

Two, a questionable belief still reigns that all political evil is of the Right. After considerable research, I concluded that fascism was an objectively rightist movement since it was a culturally determined reaction to the revolutionary Left. But this does not mean that generic, essentially Latin fascism finds its fullest expression in Hitlerian genocide. The Nazis, who have been falsely turned into the quintessential fascists, were far more revolutionary and more totalitarian than generic fascists. What's more, the Left has been capable of producing its own wicked acts and totalitarian temptations without borrowing anything from the Right or the Nazis. Philosopher John Gray has made this point eloquently in the *Times Literary Supplement*, when he attributes to a failure of the leftist imagination a lack of any awareness of the "radical evil that comes from the pursuit of progress."

And three, bringing up fascism, which is meant to bring to mind Hitler, is a thoroughly dishonest way to approach our present-day political and social problems. It is an attempt to play on the emotions of the listener to incite us to political or military action. One does not have to like the individuals or groups being targeted to recognize that we are not dealing with the Third Reich in any of today's examples. Even less when we look at contemporary cases are we dealing with the Latin fascists of the 1930s, who were merely a footnote in modern history. Calling something or someone fascist has come to involve emotional blackmail that should no longer be tolerated by the public. It is related to the parallel attempt to compare every foreign-policy crisis to "Munich 1938" before insisting that we send in the US military to handle the situation.

Citing and documenting these false parallels may have some effect, if more people begin to notice this outrageous misuse of the past.

Halting the Leftward Lurch

Chronicles

JUNE 2022

I N RECENT decades, a rhetorical style, centered on warning us about a "far right" takeover of Western countries, has developed. This has nothing to do with our present situation or with anything that seems about to happen. In the recently concluded French presidential race, Éric Zemmour, head of the French Reconquête party, was consistently depicted as a far right danger to French democracy. Perhaps Zemmour, an Algerian Jew who warned against the threat of Muslim immigration to traditional French republican values, belongs to the "French far right," but only if we stretch that term to utter absurdity. As Geoffroy Lejeune, editor of the French weekly *Valeurs actuelles*, has forcefully explained:

> The party of Jacques Chirac, Rassemblement pour la République, which now is called Les Républicains, represented in the 1980s exactly the same positions as Zemmour. And the French Left in the 1950s was in some significant ways further to the right than Zemmour. In the last few decades there has been such a lurch to the Left in France that Zemmour now appears to be the far right.

Lejeune has barely touched the surface of this lurch. Marine Le Pen, who ran for the French presidency against Emmanuel Macron (the woke globalist incumbent), has been repeatedly described in the *The Wall Street Journal* as a scary representative of the "far right." Our "conservative" press pulled out all the stops to make sure that Macron, Le Pen's culturally leftist but pro-Atlanticist opponent, won the runoff, even dragging out an eighteen-year-old embezzlement charge floated among Le Pen's opponents when she was a French representative at the European Parliament. The charge against her never led to court action but recently resurfaced thanks to the European Union and the American "conservative" media, which seem at least equally determined to preserve the leftist status quo in Western Europe. On the other hand, our conservatives have said nothing disparaging about Macron's attempts to recruit the woke vote: for example, by promising to insert into the French constitution the right to an abortion and by pledging to promote euthanasia.

Although Le Pen has not been as hostile to Putin's Russia as the EU and its American "conservative" affiliates, and although she is willing to continue buying energy from the now-pariah nation, she has emphatically condemned Putin's invasion of Ukraine, even if, according to her hawkish American critics, she has not done enough to isolate the Russian leader. So I'm not quite sure what made her campaign look like a far right crusade. She favored reducing taxes on energy, making wider use of atomic power, and incorporating other measures designed to lessen the economic burdens afflicting French citizens. Unlike Zemmour, who (relatively speaking) ran to her right by stressing immigration control, Le Pen focused on cost-of-living issues and French national independence.

She could easily have run on the same issues as a French Socialist after World War II, just as Zemmour could have run for office in the same era as a French Communist. (The French Communist Party in 1946 opposed Third World immigration because of its harmful effect on the wages of the French working class.) Of course, in the matter of the LGBT agenda, the entire French political Left of 1946 and even into the 1990s was well to the right of what is called today, quite comically, the American conservative movement.

Those who lived through the second half or even the last third of the twentieth century can grasp to some degree the magnitude of this lurch to the left. First politically and then culturally, the Left has been given a free hand for many decades here, in Western Europe, and throughout the Anglosphere. As the Left advanced, the opposition grew weaker and more accommodationist. Part of what fueled this development, as I have argued in multiple books, was the fear of being identified with "fascism," although that term became so freighted with ideological baggage that eventually it lost any connection to what really happened in interwar Europe. In those few instances where one can locate connections between extremist movements, it was the anti-white, anti-Christian Left that looked much more like fascists, and even Nazis, than an increasingly weakened and retreating Right.

For those who have no desire to reverse this continuing lurch leftward, there are two effective techniques. First, one can denounce any retreat from the present degree of radicalization as a plunge into Hitlerism. The argument goes like this: "human decency" requires us to accept everything the political and cultural Left has achieved in the last sixty to seventy years as the minimal requirement for overcoming "discrimination," "systemic white racism," and "social injustice." If we retreat from this minimal base, we would soon be living in the equivalent of Trump's America or—what may be the same—the Third Reich.

Of course, Trump's America was well to the left of Eisenhower's or even Reagan's, but that's another matter. No going back or undoing what the Left has done, according to its advocates, must ever be permitted if we wish to remain a society that is working to overcome its irredeemably evil past.

Second, there is a conservative-movement variation on this argument, which may be more interesting. This variation consists of frantically and repeatedly calling attention to "right-wing extremism" while the speaker claims to represent a genuine conservative tradition. Although there are many publicists who pursue this path, one prominent group espousing this fashion are those whom the English professor Jesse Russell characterizes as "Catholic neoconservatives." These supposed voices of moderation warn against a dangerous neo-fascist Right that is ready to corrupt both Christian humanism and "our liberal democracy."

One noteworthy example of this technique is Matthew Rose's book *A World After Liberalism* (2021). Suffice it to say that Rose's polemic against the right-wing "enemies of liberalism" made plangent waves in the conservative policy foundation community. Heritage is still reeling in ecstasy from the book's message, and recently the Witherspoon Institute posted a long panegyric to Rose, who, we are led to believe, is helping the Right out of the fascist, authoritarian fog that may otherwise be engulfing it. Rose's book is sometimes discussed in conjunction with *The Oxford Handbook of the Radical Right* (2018), which features some of the same villains whom Rose takes to task.

There is a cottage industry on the genteel "moderate" Right, perhaps going back to George Will and even earlier to Peter Viereck in the 1950s, which specializes in exposing right-wing extremist dangers. Entire careers have been built on this richly rewarding preoccupation.

Longtime *Chronicles* editor Sam Francis figures prominently in such recent vaticinations about "illiberal" right-wingers, who are apparently threatening our exemplary democracy. My late friend is invariably portrayed as a raging white nationalist, whom our wannabe centrist conservatives denounce as an inexhaustible fount of bigotry. Although one finds appeals to white racial solidarity in Sam's later political stemwinders, almost all of his published writings place the thematic emphasis elsewhere. They focus on the emergence of the modern managerial society and the paths that remain open to those who would like to give power back to the "people."

The leftist journalist Michael Lind has borrowed heavily (without acknowledging his obvious debt) from Francis's conception of interlocking managerial blocs, while Francis in turn borrowed some of his ideas from C. Wright Mills and Antonio Gramsci as well as from James Burnham and Machiavelli. The essential Francis was not an obsessive white nationalist but an outstanding social analyst. And not at all surprisingly, his devotees today include scholars of different ethnicities from different continents. In a word, Sam Francis was too towering a mind to be associated with the careerists who are now railing against his "racism."

Although there have been bumps in the Left's ascent to dizzying power, these obstacles have been at most temporary, like the hyped up "Reagan Revolution," the proliferation of GOP think tanks in the DC Beltway, or the supposedly transformative Trump presidency. Almost everything that has been billed as a counterrevolution has not actually stopped the continuing march of LGBTQ, anti-white racism, a leftist managerial state in alliance with globalist capitalists, and lately a government crusade against the populist Right.

In the face of these challenges, the authorized "center Right," in an exceedingly narrow political spectrum, has usually reacted by coming to terms with the cultural Left—and thereby attacking true conservatism as "far-right extremism"—or else by turning the conversation toward building up military defenses and fighting a mostly nonexistent Marxism.

The question is whether there will be a cataclysmic reaction to this leftist hegemony. Will the pendulum swing back, or will things just go on as they have, with a crazier and crazier Left doing what it wants, without effective pushback? On the now-marginalized Alt-Right, one does find genuine interest in interwar revolutionary nationalists and in other anti-liberal thinkers of the early twentieth century. But most of the long-dead targets of Rose and the *Oxford Handbook* have little relevance in our society. The fact that I produce historical monographs on some of these interwar figures or that members of the Alt-Right translate their work does not indicate that what little still exists of a serious opposition to the Left will assume the character of the interwar European Right.

The closest to a still-relevant guide for a populist Right in the United States is Sam Francis, but even with him, we are not speaking about a perennial model for change that should be strictly followed. Rather we are referring to someone who predicted what an upsurge of the Right might look like in our time.

Equally important, when considering what a reaction to current leftist successes might entail, is the political theorist Carl Schmitt's stress on the uniqueness of each historical moment. We cannot reproduce the political or cultural past, because "an historical truth is true only once." But we can absorb the wisdom of thinkers from the past while trying to relate what they said and wrote to the present crisis. Even in uncharted waters, we do still have a map provided by those who came before.

There is also a possibility that the leftist, woke hegemony cannot be broken and that the incalculable social harm it has done may be irreversible. Although this gloomy thought would not remove the need to mobilize against a crazed Left, drunk with power, there may be no end to our crisis. Nevertheless, a real reaction can and should be mounted. The warnings against such a reaction and the attempt to relate it to the "critics of liberalism" are part of what *Chronicles* senior writer Pedro Gonzalez describes as "the counterrevolution of the Left." The so-called conservative opposition to the Left is allowed to prosper as long as it rails against a supposedly dangerous Right.

But the concern about right-wing illiberalism seems exaggerated since the so-called extremists are not attacking a true liberal tradition. Traditional liberalism was the worldview of the nineteenth-century Western bourgeoisie. It is a thing of the past, which is no longer "our tradition," as opposed to managerial rule, global capitalism, and government-enforced wokeness. While I profoundly admire that older liberal tradition and wrote a book in its defense, unfortunately it has no influence on our present political class. Perhaps it is now "illiberal" to mourn the passing of liberalism, a worldview that was already dying when Senator Robert A. Taft tried unsuccessfully to defend Anglo-American constitutional traditions and other middle-class decencies. Taft and others of his persuasion were coming to look like liberal dinosaurs already in the 1940s.

By now, liberalism properly understood exemplifies what Sam Francis characterized as "archaic conservatism." It is an idea and practice that survives in increasingly deformed manifestations. When the *The New York Times* journalist Ezra Klein cites Rose, quite approvingly, about how "liberalism is losing its hold on Western minds,"[18] I have to laugh out loud. Klein is no more of a liberal—as the term has been understood historically—than Adolf Hitler was a German constitutionalist. Klein is a woke leftist, who is happily making war on biological gender identities and who enthusiastically excused a *Times* editor, Sarah Jeong, who called for the disappearance of white men.

Klein's gripe of late seems to be that Vladimir Putin is still Russia's president, which means that "liberalism" (whatever that signifies in Klein's mind!) is being threatened. Presumably, if leftist journalists want to call themselves "conservative," we'll have to concede that term to them as well.

CHAPTER TWO

The Post-Marxist Left

Left

– ◆ ◆ ◆ –

The Old Left Wasn't Very Leftist

Chronicles

APRIL 19, 2020

W HILE RESEARCHING a book on anti-fascism, it became clear to me that the contemporary Left has strange ideas about what earlier leftists believed. This is especially true in the ascription of a certain timelessness to intersectional politics, which today's anti-fascists are all about. In *How Fascism Works* (2018) by Yale philosophy professor Jason Stanley, and in Mark Bray's *Antifa: The Anti-Fascist Handbook* (2017), one learns, or so it appears, that the Left has always been fighting for the same ideas.[19]

Among these permanent ideas is feminism, which Jason Stanley stresses as foundational for any true leftist identity. According to Stanley, "fascist opposition to gender studies in particular flows from its patriarchal ideology. National Socialism targeted women's movements and feminism in general." Moreover, according to Stanley, the Right, including the American isolationist Right of the 1930s, has spared no venom attacking "the acceptance of homosexuality together with its supposedly attendant sin of 'degeneracy.'"

Supposedly, hatred of gay activities and the objection to feminist courses (which, by the way, didn't even exist in the interwar period) render the Right a truly persistent evil. The good guys on the eternalized Left have, in Stanley's view, always been out there rooting for the feminists, gay pride parades, and open borders. In Bray's *Handbook*, one finds the present Left joining up with the interwar communists and anarchists in what looks like an alternate universe.

Almost everything about this image of a timeless Left is flawed. What Stanley, Bray, and other leftist authors attribute to fascists was until recently (and even still, in the case of communist Cuba)[20] characteristic of the Left. For example, communist hero Che Guevara expressed absolute "loathing" for homosexuals. That is, when he wasn't raging against blacks, whom he considered to be naturally primitive. In communist countries, such as Cuba and China, those who engage in homosexual practices have landed up in concentration camps.

The Communist Party USA was always happy to go after anticommunists or communist deviationists by spreading lurid accounts of their homosexual practices. This was done to particularly good effect in the case of Whittaker Chambers, when this former communist showed himself eager to reveal the machinations of his former associates. Not only communists but most of the American Left had a field day exposing Chambers' youthful indiscretions. My late friend Will Herberg, who had been once a high-ranking communist, told me emphatically that "homosexuals were summarily thrown out of the party." *Pace* our mythmakers about an ageless intersectional Left, I saw no reason to question Will's account.

Our present Left hardly existed in the 1930s. I am also puzzled by the efforts made by our intersectional Left to claim the legacy of the Frankfurt School and its criticism of "fascist patriarchy." Although I've certainly criticized Critical Theorists like Theodor Adorno and even my own teacher Herbert Marcuse for pushing us culturally toward the left, we should be fair to these figures. While they associated patriarchy with both fascism and capitalism, they never advocated the obliteration of gender identities. Even more importantly, they were blistering in their remarks about homosexuality as a form of sexual deviance.

In *Dialectic of the Enlightenment*, which Adorno and his collaborator Max Horkheimer produced in American exile during World War II, there are so many homophobic statements that their authors might have been put on the Southern Poverty Law Center hit list if they had published such a work at the present time.[21] In their lyrically composed critique of capitalist modernity, Adorno and Horkheimer stress the connection between fascist control and homosexual practices. Supposedly, "inverted" sexuality is the price that we pay for living in an irrational society; this inversion involves a degraded form of sexual behavior. Adorno and Horkheimer follow Freud in viewing homosexuality as an "inversion," in which the person thus afflicted finds an "inverted sexual object."

A sad note to add to this account is that for years Adorno and Horkheimer spread rumors far and wide targeting Golo Mann, the son of Thomas Mann and a learned historian of Germany, as a homosexual. Although Golo was that, he was quite discreet about his orientation, and the real reason for the attacks were his critical comments about the German anti-fascist Left.

Since I assume our present anti-fascist Left never picked up on the inconvenient fact of their group's homophobic past, let me offer a few other indigestible, though easily accessible, truths about their intellectual forebears.

The communist Left in postwar France and Italy strongly opposed open borders and the importation of a Third World labor force, which they properly understood would hurt the living conditions of the indigenous proletariat. This was also the view of leftist labor union organizers across the world, from Samuel Gompers to Cesar Chavez and, up until very recently, the position of socialist Bernie Sanders.

In Annie Kriegel's classic *The French Communists* (1972), which examines the culture of French communism into the 1970s, one encounters situations that would utterly baffle Stanley, Bray, and other modern exponents of the intersectional Left.[22] According to Kriegel, who herself started out as a communist, party members were overwhelmingly male, looked with suspicion on female communist activists, and usually sounded like a "pre–Vatican Two gathering of Catholic prelates" in discussions of family matters.

It would be impossible to imagine any shared moral ground between these people and what today presents itself as the Left. Without being overly polemical, it would seem the old communist Left has about as much in common with today's Left as the American conservative movement of the 1960s does with its present, would-be incarnation. Like times, movements change—sometimes in ways that render them unrecognizable to past members.

The Left Has Gone Far Beyond Relativism

The American Conservative

JUNE 19, 2020

A ROUND THE middle of the last century, American conservatives came to regard "relativism" as an essential characteristic of the Left. Political theorist and onetime Yale professor Willmoore Kendall, who had been the teacher of William F. Buckley, was the best-known exponent of this position. Kendall was particularly concerned that liberals in post–World War II America were unwilling to stand up to communist infiltration and Soviet aggression, at least not in the decisive manner that he and his student, who became the animating spirit of the conservatism of that age, would have desired.

Kendall's explanation, which others echoed and, in some cases, anticipated, was that many intellectuals believed "in an unlimited right to think and say what you please, with impunity and without let or hindrance." Particularly in the face of the communist threat, Kendall thought that Americans would have to give up the idea of an "open society." They would have to grasp that "any viable society has an orthodoxy—a set of fundamental beliefs, implicit in its way of life, that it cannot, should not, and, in any case, will not submit to the vicissitudes of the marketplace."

Kendall viewed English democrat and feminist John Stuart Mill as a particularly dangerous thinker on political questions. He was convinced Mill's best-known work, *On Liberty* (1859), had gone too far in advocating an "open society."[23]

Mill set out to defend the right of totally free inquiry but, according to Kendall, landed squarely on relativism. In *The Conservative Affirmation* (1963), Kendall traced the non-judgmentalism of many Americans when faced by the communist threat to Mill's willingness to consider all views and opinions.[24] According to Kendall, Mill helped create America's "national religion of skepticism" and made it increasingly difficult for Americans to hold on to what was left of a traditional society. Mill also dealt with moral issues by encouraging the pursuit of truth without accepting "truth itself with all its accumulated riches to date."

In a moving tribute to Kendall, Tony Woodlief, writing recently at *The American Conservative*, declared that "this outcast Yale professor predicted 2020 better than his erstwhile colleagues."[25] Kendall had warned against "the suicidal pact with relativism," which is now driving the anti-fascist Left. According to him, "the doyens of the suicidal society will feel an irresistible compulsion to silence the voices insisting that there is truth, even Truth, and that therefore many other beliefs are in error."

Please note that I fully share Woodlief's admiration for Kendall and especially for his writings on the formation of American constitutional government and his perceptive reading of the political theory of John Locke. Where I must part company is in Kendall's attribution to the Left of a fixation with an "open society." Equally open to question is Kendall's treatment of Mill's *On Liberty*, a work that Maurice Cowling, Linda Raeder, and Joseph Hamburger have all interpreted differently from Kendall. These scholars have documented that Mill was far less interested in open discussion than he was in other ends. Above all, he was trying to build a secular society based on a consensus centered on scientific truth. Mill was an explicit nineteenth-century progressive who believed that open inquiry would advance his teleological goals.

Moreover, with due respect to Woodlief and Kendall, those who support Antifa and Black Lives Matter have hardly failed to recognize that there is "Truth" in the world. They simply reject the moral right of their enemies to express other views. This is a moral stand, hardly a relativistic one, and it is a political-existential one, in the sense in which Carl Schmitt understood "the Concept of the Political" as the most intensely antagonistic of human relationships. It is unimaginable that the more fervent and more activist side in our culture wars is not driven by its own morality, which expresses itself in rage.

One might also question whether the Left has ever believed consistently in something called "moral relativism" or whether it has merely appealed to it as a tactic to disarm opponents. Certainly the pro-communist leftists with whom Kendall debated were not likely to "relativize" Nazism or even the Francoist regime in Spain or South African Apartheid the way they did Soviet tyranny.

Russell Kirk liked to tell the story of a leftist acquaintance who claimed to have a perfectly open mind. When Kirk asked his interlocutor who was morally superior, "Jesus of Nazareth or Stalin," this fellow seemed unable to rate those figures by the required standard. But when he was asked who was worse, Hitler or Stalin, Kirk's acquaintance would immediately respond "Hitler." I had similar experiences with advocates of the "open society" before the Left gave up its facade of universal tolerance. It may be that dishonesty, not relativism, was the problem with how the Left has presented itself.

If one were to ask what exactly the Left has believed about morality over the decades, I would begin by pointing out that the most important concept is equality. The Left has never denied this, and I see no reason to question that commitment. What seems to me striking is the Left's preoccupation with equality to the neglect of other values that seem at least as much deserving of respect, such as deference to elders, respect for the achievements of one's civilization, piety, freedom, and so on. We might also question how the Left understands its highest value, which is clearly different from the way non-leftists might approach it. For example, some may think that equality before the law is enough; others may want equal voting rights, and still others may believe it is the duty of the state to reduce its citizens or subjects to the same living conditions.

The present Left also seems interested in imposing equality of esteem for those whom it designates as historical victims. This is certainly not an expression of relativism but an attempt to carry a highest value one step beyond where it was carried in the past. The drive toward a more total equality brings with it a host of human problems, anarcho-tyranny as seen in cities like Seattle right now being the most obvious. But the belief that all values are relative does not in any way seem to have influenced this course of events.

Another curious characteristic of the Left is how furiously it reacts to Western failures to meet its fastidious standards of equality. The existence of economic disparities in Western countries drove generations of leftists to look for answers in communism, or at least to treat communist governments as efforts to create more "just" or more "scientifically run" societies. The enemy then and afterward was "fascism," and it remained so long after the Second World War. Fascism has been defined as a chronic Western disease, arising out of specifically Western cultural and religious attitudes rooted in bigotry. Fascism used to be explained with reference to those who controlled the means of production. It was an ideological tool for oppressing the poor and maintaining colonial empires. In its more contemporary form, fascism has become whatever the intersectional Left considers to be morally reprehensible. Since the list of fascist offenses continues to grow by the minute, the only moral way to deal with this right-wing pestilence is through "cancel culture." Only by getting rid of all reminders of a traditional Western society can we protect ourselves from the pervasive fascist menace.

Yet somehow the evils we are supposed to combat never appear anywhere outside the West. Other societies live in a perpetual state of grace as victims of the West or as examples of what we might become with the proper reeducation. The late Paul Hollander wrote a voluminous study on "political pilgrims" who visited "progressive" or Marxist societies, where they hoped to find human perfection. Hollander's "pilgrims" were hardly relativists. They were fixated on a highest value, usually equality, but equality combined with scientific management, which they imagined was being realized in some distant place but not in their own country.

Where Kendall was correct was in grasping that the Left was destroying traditional human attachments, where people are integrated into families and communities. There, morality operates in an inherited social context, and not in the pursuit of highest values. Although one may be skeptical about the portentous importance that Kendall ascribed to relativism, his description of a society without shared premises descending into "ever-deepening differences of opinion" is accurate. So was his prediction that such a society would descend "into the abandonment of the discussion process and the arbitrament of public questions by violence and civil war."

Persistent Leftists Aren't Necessarily Persistent Marxists

American Greatness

MAY 1, 2021

A QUESTION that has been batted about on this website is whether the woke Left is Marxist, albeit representative of a Marxism that stresses racial, gender, and expressive inequalities rather than socioeconomic divisions. My answer to this question is at least provisionally "no." Unless I see evidence to the contrary, it seems to me the differences between traditional Marxism and the Left that is now oppressing onetime Western democracies are too great to warrant an affirmative response. Like another contributor to this website,[26] I do not believe that the cultural and political struggle in which we are engaged is primarily about race. American blacks are expendable foot soldiers in a struggle that white elites are waging, mostly against white Deplorables.

In Germany the supposed Right, whom publishing houses and newspaper editors are now ostracizing, include former East German freedom fighters,[27] like Vera Lengsfeld, Uwe Tellkamp, and Monika Maron, who should be hailed as friends of liberty. Such literary figures have dared to complain about censorship and government-encouraged violence against dissenters, particularly as regards immigration and COVID restrictions. In France, it is the Muslim population that the Left mobilizes to fight a "fascist" threat; and critics now refer to the French Left as "Islamo-gauchiste." In Germany, Turks, Syrians, and other descendants of Third World immigrants (only a minority of whom are black) are joining the government- and media-supported "Struggle against the Right." Non-American elites are pushing the same anti-Western, anti-bourgeois, and totalitarian leftist agenda as their American counterparts but doing so mostly without black protesters.

One may, however, question whether these activists are Marxist. As Victor Davis Hanson points out: "Those whites smeared for having privilege, usually do not have it; those who smear them, white and non-white, usually do."[28] There is no Marxist movement I am aware of whose members come largely from Martha's Vineyard, the Chicago North Shore, Kamala Harris's Los Angeles Country Club, and other locations where the leisure class hangs out. We are now witnessing limousine liberalism on steroids, and it looks nothing like European communist parties circa 1948, with their working-class base and generally puritanical morals. Genuine Marxists, like Gyula Thürmer, head of the now reformed Hungarian Communist Party, are grousing about the false identity of the Western rich, who falsely claim to represent the radical Left. According to Thürmer, Eastern Europe has abandoned communist regimes to be taken over by George Soros and his anti-national, socially radical cohorts. This old commie may have a point.

Further, one ceases to represent Marxism if one shifts the conversation from socioeconomic conflict to the social discrimination bewailed by the transgendered and gays. These psychological concerns do not flow from a recognizable Marxist ideology. There is, moreover, little shared ground between traditional working-class grievances and the demand for sex hormone therapy for grade school children who wish to change their gender. One must show a greater similarity between these alleged victims of discrimination to prove a significant relationship.

Hitler claimed to be struggling for disadvantaged Aryans. Did that mean that the Nazis were Marxists? Mussolini, in declaring war on the English and French in July 1940, spoke of waging a crusade for his proletariat nation against "democratic capitalist plutocrats." Was Mussolini then a Marxist because he appealed to a victimized nation against its supposed victimizers? Calling for a struggle against enemies designated as victimizers does not by *itself* prove Marxist credentials.

Characterizing one's enemies as Marxists, however, has become an established practice in the American Conservative Movement because that movement's founders came out of the Cold War and the protracted battle against communism. But that habit does not turn all the adversaries of American conservatives into communists or Marxists. Although new enemies may be as pernicious as old ones, they are not necessarily the same.

But there is continuity in the radical Left (as I have discovered from my own research). A certain pattern can be discerned in adherents of an older Left moving on to champion a later one. Often the same people have traveled from one Left to another because of their cultural and emotional orientation. Does anyone believe that Jerrold Nadler and those of a certain age in his 10th Congressional District in Lower Manhattan had the slightest difficulty moving from communist-front causes into solidarity with BLM and LGBT? The late Congresswoman Bella Abzug went from being a hardline communist (who supported the Soviet–Nazi pact in 1939)[29] to a radical feminist and a fan of Castro's Cuba. Carl Bernstein, who came from a radical leftist home, has embraced just about every Left that has come along during his long lifetime. Minnesota progressives (who are mostly of Scandinavian ancestry) have seemed equally happy voting for socialists or supporting the very BLM-friendly Governor Tim Walz[30] and the Antifa-sympathizer Attorney General Keith Ellison. It might be best to focus on those who reflexively align with the Left rather than worrying about a persistent Marxist ideology.

The Free Speech Facade

American Mind

I N A thoughtful commentary on "The 'New Normal' and the Assault on Reason," Glenn Ellmers makes this historical observation:

> For several centuries, at least since John Stuart Mill, the Left has defined itself by its commitment to freedom of speech. This was practically the *sine qua non* for calling oneself a liberal. Yet some time around 2019–20, in the historical blink of an eye, free speech was simply . . . dismissed. It became obligatory on the Left to support systematic control of our public discourse by a handful of massive tech companies, in cooperation with the government.[31]

Professor Ellmers is correct that the Left, especially that part of it that has described itself as democratic, has traditionally flaunted its "commitment to free speech." The American Civil Liberties Union, since its founding in 1920, has urged its members "to defend and preserve the individual rights guaranteed by the Constitution and the laws of the land." And some of us are old enough to remember when the ACLU came out in support of the right of Nazis to march in the heavily Jewish community of Skokie, Illinois. A defense of that march,

43

which took place in 1978, was interpreted as the *reductio ad absurdum* of the Left's commitment to expressing unconventional views, a freedom that was to be exercised even if it produced an inexcusably insensitive outcome.

Most college-educated Americans of my generation were exposed to another statement of the supposed dedication to freedom among progressives. We had to read John Stuart Mill's *On Liberty* (1859), one of the most oft-quoted defenses of freedom of opinion in the Western world. Chapter Two includes these words about freedom of the press:

> The time, it is to be hoped, is gone by, when any defense would be necessary of the "liberty of the press" as one of the securities against corrupt or tyrannical government. No argument, we may suppose, can now be needed, against permitting a legislature or an executive, not identified in interest with the people, to prescribe opinions to them, and determine what doctrines or what arguments they shall be allowed to hear.[32]

The Englishman who wrote those lines represented the Left of his time. He advocated an expanded franchise that included women, favored the emancipation of slaves in America, and supported the use of state power to redress economic inequalities. Mill also famously opposed any restriction on having people express their opinions, and apparently believed that even views that had been to all intents and purposes refuted, might still contain a grain of truth, and needed to be discussed, as long as there were those around who were willing to present those positions.

The populist conservative Willmoore Kendall famously attacked Mill in the 1950s for previewing the liberal fetish of free speech. Kendall regarded Mill's defense of "the open society" as "inseparable from his assault on truth." It was a defense that left no room for religion, tradition, and other sources of authority. Mill's "all questions-are-open-questions society" could not even recognize "truth, itself with all its accumulated riches to date," because it was grounded in relativism. It was an attempt to escape from both the quest for truth and any acknowledgment of those truths that our civilization embodies. Kendall underscored what became a leitmotif in the post–World War II conservative reaction to the cultural and political Left. Significantly, critiques of relativism punctuated the writings of Leo Strauss, William F. Buckley, Russell Kirk, and other thinkers of the period, though their formulations were not always the same.

Strauss's relevant comments were a recognizable extension of a scholarly discussion in Germany, one that started with Max Weber in the late nineteenth century and addressed the nature of values. Although Strauss famously assaulted Weber's fact-value distinction, he nonetheless held on to Weber's understanding of values as an expression of the individual will. A person posits values as an individual judgment that he expects others to agree with and act on. If that person decides to privilege a particular value, say tolerance, he may then change his mind and prefer intolerance to his earlier, now-rejected value. In either case I am expressing an individual preference. In his critique of relativism, Strauss was indicating that values are arbitrary individual constructions, unless grounded in an ethical tradition or, even better, ethical reasoning that communities accept and are willing to live by.

In *Natural Right and History* (1953), Strauss also attacks the escape from moral judgment among social scientists and singles out his fellow Central European émigré, the legal scholar Hans Kelsen, for treating all forms of government at least by implication as morally equivalent.[33] Without getting into this censure (with which I have elsewhere disagreed), I would note that Strauss was not here attacking the Left specifically. His comments were directed against social scientists and therefore may not relate to the topic at hand. In any case, Strauss's value critique may be the stronger part of his assessment of relativism.

Kendall attacked relativism in his own way. He saw the relativism he thought was reflected in Mill's "open society" and on the mid-twentieth-century American Left as an acid eating away at America's onetime moral consensus, founded on biblical morality and common law. Relativists were destroying what was left of an America held together by a shared sense of the Good. Although the two critiques of relativism were not identical, Kendall eventually became a devotee and regular correspondent of Strauss. (Kendall's famous essay "Conservatism and the Open Society," which appeared as Chapter Six in *The Conservative Affirmation* [1963], may offer his most extensive polemic against Mill's and the Left's value-relativism.)

While we may still find merit in the axiological critique of values presented by Strauss and his predecessors, it may be harder to accept Kendall's contention that the Left in its essence is open to all points of view. The Left has had its own conception of Truth, but, unlike the traditional Right, has carefully disguised it. Maurice Cowling and Linda Raeder, both Mill scholars, have shown how their subject planned *On Liberty* as a preparatory step to leading humankind into a new scientific age free of religious superstition. Already in the introduction to this work, we are presented with Auguste Comte's three stages of human development, culminating in an Age of Positivism. Mill may have believed that we could afford to promote open discussion because such a situation would lead to the positivist future that he envisaged for the entire human race.

William Donahue's *The Politics of the American Civil Liberties Union* (1985) is the perfect eye-opener for anyone who is deluded enough to believe that the ACLU has ever been entirely or mainly about what it claims to be defending.[34] From the beginning, as Donahue carefully documents, the ACLU was packed full of communist sympathizers, whose primary concern was legalizing speech for the revolutionary Left. Defending the expressive rights of Nazis or the Klan was mostly a diversionary tactic. It helped create an appearance of balance so that the ACLU could do what interested its staff and its donors the most—namely, stripping the public square of religious traditions, legitimizing left-wing subversives, and rushing to defend those who made obscene attacks on traditional religious institutions. Everything else, Donahue maintains, was window dressing. Though there have been ACLU officers, like Nadine Strossen, who have opposed the organization's efforts to enforce Political Correctness, they have been rare exceptions, particularly in recent years. And they certainly have not influenced where the ACLU is now, which is behind every culturally leftist plan being pushed by the Democratic Party.

There were moderate center-leftists in the past, like Hubert Humphrey and Henry Jackson, but such moderate reformers have ceased to matter for grasping what the Left has become in the present age. Although past center-leftists may have worked to increase public administration, which was far from a blessing, and may have underestimated the effect of the social policies they supported, they were not openly contemptuous of freedom. They were also hostile to communism and supported the struggle against Soviet expansion; not all advocates of an expanded welfare state were intent on destroying our inherited right of dissent.

That said, the current Left's desire for "systematic control of public discourse" may not be a dramatic departure from where many leftists stood in the past. The totalitarian Left is just tightening its grip on the rest of us while no longer feeling obliged to maintain the civil liberty stance that it assumed in the 1950s. When Kendall and other American conservatives active seventy years ago concluded that the Left wanted the kind of society that is open to all points of view, they were generalizing by looking at a Left then under assault from anti-communists. It was then in the interest of the Left to defend dissent. The question that these conservatives might have addressed more thoroughly was how the Left would have behaved once it achieved an unassailable position of power. The Left attacked the House Committee on Un-American Activities when it investigated suspected communists and communist agents in the 1940s and early 1950s. But with few exceptions, these "civil libertarians" hardly protested when the same committee went after those suspected of fascist sympathies, including Christian pacifists, in the preceding decade. The ACLU never really stood for the kind of open society that Kendall and Buckley mocked.

An obvious reason for this, in my considered view, is that the present Left and earlier Lefts have not been relativistic in the sense of having no moral orientation. While that orientation or disposition may not appeal to most readers of this book, it does suggest a definable moral stance. In pursuit of its morality, the Left has no qualms about disarming its opponents, either by guile or, more recently in the West, by force.

That's because the Left wishes to abolish the Western past, which it regards as evil. This past is evil because Western societies until recently attributed unequal identities to different groups of people, and they supposedly still oppress the virtuous of the Earth, who are non-Westerners or victims of the West. This may not offer a serious example of moral reasoning, but it also does not betoken relativism or the wishy-washiness that Kendall associated with his political opponents. The Left is venting moral fury on what it perceives as an unjust situation and against those who are held responsible for real or imagined inequality. This outrage together with its war against civilization renders the Left, certainly in its present form, utterly destructive.

Marx Wasn't Woke

Chronicles

APRIL 2023

Y ORAM HAZONY provides what is perhaps the best exposition of how the woke Left represents an "updated" form of traditional Marxism. His argument, which is ably presented in his book *Conservatism: A Rediscovery*, is summed up as follows:

> Marx's principal insight is that the categories liberals use to construct their theory of political reality (liberty, equality, rights, and consent) are insufficient for understanding the political domain. They are insufficient because the liberal picture of the political world leaves out two phenomena that are, according to Marx, absolutely central to human political experience: the fact that people invariably form cohesive classes or groups and the fact that these classes or groups invariably oppress or exploit one another, with the state itself functioning as an instrument of the oppressor class.[35]

Part of this argument is undoubtedly correct. The form of liberalism that came out of the eighteenth-century Enlightenment did indeed stress individual rights and liberties, and it placed less emphasis on national and class identities than on individual advancement. This liberal tendency continued to manifest itself into the late twentieth century, although liberalism itself underwent significant changes with the modern welfare state and the introduction of universal suffrage. Moreover, while self-identified liberals supported nationalist movements and movements of national liberation throughout the nineteenth century, to whatever extent they reflected Enlightenment liberalism, they stressed individual rights and individual self-fulfillment.

Hazony is correct that the woke Left has outflanked self-described liberals in the media and the academy by defending collective identities. These privileged identities are ascribed to exploited members of designated victim groups. The contemporary Left has therefore developed its own collectivism by incorporating a vocabulary and conceptual framework borrowed from the Marxist tradition. Like Marxism, the woke Left divides humanity into oppressors and the oppressed, and it views the state as an instrument of power that should be made to fit the needs of the supposedly downtrodden. The woke Left has abandoned the socioeconomic perspective of older Marxist theory but, according to Hazony, continues to imagine reality along similar lines: that is, as a confrontation between cohesive classes, consisting of the oppressors and the oppressed. Thus the woke Left conjures up a situation that calls for a revolutionary solution.

Hazony relates his treatment of this Left as an updated form of historic Marxism to the waning of anti-Marxist liberalism. In his judgment, liberals who fight Marxism in the name of individual rights are holding a poor hand. They are upholding individual natural rights against collective identity, a concept that now dominates in Western societies. The battle lines are no longer between the liberal defense of the individual and various forms of collectivism. Rather the lines are drawn between conservative nationalism, that is, "conservative democracy," and Marxism in its regnant woke form.

Hazony's argument about the connection between Marxism and the woke Left is carefully developed and does not seem aimed at promoting the talking points of self-interested conservative establishmentarians. Hazony is not pointing to a Marxist bogey to avoid battle with what has become a much more formidable adversary than "creeping socialism." And he is certainly not trying to divert our attention from the necessary struggle against the woke Left. He is offering what seems to me the most effective argument for assigning a Marxist derivation to woke ideology.

Unfortunately, Hazony cannot escape the materialist foundation of Marxist historical theory. Marx was not in the least concerned with nonbinary oppression, raging homophobia, or the inherently evil nature of being white. This father of "scientific socialism" focused on socioeconomic antagonisms expressing themselves as class conflict. His historical materialism, however, was overhauled in interwar Germany, as the Frankfurt School and its Critical Theory came onto the scene. This new iteration of the Left developed what has been called "cultural Marxism," and it defined as a pressing socialist task the reconstruction of the bourgeois Christian family. This reconstruction was supposedly necessary to stand firm against the rampant spread of fascism. Among Frankfurt School theorists, attempts were also made to assimilate Marxism to a variant of Freudian psychology; and in Herbert Marcuse's work, Marxist socialism was fused with the vision of polymorphic sexuality.

It was also the Frankfurt School theorist Marcuse who paved the way for the New Left neo-Marxism of the 1960s and 1970s by advocating an alliance of counterculture revolutionaries with anti-colonial rebels in the Third World. Marcuse's "Berlin Lectures," delivered to cheering young German radicals in 1973, looked forward to a period of extreme change driven by collaboration between Third World revolutionaries and the Western student movement. By the 1970s, it was also becoming clear that the Western working class, which was moving decidedly to the Right, could no longer be instrumentalized as a leftist revolutionary class. Marcuse added to his revolutionary brew, perhaps as an afterthought, the rage of angry young blacks.

This was a useful course of action because, by the 1960s, blacks had become more and more drawn into revolutionary activism, although they would soon be joined by others in what can be described as the post-Marxist Left. Although members of what eventually evolved into the woke, anti-fascist Left looked for an "oppressed class," their choices had nothing to do with Marx's proletariat. The real working class wanted nothing to do with cultural revolutionaries, and fights broke out between the two groups in American cities in the 1960s.

Marcuse and his followers also fatefully redefined the "realm of needs," as understood in traditional Marxism. No longer was it the labor required to sustain the working class but rather the acquisition of psychological and esthetic fulfillment. This lent weight to the complaint that capitalism was emotionally repressive. In the post–World War II Western context, the capitalist form of production was accused of leaving the youthful vanguard of a future revolution inwardly stunted. Marcuse believed Western countries were materially able to create a "rational economy"—that is, a socialist one—but simply lacked the will and the vision to establish the sexually and economically liberated society that he desired.

Such ideas represent a countercultural alternative to traditional Marxism as well as to the still recognizably bourgeois Christian society that Marcuse and other Critical Theorists hoped to transform. Communist parties throughout the West as well as Soviet critics condemned this reconfiguring of Marxism as a distortion of Marx's dialectical materialism. Instead of highlighting the class struggle centered on the ownership of productive forces, Critical Theorists were talking about fighting prejudice and increasing erotic satisfaction. If such notions passed for Marxist theory, so went the critique, they would reduce a true revolutionary doctrine based on an analysis of material forces to a bourgeois campaign against emotional repression and discrimination. The invective against this transmogrified Marxism among communists and orthodox Marxists was every bit as furious as those denunciations against the Frankfurt School that have issued from the Christian Right.

The woke Left is an even more grotesque distortion of Marxism than anything the interwar and postwar Frankfurt School brought forth. This Left has shed any recognizable Marxist theory, but it continues to venerate communist heroes while appealing to the interwar struggle between the communist Left and "fascism." Despite socialist proposals that occasionally enter woke wish lists, corporate capitalists are integral to the post-Marxist Left. Nor are such capitalists likely to suffer any ill effects even if the green agenda that most Western countries are pushing is put more broadly into effect.

Corporate capitalists who donate money to the Democratic National Committee and to its counterparts in Western Europe and the Anglosphere will not go begging if the eco-militants get their way. The state-protected rich are already making profits by converting to green energy. The corporate class enjoys the benefits of government contracts and having their earnings protected in tax-exempt funds. If capitalists pour their money into Black Lives Matter, critical race theory, and LGBT, it is not because they are Marxists. Rather, they represent what Pedro Gonzalez characterizes as "the counterrevolution of the Left." Citibank, Walt Disney, Coca-Cola, Pfizer, etc., belong to the privileged class in woke America, and it is the predominantly white working class who will pay by taxes for the woke regime in which our corporate giants are invested.

Even the Biden administration's proposed hike in corporate tax rates from 21 percent to 28 percent will likely impact wage earners far more than the upper 5 percent of the income scale. It has been predicted that 50 percent of these added costs will result in wage reductions and increased prices for consumers. The inflation already produced by our present administration has hurt the working and middle classes far more than the earnings of those making annually $500,000 or more, yet that is the class on which the Biden administration claims to be imposing the cost of green energy and social redistribution programs. In the end, the rich may have the least to fear from the government-manufactured rise in the price of essential goods, starting with food and fuel. According to the Ways and Means Committee, by June of last year, Biden's inflation had wiped out the life savings of more than twenty-six million low-income families.

Behemoth (1942), Franz Neumann's classic Marxist study, seems to be as applicable to our present ruling class as it was to economic elites under the Third Reich.[36] Neumann's study may be describing our woke capitalists even more plausibly than those German plutocrats whom Neumann thought were building a corporate state in alliance with Hitler. Curiously, German industrialists and bankers may have been more reluctant to jump onto the Nazi train than our corporate elites have been to join the cheering gallery for gender reassignment and anti-white racism. In any case it is exceedingly difficult to imagine that "American Marxists" would threaten the corporate wealth of our crony capitalist wokesters.

Unlike Marxism, moreover, the woke Left has long ceased paying homage to science and rationality. The Left is driven by hate against traditional Americans with fixed gender roles, communal hierarchies, and some form of inherited religious faith. Truth, for the woke Left, is determined and redefined by those in power. Woke beliefs have no necessary connection to what is empirically provable, since from the woke perspective Western science and empirical demonstration are tainted by white, masculine, racist prejudice. Communism in Europe, at least in practice, never showed the frenzied nihilistic energy that seems endemic to the woke Left. From tearing down statues to abolishing genders to inciting mob violence against white Americans to throwing open borders for invasion by Third World migrants, the woke Left seems far more socially and culturally destructive than most past communist governments.

The end goal of wokeism is universal equality, which is to be brought about through a universal state. It opposes particularity, at least in the Western white world, and works to obliterate anything that is specifically Western. Indeed, wokeism offers the example of a thoroughly unhinged Left that communist governments and parties, as well as the Cold War in the West, all kept in check. Wokeism privileges those with deviant sexual appetites, anti-Christian and anti-white fixations, and repugnance for bourgeois institutions, groups whom the communists quite properly kept from rising in their parties and governments. The communists held generally traditional moral views even if they practiced tyranny.

Unfortunately, the postwar conservative movement became so obsessed with "fighting communism" that it failed to notice the far more dangerous enemy gathering its forces domestically. And by the end phase of the Cold War in the 1980s, neoconservatives were frequently making the charge that communist regimes discriminated against homosexuals. This charge was perfectly true because in comparison to leftward-drifting Western countries, communist governments were, in some sense, more socially conservative.

Moreover, those Eastern European governments—including the northeastern parts of Germany—that were formerly under Soviet control have resisted woke takeover far better than Western Europe, the United States, and the Anglosphere. The complaint that these regions never underwent proper anti-fascist instruction, a charge that I address in my book on anti-fascism, is, all things considered, correct. The "all things considered" in this case would refer to their undergoing a process of change that would make these regions look and think like Canada, the German Federal Republic, or the American state of California at the present hour.

Also worth noting is the duplicitous role of the woke Left regarding Islamic inroads into the West. Since promoting a Muslim presence and Muslim influence in Western societies is now linked to the multicultural Left, critics of Islamization are assigned by virtue of this practice to the far right. In reality, pushback against Islamic culture comes from the woke Left more than from any recognizable Right. Those who loudly protest that Muslims oppose feminism and discriminate against homosexuals are by no means conservative. They are simply more consistent in their progressive views than those on the woke Left who treat Islamic patriarchy indulgently, that is, those on the Left who make excuses for non-Western male chauvinism and non-Christian theocracy.

Hazony's key point in identifying the woke Left as Marxist is their shared focus on the historical struggle between the oppressors and that oppressed. This struggle is certainly foundational for Marx and the Marxists, but it is one that other ideologies and movements have embraced as well. This dialectic has roots in both the Old and New Testaments, in which the suffering servants of the Lord or the chosen people eventually triumph over their oppressors. In the Bible, the righteous are destined to prevail over those who are persecuting them, thanks to divine assistance. Marx, it may be argued, was putting a scientific covering over an ancient belief, the lineaments of which he did not invent. He was adapting an ancient narrative to new material circumstances while invoking the mystique of nineteenth-century science.

A similar narrative has surfaced among those who are not typically associated with the Left. From the time the Italian fascist movement was founded in November 1921, references were made among their leaders to the Italian people as an oppressed nation, a theme that already surfaces in the nineteenth-century Italian anthem, "Fratelli d'Italia." Mussolini's orations featured unkind references to democratic plutocrats, by which he had in mind English and American capitalist regimes. The speech that Il Duce delivered on June 10, 1940, when he declared war on England and France in alliance with Nazi Germany appeals to L'Italia proletaria e fascista ("proletarian and fascist Italy").

This does not prove that Mussolini was a Marxist; nor were the Nazis, who compared Germany after the Treaty of Versailles to the crucified Christ; nor are the Poles who have called themselves "the Christ of nations." Many groups and nations have drawn on images of the suffering Just, unjustly exploited, to characterize their struggles against putative oppressors, a characterization that hardly qualifies them as Marxists under a different name.

In the seventh chapter of *Conservatism: A Rediscovery*, Hazony highlights the replacement of post–World War II liberalism by woke collectivism. Such a changing of the guard is seen in the abandonment of the principle of open discussion, and even disagreement, in favor of group cohesion. We also find self-identified liberals expressing horror at the closing of open discussion by others on the Left. This closed-mindedness has caused those who cling to a "liberal" identity to protest woke cohesiveness and to call for a return to a free society.

Hazony's observation is accurate but may require qualification. The liberalism that the woke Left canceled was a greatly weakened form of the liberal persuasion, the exponents of which had already ceased to argue very convincingly for open discussion. For decades, that attenuated liberalism excluded the Right, except for a moderate centrist version of it that would not upset leftist gatekeepers. The parameters of allowable discussion on many issues had become more and more restricted before a late modern form of liberalism gave up the ghost entirely. By then, universities were already being ideologically controlled while both government and the media had prepared the way for this postliberal age.

Liberalism in its last stages did not suffer from an indiscriminate tolerance, a condition that thinkers as diverse as Joseph Schumpeter and

Carl Schmitt viewed as liberalism's great weakness. Quite to the contrary! Late modern liberalism moved in the direction of what became the woke Left even while clinging to the illusion of openness. And those who complain about leftist intolerance practiced the same vice in relation to the Right, until they were overtaken by greater powers on the Left. They then became the fashionable mourners of a lost tolerance, the loss of which they themselves helped bring about.

This observation is not meant to invalidate Hazony's larger point, which is correct. At some point in the last twenty years, the very ideal of open discussion and debate fell into disrepute both in institutions of higher learning and in the media. What had become a shrunken, denatured liberalism was abandoned for a successor ideology: wokeism. Further, there may be no way back to what has been resoundingly repudiated and what took generations to collapse. Only an equally determined collectivism can effectively resist those who have ended the liberal era, or what became the pale imitation of one.

Marcuse, the American Philosopher

The American Mind

AUGUST 29, 2023

C HRISTOPHER F. RUFO recently published a bestseller on the impact of predominantly foreign leftist ideas on American politics and culture. In his review of the volume for *The Washington Post*, Hugh Hewitt compares Rufo's considerable work to such examples of "intellectual history" as the political tracts of George Will, Matthew Continetti, and Jonah Goldberg. As a trained intellectual historian, I raised an eyebrow when I encountered Hewitt's idea of historical studies that are "well done" and "full of illuminating ideas." Also, Hewitt used the space allotted to him to attack my favorite graduate professor, Herbert Marcuse, a large photograph of whom graces his review. My former mentor functions in Hewitt's account largely as a whipping boy.

According to Hewitt, Rufo focuses on Marcuse, "whose Marxist- and Freudian-inspired critical social theories had an astonishing lasting impact on the American Left." Among the notorious activities of this German refugee scholar, who came to the US in the 1930s, was training Angela Davis, the black radical Marxist, and this relationship (as we are not told) came during the twilight of Marcuse's career, at the University of California at San Diego. Hewitt believes that though Davis was a "marginal figure in the violent upheavals of the 1960s and 1970s," her complicity in the attempted escape of murder suspects in a courtroom drama in Marin County, California, which resulted in four deaths, was somehow related to Marcuse's teachings. Hewitt, like Rufo, does mention homegrown radicals like Derrick Bell, the first black law professor at Harvard, but the major focus for both the author and the reviewer is the poisonous fumes of foreign ideologies, particularly the radical revolutionary doctrines of Marcuse.

Although it is not my intention to deny such influences entirely, I believe the American conservative establishment has focused excessively on foreign contaminants while denying the extraordinary receptiveness of American political culture to certain European fashions. Works by conservatives attacking Marcuse and his followers as "termites" eating away at the otherwise sound structure of American democracy go back to Eliseo Vivas's *Contra Marcuse* in 1971.[37] This work by a prolific Colombian American aesthetician, which offers a penetrating critique of Marcuse's social theory, gives the impression that nothing essentially American was responsible for the spread of Marcuse's ideas. We were taken unawares, runs the argument, by dangerous foreigners whom we let into our country out of misplaced generosity.

Allan Bloom's *The Closing of the American Mind*, which became a conservative bestseller in 1987, does not dwell on Marcuse, but Bloom looks critically at other alien ideas that he believes polluted the real America.[38] These ideas entered our culture through "the German connection," and apparently college students, according to Bloom, were becoming radicalized after devouring Friedrich Nietzsche and Martin Heidegger. Though Bloom's central argument seems to beg for evidence, it had the indisputable advantage of not blaming what was indigenously American for the straying of American political culture. A patriotic reader could deplore our radicalization without having to believe that what was taking place was owing to things originating at home.

My own view on this matter, to which I devoted several books, argues the opposite position, namely that there were already developments in the United States that led to the breakdown of our traditional social and political institutions. There is no need to point to foreign contaminants to explain our condition. Frankfurt School theorists like Marcuse, Theodor Adorno, and Max Horkheimer acquired fame and fortune in American exile. They only acquired comparable status in their native Germany with the American post–World War II occupation, when the American government sent critical theorists back to "reeducate" the Germans.

In the United States, as Christopher Lasch argues persuasively in *The True and Only Heaven: Progress and Its Critics* (1991), what were considered radical social ideas in interwar Germany, e.g., massive social engineering, the imposition of gender equality, the acceptance of homosexual relations, and a continuing crusade against the "fascist" mentality, resonated nowhere else as well as they did here.[39] *The Authoritarian Personality*, which Adorno and Horkheimer coedited in 1950 and which was published by the moderately left-of-center American Jewish Committee—which, by the way, also put out *Commentary*—became a standard work in the social sciences.[40] The F-scale devised by Marcuse's friend Adorno for determining "pro-fascist" attitudes was adopted in both the US and Canada as the basis for testing the mental soundness of students and public administrators. The highly respected social scientist Seymour Martin Lipset viewed *The Authoritarian Personality* as a valuable guide not only for understanding the fascist danger but also for mobilizing Western democracies against Soviet communism.

By the time Lipset offered this judgment, members of the Frankfurt School had run afoul of the House Un-American Activities Committee for having leaned too noticeably toward the Soviets during the Cold War. This however may be less relevant for our consideration than the widespread cultural and social acceptability in the United States of what in interwar Germany had been considered "cultural Bolshevism." In the United States the founders and early members of the Frankfurt School, including psychologists Erich Fromm and Karen Horney, found an enthusiastic home.

By 1968, when Angela Davis was studying with Marcuse in San Diego,[41] her teacher had become much more of a political activist than he had been when I first encountered him five years earlier. In the intervening time, events occurred that may shed light on this change. Brandeis University had refused to extend Marcuse's professorship beyond the fixed age of retirement; and Yale, while I was studying there, turned down the plan to offer this dignitary a special chair in the history of Marxism. I suspect Marcuse took the offer from San Diego because nothing better came his way. It is also hard to recognize from Davis's descriptions my own professor, although I have no doubt that after my relationship with him, he became more negative about Western "repressive capitalism."

In one of Marcuse's classes I attended, many of his students were patriotic anti-communists. I myself have not changed my political opinions significantly since that time, but I don't recall Marcuse ever trying to censor or cancel any of us in class for not parroting his political convictions. We assumed what his opinions were since he never stated them explicitly. To my surprise Marcuse liked Joseph de Maistre's profoundly reactionary dialogues, *Soirées de Saint-Pétersbourg* (1821), which he could quote from memory, while naming different editions of that work. Compared to my other professors, who were mostly pedestrian liberal Democrats, Marcuse stood out as an old-world scholar.

In the 1960s, the United States underwent enormous political ferment, which likely would have been the case even if political activists were not reading Marcuse, Frantz Fanon, and other non-American radicals. The anti-war and civil rights movements and the burgeoning of the feminist rebellion against a male-dominated society were all taking place simultaneously. Meanwhile the administrative state was assuming a larger and larger role in fighting "discrimination" and righting what were perceived as historic wrongs. There was also a movement in the counter-culture that rejected bourgeois standards of social conduct, and which was open to both sexual promiscuity and psychedelic experiences. European thinkers like Marcuse definitely influenced those fashions, but they were not necessary for their flourishing. It is quite conceivable that most of these developments would have transpired even without the effect of European radical thinkers. There was enough combustible energy in the US to have produced these results without foreign stimulants.

Moreover, Europeans were reading American progressives like Betty Friedan, Paul Goodman, and C. Wright Mills while Americans were reading European radicals. The radicalizing influence was certainly not all in one direction, as I noticed from visiting European bookstores in the 1960s and 1970s. Rufo's subject, Marcuse, became in some sense an American author. His books were published in English for American readers from 1941 onward, which was the date of the appearance of *Reason and Revolution: Hegel and the Rise of Social Theory*. (A German edition of this work did not exist until 1962.) *Eros and Civilization: A Philosophical Inquiry into Freud* came out in English in 1955 and was then translated for German readers two years later. *One-Dimensional Man: Studies in the Ideology of Advanced Industrial Society* was also first produced in English, for a predominantly American readership, in 1964, and wasn't available in German translation until three years later. Marcuse's *An Essay on Liberation* was likewise published first in English in 1969, although the German version *Versuch über die Befreiung* came out shortly afterward.

I mention these publication dates to indicate where Marcuse's primary audience was found for decades. No one would deny that he came from a German cultural world and spoke with an accent. But he found a fervent fan base here long before he became a rock star in Europe. Already by the 1970s, I no longer thought that the United States was being transformed by an invasion of foreign authors. I realized that the cultural and social changes that we were experiencing were mostly internally generated. European radicals resonated with American academics, journalists, and college students because they fitted in with what this country was becoming. The success story of the "American" Herbert Marcuse is a case in point.

CHAPTER THREE

Dead Right

–◆ ◆ ◆–

The Historical Realism of James Burnham

Intercollegiate Review

WINTER 1984

READING SAMUEL T. Francis's terse biography *Power and History: The Political Thought of James Burnham* made me aware of the general neglect that Burnham has suffered as a thinker. Although a recipient of the Medal of Freedom and, more recently, of an Ingersoll Prize, neither can compensate for the indifference and often contempt that academics and journalists have shown for his accomplishments. It should be noted that the Medal of Freedom was a political honor that the President, who periodically looks to his right flank, paid to an aging conservative theoretician. The awarding of an Ingersoll Prize was likewise a political statement, designed to embarrass the liberal intelligentsia; the judging committee for the Ingersoll Prize wished to honor a great thinker scorned by the Left. In making an equivalent award to Jorge Luis Borges, the same committee was sending a message to the Nobel Prize judges, who had passed up repeatedly a brilliant anticommunist man of letters.

Burnham has aroused considerable and justified hostility from the Left. For example, the usually civil (but then leftist) author of *Up from Communism* (1975), John P. Diggins, became rather abusive in 1973 when he described Burnham's post-communist career.[42] In the 1930s Burnham was a high-ranking Trotskyist and close friend of Leon Trotsky. By 1940, however, he had disavowed communism without showing any apparent signs of emotional turmoil, and several years later was denouncing liberal idealism as well as communist duplicity. Francis argues (convincingly in my opinion) that Burnham abandoned communism less because of a moral judgment than because of his growing doubts about the communist view of history. Capitalism, which he identified with an economy that was entrepreneurial and largely unregulated by government, seemed to be increasingly a thing of the past. Yet Burnham also viewed socialism as an unrealizable ideal. The movement of industrialized countries toward welfare economies and the emerging alliance between corporate business and bureaucratic government did not represent the beginnings of a classless society. These developments dramatized the political ascendancy of a managerial class, which concealed its bid for power behind various ideological slogans—democratic socialist, fascist, and communist. The class struggle, which Burnham believed that Marx had only partially understood, was bringing forth a managerial hierarchy in post-capitalist society.

Although Burnham maintained ties to the democratic Left throughout the early and mid-1940s, Francis correctly stresses the conservative thrust of his thinking even in that period. *The Machiavellians*, which Burnham published in 1943, aims its most savage attacks at the democratic Left.[43] Despite his distaste for the medieval concept of a Christian commonwealth (expressed in the opening pages of *The Machiavellians*) and his recurrent praise of Machiavelli's "science of politics," Burnham, as Francis reminds us, set out in his book to criticize crusading democratic internationalism, not traditional Christian values. His villains were the self-styled anti-fascists who found no enemies on the Left. His heroes were Gaetano Mosca, Vilfredo Pareto, Robert Michels, and other social thinkers who had recognized that the pursuit and exercise of power went on in even so-called democratic societies, but more insidiously and hypocritically than in the past. I for one am astonished that some American traditionalists still refer to *The Machiavellians* as an "anti-traditional, positivist" work. It is in fact quintessentially Augustinian in its analysis of corrupt, unchanging human appetites, and in its defense of the state as a flawed but necessary instrument of governance in what can only be described as Burnham's version of the City of Man. It is also a grim indictment of the utopian impulse in American politics, which foreshadows the argument of *Suicide of the West* (1964).

Burnham has aroused not only anger born of a sense of betrayal among leftists, but also deep suspicion among neoconservatives. Despite the neoconservative's celebration of George Orwell as one of their precursors, they have still not discovered the thinker who, by Orwell's own admission, had first sketched for him the gruesome landscape of *Nineteen Eighty-Four*. An editorial column in *Encounter* (May 1975) posed the question whether Orwell could have really been affected by such insubstantial books as *The Managerial Revolution* and *The Machiavellians*.[44] The author proceeds to give his own judgment: "I doubt that anyone reads them today except, like Professor Steinhoff [an Orwell biographer], for historical reasons." Lest there be doubt that the writer is stating his own opinion, he then adds:

> Even the works of James Hadley Chase, whom Professor Steinhoff includes among those who influenced Orwell, have probably stood up better to the test of time than Burnham's. But it isn't the best books which necessarily influence us most. In bad books one finds what one is looking for, especially if they are things which are not to be found in the best ones; and in Burnham, Orwell found as it were a scenario which fitted in ideally with his own preoccupations.

The disparaging judgment of Burnham implicit in this comment raises the question whether its author, or the journal that included this judgment as part of an editorial column, has not allowed malice to color scholarship. As Samuel Francis has shown in arguing the obvious, Burnham throughout the 1940s and into the 1950s was a highly respected social and political analyst. Raymond Aron, Benedetto Croce, Leon Trotsky, Reinhold Niebuhr, and Sidney Hook were only a few of the intellectual celebrities who published critical responses to his analytical studies. Nor were Burnham's conclusions about American society and the international scene foolish and trivial as *Encounter* suggests. His view of long-term Soviet advantages in a protracted Cold War and his observations on the growing bureaucratization of post-capitalist Western society turned out to be unfortunately accurate. *Encounter* tries to discredit *The Managerial Revolution* by stressing Burnham's faulty prediction that Nazi Germany would defeat Soviet Russia. But the prediction was plausible enough when it was made in 1941. Besides, Burnham's work was not primarily an exercise in futurology. It was explicitly a study of social change in advanced industrial societies that is still read and quoted today.

The blast against Burnham in *Encounter* was not a random shot. It came from those who still held to the values and positions of what was once the anti-communist moderate Left. The overlapping bodies of contributors to *Encounter* and *Commentary* recognize their unbridgeable differences with Burnham.

It would be wrong to reduce Burnham's quarrel with neoconservatives to tactical questions. It has been argued, for example, that what divides Burnham's conservative realism from neoconservative thinking is their differing degrees of toughness. While neoconservatives still defend the containment strategy of the Truman administration, Burnham, particularly right after the Second World War, advocated a vigorous offensive response to Soviet aggression in Eastern and Central Europe. Both parts of the assertion are correct, but must be qualified. Although Norman Podhoretz, Jeane J. Kirkpatrick, and other neoconservatives idealize the Truman administration's policy toward the Soviets, they do so defensively: against the outright Soviet appeasers on their left. They also defend Truman's foreign policy symbolically, in looking for a precedent for their own attempt to merge the welfare state with hard-line, anti-Soviet positions. Moreover, *Commentary* has published policy analysts such as Richard Pipes and Edward Luttwak whose advice for dealing with Soviet imperialism recalls the tone of Burnham's postwar tracts. Nor is it clear that Burnham has been consistently hawkish since 1945. His response to the Soviet suppression of the Hungarian uprising in 1956 was surprisingly mild: he called for negotiation, not confrontation, with the Soviets. Significantly, Burnham has never associated himself with free market economics. He has generally viewed the welfare state as socially inevitable in a post-capitalist managerial world. Despite his passionate defense of freedom of property in *Suicide of the West* (1964),[45] he sees that freedom as a necessarily eroded one. The managerial revolution that has occurred can no longer be undone in the name of nineteenth-century ideals.

But unlike the neoconservatives, Burnham never praises the welfare state as an agent of social justice. In *Suicide of the West* he ridicules the advocates of material redistribution and all other apostles of "democratic egalitarian and universalist beliefs." He notes that the American political Left refuses to accept the fact of natural human inequalities. Because of this self-imposed blindness, liberals insist on giving the state ever more power to legislate equality. They persist in believing that education will make everyone the same and see no danger in embracing as political equals groups that are "inferior on the average to other men in their ability to create and maintain a civilized society." Liberals, one may infer from Burnham, descend from a higher to a lower level of illusion. They move from the high-minded illusion (which he identifies specifically with Sidney Hook) that education will remove intellectual and moral disparities among men to the more pernicious position of value relativism, which denies cultural inequalities entirely. Although Burnham does not consistently distinguish degrees of liberal illusion, and sometimes sees all liberal beliefs as part of a single pattern, it may be possible to recognize neoconservative positions as those of the less extreme liberals whom he describes.

In an incisive review of Jeane J. Kirkpatrick's book *Dictatorship and Double Standards* (1982), Aileen S. Kraditor characterizes Kirkpatrick as a "champion of welfarism at home who has fought against its unintended—and in many cases intended—consequences abroad." Despite her denunciation of communism in practice, Kirkpatrick gives repeated evidence of admiring socialism as an ideal. She believes that the state should actively attempt to reduce economic differences; and while she expresses reservations about the use of government-enforced quotas to reduce racial inequalities, she adopts the more ambiguous liberal position of calling for "affirmative action" programs. Kirkpatrick follows the neoconservative practice of identifying herself with the vital center, between what is a caricature of the New Right and the pro-communist Left. In *Breaking Ranks* (1979), Norman Podhoretz depicts himself and other Moynihan-Democrats as in a similar position, between James Buckley Republicans and Bella Abzug liberals. In the summer 1984 issue of the neoconservative publication *This World*, a member of the advisory board, Max L. Stackhouse, calls for an ecumenical public theology for America, equally removed from both Fundamentalism and Marxist Liberation theology. Martin Luther King Jr., "who touched the consciousness of the nation on racism and segregation, one of the greatest flaws of our national history," is seen as having provided a theological "model for twentieth-century America"—along with the Cold War liberal, Reinhold Niebuhr, and the secularized Christian-turned-socialist, Walter Rauschenbusch.

Clearly neoconservative sensibilities, values, and heroes are quite different from those of James Burnham. Burnham, from their standpoint, expresses an extremist position on social issues, as repugnant as the views of the Marxist Left. For Burnham, on the other hand, the neoconservatives, despite their hostility to communism, may be part of the problem that is overwhelming the West. This is the pursuit of the fantasy of social equality undertaken in a secularized society that leaves "no room for qualitative distinctions among men." Needless to say, there are exceptions in terms of the neoconservative's dedication to social equality, as the writings of Irving Kristol demonstrate. (As I have argued elsewhere, there are obvious affinities in thinking between Burnham and Kristol, whose relationship to the neoconservative camp seems to be ethnic and regional rather than ideological.) But there remain characteristic, even commonplace, neoconservative positions, which supposedly occupy a middle ground somewhere, between the Marxist or Bella Abzug Left and the anti-communist, anti-egalitarian Right.

A more demonstrable, or less hypothetical, difference between Burnham and the neoconservatives pertains to their differing views of democratic universalism. In his book, Francis stresses this difference in outlook and uses it to clarify Burnham's thinking as an historical conservative. Understanding what is at the heart of the matter, Francis quotes from Burnham's response to a call by Peter Berger in 1972 for the construction of a "conservative humanism." Berger believed that the struggle for social and moral traditionalism was entering a new phase in the late twentieth century. It was finally possible and necessary for conservatives throughout the world to define their shared universal concerns in the name of mankind. In a trenchant critique of Berger's undertaking, Burnham observed:

> Conservatism can be considered humanist only if humanism is interpreted to mean a concern with the interests and well-being not of abstract Man or Mankind but of existential Man, historical Man, or actual men as they actually exist in space and time. Existential man is not a bare identity, a featureless constant, but a node of particularities, distinctive relationships, differences, qualities, peculiarities.

It may be possible to compare Burnham's reaction to Berger with Burke's eloquent rejoinder to the English friends of the French Revolution and their spokesman, Dr. Richard Price. In *Reflections on the Revolution in France* (1790), Burke assailed Price's contention that the French Revolution's Rights of Men and Citizens were merely an extension of the established liberties of Englishmen.[46] Burke attacked not only the comparison that Price had drawn, but also the very notion of abstract or "metaphysical rights." It is ironic that the self-labeled Machiavellian Burnham replied as a Burkean to the universalist proposals of a sociologist who long associated himself with Burke. Francis senses the overshadowing role of history, or more specifically historical particularities, in shaping Burnham's conservatism. Burnham might have written the following passages as easily as did Burke (who was here responding to the admirers of the French Revolution):

> The nature of man is intricate; the objects of society are of the greatest possible complexity: and therefore no simple disposition or direction of power can be suitable either to man's nature or to the quality of his affairs . . . The pretended rights of these theorists are all extremes; and in proportion as they are metaphysically true, they are morally and politically false. The rights of men are in a sort of *middle*, incapable of definition, but not impossible to be discerned.

Like Burke, Burnham believes that the lust for power has often motivated the exponents of universalist political theories. Yet in the modern Western context, Burnham identifies the stress on humanity and human rights primarily with liberal self-delusion. By assuming the existence of the imminence of a universal political community with shared democratic-egalitarian values, liberals mistake an empty vision for an emerging reality. Burnham's remarks on Peter Berger in 1972 were prophetic. In November 1983, Berger, in an essay for *Commentary*, exhorts his fellow Americans to undertake missionary activity in the Third World as the representatives of liberal democracy. Berger's earlier attempts to universalize the lessons of Burkean conservatism, and, on other occasions, to study the applicability of the Protestant work ethic to "emerging nations," were now being replaced by the militant creed of democratic universalism. Berger was also expressing two cardinal principles of the neoconservative worldview that were diametrically opposed to Burnham's thinking: the universal applicability of democratic procedures and the moral superiority of democracy to other forms of government and ways of life. In March 1984, *Commentary* printed an article that recommends a new bipartisan American foreign policy: basic to this policy will be the nurturing of democracy throughout the world. The same article favorably compares the success of Indian democracy to Argentine authoritarianism. The fact that India is a bloated, bureaucratic, politically corrupt, usually pro-Soviet socialist state should matter less to the American people than its ostentatious use of the ballot box in what are often rigged elections.

It may be fair to say that while for the neoconservatives the best of all worlds would be a collection of interchangeable democratic welfare states, for Burnham the best of all worlds would be one in which social and national diversity could be expressed. He opposes communism as an enemy of utopian visions and as a realistic critic of the passion for power masquerading as idealism. Unlike the neoconservatives, who have studiously ignored him, Burnham does not seek to replace the Bolshevik crusade begun in 1917 with the armed doctrines of older European revolutions. Although he sometimes has been criticized as mean-spirited and coldly cerebral, Burnham's historical conservatism is based on tolerance of men in their distinctive cultural and social relationships. Yet such a position does not incorporate the value relativism that Burnham properly identifies with self-hating Western liberals. His understanding of men in their own cultural context stems from an appreciation of the intricate arrangements needed to build and sustain civilized society.

It may also be that that comparative historical perspective which Francis finds in Burnham is related to a growing pessimism about the modern West. In *Suicide of the West* Burnham laments the guilt-ridden retreat from empire that took place among postwar European states. He also bewails the dreariness of the partly realized liberal vision of society, no doubt as he contemplates the peaks and accomplishments of other world civilizations and the happier moments in the Western past:

> [M]odern liberalism does not offer men compelling motives for personal suffering, sacrifice, and death. There is no tragic dimension in its picture of the good life. Men become willing to endure, sacrifice, and die for God, family, king, honor, country, from a sense of absolute duty or an exalted vision of the meaning of history . . . Except for mercenaries, saints, and neurotics no one is willing to sacrifice and die for progressive education, medicare, humanity in the abstract, the UN, and a ten percent rise in social security payments.

No words have portrayed as well as these the liberal wasteland into which bureaucrats and intellectuals are pushing America. This wasteland, Burnham warns, will not last long, for a hard tyranny will quickly follow the reign of decadence.

Robert Nisbet, R.I.P.

Chronicles

JANUARY 1997

T HE RECENT death of Robert Nisbet has removed from our midst one of the premier social thinkers of the century. His works, particularly *The Quest for Community* (1953) and *The Sociological Tradition* (1966), will be read as long as literate people consider the nature of human relations.[47] Nisbet brought to his discipline both a rich historical sense and a justified anxiety about the modern state. He viewed the "national state" as an administrative mechanism run by social engineers and born and sustained by the breakdown of traditional community. And he saw the rise of this regime as being tied to another social crisis, the frenzied search among the uprooted for new forms of association and security. For Nisbet, this constituted the greatest danger of modern political life: the continued need for authority in a society that preached individual autonomy. This need for direction turned people toward redemptive political movements and encouraged the state's attempt to socialize its subjects. Contrary to a recent commentary in *The Wall Street Journal* which argued that the statists, after "making a mess of things economically," have turned their "penetration point to the arena of family life," Nisbet maintained that social democracy has always been primarily about social reconstruction. Those who support this patently intrusive system, he explained, are looking for control, not only social services.

Against these flights from freedom, Nisbet had little to offer, except sound warnings and prescriptions about "intermediate institutions." Though he praised such institutions, the buffer he saw between isolated individuals, often colluding in their enslavement, and an encroaching state was never more, for him, than a last defense. Nisbet thought that the Western welfare state, with fortunes to spend and a monopoly of power, would probably continue to get its way. In the United States it would manage opposition by offering entitlements and by waging crusades against ideological enemies.

The compasses for his social thinking were the genteel skepticism of David Hume and the counterrevolutionary thought of the early nineteenth century. From these sources he drew his critical views about the superstition of rationalism and about plans to redo societies from the bottom up. Of all social doctrines that Nisbet criticized, the one he found most absurd was the belief that individuals could be trained by the state to be autonomous. Men, explained Nisbet, replicating Hume's critique of John Locke, had never existed outside of fairly constant social units; it was therefore highly doubtful that they could live in any other way or that our social existence until now was somehow unnatural. The state's offer to help human beings rise above natural social groupings seemed to Nisbet a call for control, one whose advocates would apply force on behalf of a whimsical but far-reaching social project.

Nisbet singled out for praise the critics of the ideal of the socially autonomous and self-defining individual. But his respect for such critics and corresponding distaste for libertarians did not prove Frank Meyer's passionately held view that Nisbet worshipped the state. The truth is more complex: Nisbet held organic authority to be essential for a stable and satisfying human existence, and he accused libertarians of weakening social resistance to the modern state by imitating its appeal to individual rights and pleasures. Despite this particular censure, it would be a mistake to consider Nisbet a friend of the welfare state. His published remarks on this subject are as vitriolic as those of Murray Rothbard.

It may be permissible for me to express my own considerable debt to Robert Nisbet, the scholar and the man. Whatever I have done in my own field would certainly have less value if his books had not come to my attention as a graduate student. And I studied them closely without knowing of Nisbet's strong views about American politics. While he and I, as I later discovered, held generally the same political opinions, those opinions were not what drew me to his world of ideas. Though, like him, a conservative, I shared his appreciation of Marx and Émile Durkheim, both men of the Left, whom he preferred to that dreary proto-liberal John Locke. Nisbet's writings had in my case another long-range effect: they led me toward social history and the history of sociology. Indeed they illustrated that one can be interested in both and respect traditional societies. This pairing of attitudes is also exemplified by the social anthropology of Grace Goodell, an admirer of Nisbet, but it might have taken me decades more to become aware of it if I had not encountered *The Sociological Tradition.*

Late in life, after I had met him, Nisbet wrote generously about my books and more than once worked to salvage my derailed academic career. What made these efforts particularly noteworthy is that by then he was gravely ill but gave no indication that his health was failing. No matter how afflicted he was, he sounded cheerful in phone conversations. And though an internationally honored author, an Albert Schweitzer Professor of Humanities, and recipient of the Ingersoll Prize for Scholarly Letters, Nisbet spoke to his disciples as an equal. His lack of condescension was obvious to his acquaintances, though Bob's friendliness never caused me to forget in whose shadow I stood. This always elegantly dressed, affable, and strikingly handsome gentleman looked as academic luminaries should but rarely do. He also bestowed on me and others lifelong ideas; and once while he was complimenting me for something I had published, I joked that he was only noticing what I had cribbed from him. "Go ahead and crib more!" was his jovial response. Those of us who learned from his genial mind will inevitably take that advice, *calcando passus gigantis.*

A Man of Letters

Chronicles

AUGUST 1994

R USSELL KIRK's death on April 29 deprived both the world of letters and high-toned American conservatism of one of its premier representatives. Author of numerous studies on topics ranging from constitutional law to economics and creator of Gothic mysteries and ghost stories, Kirk left behind a corpus testifying to his rich learning and literary gifts. His best remembered work, *The Conservative Mind*, which has gone through seven revised editions since 1953, gave to the then-nascent postwar Right a lustrous pedigree.[48] Here Kirk traces the conservative mood and principles, which he saw threatened but still operative in postwar America, back to their provincial English and early American sources. He demonstrates a certain continuity running from John Adams, Edmund Burke, High Federalists, Southern regionalists, and other early nineteenth century Anglo-American critics of both equality and the modern state to later spokesmen for the same critical positions. It may be useful to look in this line of succession less for more of the same than for a continuity of spirit, which Kirk convincingly defines as the Anglo-American conservative tradition. It is the author of *The Conservative Mind* who first uncovered that tradition and allowed American conservatives to view themselves as part of a unified and venerable heritage.

Among Kirk's other contributions, for which Thomas Fleming and I are particularly grateful, is the prominence he gave to conservative thinkers and statesmen whom scholars might otherwise overlook. Among these cases in point are James Fitzjames Stephens, John Randolph of Roanoke, and William Lecky. Kirk not only theoretically resurrected neglected Anglo-American conservatives, but he brought out the conservative side of figures not often viewed as being on the Right. His commentaries on Nathaniel Hawthorne, James Fenimore Cooper, and Herman Melville, all Jacksonian Democrats, have helped to explain these literary figures in a theological light. Because of his own interest in his Calvinist forebears, Kirk looked at the ways in which the idea of Original Sin affected early American culture.

Any biographer of Kirk will face the daunting task of integrating into a single study a body of writing that would take an entire library room to house. These writings include a magisterial biography of Kirk's friend, T. S. Eliot, a learned history of the United States as seen within the Western experience, *The Roots of American Order*, and *The Conservative Constitution*.

Those eulogies that movement conservatives have showered on Kirk in the wake of his death and during a testimonial to him at Dearborn last October are entirely deserved. Without Kirk the postwar conservatism to which I have devoted considerable scholarship would have been far less respectable—and without any serious claim to a past. However, the surprise is not that New York–Washington conservatives have praised Kirk at the end of his life, but that so comparatively little was made of him in his later years. His Heritage Foundation lectures, while they did lend dignity to the shop-and-till conservatism of the Reagan years, seemed to attract attention only when he courageously spoke out about the decadence of his movement.

While older conservatives at Hillsdale College, the Intercollegiate Studies Institute, and Heritage continued to provide Russell Kirk with opportunities, newcomer institutions seemed far more interested in promoting Dinesh D'Souza's collected academic horror stories, *Illiberal Education* (1991). The *Festschrift* that appeared in Kirk's honor several days before his death waited years for subsidies. It was finally published on a shoestring by a less-than-distinguished conservative press. When the neoconservatives assailed Kirk in 1987 for making surprisingly strong remarks about their involvement with the American-Israeli lobby, few conservatives rose to his defense. Some, like William Buckley, offered to mediate once Kirk had atoned for his indiscretion. Making baseless charges against Kirk as an "anti-Semite" was obviously not considered indiscreet, particularly when the name-callers controlled newspapers and fortunes.

Some paleoconservatives have been heard to grumble that Dr. Kirk might have done more for "the Cause," but there was, in fact, little he or anyone could have done in the declining decade of his life that would have made any difference in the current conservative wars. Not even during his period of fame had he exercised political influence. His own abiding interest was culture, and as he grew older and the left-liberal ascendancy over America became frenetic, his role as a cultural critic grew correspondingly weaker. In 1971, his biography of Eliot, published by Random House, had been widely reviewed by the elite press. Twenty years later his books went unnoticed, except by a few conservative magazines with rather limited readership.

Russell Kirk stood for an older cultural conservatism, which did not "reach out" to those whom Washington conservatives were rushing around to pacify. He did not strike or change his colors; nor did he whine about the lack of "indecisiveness" among conservatives. Despite his "insensitivity" here, he and his wife beggared themselves by caring for Third World refugees, but neither made a political statement out of their acts of Christian kindness.

Kirk's one overshadowing fault revealed the naive goodness of his character. He bestowed selfless love upon a largely unworthy political cause, and though this did not transform that cause, he dramatized the disproportion between his devotion and its object. For many of us there are lessons to be learned from this example, and the most palpable is the need to judge harshly those who refused to defend and even lent themselves to humiliating a noble teacher. For all these ingratitudes, Kirk led a fulfilling life as a husband, father, and as the revered mentor of those youthful devotees who sojourned at his house in Mecosta. Here this benign and erudite man of letters did enjoy a suitable reward even in this transitory existence—and a foretaste of the world to come.

Loss of a Principled Critic

Chronicles

JANUARY 1995

W ITH CHRISTOPHER LASCH's death last March, our society lost a probing and principled critic. According to one by now standard biography, Lasch started his career as an anti-war activist and Marxist-Freudian synthesizer and by the end of his life had moved to the right with a defense of traditional communities. There is truth in this account, as anyone who knew and read Lasch can testify, but equally important, there were striking continuities in his work. Whatever else Lasch was, he fought relentlessly against the liberal tradition. And by that tradition he understood not only the latest PC outrage but the beliefs in individual gratification and the profit motive as the foundations of social life.

In a cascade of books from the 1970s on, including *The Culture of Narcissism* (1979), *The Minimal Self* (1984), and *The True and Only Heaven* (1991), Lasch lamented the liberal presuppositions of American politics and culture. Americans, he maintained, had sacrificed the value of community to pursue self-centered pleasure and material riches. Our greatest writers, he explained, had observed this problem, and some had come to view it as an inescapable fate. In his later writings, particularly in a spirited piece for *Harper's*, Lasch also went after the feminists; and in his last book, he even dared to castigate an icon for both liberals and conservatives, neoconservative hero Martin Luther King Jr., for demanding that the federal government alter the residential patterns of urban ethnics. But all of these strictures, especially those directed against the alliance of big business and the managerial state, reflect a premise found in Lasch's early work, that liberal individualism saps communal life and prepares the way for administrative, therapeutic tyranny.

Lasch became a personal friend of mine, despite the untoward circumstances of our first meeting. As a candidate for an associate professorship at the University of Rochester more than twenty years ago, I encountered him as an illustrious senior member of the history department. Lasch opposed my candidacy, seeing in me a potential instrument of an enemy faction. (His political judgment was, by the way, entirely correct.) When we met again in what turned out to be the twilight of his career, we discussed his fateful opposition to me. I assured him that he had quite properly acted in self-defense, though his action had ended for me any possibility of professional advancement. Lasch disagreed. He spoke of the need to turn enemies into friends, and he noted that our friendship might have begun sooner if he had supported rather than opposed me.

Balancing his feistiness was the other side of Lasch's personality: his proverbial kindliness toward family members, friends, and students. A warm disposition was the characteristic that those closest to him remember best. And though descended from a distinguished St. Louis publishing family and the son-in-law of the historian Henry Steele Commager, Lasch reveled in the company of working stiffs. He was a populist not only in his politics but also in his genuine appreciation of unabashed Middle Americans. Unlike those ersatz communitarians who wish to construct victim-friendly settings with the aid of government agencies, Lasch did not look to coercive sensitizers to restore the social good. By community he meant what the Germans call *Gemeinschaft*, organic associations derived from kinship and a shared history. Though Lasch was willing to accept variations on this model, given the present shattered condition of the real article, he rejected academic redefinitions of what community is about. Least of all did he view it as a collection of itinerant yuppies and sexual deviants looking for an idol to replace the god that failed.

A certifiable Brahmin, he nonetheless appealed to those uncorrupted by wealth or academic pretension. Both his celebration of the lower middle class and his yearning for a localist, family-based socialism show the unseasonable nature of his anti-liberal radicalism. More distributist than leftist and more traditionalist than would be tolerable to our official Right, Lasch defies simplistic labeling. He also continues to be a source of inspiration to those on the true Right, those of us whose conservatism has nothing to do with the defense of multinational consumerism.

Panajotis Kondylis and the Obsoleteness of Conservatism

Modern Age

FALL 1997

P ANAJOTIS KONDYLIS, a Greek scholar who lives in Heidelberg
and writes in German, may be, unbeknownst to himself, one of
the great conservative thinkers of our age. Describing Kondylis
as a conservative might leave him and his readers puzzled. His 500-page
work *Konservativismus* ("Conservatism," 1986) examines "the historical content and *decline*" of its subject.[49] For Kondylis, conservatism had
already declined in the last century as a major political force. It was the
ideal of an essentially medieval hierarchical society defended by landed
aristocrats and their intellectual followers. What Americans have usually presented as conservative values, Kondylis explains, belongs to a
"bourgeois world of thought." Indeed the historical constructions of
American traditionalists have been at most attempts to "exalt an older
conceptual legacy and a long dead way of life against the newest developments in the direction of a consumerist mass democracy."[50] Kondylis
cites Russell Kirk and the Southern Agrarians as examples of this ten-

82

dency to conjure up an ideal organic past in a society that has always been nearer to mass democracy than it has to European traditionalism.

Kondylis identifies himself with Marxism, broadly understood. In a recent essay, "Marxism, Communism, and the History of the Twentieth Century," Kondylis offers this revealing opinion: "The planetary social project of communism failed not because of moral or economic inferiority but because the national power of Russia encountered the superior national power of the United States." Furthermore, "Never before has the Marxist view of history been as true and current as it is now in the initial phase of a planetary history," particularly in determining social relations and the "ideological" forms that they take.[51] In my German correspondence with him, Kondylis makes the point that, unlike me, "he stands far closer to Marx than to [the German legal thinker] Carl Schmitt."[52] His detailed analysis of social class and of ideological consciousness as reflected in culture point back to Marx and to the twentieth-century Marxist interpreter of intellectual history, Georg Lukács. Kondylis underlines these connections whenever he can.

His transparent dislike for the United States and its current devotion to "human rights" may offend some American patriots. He reduces the American faith in democracy and in universal rights to an instrument of national power. In a caustic piece for the *Frankfurter Rundschau* (August 18, 1996), "Human Rights: Conceptual Confusion and Political Instrumentalization," he notes that the United States speaks of human rights in the context of international affairs, not as a replacement for its own national laws that still distinguish between citizens and noncitizens: "No state can grant all of humanity the same rights—e.g., rights of settlement and voting—without ceasing to exist." For the American government, "human rights are a political tool within a planetary context whose density requires the use of universalist ideologies; within this framework, however, great nations continue to determine the binding interpretation of those same constructs."[53] Kondylis dislikes not only Americans for what he perceives as political hypocrisy but for their consumerist mentality. He has editorialized against the corrupting effect of American hedonism, which he thinks is now infecting Europeans.

Kondylis's brief against the United States occasionally descends into superficial generalization. "Human rights" ideology is by no means accepted by all Americans; and contrary to what Kondylis asserts, "human rights" ideologues are willing to blur the distinction between the rights of citizens and of non-citizens. Recent judicial decisions that bear on the "rights" of illegal aliens have interpreted the Fourteenth Amendment as establishing universally binding human rights. Meanwhile, advocates of a human-rights-based foreign policy, like the editorial boards of *The New York Times* and *Wall Street Journal*, have been equally zealous in upholding an expansionist immigration policy. Conversely, American nationalists on the Old Right have been both isolationists and critics of "human rights."[54] As for the assurance given that "economic inferiority" had nothing to do with the disintegration of the Soviet empire, this particular statement is never demonstrated. Kondylis goes on to speak of the "superior national power of the United States," which may be another way of referring to the working economy of the United States, as opposed to the fatally paralyzed one of the former Soviet Union.[55]

Despite Kondylis's Marxist self-labeling and distaste for the United States, one can find in him an identifiable man of the Right. But the Right to which Kondylis belongs is not the European counterpart of the American Right-Center, made up of pro-business supporters of a democratic welfare state and of a consumer economy. Like the intellectual movement called the European New Right, which often quotes him, Kondylis stresses the merits of traditional community, which he believes to be threatened by American mass democracy and American economic expansion. Unfortunately, anti-Americanism has become instinctive for many on the European Right.[56] I say "unfortunately" not because this sentiment is never justified. I think it often is, given the human rights and globalist triumphalism of American state department spokesmen and journalists and the moral pollution produced by our entertainment industry. But anti-Americanism gets in the way of understanding our current political context. Much of what the European New Right blames on the American people are recent developments, such as crusades for human rights with an often-changing content, while what is perceived as quintessentially American is equally characteristic of other Western societies. Here a sense of historical change may be necessary. For example, Southern planters and the Northeastern merchant class of the mid-nineteenth century were far removed from late twentieth-century mass democracy. They were in fact as far removed from it as the world of Palmerston and Disraeli was from the social democratic and multicultural England that I visited last year.

Note that the Marxism that Kondylis expounds is highly selective and without the egalitarian and "utopian" aspects of the original product. Kondylis praises Marx and some Marxists for looking behind ideologies for the social and/or political interests that they incarnate. Like Marx, he considers "ideology" to be "false," a shared body of social and cultural attitudes that distorts historical reality, willfully or unwittingly.

Kondylis mocks ethicists for packaging as "human rights" the interests of empires or the political ambitions of particular intellectuals. For Kondylis, such ethicizing conceals a will to power or the force of an expanding consumer economy. But Kondylis rarely seizes on the terms "*ideologeme*" or "false consciousness" when he analyzes the restorationist thought of the early and mid-nineteenth century. Although a sound argument can be made that Joseph de Maistre, Friedrich Julius Stahl, and Louis de Bonald were defending a dying European order against a rising bourgeois society, Kondylis discusses such counterrevolutionaries with profound respect. Not all of the foredoomed battles in his work or in his view of world history are traced to "false consciousness," and it may be observed that the closer he gets to the modern era of "mass democracy," planetary politics, and a consumerist culture, the more Kondylis talks about dishonest ideologues.

This selectiveness may be partly the result of ingrained attitudes. Though a visceral anti-American fond of Marxist terminology, Kondylis has no use for mass democracy and its cultural and economic accompaniments. Sprung from an illustrious Greek family that produced both statesmen and military officers, he remains proud of his own antecedents. As he explained with self-deprecation in a letter to me, unlike other Kondylises who accomplished much, "all he has managed to do is write long books in German." His books, by the way, are not only long but recondite, written in exceedingly dense prose and marked by tortuous explications.

This stylistic difficulty and his questionable generalizations about Americans notwithstanding, Kondylis reveals two strengths that American conservatives would do well to imitate. One, he contextualizes ideas, without reducing them to mere epiphenomena of other historical forces. Kondylis grasps the necessary relation between cultural and moral ideals and the social and political configurations in which they develop. He demonstrates the disintegration of a conservative vision, one based on fixed orders with corresponding duties and privileges, in a society then undergoing critical changes, namely urbanization and the Industrial Revolution. Those who wished to represent an already superannuated conservative vision lost their social base and were forced to modify their public stance to include bourgeois ideals.

In this modified conservative view that emerged in the second half of the nineteenth century, defenders of medieval hierarchy and civil order made common cause against revolt from below. They and bourgeois liberals opposed democratic revolutionaries and socialist reformers. In this alliance, however, the truly conservative vision of order became increasingly vestigial.[57] The major lines of division were thereafter between "bourgeois modernity" and "mass democratic postmodernity," a topic minutely discussed in Kondylis's book *Der Niedergang der Bürgerlichen Denk-und Lebensform* ("The Decline of the Bourgeois Form of Thought and Life," 1991).[58] Social visions remain competitive, Kondylis reminds his reader, for only as long as they are tied to a dominant or powerful class. Once that class is overwhelmed by political or material changes, its ideas inevitably fall out of favor. Though Kondylis points out the historical precondition for the predominance of what he as well as Richard Weaver calls a "vision of order," he does not relativize all such visions. From his descriptions it is clear that Kondylis favors the restorationist thought of the early nineteenth century over the liberal bourgeois *Denkformen* that replaced it. Despite his attempted detachment in surveying the end of mass democracy, Kondylis despises the disorder and boundless self-indulgence that he associates with the postmodern age.

He presents mass democracy as a total way of life that develops in a favorable political and economic climate. He does not use the term simply to express contempt for what he dislikes. Nor does he try to reduce mass democracy to a side effect of some material transformation, for example, by treating it as a byproduct of industrial growth or of the shifting of population toward cities. Kondylis does note certain political and economic preconditions for the rise of mass democracy, most particularly universal suffrage, material abundance, and the identification of self-government with public administration. But he also stresses its cultural and intellectual presuppositions. Among those that preoccupy him are the avant-garde artistic movements of the early twentieth century and the kind of experimental theater that began shortly thereafter. Unlike the Marxist Lukács, who viewed such movements as sources of bourgeois amusement, Kondylis interprets them as the beginnings of a cultural war. Artists and playwrights collaborated in bringing down the bourgeois liberal world. For they despised precisely what it exalted: social constraint, rationally comprehensible art, and a coherent view of life and civic responsibility.

In their place Western society received a highly subjective, self-expressive, and ideologically inflammatory culture. Once this became wed to material hedonism, the erosion of identity, and a fixation on total equality, Kondylis maintains, a mass democratic worldview established itself.[59] Kondylis points to the cultural components of this worldview as omens of postmodernism. Rather than identifying this phenomenon exclusively with the most recent assaults on fixed or received meanings, Kondylis argues that postmodernism has been extensive with the entire mass democratic age.[60] The relativization of meaning is only the latest strategy for advancing social equality and for evacuating nondemocratic opinions associated with an elitist past.

Mass democracy, as interpreted by Kondylis, is also a global process. Moving from the West where it supplanted "an oligarchic and hierarchical bourgeois liberalism," it is now "merging with a planetary landscape," in which Marxism and communism have become the preparatory phases in a mass democratic end of history.[61] Unlike the liberal age it ended or the communism it surpassed in material productiveness, mass democratic society both proclaims and works toward providing material gratification. In a secularized and de-hierarchical setting, it does what Marxist socialism promised but only occasionally could produce. Here Marx, according to Kondylis, offered a partially accurate prediction but grafted onto it a happy historical ending that is unlikely to come to pass. Marx "had clung to the idea of a normative-eschatological unification of world history" and "had explained this unitary character of a planetary event through social and economic factors while drawing appropriate political conclusions [from his assumptions]." But this unitary world history that Marx saw as tied to economic modernization is also intensifying the war against social cohesion, in the name of individual gratification and universal sameness. Kondylis observes the irony that the struggle against communism, "fought not least of all for liberal ideals," has resulted in the victory of a postliberal society, one whose dissimilarity from the bourgeois age is greater than the distance that had separated Europe before the French Revolution from the Europe of the late nineteenth century. This exemplifies the ideological misrepresentation that Kondylis believes characterizes the promoters of mass democracy. They insist on a fictional continuity with the liberal past.[62]

Kondylis's contextualization of conservative, liberal, and mass democratic worldviews and his detailed analysis of mass democracy carry implications that he spells out for would-be conservatives. The term "conservative" is now being applied, he explains in an essay, "Die Antiquiertheit der Politischen Begriffe" ("The Archaic Character of Political Concepts" 1991), to those who have nothing to do with an agrarian aristocratic society and less and less to do with a bourgeois liberal order. Kondylis finds it useless to define conservatives as "those who defend existing institutions, no matter what they happen to be."[63] He mocks journalists and academics who indiscriminately apply "conservative" to Chancellor Kohl or to Russian insurgents. They are accused of the same semantic opportunism as those who use "liberal" not to describe the "economic and constitutional conceptions of the European bourgeois but the right to abortion or an unlimited right to asylum." Least of all does Kondylis accept the Marxist practice, common during the Cold War, of designating the anti-communist West as "conservative." Such a designation is unsuited for a "system which has revolutionized productive forces to an unprecedented extent and which places at the disposal of individuals material and mental possibilities that represent an astonishing and world-historical novum."[64]

Kondylis believes that a conservative politics, in the sense that he understands that concept, can no longer be fruitfully pursued. The socio-political context for this orientation was already disappearing by the late nineteenth century, and a similar fate overtook bourgeois liberalism, which gave way to mass democracy. Moreover, the mass democratic system that Kondylis analyzes embraces politics, the economy, ethical reasoning, and the arts. It permeates and shapes human relations and expectations and, despite its war against most of the Western heritage, is now held to be the crowning achievement of Western democratic peoples. It also condemns and dissolves traditional gender, social, and ethnic distinctions and, ethically and economically, prepares the way for a global society of uprooted and increasingly indistinguishable individuals. Whether or not one accepts Kondylis's view of the United States as the vital source of this mass democratic empire, what he describes in any case is too monolithic and popular to be effectively opposed by eighteenth- or nineteenth-century visionaries.

Inasmuch as Kondylis makes fun of political labels "with changing contents," it is hard to imagine that he would take seriously any conservatism anchored in mass democracy. While an ambitious politician or political journalist might find reasons to praise this state of affairs, their reasoning, he would conclude, has nothing to do with conservatism. Those who exalt "human rights" and call for open borders and global democracy may be taking positions that help their careers and make them part of a respectable opposition. But nothing substantive separates them from other boosters of mass democracy or links them to either classical conservatism or bourgeois liberalism. There is also no evidence that such "conservatism" slows down the dynamism of mass democracy. At most, "moderate" mass democrats may create procedural obstacles that prevent democratic change from moving more quickly; in other situations, however, they may accelerate that change by their devotion to multinational corporations and by their dislike for national and regional differences.

In contrast to the bogus, would-be conservatisms that Kondylis finds in the postmodern age, he does view the counterrevolutionary Right as a genuine alternative to mass democracy. But this Right offers not a "conservative" alternative to the present age but a force of resistance to radical change:

> The distinguishing characteristic of the Right consists of its willingness to suspend political liberalism for the sake of protecting economic liberalism and private property against leftist assault. In this sense the Right belongs to liberalism, however much the "enlightened" segment of the bourgeois might show embarrassment about this connection.[65]

In one crucial respect this authoritarian Right does resemble the counterrevolutionary conservatism of the early nineteenth century: in its willingness to impose "provisional dictatorship" to prevent "the over-throw of existing institutions through a revolutionary sovereign dicta-torship." The distinction between "commissarial" and "sovereign" dic-tatorship, one that suspends legality (as in the case of Peru) in order to restore it in peaceful conditions and one that supplants a constitutional order by force, is taken from the work of Carl Schmitt, a legal theorist who defended precisely the kind of authoritarian Right that Kondylis describes.[66] But such a Right, which may take over because of a commu-nist threat or because of the radicalization of mass democracy, can lurch out of hand. It may culminate in the sometimes irresponsible violence unleashed by a military coup or in the kind of substantive "national rev-olution" sought by idealistic Italian fascists. In either case the socioeco-nomic upheaval wrought by these events or later reactions to them will far surpass whatever order is brought by provisional dictatorship.

In other cases, alluded to by Kondylis, the "authoritarian dominance of the Right" has "created the institutional framework for moderniza-tion and industrialization in a capitalist direction, to the exclusion of socialist experiments."[67] But these charges have sometimes led, as in the case of Spain, to the establishment of a mass democratic culture. Social democracy, a consumer society, "human rights" ideology, and a disinte-grating nuclear family have all followed once a welfare state and modern economy have been established. Pointing these problems out is not the same as deploring twentieth-century technology or exaggerating the benevolence of landed aristocrats or Victorian merchants. It is to state a causal connection between postmodernity in its social, political, and cul-tural forms and a progressive vanishing of inherited identities, civil soci-ety (as opposed to the state and economy), parental authority, and any-thing once understood to be "tradition." Kondylis believes that what has caused this situation is not the failure of public administrators to teach "values" or of manufacturers to promote "democratic capitalism." For him, the problems are systemic and lie in the fit between human appetites and changing institutional arrangements. They are also rooted in what Kondylis sees as the inevitability of struggle as the human condition. In the planetary age, people are fighting over resources but do so while appealing to the human rights slogans invented by intellectuals and the media.[68]

Kondylis claims to be pursuing value-free science and stresses the distinction by nineteenth-century social thinkers between descriptive statements and concepts formed out of observation and value assertions. He insists that his scholarship does not contain expressions of normative morality and is openly contemptuous of political advocacy disguised as analytic thought. Yet the nonscientific aspect of his own judgments keeps intruding, seen in the obvious moral passion shown by Kondylis in scolding political utopians. Since 1991, when the "end of history" argument was first advanced by neoconservative publicist Francis Fukuyama, Kondylis has held forth against the notion that human history is ending with the fall of communism. He has ridiculed the idea and the presumed intent behind it, that all or most of humanity is being drawn into a democratic capitalist orbit marked by peaceful trade and orderly change.

To this Kondylis has responded that history will likely go on, as has been the case until now, with struggles and ideological self-justifications. In a world of expanding population, limited resources, and rising materialist expectations, he finds no reason to think that human conflict is about to end. Moreover, the terms "democracy," "capitalism," and "rights" have been made to mean whatever partisan politicians and intellectuals wish them to mean. All of these terms now have been given what Kondylis calls a "polemical" function: they are used to carry on a struggle against political and cultural enemies or obstacles. Here Kondylis may be entirely on the mark. As I myself found in doing research on a book dealing with the managerial state, "democracy," "liberalism," and "rights" have lost any specific meaning in "Western democracies." What provides these terms with steady points of reference are their connection to postmodern societies and their sacral use by a particular elite. Public administrators, journalists, and other segments of the political class determine or alter the meaning of political doctrine. Even so, Kondylis, no less than those he argues against, is speaking "polemically." His attempts to refute global democrats are not disinterested scientific statements. They proceed from a moral stance composed of his tragic view of life and dislike for ideological manipulation. This view does not weaken Kondylis's arguments and in fact may enhance them, but it clearly does not represent the triumph of value-free science.

His interest in the cultural and geographic extensions of mass democracy has resulted in, among other projects, a book on planetary politics published in 1992. The argument of this work features prominently in Kondylis's critical remarks on another recent study of world politics, Samuel Huntington's provocative thesis on impending cultural wars presented in *Foreign Affairs* in 1993.[69] Kondylis disagrees sharply with Huntington's view (which I happen to share) that future planetary conflicts will be fueled by the tensions among cultural-religious blocs. In opposition to this gloomy prediction, he offers another equally somber one, that mass democracy will create both spiritual stupor and a growing desire for material well-being. This will lead not to peace, but to devastating wars pursued for resources, without much regard for moral self-justification. The belligerents will simply trot out the already worn mass democratic tags about "equality" and "human rights."[70]

For all the pessimism of his work, Kondylis remains cheerful in his demeanor. He attributes this serene cheer to the kind of stoic *apatheia* that he cultivates. Already in his mid-fifties, he continues to live in austere solitude, dividing his time between two bachelor residences, in Heidelberg and in the Kifisia district of Athens. He has never held a full-time academic appointment, but has made do with a series of grants and the payment received for his political journalism. Despite the unfavorable comparison he draws between himself and better-known members of his family, Panajotis Kondylis may add further luster to an already distinguished name.

Marvels and Missed Opportunities

Taki's Magazine

MARCH 05, 2008

THE RECENT death of Bill Buckley brought forth the usual lies from the liberal-neocon establishment; and having devoted part of my latest book[71] and a slew of irate commentaries to exposing these gross untruths, I see no reason to dwell on them here. Suffice it to say that in the 1950s the late Mr. Buckley, contrary to the current fiction, did not drive out a mob of anti-Semites and racists from the conservative movement. More accurately, he kicked out a few Jewish libertarians, starting with Ayn Rand, Murray Rothbard, and Ron Hamowy. Nor did he make a moral statement in the 1960s against the anti-Semitism of the John Birch Society by expelling the society's members (to the extent he was authorized to expel anyone from anything) from American conservatism. What Buckley, James Burnham, and Frank Meyer did in 1965 in *National Review* was to condemn the Birchers principally for their opposition to the war in Vietnam.[72] As for anti-Semitism, I recall reading as a teenager the JBS publication *American Opinion* (which for some reason arrived *gratis* at my parents' home), and it contained multiple articles by a journalist named Alan Stang who looked a lot like Woody Allen.

More credible comments about Buckley's accomplishments, however, have come from members of the Old Right, and particularly from Peter Brimelow and Larry Auster on their respective websites. Peter sketches a picture of a socially driven and callous journalist who disposed of people like us when we ceased to be useful and whose vaunted oratorical abilities were rather exiguous. He recalls one social gathering with Buckley that he felt obliged to attend after Peter's wife had undergone surgery for breast cancer. Buckley was totally indifferent to Peter's worrisome problems, about which he was well aware; instead he tried to impress on the then-distracted husband the need to fawn on well-connected guests. Peter considers Buckley's proverbial charm to have been a grease gun applied for social advantage. A perpetual climber, he was nice to lefties who counted or when his apparent kindness could be used to make him look admirably tolerant.

Larry adds to the grievances resulting from Buckley's betrayal of the Right that he had claimed to be fighting for. Instead of truly "standing athwart" the age, as he said he was doing when he launched *National Review* in 1955, Buckley became the captive of a leftward moving American culture. For Brimelow and Auster, Buckley's abandonment of the immigration question, while courting neoconservative friends and allies, and his willingness to purge immigration restrictionists from his own magazine in the 1990s, indicates his lack of serious conviction. Both of his critics attack Buckley's character as well as his traceable fall from any position that might with reason be considered right-wing. Neither critic sees fit to praise Buckley for having scolded the neoconservatives for their ill-considered war policy. By the time he got around to that, he had already done incalculable and perhaps irreversible harm to the American Right by not speaking up at the moment of decision.

Except for some of the personal details in Peter's account, there is nothing in his broadside or in that of Larry Auster that has not also appeared in my occasional writings. As a matter of historical interest, I was discouraged from contributing further to *National Review* before Peter became a noted writer there; and unless I'm mistaken, by the early 1990s, no one contributing to *National Review* could have done so for very long unless he enjoyed neoconservative favor.

But the trek of this magazine toward the left did not begin in the 1990s. It was already in full swing by the 1970s, something that my monograph on the conservative movement tries to demonstrate. What rendered Peter's and Larry's "obituaries of sorts" memorable was not that they contained new revelations, or that their authors even thought they did. Rather they were imitating Buckley who, when Murray Roth-

THE ESSENTIAL PAUL GOTTFRIED, ESSAYS FROM 1984–2024

bard died unexpectedly in 1995, leapt at the occasion to settle scores with his longtime adversary. In this case, however, the charges were considerably more defensible than they had been when Buckley had gone after the deceased Rothbard, accusing him of, among other enormities, supporting the communists in the Cold War.

Chief among the particulars in the briefs under consideration was that Buckley had handed over American conservatism to neoconservative adventurers from the Left. He had done so by turning sharply against more genuine conservatives (a practice that my book heavily documents) and by making neoconservatism the only permissible form of thinking on the Right. There is of course nothing in my friends' charges that seems even vaguely untrue. I myself have made the same general charges, and often with far more ferocity. The only objection I could raise, and even this might sound hypocritical considering its source, is that it looks bad to say bad things about someone who has just died, and especially if that someone has attracted decent people as admirers.

But there is another reason I would hesitate at this point to go after Buckley. When all is said and done, there must have been something in him that caused me (as well as the young John Zmirak) to have once admired his achievements. It was not until I had entered my forties that I began to disapprove, and quite openly, of this onetime idol. But before then, for more than twenty years, I had followed his columns, read his anthologies, and watched him on television with undiminished respect for his literary gifts and remarkable aplomb. His manipulation of English syntax, his capacity for sarcasm, and his unending output had all turned me into his loyal devotee. On the few occasions I met him, I was almost speechless with wonder, just as I would later become inexpressibly angry when he was foolish or cavalier enough to have shoved what he had built up into unworthy hands. Although I now see how deeply flawed he was as a person and how ridiculously contrived his "movement" had been, the question remains whether I had been entirely deluded in my judgments about him from the beginning.

The closest I have come to resolving this question is to recognize the possibility that figures with considerable gifts and often brilliant insights are not always especially virtuous. I remember being wild about the movie *Amadeus* (1984) because it revealed a profound truth, and one that the film's writer and producer might not even have been aware of. The movie taught that God, for His own inscrutable reasons, awards great gifts to people who are not otherwise particularly nice, or in Mozart's case, not even adult in their behavior. There is simply no democracy at work here; nor should one expect to find it. God is not a global democrat, and He is not required to practice equality or affirmative action or even to notice those who are virtuous when He distributes intellectual or artistic gifts. Antonio Salieri, a pious Catholic and plodding composer, was justified in taking offense at Mozart's (allegedly) childish, dissipated ways. He was also understandably upset that such a flawed adolescent could produce such lilting operas, euphonious symphonies, awe-inspiring Masses, and other unforgettable musical compositions. But that is the nature of reality: those who have gifts in one area do not necessarily stand out as moral exemplars. And we must be broadminded enough to respect the gifts of morally flawed, even reprehensible individuals, without having to overlook their weaknesses. (And with due respect to Salieri, musical historian Robert Stove suggests that he was a far better composer than most have been led to believe.)

As an illustration of this capacity, I would point to the example of the Southern traditionalist Richard Weaver, whose family had fought and bled for the Confederacy in the War Between the States but who deeply respected Abraham Lincoln as an orator. To the consternation of his fellow Agrarians, Weaver let it be known that he considered Lincoln a far greater and more morally focused rhetorician than the father of nineteenth-century European conservatism, Edmund Burke. While Burke appealed to expedience in his arguments before Parliament, Lincoln in his famous speeches "argued from principle." Although I would suggest that Burke argued as strongly from principle as did Lincoln, Weaver was correct to hold up Lincoln as a model of principled oratory, whatever he might have thought of his controversial invasion of the Southern states. Note Weaver here was not commenting on Lincoln's war politics, which he plainly deplored, but on his qualities as a rhetorician. (Weaver was, of course, a distinguished professor of the history of rhetoric at the University of Chicago.)

Without boring the reader with other examples of such broadminded respect drawn from the past, I would note that my reaction to Buckley's career follows Weaver's regard for Lincoln as an orator. One does not have to overlook his flagrantly opportunistic career, especially his passion for neoconservative dinner companions and for taking instruction from these grotesques, to appreciate Buckley's magnificence as a polemicist and wit. Even now I read *Up from Liberalism* (1959) and other samples of Buckley's early oeuvre and continue to thrill to the clever phrases and epigrammatic style.[73] Buckley's descriptions of Eleanor Roosevelt, the ultimate do-gooder, in the 1960s are at least as funny as Mencken's earlier, devastating snipes at Woodrow Wilson, the world missionary. And Buckley's arguments against the Civil Rights Act of 1964 and the Voting Rights Act of 1965 were entirely on target, no matter how far he would later move from these sound positions out of social anxiety or rank opportunism. For years I walked among my leftist academic colleagues armed with Buckley's well-framed refutations of what were then fashionable political opinions. The fact that Buckley made a later, fateful alliance with even more obnoxious leftists than the ones I was then forced to associate with does not diminish the force of what he had said and written at a more principled and more spirited time in his life.

Admittedly Peter might have a point that Buckley's speeches sometimes fell flat; and certainly he took on tasks that went beyond his perpetually cluttered publishing schedule. What for me, however, is noteworthy is that he was as good as often as he was, given his endless obligations and considering all the novels and columns that he was grinding out. In the early 1990s, I began to correspond with Buckley at the urging of a shared friend, and in one abrasive, no-holds-barred letter, let him know how disappointed I had been by his odyssey over the preceding twenty years. I carefully spelled out his "tergiversations," one of his favorite bookish terms, and I cited examples of those he had once reamed out—for example, the atheist philosopher at Yale, Paul Weiss—with whom he later struck up much publicized, socially celebrated friendships. I strongly hinted that he had "put off the Old Adam and put on the New one" as an exercise in social climbing. Buckley wrote back an even longer letter, and it was full of the statements that he had made about his present friends over a long period of time, citations that were meant to indicate a lack of contradiction between his current and past views. He also tried to prove that his apparent about-faces on a wide range of social issues had never really occurred, and indeed his present stands were the ones he had held decades earlier.

Two things about Buckley's letters, and this text in particular, impressed me. One, my correspondent did not have to provide me (of all people) with an elaborate self-justification. His neoconservative buds had already marginalized me, and although I was corresponding with my one-time hero, I would be of absolutely no use to the movement that his then-current friends were creating with his cooperation. In fact, I would never be allowed to participate in any way in their zombie army. Two, he managed to play the bad cards I had dealt him superbly. He had put me on the defensive, despite the abundant proofs for my implied charges. He was like a chess master taking his multiple opponents apart one after the other.

Presumably I was not the only person with whom my correspondent was discussing his "tergiversations." He had undoubtedly tried some of his polemical weapons on other "Dear Bill" critics before getting around to my brief on July 22, 1992. Still, it seemed unlikely that in all cases he had had to respond to exactly the same set of evidence. There is probably a ton of evidence for what I was suggesting, and his attackers would have had no problem finding many illustrations of his volte-face. Nor do I consider my debating abilities to be anything but first-rate. But I was clearly embroiled with someone who was much better than I. Moreover, a letter he had written that was brought to my attention soon after (in circumstances I am not allowed to reveal), one that had been sent to the neocon ranter Irwin Stelzer, who had predictably called Pat Buchanan a "Nazi," testified further to Buckley's argumentative and verbal skills. I could not imagine having come up with a refutation even remotely as good, and certainly not as a literary exercise produced en route to a speaking engagement.

Having paid this compliment, I also find it inconceivable how such a writer of quality could have surrounded himself with the mental midgets he enlisted for *National Review* or the untalented social vulgarians who snatched up his mind in the 1970s. One is sadly reminded here of how Carl Schmitt and Martin Heidegger, both surpassingly brilliant thinkers, tried to pass in the social world of the Third Reich. The renowned composer Shostakovich had engaged in a similar form of slumming under Stalin. But these celebrities eventually recoiled from those they had forced themselves to court, unlike Buckley, who sank deeper and deeper into the fatuous world of his patrons.

Despite his slide downward, WFB showed talents that I could never dream of equaling and particularly not at this stage in my life. He deserved at least some of his moments in the sun; and I am glad that he enjoyed the ones he was entitled to. As in our views of other badly flawed men of talent, let us pay fitting tribute to Bill Buckley, without willfully ignoring what the Germans call the *Schattenseite*, the shadowy, negative aspect of people and things that honesty requires us to notice.

Eugene D. Genovese, R.I.P.

The American Conservative

SEPTEMBER 27, 2012

T HE JUSTLY renowned social historian Eugene D. Genovese died yesterday at the age of eighty-two in Atlanta. His death followed several years of dealing with a worsening cardiac ailment and with a jolting loss in 2007 from which he never recovered. This was the death of his beloved wife Elizabeth (Betsey), who was his frequent collaborator on books and whom he celebrated after her passing in moving memoirs. In my professional opinion, Genovese may have been the greatest social historian this country has given us; and the fact that he wrote like a dream makes his accomplishment even more noteworthy. In *Roll, Jordan, Roll*, a work that won the Bancroft Prize in 1974, *The Political Economy of Slavery* (1965), and *The Mind of the Master Class: History and Faith in the Southern Slaveholders' Worldview* (2008), Genovese presents an unsurpassed analysis of the mindset of the once-dominant planter class in the Old South. Although Genovese wrote his early works as a Marxist and his later ones as a Catholic traditionalist and an avowed man of the Right, it is sometimes hard to distinguish his writings in terms of these personal changes. There is something that, from the current political perspective, is remarkably reactionary about

Genovese's oeuvre, even in those books he published as a Marxist who once came out openly for the Viet Cong. But that was when it was still possible to be a left-wing radical without having to be politically correct.

Absent from Genovese's work is the tiresome moralizing that now characterizes academic historiography. Even in his most radical phase, he wrote admiringly about the Antebellum Southern slave-owners, who believed deeply in their right to rule. This doomed class, which would give way in the Civil War to the dominance of the capitalist bourgeoisie and to the victory of free labor, did not lack for courage or manliness, according to Genovese. The planter class however represented the past, one that was destined to fall to the capitalist North, which eventually, Genovese hoped as a Marxist, would be overthrown by world socialism. By the way, Marx and Engels did not exhibit any of the tender feelings for the Southern side that one finds in their onetime follower. They saw the Civil War, like our liberals and neoconservatives, as an unvarnished struggle between Good and Evil.

Toward the end of his life Genovese turned to a somewhat different interest, which was the religious thought of Antebellum Southern theologians. Essential to these studies was a detailed explanation of how learned Protestant thinkers, like James Henley Thornwell and Robert Lewis Dabney, justified from a religious, biblical perspective Southern plantation society with its embedded hierarchy. Even more important, Genovese and his wife, who closely collaborated on this study, looked at how Southern theologians and Southern preachers came to terms with Southern defeat. Despite his Catholic loyalties, it is obvious from these studies that Genovese was strongly attracted to the Southern Calvinist mindset. He reveled in its discussions of divine Providence and in its tortuous attempts to make sense out of human history. One cannot read these texts without noticing that the interpreter is pondering his own theological quandaries while explicating those of others. Genovese's themes over a working lifetime ranged from a unique application of Marxist materialism to the Southern experience to learned explorations of Protestant theology.

It would be remiss of me as Gene's friend not to mention what I found to be his most endearing quality, his total openness about those he liked and disliked. Gene never hid behind righteous poses. He had a Latin exuberance, which he probably inherited from his ancestors and which made his letters to me a delight to read. He was always about settling scores and awarding senatorial honors. Never (to my knowledge) did he indulge in moral righteousness or in talk about the suffering just. It is hard to think of Gene as someone in the past tense. Never have I known a more animated personality or such a brilliant historian.

Dancing on a
Hero's Grave

Taki's Magazine

MAY 29, 2013

S A college student I would buy copies of *The New Yorker* to
sample the sparkling prose of James Thurber and S. J. Perelman
and to appreciate the clever cartoons that graced each issue.
Despite the magazine's veering toward the trendy Left thereafter, I could
still find material in it worth reading well into the 1980s, such as John
Updike's elegantly phrased erotica or the occasional vignettes of interwar Hungary by John Lukacs. Then *The New Yorker* took a further
slide into sheer madness, and the results are visible in a libelous obit that
came out last Wednesday by a certain Judith Thurman.[74] Seething with
rage syndrome, Thurman announced the "Final Solution" of my onetime correspondent and one of France's most illustrious historians of the
last century, Dominique Venner (1935–2013).

On May 21, Venner, acting desperately in the face of events he could
no longer control, committed suicide by shooting himself in the mouth
in Notre Dame Cathedral in Paris. Venner left behind a suicide note
explaining his horror at the gay-marriage law that French President
François Hollande had just pushed through the National Assembly.
Venner further lamented the self-destruction of his country and of Euro-

pean civilization that he ascribed to gay marriage and to Western Europeans' unwillingness to keep Muslims from resettling their countries.

It continues to be disputed whether Venner was a believing Catholic, although the "Catholic traditionalists" in whose company Thurman places Venner admired his cultural stands and continue to hope that he'll make it into heaven despite the mortal sin he committed by hastening his departure from this world.

Venner was also a hero to the neo-pagan European Right, and since the 1960s he was active in laying and extending the foundations of the emphatically anti-Christian French New Right, together with his frequent collaborator Alain de Benoist. Venner had a clear record of standing defiantly in the face of the French Communist Party. Unlike the communists and other French leftists who supported the Algerian rebels, Venner fought gallantly and was decorated as a sergeant in the French forces in Algeria.

Contrary to what Thurman tells us, Venner did not get his political start as a fan of the Nazis and their French collaborators (although his parents had once rallied to Jacques Doriot's French fascist party). He rose to fame as a fervent anti-communist and European nationalist. The young Venner risked his life as a volunteer in the Algerian War, went to Budapest in 1956 to stand with the outnumbered Hungarian rebels against the Soviet occupational forces, and later was caught sacking the premises of the French Communist Party, whose allegiance to the Soviets he detested.

In the last twenty years of his life, this "unapologetic Islamophobe," to use Thurman's phrase, showed the audacity to characterize both the takeover of European inner cities by a hostile Muslim population and "the declining white birth rate in France and Europe" as "a catastrophic peril for the future." Several blog respondents to this screed noted the embarrassing coincidence that Thurman's expression of rage against the "Islamophobe" Venner appeared at the very time that predominantly Muslim riots had broken out in Sweden and a Muslim convert cut off the head of a hapless off-duty soldier in London.

In a final nod to PC, Thurman tells us that Venner's commentaries "evoked the racist, xenophobic, and anti-Semitic rhetoric of the fascist European Right between the two World Wars, which has been moderated, though not abolished, by postwar hate-speech laws." Thurman does not offer even a sliver of proof that Venner imitated the style of Hitler's *Mein Kampf* (1925); having read both Venner and Hitler, I would have no trouble distinguishing between the two, even if I'm not a certified "anti-fascist." But we should be grateful for small improvements: now we have the enforcement of "hate-speech laws" in Europe to protect us from what Thurman doesn't care to hear. As one of her respondents asks very much to the point: Is Ms. Thurman out to ban, as reminiscent of fascism, any oral or written communication that doesn't meet her criteria of sensitive speech?

Thurman's treatment of Venner as a trained historian specializing in military affairs is almost as perplexing as it is glaringly biased. Thurman tells us that Venner wrote a work "admiring of the Vichy collaboration with Hitler" and other presumably pro-Nazi polemics, but she then identifies the dead author with "a history of the Red Army that received a prize from the Académie Française." Venner was widely respected for his objective two-volume *Histoire de l'Armée Rouge* (1984), which starts with the creation of the Soviet army during the Russian Civil War and then examines the further development of Soviet military forces through World War II.[75] Venner also compiled an eleven-volume encyclopedia on firearms that continues to enjoy academic favor. The works that obviously irk Thurman, however, are Venner's sympathetic studies of the white forces that combated the Red Armies and his work on French divisions that fought alongside the Wehrmacht in Russia during World War II.

Perhaps most inexcusably for his leftist critics, Venner published a critical work on the French Resistance in 2000, presenting its shadow side in a way that the French Left or its American journalistic appendix do not care to hear about. Venner reminded us of the frequency with which communists in the Resistance carried out assassinations against political enemies, a tendency that became pandemic after the Liberation. He also dwells on isolated terrorist acts by the Resistance that did little to advance the cause of freeing France from a foreign occupation.

I knew Venner best for having edited two stimulating journals that I would devour whenever I could get my hands on them: *Enquête sur l'Histoire* (in the 1990s) and its recent successor *La Nouvelle Revue d'Histoire*, a publication that displays the same willingness to defy leftist taboos as everything else Venner wrote.[76]

A kindly leftist historian, Benoît Rayski, wrote after he heard of Venner's death:

> I rarely agreed with his ideas, but he was a man who escaped with his courage and nobility from the usual ideological trappings and he wore his independence as a badge of honor.

Too bad our leftist hacks in Midtown can't show a similar generosity toward a dead, non-conformist scholar.

Remembering Eric Voegelin: Anti-Gnostic Warrior

Chronicles

AUGUST 2021

THAT POLITICAL ideology and activism have become a new religion is something the average individual sees signs of nearly every day. A black man is killed in an altercation with police, and his face instantly becomes an icon to be carried in protests, his name a phrase to be repeated with adoration. A slogan such as "Black Lives Matter" or "Defund the Police" is repeated with the regularity of praying beads on a rosary. And critical race theory is taught with fervor to schoolchildren, catechizing them in the doctrines of this leftist ideology.

Yet while these signs of political religious fervor are relatively new, the idea of politics as religion is decades old, fostered largely through the political and historical thinker Eric Voegelin. A German who fled Austria for America during the Nazi takeover, Voegelin had firsthand experience of how political ideology could be infused with religious fervor, and the connection between the two would become the critical thrust of

Voegelin's assessment of political science and his approach to the ideological temptations of the modern age, ones we are facing with an even greater intensity today.

Born in Cologne, Germany, in 1901, Voegelin moved with his parents to Vienna as a child and was later educated in political science at the University of Vienna. At that institution Voegelin studied with such outstanding scholars of the age as the jurist Hans Kelsen and the conservative social theorist Othmar Spann. He also developed long-lasting friendships with the phenomenologist Alfred Schütz and the social economist Friedrich Hayek. Both these figures were close to the Austrian School of Economics, as was another scholar, Ludwig von Mises, with whom Voegelin also formed a connection in Vienna.

This transplanted Rhinelander eventually became an associate professor of political science while also a member of the University of Vienna's law faculty. In these positions he produced *Political Religions* (1938), a work that contained the theoretical seeds of later studies and which he wrote while both Nazi and communist ideologies were on the rise.[77]

Voegelin and his wife became American citizens in 1944, only six years after emigrating to the United States following the *Anschluss*. He then spent most of his later academic career at Louisiana State University, the University of Munich, and the Hoover Institution of Stanford University.

Voegelin's youthful work focused on the adaptation of religious myth to modern political movements and was obviously influenced by the German legal theorist Carl Schmitt, a pioneer in analyzing the interrelationship of religion and political concepts. But the young Voegelin went beyond Schmitt in underscoring the religious origins of modern ideologies, something that would become an overshadowing theme in most of his post–World War II publications.

The range and variety of his work revealed an extraordinary knowledge of both ancient and modern history, classical languages, philosophy, and theology. Reading his five-volume *Order and History* (1956–87), with its erudite overview of Plato, Aristotle, the ancient Jews, and early Christianity, one stands in awe of the knowledge and insight that the author reveals.[78]

Particularly noteworthy is Voegelin's attempt to do justice to the mystical search for the source of being in both Greek and Hebrew teachers, a search that he believed found its most dramatic "leap into being" in the visions of Saint Paul. Unlike his contemporary and longtime correspondent Leo Strauss, Voegelin was struck by the overlaps rather than the line of demarcation between Hebrew revelation and Greek philosophy. He characteristically treated the mystical outgrowths of Platonic philosophy not as a distortion of what Socrates and Plato taught, but as an understandable and defensible extension of their teachings.

In shorter post–World War II works, like *The New Science of Politics* (1952) and *Science, Politics and Gnosticism*, (1959), Voegelin presents the main problem that political scientists and others should be considering (but are obviously not), namely, the spiritual derailment (*Entgleisung*) that has led to the destruction of social and inner human order.[79] In its most virulent form this derailment has contributed to totalitarian regimes like the Nazi and communist ones, but even in less-derailed Western societies the same moral disintegration was evident. Voegelin identified this spiritual and political problem with the rise of ideology as a "political religion," a situation that he began examining after the rise of Nazism.

He also famously traced this outburst of ideological fervor to Gnosticism, the ancient and medieval Christian heresy that scorned the world in its present form as irredeemably evil. Voegelin did not contend that modern ideologies or political religions entirely replicated the Gnostic heresy. Rather he found aspects of these political religions—for example, revulsion for the world as it has existed, the expectation of a sudden cosmic transformation, and the distinction between those who carried the inner light and a fallen humanity—in modern revolutionary ideologies.

Voegelin was critical of the left-wing of the Protestant Reformation, which he maintained became a vehicle for carrying Gnostic and apocalyptic themes and expectations into modern political religions. A Lutheran by birth, he showed no discernible sympathy for his ancestral religion, which he may have identified with the willingness of the Evangelical Church in Germany to cooperate with the Third Reich. Although not an orthodox Christian, Voegelin defined himself at least temperamentally as a "pre-Reformation Catholic." This self-description may have been why most of his American followers and his patrons (at Notre Dame and in Bavaria where he also taught) were traditional Catholics. Yet these devoutly Catholic disciples were forced to acknowledge that he was not really of their persuasion each time Voegelin published a book.

As far as his own theological position was discernible, he was a Neoplatonist with strong mystical proclivities who hated modern totalitarians. His widely expressed distaste for Gnostics may have hidden Voegelin's own attraction to Gnostic ideas, for example, his stress on an inward awareness of spiritual truth and his lack of interest in conventional religious ritual.

Most Gnostics came out of a Neoplatonic tradition of thought but moved from there into a heretical form of Christianity. Still, according to Voegelin, they had fallen into disastrous error. They allowed themselves to become derailed and went from their exploration of being into projects of cosmic transformation. From there it was only one more step to the dangerous revolutionary religions of the modern world, in which Gnostic elements were still allegedly present.

Voegelin outlined his own religious belief perhaps better than anywhere else in a 1943 German essay on the philosopher and metaphysician F. W. J. Schelling. In that essay, Voegelin wrote that theology was to be "grounded in a system of symbols which expresses the relationship between consciousness, as transcendent, and inner-worldly classes of being, and the world-transcending ground of being in the language of immanently understood process."[80] In other words, religion and philosophy both yield truth, but are equally required to interpret "worldly transcendence" in language that is humanly comprehensible. Although this statement does not rule out the Christian system of symbols, it also does not categorically affirm it.

Like Nietzsche, Marx, Hegel, and other critical thinkers whom Voegelin declaimed against, it may be necessary to protect this polymath against his own enthusiasts.

Voegelin's key ideas, about Gnosticism and its ramifications, apocalyptic ideologies, and even the history of humanity as punctuated by "leaps into being," were not entirely original. Karl Jaspers, Hans Jonas, Carl Schmitt, and Schelling all contributed to Voegelin's conceptualizations. What made him stand out was the use that he found for ideas that were then circulating in the Germanophone world.

Curiously, Voegelin treated that world quite critically and never ceased looking for aberrant German thinkers whom he believed had prepared the way for the Nazi catastrophe. But his mind was obviously shaped by a German conceptual framework, and its imprint can be seen in his work. He also synthesized the insights that he drew from an older generation in a way that profoundly affected posterity. What he achieved theoretically and analytically became distinctly Voegelinian.

Voegelin's American disciple, Ellis Sandoz, who wrote *The Voegelinian Revolution* (1981), posited that his subject pointed the study of politics in a new direction.[81] Although Sandoz may have overstated the point, the focus on ideology as a religious heresy owes more to Voegelin than any other thinker. And what the Italian historian Emilio Gentile says about Italian fascism as the "sacralization of the political" is as relevant for the cult of liberal democracy as it was for the fascist enthusiasms of interwar Italy. For Voegelin the contagion of ideology and the derailment of being were problems for modern Americans as well as for Italian fascists and *a fortiori* German Nazis and communist zealots.

It is hard to imagine that Voegelin would have recognized his project fully in the praise bestowed on him by *National Review* editor Frank Meyer. According to Meyer, Voegelin, in *Order and History*, had set out to "controvert the two related theories of history which have created the worldview that dominates our age: Marxism and the Liberal theory of progress."

Although Voegelin was certainly no friend of Marxism, it's unlikely that he was motivated to study the Greeks and the Hebrews because of a crusade against Soviet communism. If anything, Voegelin was more deeply marked by the Nazi takeover of Europe than by the Cold War, an attitude that was equally true of his fellow refugee Leo Strauss. Despite their anti-communism, these refugee scholars thought of the Nazis first when they spoke about the totalitarian danger. A look at Voegelin's posthumously published *Hitler and the Germans* (1999) should indicate how obsessed he was by the collaboration of German academics with the Third Reich.[82] Although he may have been overly critical of former colleagues who stayed behind in Nazi Germany, clearly Nazism was an evil that Voegelin never forgot.

It may also be necessary to reassess Voegelin's relationship to the American conservative movement that venerated him from the 1960s on. In a response to a request from George Nash for a photograph to be included in *The Conservative Intellectual Movement in America Since 1945* (1976), Voegelin caustically rejoined, "Just because I am not stupid enough to be a liberal does not mean I am stupid enough to be a conservative."[83] This response may have encapsulated how Voegelin regarded the American conservatism of his time. It failed to meet his fastidious intellectual standards and seemed overly absorbed in partisan, ephemeral politics.

Significantly, Voegelin did not come out of the European Right but, like his professor Hans Kelsen, leaned strongly toward the social democrats during his youth. His German disciples, Jürgen Gebhardt, Gregor Sebba, and Peter Opitz, were also not identifiably on the Right, contrary to his American conservative admirers, who seemed more anti-communist than his European exponents.

None of this is said by way of criticism. Rather we are suggesting that Voegelin's greatest accomplishments transcend the context of the Cold War and American Catholic anti-communism. More than any other political analyst, Voegelin grasped the derailment of religious impulses and principles that is inherent in modern ideologies. Whether ideologies are really Gnosticism in disguise, if that was Voegelin's position, is open to dispute.

Less contestable to this writer is that all leftist belief systems present themselves in a heretical Christian gestalt. While the Nazis drew from the Gnostic heritage their own forms of a transformational myth, Voegelin would have contended that the Nazi adaptation failed to resonate as well as that form of the Gnostic myth that has endured through the modern Left.

Voegelin had no trouble seeing through the Left's claim to be "scientific," and already in the 1930s he recognized this claim as false. The Left, particularly in its most current form, is exactly what Voegelin revealed it to be, an agglomeration of religious heresies pretending to be true "science." To Voegelin's credit, he also perceived the need to show historically how these Gnostic derailments occurred. They did not just appear. They arose out of a deep emotional need and a failure to recognize what is permanent in human nature.

Frank Meyer's Fusionism and the Search for Consensus Among Conservatives

Chronicles

SEPTEMBER 20, 2022

The following speech was presented at the third annual National Conservatism Conference, held in Miami, September 11–13, 2022. Paul Gottfried gave the lead-off presentation for a panel on fusionism on the afternoon of September 13.

E VER SINCE I can remember, fusionism has been a reference point for those trying to make sense of the American conservative movement. Although not entirely one man's creation, an embattled anti-communist and spirited debater, Frank Meyer, gave fusionism its first form. It was Meyer who in 1962 produced *In Defense of Freedom*, an exposition of fusionism in which American conservatism was presented as a blending of individual freedom with inherited moral authority.[84] Both principles were seen as grounded in Anglo-American political and moral tradition, which supposedly stressed the paramount value of the individual.

After the publication and distribution of his book, Meyer was exposed to sharp rebukes, particularly from the Christian Right, representatives of which objected to his confounding of individualism with the Christian doctrine of the person. Willmoore Kendall mocked the book for being overly doctrinaire, while Russell Kirk, who had tangled with Meyer previously, complained that Meyer's attempt to present himself as the theorist *par excellence* of the conservative movement exposed him as an arrogant ideologue. Behind this endeavor to fuse freedom with tradition and to create a synthetic American conservatism was someone whom Kirk accused of being "filled with detestation of all champions of authority," indeed, someone who was trying to "replace Marx with Meyer."

This scolding should have been expected since roughly a third of Meyer's polemic is directed against the "New Conservatism," which was then associated with Kirk. Meyer portrays traditionalist communitarians as the right-wing counterparts of his hated "liberal collectivists." Both fail to recognize that the individual is "the locus of society," and each seeks in different ways to keep the Leviathan state unfettered.

Faced by these censures, Meyer suggested that his work resonated better with those who came out of an Anglo-Saxon Protestant culture than with his snarling Catholic detractors. But there is no evidence this group was more attracted to Meyer than his other critics. We might also observe that some libertarians were deeply displeased with his theoretical construction. The anarcho-libertarian Ronald Hamowy expressed strong disagreement in *Modern Age* with Meyer's intended "middle way" between authority and liberty; and from what I can gather, the great Friedrich Hayek was equally unhappy with how close to neoconservatism Meyer placed his intended fusionism.

Fusionism's creator refused to abandon his project despite these rebuffs, and two years later, he brought out an anthology of essays that was aimed at lowering temperatures on the Right. In preparing this anthology, *What Is Conservatism?* (1964), Meyer made sure it was he who provided the concluding essay, which stated those broad principles on which all conservatives were supposed to agree.[85] These included "opposition to the growth of government power" and "leveling egalitarianism" but also an emphatic rejection of "the presently established national policy of appeasement and retreat before communism." Meyer's model conservatives would "stand for firm resistance to communism's advance and for a determined counterattack as the only guarantee of the American Republic and of our institutions generally."

This presentation was at least partly a response to a concern expressed in 1964 by theologian and political philosopher John Hallowell that conservatives "are having difficulty agreeing with themselves as to what they stand for." Meyer attempted to address this concern by cataloging those beliefs that Americans who called themselves conservatives might or should have shared in 1964. Quite significantly, at the core of this belief cluster was fighting the communist enemy and prosecuting that struggle with far more determination than postwar presidents had shown until then.

We may properly ask how this Herculean goal could be achieved without putting on the backburner the struggle against centralized federal power. The contradiction between these affirmations, however, may never have entered the author's mind. Meyer, a fierce anti-communist who had once been a dedicated communist himself, believed passionately in an expanded military crusade against the enemy. But he hoped this undertaking would not interfere with either dismantling the welfare state or strict constitutionalism in most other areas of government activity. His friend William F. Buckley was less sanguine about this juggling act and at least once frankly admitted that the United States would have to live in what amounted to a police state for the duration of the struggle against the Soviet Empire.

The common mission for Buckley, Meyer, and others who founded *National Review* in 1955 and who fashioned the postwar conservative movement was anti-communism and the hope of seeing the Cold War pursued more aggressively. *National Review*'s conspicuous devotion to Senator Joseph McCarthy and his crusade against communists in American government and the military flowed from this preoccupation. Although some figures associated with the magazine did not share that characteristic militancy (Russell Kirk comes immediately to mind), no one who repudiated the common goal would survive as a *National Review* contributor. In the 1950s and even later, Buckley pronounced a ban of excommunication on anti-war libertarians, including Murray Rothbard, Ron Hamowy, and perhaps less explicitly, Frank Chodorov. Even the expulsion of the John Birch Society from the *National Review* fellowship, a ritual that covered most of an issue in July 1965, was based partly on divergent views about the Cold War. The Birchers opposed the Vietnam War as wasted American energy and sought to focus on the domestic communist threat exclusively.

This isolationism was not peculiar to the Birchers' brand of conservatism but an essential characteristic of the Old Right that had existed in the United States during the interwar years. When the late Ralph Raico praised Chodorov as "the last of the Old Right greats," he was recognizing what, for Raico, was the legitimate American Right, the anti–New Deal isolationist one. Opposition to American involvement in foreign wars was foundational for what had once been viewed as American conservatism. The America First movement, which tried to keep the United States out of the European war in 1940 and 1941, was not composed entirely of Old Right supporters. Quite a few members, as Justus Doenecke documents in his work on this movement, came out of the American Left. But the anti-interventionism promoted by the America Firsters did not differ significantly from that of such Old Right stalwarts as John T. Flynn, Albert Jay Nock, and Garet Garrett, all of whom identified "fascism" with military interventionists and the growing welfare state.

Although the very interventionist postwar conservative movement could accommodate inoffensive remnants of the Old Right, their opinions were peripheral to the war against communism. An established procedure evolved for dealing with these remnants of older rightists. Postwar conservatism could be gracious toward hard-money libertarians, Southern Agrarians, Burkean traditionalists, or pro-Franco Latin authoritarians, providing this outreach did not clash with the magazine's *raison d'être*, which was, of course, fighting communism.

While Meyer's *In Defense of Freedom* tells us that he will not dwell on the communist threat because he "is concerned with the development of ideas within the Western and American traditions," he then denounces communism as "Nazism's older brother," which "dominates a third of the world and advances messianic zeal and cold scientific strategy toward the domination of the whole world." Further, "Everything projected in this book presupposes the defeat of this monstrous atavistic attack upon the survival of the very concepts of moral order and individual freedom."

It is difficult to discuss Meyer's fusionism without considering his leitmotif. Clearly, he sought to supplant an older version of the Right with one specifically geared to fight and defeat "Nazism's older brother." Reviving the libertarian isolationism of the 1930s would not have served the present purpose, and Meyer's fusionism was an attempt to summon into existence an anti-communist conservatism fitting the exigencies of what James Burnham characterized as "the protracted struggle."

THE ESSENTIAL PAUL GOTTFRIED, ESSAYS FROM 1984–2024

Unfortunately, this effort did not succeed in winning over Kirk and those whom Meyer called, misleadingly, the "New Conservatives." Nor did it greatly please those staunch libertarians who thought that fusionism was making too many concessions toward traditionalists. There was also no praise for Meyer's theorizing from Burnham, that political realist and neo-Machiavellian who may have regarded fusionism as mere metaphysical twaddle.

One might retort to my argument that there were other forms of fusionism besides Meyer's, and some of these variants may have worked better to advance conservative unity. Ronald Reagan may have been practicing his own fusionism when he spoke about the "tripod" upon which the Republican Party and American conservatism both rested. This tripod consisted of a defense of the free market, military preparedness, and traditional social values. Although Reagan was more rhetorical and less theoretical than Meyer, his formulation seems to have aroused less opposition.

Even more relevant, as George Nash points out in his magnum opus on the postwar conservative intellectual movement, is that Buckley in the 1960s praised Meyer's attempt to outline the "conservative consensus."[86] Obviously, there was something substantive that brought together those who identified themselves as conservatives at the Philadelphia Society, an organization for conservative discussion Meyer helped found in 1964. When the father of fusionism died in April 1972, after converting to Roman Catholicism, many saw in his conversion "the great symbolic reconciliation, the ultimate fusion."

Allow me to quibble with these efforts to identify conservatism with a fusionist vital center. A critical difference exists between an intense political engagement and the laying out of an ideological position.

Mind you, I'm not disparaging the importance of trying to persuade a political group that one hopes to influence. But such an activity is usually not of the same magnitude as a more life-consuming, let alone life-endangering, mission. Trying to sell a fusionist doctrine is not like staking one's life for a cause. This endeavor is not the existential equivalent of what Ukrainians, who are fighting under siege to preserve their independence, are now doing; nor is it similar to the risky undertaking of those American colonists who declared independence from the British Crown. Although proposing one's consensus position to a divided political group may be noteworthy, it falls well short of an existentially defining mission. To restate Carl Schmitt's deservedly famous distinction, we are speaking in this case not about the "political" as a life and death engagement but about a far less consequential activity.

Allow me then to make a further point. Sharing slogans or stating similar views at an annual conference—however exhilarating that experience may be—is not the same as struggling to save an inherited way of life. Hungarian-German sociologist Karl Mannheim defined "conservative thought" as precisely that, the fashioning of a worldview related to an existing social situation. Conservative thinkers, like Burke and his continental counterparts, were neither designing slogans for political campaigns nor drawing up unity statements for their colleagues. They were rallying to a way of life that was under attack, an agrarian hierarchical one they intended to preserve.

This articulation of a worldview that results from a defense of a threatened way of life seems to me an essential aspect of conservatism, historically understood. Meyer's manifesto was designed to unite his fellow intellectuals in a polemical campaign against the Soviet Union. Whatever its merits, this statement of fusionism does not rise to the historic importance of Burke's *Reflections* or Maistre's *Considerations on France*. Meyer's book is a document among other documents telling us about the internal disputes besetting the American conservative movement at a particular time. Thus, I would contextualize Meyer's endeavor as one trying to find common ground for his fellow conservatives even as their movement was attempting to define itself.

Although well worth studying, that movement never acquired the large social base of an older conservatism, such as the one that mobilized followers against the "ideas" of the French Revolution. That crusade gave rise to a conservatism that lasted throughout most of the nineteenth century. It was socially situated, something our populist Right has recently tried to become. This populist Right that is still taking shape could become a political game-changer. Its protests even now are signaling more of a revolt against the leftist ruling class than all the recent editorials in *The Wall Street Journal* about what new or old faces are admitted to Conservatism, Inc. This populist upsurge (and I'm saying this with more than a tinge of regret) may be historically more critical than even those learned disputations by founders of *National Review*, on whose every word I hung as a young man.

Not surprisingly, the anti-communist alliance that Meyer and the fusionists hoped to forge took a strange historical turn. What became the dominant force in that movement by the 1980s were the neoconservatives, who by then were well-placed advocates of an anti-Soviet foreign policy. On most issues, the new conservative leaders stood well to the left of Meyer and his critics of the 1960s. Arguably, Meyer's fusionism ceased to be relevant as the neoconservatives imposed their own set of ideas on a changing movement.

Despite these twists and turns, self-described conservatives, many of whom worked for the administrative state or as lobbyists, continued to attend the same yearly conferences. But I doubt they were there because of an existential commitment or an intensely shared worldview. From what I recall, these attendees were networking professionally or else attended the meetings with their friends the way Englishmen of an earlier era went "to the club." Those who came to these gatherings were motivated up to a point, but they in no way reminded me of Aleksandr Solzhenitsyn or of another spiritually driven anti-communist, Whittaker Chambers, whom Dan McCarthy graphically depicted for *The American Mind*. The conference-enthusiasts whom I remember mostly lacked the fighting spirit that Frank Meyer so richly embodied. Lastly, I should stress that nothing I have said is intended to demean the founder of fusionism, who is someone I deeply respect and of whom, as a graduate student, I stood in awe. As a writer and speaker, I have always emulated Frank Meyer's contentious style, even when I disagreed with him. As an historian of political movements, however, I have tried to put fusionism into historical perspective. Others are free to, and I would expect them to, dispute my judgments.

CHAPTER FOUR

The Liberal Tradition

– ◆ ◆ ◆ –

Therapeutic Democracy

Chronicles

JUNE 1993

I T IS impossible to judge what is wrong with democracy unless we first understand its changing and constant features. The democratic principle as we now encounter it is both ancient and rudely contemporary. Among the ancient aspects of our contemporary democracy are the spirit of equality and the dangers that result therefrom. Aristotle properly perceived that democracy involves a regime of the have-nots, and, as he tells us in *Politics*, Book Three, the connection between democracy and indigence, real or imagined, is more important than whether the poor become the popular majority.[87] Rule by the multitudes would not be democratic, Aristotle notes, unless that multitude was, or saw itself as, materially deprived. In the *Republic*, Book Nine, Plato depicts democrats as drones avid for the honeycomb produced by the industrious few.[88] Lack of discipline, exemplified by a demand for endless oration and a boundless appetite for the fruits of others' work, characterizes democratic man, and by degrees, Plato shows, the lawlessness of democratic life gives rise to tyranny.

The coupling of democracy and equality was axiomatic among Greek political theorists, and it has remained thus for modern critics and exponents of democratic institutions, from Rousseau and Tocqueville to Carl Schmitt, John Dewey, and Harry Jaffa. Whether these theorists advocate or deplore democracy, clearly none of them dissociates it from the expanding application of the principle of equality. Legal equality must move toward political and, to some extent, social equality if democracy is to remain true to its essence. The toleration of privilege, it is said, works against the inculcation of a democratic ethos; thus, as Professor Jaffa is fond of reminding us, American political leaders pointed back to their nation's doctrinal origins while fighting a war against slavery and carrying through a belated civil rights revolution.

But also present in classical democracy and in the Swiss, Italian, and American republicanism of an earlier age (though increasingly absent from modern Western democracies, including our own) was the practice of self-government. Among Plato's chief objections to democracy was that the demos in fact governed and were preeminently in a position to inflict their greed and sloppiness on society in general. It was *homonoia*, spiritual and ethical unity, not *isegoria*, allowing everyone to have his say, that Plato believed produced a good government and a public-minded population. To achieve a citizenry capable of self-government, ancient democracies and ancient democratic statesmen engaged in what today would be considered hate crimes. With due respect to Donald Kagan, who celebrates him as the forerunner of global democracy, Pericles—an advocate of the people and later a virtual tyrant—began his political career by striking from the voting roles Athenians who were not descended from *astoi*, registered citizens, on both sides. This act was genuinely popular and was thought to underline Pericles's respect for the lineage of all properly born Athenians, whatever their social status. In *Politics*, Book Seven, Aristotle pointedly warns against allowing *xenoi*, aliens, to overwhelm an already established polity. Such an oversight could result in social disruption and, as Bertrand de Jouvenel explains in *The Pure Theory of Politics* (1963), undermine effective self-government by lessening the recognized value of each individual citizen.[89] The larger and more heterogeneous the population base of a political society, Jouvenel observes, the more difficult it is for citizens to run public affairs in a meaningful way. Whence the attempt of ancient democracies to limit rigorously the right of citizenship.

Such facts, it can be argued, illustrate the impoverished imaginations and bigoted mindsets of the ancient world. If Aristotle had only known about democratic capitalism, he would have established his own Heritage Foundation, propagating the ideas of open borders and universal nations. And Plato, once enlightened about global economies and the propositional nature of an American democracy in which anyone can be a citizen by believing selectively in the Declaration of Independence, would have insisted on the ultimate *beau geste*: bringing the ancestors of the Haitian boat people to ancient Greece, as full citizens.

At the very least, we are led to believe, James Madison would have been suitably broad-minded. Had not that American Founder praised (in *Federalist*, no. 51) the merits of an extended republic, a regime that would avoid the claustrophobia and strife of ancient republics by opening American society to as many groups as might want to come in?[90] The ensuing diversity would presumably protect us against the danger of majority factions, as proliferating heterogeneous groups would spread out along the Eastern seaboard. This appeal to Madison as a multiculturalist is stupid, dishonest, or, what is more likely, both. Madison, in his comments on the composition of an extended American republic, was referring to artisans, merchants, farmers, Presbyterians, Anglicans, Methodists, and possibly Catholics and Jews. But he was surely not speaking about unemployed Rastafarians. He was not indifferent to the kind of cultural base American republicanism required to maintain the ordered liberty under English Common Law that was then, more than now, the birthright of American citizens. Mel Bradford may have turned himself into a moving target by devoting his career to glossing this obvious point, but it is obvious nonetheless. And what renders Bradford's observation on the inherently restrictive nature of American republicanism so obvious is that the Founders intended to have communities look after themselves. On this there was no disagreement between Federalists and Anti-Federalists—or among most Americans until the present century. The Madisonian system by which Americans lived assumed that regions and localities would attend to their own affairs while operating together in dynamic tension. The federal government would mediate their differences, provide for the common defense, and regulate interstate commerce. But it was not there, at least not until recently, to impose thought control on groups that in the absence of sensitivity training and handouts would be unable, or so it is feared, to coexist in the same society.

Contrary to what Edwin Yoder states in his December 19, 1992, syndicated column, the Bill of Rights did not first come to be taken seriously "twenty or thirty years ago," when the federal government began applying it against states and localities. It had originally served as a safeguard for states' rights as well as for the rights of citizens within states against congressional encroachments. That document goes back to a time when a smaller and far more culturally homogeneous America still practiced self-government, which presupposed state and local control over access to voting and offices. As the Ninth and certainly the Tenth

Amendments indicate, that exercise in self-rule depended on keeping federal power limited to certain specified tasks. To the question of whether that self-rule guaranteed equality to all American residents, the answer is plainly no.

Until the twentieth century, with the problematic exception of revolutionary France, democratic citizenship was never open to everyone, not even to all residents of self-described democracies. Such regimes have followed the principle that those who are not of the political community, which sets up its own rules for membership, do not exercise its political rights. Thus the Swiss cantons only conferred full citizenship on males who had been born in them and belonged to their established churches. Such circumscribing of citizenship does not indicate disregard for the practice of self-rule. Rather, it demonstrates the continuity of the classical republican assumption that the possibility of self-rule hinges on the presence of cultural unity and of jealously guarded limits on citizenship.

Democratic pluralists reject this idea categorically. They insist that Americans and other Westerners think of their societies as perpetually incomplete and in need of diversity. They are not deterred by the prospects of the instability that results from trying to absorb more unlike things into a society whose collective existence has become steadily more precarious and violent. Speaking on behalf of the pluralist experiment, Leon Wieseltier in the *New Republic* last year scolded long-time social democrat and British poet Stephen Spender for disapproving of further Third World immigration into Europe. Spender saw such added pressure on countries already afflicted with violence and social unrest as something one ought to avoid. Besides, he concluded, "the immigrants themselves are by no means always upholders of democracy." Wieseltier, unsettled by his argument and by his reference to a "global population hotch-potch," stated in response that Spender had confused the object and the source of the hatred: "Reactionary forces are not reacting at all, they are seizing an opportunity to act on a desire." Moreover, "democrats are not born, they are made. Democracy is an instruction, a taught discipline, and the instincts that it inhibits are common to clay."

Wieseltier's own conception of democracy has nothing to do with the practice of self-government or with training for citizenship in a community living by its own lights and customs. It is a "taught discipline" that requires us to rise above what we are or, more accurately, used to be as a result of our political and cultural heritage and to open ourselves to imposed change. And it is not we who are supposed to make or unmake that change as a prudential decision; we are only to allow it to happen to us—as "an instruction," to use the pseudoclassical rhetoric typical of the new democratic ideologues. As I argue in my book on Carl Schmitt and the nation-state, what democratic pluralists chiefly want is a return to erotic politics, to the bonds of civic fraternity present in the ancient city, albeit under altered circumstances. In the new erotic politics, we shall live together in a global society that absorbs but never excludes. Any retreat from that ideal is now identified in the popular press with tribalism or with a slippery slope leading precipitately into Auschwitz.

Therapeutic democracy, as practiced by a growing welfare state, has a symbiotic relationship to erotic politics. Indeed, that politics has become the ideal that fuels managerial tyranny at home and abroad. In the absence of cohesive societies capable of looking after themselves, sensitizing bureaucrats, particularly social workers, have risen to political power. And to some extent this ascendancy has been necessary to maintain civil peace among otherwise warring minorities. A vast bureaucratic structure has sprung into being in France to help absorb incoming North Africans under the banner of "the rights of man." This bureaucratic network has also been charged with the *"sensibilisation"* of the French population, whose dislike of the new immigrants is all too apparent. Of course, it is hard to imagine any group that would clash with the French more dramatically than North African Muslims, with whom they fought a long and bloody war in the postwar period and who insist on bringing Muslim dress and religious practices into French public schools. Though there is surging popular resistance, French journalists grouped around *Le Monde*, social professionals, and human rights advocates in the government have protested any change in immigration policy. It is the French, not the growing and largely unassimilable minority, that are seen as being at fault. Democratic pluralists are always stressing the need for constant adaptation to alien and even shocking lifestyles. This adaptation, it may be inferred, will have to continue until we have shed all established identities in favor of a coercively homogenized and bureaucratically sensitized world community.

I remember a December morning in 1991, when I made the mistake of allowing my eyes to stray over breakfast coffee onto a newspaper column by Richard Cohen. A human rights maven who ranted against a congressman for appearing in public with Pat Buchanan (whom he had personally excommunicated), Cohen was exercised that morning over new insensitivities. The United States was stubbornly refusing to admit twenty thousand more Haitians; and this callous behavior made him think of how America had turned back German Jews fleeing Hitler in 1940. What one situation has to do with the other, save for the desire of various people in the twentieth century to enter our country, is, to me at least, unclear. Certainly there is no reason to assume that Haitians who return to their homeland will meet a fate as dire as the one that overtook Jews in Nazi Germany. But, even more to the point, are the Haitians whom Cohen and Jesse Jackson and their ilk encourage us to take in likely to yield the same types of citizens as the German Jews who were turned away in 1940? Such an outcome seems highly improbable, on the basis of what can be learned about both groups. But for Cohen and other democratic pluralists, such qualitative distinctions or the unequal dangers faced by different refugees from different societies are ultimately irrelevant. The issue comes down to determining how many diverse minorities we can stick between the two oceans for social workers to assist and human rights advocates to represent. There are no legitimate communities, national or otherwise, in Cohen's and Wieseltier's universe, except for designated victims, social therapists, and concerned intellectuals. Unfortunately, these same lobbies stand in the way of any attempt to restore real political communities or even a semblance of self-government in America.

The Twilight of National Sovereignty

Taki's Magazine

AUGUST 14, 2008

This essay is the final installment in a three-part symposium on the problem of sovereignty. Earlier contributions were made by Thomas E. Woods Jr. and John Zmirak.

U NLIKE AT least some of my readers, I find nothing intrinsically offensive about the idea of state sovereignty. That is because I don't see individualism or anarchy as the preferred perspective for understanding political relations. In the fictitious dream world in which some libertarians operate, the state is evil, regardless of whether it's necessary or not. Only by weakening political institutions, we are told, so that the state could do nothing but defend life and property with minimal means, would it be possible to preserve our individual identities. Some libertarians I have known also seem to believe that the "state" has existed in opposition to individual self-actualization since ancient times, and whether we are talking about the Old Kingdom of ancient Egypt or the Anglo-American welfare state, it is always the same adversary that enterprising individuals have had to face, as best they can.

Needless to say, this view, which I may be guilty of parodying (but not by much), is based on a totally skewed conception of the past. The "individuals" whom the state has supposedly oppressed throughout recorded history did not exist until recently, at least not in the atomistic form in which self-described individuals are now depicting their true selves. Until the modern period, individual members of any established community took on their identities by belonging to classes, genders, prevalent confessions, and ethnic groups. And though New Testament Christianity, prophetic Judaism, Platonic philosophy, and Stoicism all prefigured in some sense the possibility of the individual standing outside of his inherited communal associations, what these forces represented were glimpses into an alternative human identity rather than substitutes for the way situated people lived.

It was the state, which came into existence in the late Middle Ages and early modern period, that created the political precondition for the spread of individual identity. It did this by enacting legal systems that embraced all citizens or royal subjects and by imposing uniform taxation that applied to all classes equally. The growth of the state was accompanied by two forces from which it drew considerable strength. It represented in its European place of origin self-conscious nations; and it found its most enthusiastic promoters in the rising bourgeoisie, which supported the authority of the state and its association with particular nations and national patrimonies. Charles de Gaulle was correct when he described the French motherland as *"une nation de quarante provinces et de trente rois."*

It was, however, kings who had subverted the cohesion of French provincial life when they had imposed, along with uniform administration, *une langue française pure,* a refined and homogenized French tongue that presumably all royal subjects would speak and pass on to their children. The same monarchs took care to provide a standard French literature and a national history that was made to go back to Vercingetorix and the ancient Gauls or to the Roman Empire, whichever the preferred antiquity that rulers wished to stress for expediential reasons. Certainly in some cases nations pre-existed the achievement of national unity, and particularly in Eastern and Central Europe. But it was just as often the case that state leaders enhanced and instilled national consciousness as a means of consolidating political power and administrative unity.

In the nineteenth century, the ascendant professional and commercial class had a special affinity for national cultures and nation-states. And it is also no mystery why the bourgeoisie threw themselves behind these institutions. Their own rise to prominence depended on replacing the feudal aristocracy as the dominant social class. Equally significant, their upward mobility presupposed the kind of national order in which careers were open to talent and wealth, both of which the bourgeois had in abundance. Moreover, membership in nations was more attractive to these *novi homines* than being locked into their once-inherited social status, and particularly inasmuch as the older social order had excluded them, unless they were allowed to buy patents of nobility from the aristocracy. This had meant for most of the early bourgeois exclusion from government positions and the indignity of being treated as commoners. Unified national governments also brought expanded opportunities for wealth, by breaking down provincial tariff barriers, by establishing a uniform currency, and by generating a growing pool of credit. Finally national monarchies supported overseas exploration and colonial settlements, both situations from which the bourgeoisie drew disproportionate benefit.

To the extent there existed the political and social world of Western modernity, one based on constitutional monarchy, a bourgeois culture, and some kind of a free market economy, its origin lay in what had preceded that stage of history. The individualism and libertarianism that some of my colleagues are now celebrating did not come along simply in opposition to the historical state. They are the late modern products of social developments that the prior existence of the state had made possible. And without this earlier sequence of events, a peculiarly late modern libertarian consciousness would not have become as widespread as it is (or used to be).

A certain qualification may be in order here: Not all good states were nation-states, and the Habsburg monarchy, particularly during its last seventy years, exemplified the possibility of a refurbished medieval empire, held together by the dynastic principle, serving the needs of a changed European society. The same might have been possible in a reformed Ottoman Empire, if the First World War had not destroyed its opportunities for further adaptation.

On the whole it was within nation-states that the modern West developed politically, culturally, and economically. And the breakdown of this political system has had a deleterious effect on the survival of a recognizably European civilization, especially when it has been replaced by supranational bureaucracies preaching multicultural ideology.

But even before a monstrosity like the European Union came on the scene, the institution of the nation-state was becoming a remnant of an obsolete modernity. The "democratic welfare state" that our neoconservative and liberal adversaries glorify is not an extension of an older political structure. It is a dreadful distortion of that structure. How that distortion took place is the central focus of my study *After Liberalism* (1999) and is given further attention in the two books that followed.[91]

What distinguishes the "liberal-democratic" or "social-democratic" regime from a nineteenth-century Western nation-state is the arrogant, intrusive role assumed by public administration, one that allows it to interfere in a wide range of social relations. In fact the authorized spokespersons for the democratic masses now everywhere in power in "the West" have set about reconstructing their subjects, revamping their families, redefining gender relations, and banishing "prejudice" from the minds and hearts of white male Christians. In the case of the European Union, "democratic" administrators have also set about transferring national sovereignty to supranational organizations, preferably as in the German case without permitting unenlightened national subjects to have any say about who exercises sovereignty over them. Public administrators and their judicial and media allies have also succeeded in de-Christianizing Western Europe, not only through their control of education but also by repopulating Europe with Muslims, many of whom are explicitly hostile to Western Christian civilization.

In this system the re-socialized masses go along for at least two discernible reasons.

1. The organs of the state and their media allies shape and control popular consciousness, and once all intermediate institutions between the individual and public administration have been diluted, partly by being associated with insensitive attitudes and partly by being colonized by the state, it is relatively easy to get uprooted individuals to think and act as they are told.

2. "Democracy" itself has been redefined as political correctness, and therefore the demand that people be allowed to act contrary to the wishes of "scientific," sensitizing elites has been effectively condemned as "fascistic," "racist," "anti-Semitic," "anti-democratic." Democracy as indoctrination rather than as self-government has won the day throughout the West, and at this point one has reason to doubt whether this process is reversible, outside of small pockets of defiant ethnic minorities, for example in Flanders and Switzerland.

But this is only one side of the totalitarian essence of the ultramodern "democratic" regime. Equally important, at least in its American heartland, is the haughty unwillingness on the part of its journalistic and political elites to recognize the sovereignty of states that don't suit their vision of how the world should look. Wars are launched to "make the world safe for democracy," and as in the bloody case of World War II, entire civilian populations belonging to undemocratic enemies are targeted for destruction. The modern democratic state is an increasingly ideological construct, and the fact that the European Union, following the model of the degenerate nation-states of Western Europe, is now imposing on its subjects "gay rights" codes, "hate speech" laws, and other features of leftist totalitarianism, without being viewed by our leftist and neocon press as outrageously anti-democratic, speaks volumes about how we now understand "democracy." It is PC indoctrination to be carried out by elites, who are viewed as the bearers of "democratic values."

Michael L. Desch has made the perceptive observation that the true inspiration for American democratic crusades is not the World War I president who is now celebrated for this dubious achievement. Rather it is the German philosopher Immanuel Kant (1724–1804), who pointed the way, unintentionally, toward what David Gelernter calls proudly "the American religion." It was Kant who, in his tract *To Perpetual Peace* (1795), evokes a world teeming with legislative republics.[92] This situation, Kant insisted, was the necessary basis for global peace, for it was the prerequisite for a universal society in which individuals would act in accordance with their rational wills, in such a way as to treat "everyone as an end rather than as a means toward something else." It was as a moral exhortation rather than as a description of reality that Kant offered the observation that "nobody would obey laws to which he has not already given his consent." People, of course, have done this constantly, in Kant's time and certainly in ours.

Kant's republicanism was based on "the pure idea of the authority of the law," a position that leads him to support not only universal republicanism but a "world citizenship right." In his new order, all people who entered a particular society could expect to receive "hospitality" (*Wirtbarkeit*), presumably at the expense of the local population. Although Kant does not specify how far rationally guided citizens would have to go to accommodate the influx of strangers, he indicates that "a world citizenship right is not an eccentric conception of some visionaries but basic to world republicanism."

131

Each individual, as a self-conscious bearer of Reason, had to imagine that what he considered to be moral had universal application. What this added up to was the conceptualization of an individual who imagined himself liberated from historical contingencies and private sentiments, handing out his supposedly dispassionate, universally valid principles and axioms to the rest of the world.

Let me make clear that this is not the totality of Kant's complex ethical theories. (I am also unhappy about criticizing a philosopher from whom I continue to learn, and particularly from the thirteen-volume Cassirer edition of his work that I hold as a family heirloom.) What has been exposed is only a particular recycling of selective passages from Kant, the ones that directly or indirectly have foreshadowed the American religion of global democracy. Lurking behind the self-righteous contempt for the principle of sovereignty and the media-generated noise about "Western democratic values" is this vulgarization of Kant, or at least those visionary ideas that Wilson and his spiritual descendants have helped inject into our political bloodstream. Kant believed perpetual peace was only feasible if rational individuals forced their leaders to abandon standing armies. What would take their place would be military forces under the command of rational citizens, an arrangement, we are made to believe, that would provide collective security against presumed warmongers. A League of Nations, a United Nations . . .

The Kantian worldview arises in some surprising places, such as in the writings of the German-Jewish philosopher and supporter of the *Kaiserreich* Hermann Cohen. It's now a cliché to lump the German Empire in with Nazism, or at least view it as a backward, authoritarian deviation from the European modernity of the victorious Allies. But in Cohen's 1915 polemic *Deutschtum und Judentum*, he intended to convince Jews worldwide to support the Central Powers in the Great War as a new version of Kant's world federation.[93] Presumably after Cohen's side had won, and the Jews in Eastern Europe had been liberated from tsarist oppression and attended the schools that the German and Austrian occupation forces had already set up for them, they would become the adherents of a Kantian world order. At that point they and others would grasp that the real obstacle to world peace were not standing armies but unsettled social problems: "[T]he social politics of individual states must prepare the way for perpetual peace by advancing the concept of a federation of states. This is the essence of the state's task, and through the application of its power it was possible to advance the social end for which it exists." The imperfect Europe of the present would give way to a new order that would maintain international fraternity by ensuring the proper distribution of profits and social services. The German government happily distributed Cohen's tract to those it hoped to influence.

Cohen was a German patriot who believed the Jews had fared well in his homeland. Nevertheless, his claim to having privileged access to universal values, which we are made to think are superior to the historically grounded and particularistic, has consistently been present in the war against national sovereignty. And the values privileged in this struggle point in more than one political philosophical direction, to either international social democracy or libertarianism, two concepts that are equally far removed from the older tradition of nation-states and historic nations. Movement in this abstract, universalistic direction has continued to progress, so that today what is mistakenly called "conservatism" has abandoned the principle of national and state sovereignty in favor of a periodically updated "human rights" talk. This might be seen as the religious aspect of the political and administrative crusade that has been successfully waged against the idea of nation-states.

The nonstop appeal to a highest "human" value in the matters of immigration, the determination of national interests, and the preservation of historical patrimonies has worked to undermine the politics of a world of independent states, bound together by the making and keeping of treaties.

Barry Alan Shain, in a recent essay in *Modern Age* (Summer 2007), mocks the idea of defending the West by imposing what are supposedly universal, democratic values.[94] This value-imposition, in Shain's view, has become the defining element of a creed that has been misleadingly packaged as "conservatism." In place of the defense of "cultural particularity" and established hierarchy, "conservative" value-merchants are now offering something that is alien to what they claim to be upholding: "It is the creation of an intellectual bulwark against modern egalitarian utopianism, not the suppression of a phantom nihilism, which defines conservatism."

One is reminded here of Nietzsche's mocking characterization of nihilism as the devaluing of what someone else considers his highest value. In the end, it may be impossible to go back to a less ideologically driven point of reference, but it is foolish to imagine that universalized individual value-preferences, to be imposed internationally, or pronouncements in favor of an imaginary world of self-actualizing individuals, are carrying us in the right direction. Such Kantian or neo-Kantian practices belong to the very problem that brought us to our present mess.

Bourgeois Liberalism

Chronicles

S INCE SOME of the articles in this number offer a critical discussion of liberalism, it might be helpful to consider what exactly that term means. Keeping in mind that the meaning has been changing since the end of the eighteenth century, I'll start by listing four definitions, only the last of which seems to me to work.

First, we should reference what the media and chattering class label as "liberal," which signifies whatever the user wants it to mean. For Ezra Klein at *The New York Times*, liberalism is perfectly compatible with abolishing gender distinctions or with Sarah Jeong's tweet calling for the disappearance of white men, an apparent indiscretion that Klein passionately defended. This arbitrary use of "liberal" is comparable to the looseness with which the GOP media wield their god term "conservative," which has been extended to such signs of the age as gay marriage and transgendered Republicans. In neither case do we learn what the terms under consideration mean historically, as opposed to what politicians and political journalists would like them to mean.

A second definition brings us to the common understanding of "liberal" among advocates of the welfare state and government-enforced social policy. It was the rise of what the socialist philosopher John Dewey called "the new liberalism" that inspired me to write *After Liberalism* (1999), a book that focuses on the differences between the nine-

134

teenth-century concept of liberalism and twentieth-century social democracy.[95] The semantic extension of "liberal" was already going on in earlier attempts by the modern administrative state to alter the income curve and to colonize the family. Despite the effort to treat this massive interventionism in civil society as an affirmation of "freedom" based on self-government, it was exactly the opposite of what it claimed to be. Self-described libertarians like Albert Jay Nock, H. L. Mencken, Friedrich Hayek, and Murray Rothbard were right to notice this obvious contradiction.

Still, our third definition, the libertarian alternative—particularly when yoked to a defense of radical lifestyles—hardly represents a return to the liberal ideals of an earlier time and society. Terms like "classical liberalism" and "nineteenth-century liberalism" are now routinely linked to expressive individualism and the right of each person to do his own thing. This linkage has arisen from the selective citing of certain nineteenth-century sources, whether in defense of anarcho-capitalism or of a right to pursue certain peculiar moral practices. Some of the personalities who are associated with this idea of liberalism, like James Mill, his son John Stuart, Richard Cobden, and the German anarcho-individualist Max Stirner, were not really "classical liberals." In the age in which they lived, they were viewed as being on the political fringe. Unlike most liberals of their time, James Mill and Richard Cobden were in favor of both universal suffrage and international free trade. John Stuart Mill, who offered an extravagant defense of listening to all points of view in *On Liberty*, was an early feminist and advocate of the welfare state.[96]

But outside of England, most self-described liberals in an earlier time were protectionists and defenders of the nation-state. Like the English judge and philosopher James Fitzjames Stephen and François Guizot, the French premier in the 1830s and 1840s, these liberals resisted the plan to extend the suffrage to those without real property, who paid below a certain tax rate.

Which brings us to our fourth definition: liberalism, properly understood in those earlier times, was the lens through which the educated and propertied bourgeoisie (and note we are not just speaking here about an income group) understood the world and their place within it. Although evidence of this class could be found much earlier, the golden age for the bourgeoisie was the nineteenth and early twentieth centuries. And contrary to what Marxists tell us, the bourgeoisie was not just running around amassing and investing capital. The bourgeoisie built a civilization centered on glittering cities, palatial homes, and the fostering of the arts and education.

Although there were Catholic liberals, perhaps most famously Lord Acton, liberals in general fitted more easily into Protestant rather than Catholic societies. For centuries, liberals had battled "clerical" enforcement of "just prices" and laws against usury (with roots going back to Aristotelian economics), societal influences of the Catholic Church. The Church also backed guild control of crafts and commerce, which limited trade competition and access to certain vocations. Needless to say, the bourgeoisie opposed such checks on trade and finance from wherever they came, and the Catholic Church represented for liberals the most unified opposition to desired economic change.

Again, there were exceptions, and both Catholic Belgium and the mostly Catholic regions of the Rhineland were among the pacesetters in industrial development and the expansion of investment credit. But there, too, the rising economic sector faced resistance from ecclesiastical authorities. This was true even in England, where the Anglican Church, into the early nineteenth century, opposed what it considered high interest rates. (Not surprisingly, a disproportionately large number of the English entrepreneurial class came from nonconformist Protestant backgrounds.)

This anticlerical tendency, which prevailed among the bourgeoisie in Catholic countries, did not translate into anything even distantly foreshadowing modern wokeness. Victorian morality thrived among the bourgeoisie; and the practice of separating the sexes socially was far more typical of the bourgeois class than of the older aristocratic order, in which philandering and the keeping of mistresses were hardly frowned upon. Although the affluent bourgeoisie avidly supported opera and civic festivities, their poorer cousins were often engaged in what Leo Strauss, paraphrasing the teaching of John Locke, described as "the joyless pursuit of joy." Hard work was viewed as godly work, even if it brought, at least initially, scant reward. The prospering capitalist economy did not favor every interest and group equally, and far more ventures foundered than prospered in those regions of the West that were modernizing. Not every ship benefited to the same degree or at the same time from the rising flood of economic growth.

Although the bourgeoisie spoke about expanding freedom, they also stressed its moral limits. Public order took precedence over individual expressiveness, and discussions that were suitable for debating societies and academic lecture halls were not always acceptable in other social settings. Liberal societies were not only tolerant of what are today called "family values." Indeed, such values were basic to their existence, as was the emphasis on women as mothers and wives. The expectation of most girls with whom I went to school in the 1950s was that they would become "homemakers," and this did not testify to low self-esteem. Rather, it showed to what extent my fellow students were imbued with the social values cherished by our traditional social elites. What Amy Wax has referred to as "our Anglo-Protestant values"—values that once shaped American life and marked all religious denominations—are what sustained the traditional liberal society that existed by the nineteenth century.

Condemning that liberal order for practicing discrimination or for not imposing our present egalitarian ideology is an example of foolish presentism. Probably no one on the planet a hundred years ago held the social views of our present woke ruling class. Even the suffragettes, whatever their rhetorical excesses, made far less extravagant demands than did later feminists. The suffragettes wanted the right to vote and access to certain professions, and they sought more control over their property. These women also didn't want their husbands to come home drunk, and many of them were staunch prohibitionists. But these advocates of "women's rights" did not insist on abortion rights and were generally well-disposed toward being homemakers. Although more sweeping demands may have been implicit in their movement, there is no reason to treat these harbingers of a later feminism as being more radical than they actually were.

Although the liberal bourgeoisie opposed the slave trade and called for "putting slavery on the road to extinction," they would not have been racial egalitarians even if they thought about such matters. These burghers usually had little contact with blacks, unless they were living in the American South or near a black urban neighborhood. The homage they paid to diversity might have been limited to a recognition that, at least in the sight of our Maker, all humans are in some sense equal. Our liberal bourgeoisie most certainly would not have favored extending voting rights to poor, illiterate blacks, but they also would not have wanted to give those rights to white people of the same economic and educational background. If these civic leaders and captains of industry were glaringly insensitive to any demographic, it would have been toward the predominantly white working class, a group that we on the populist Right now champion.

But there is a difference in terms of the historical situation between the present populist Right and workers' organizations circa 1900. The latter were generally on the socialist Left and favored government control of the economy and major income distribution. Today the working class has become a source of relative social and cultural stability. Because of both a managerial revolution and the cultural radicalization of the corporate class, our circumstances now differ dramatically from those of earlier times. The working class has been transformed into an ally of the Right, a mainstay of the historical nation-state, while corporate capitalists are now usually found on the cultural Left. The onetime liberal order has now mostly passed; and older confrontations—e.g., between the bourgeoisie and an alliance of church and altar or between the bourgeoisie and the working class—have given way to a new struggle. It is the confrontation between the populist Right and a globalist managerial class allied to a woke intelligentsia. This struggle is taking place in a postliberal West; and while we may lament the erosion of our liberal past, it is not about to come back.

Lest there be any confusion on this point, let me state that I'm not calling for the right to ditch traditional constitutional morality or respect for public order. We should uphold such guiding principles to whatever extent that course remains open to us. Unless I'm mistaken, however, such vestiges of the liberal past may be less and less operational going forward. We should therefore not be surprised if the power grabs by the woke Left become even more outrageous as our postliberal fate unfolds.

Woke Liberalism?

American Greatness

APRIL 20, 2023

E ARLIER THIS month, an article I had just published in *Chronicles*, "Marx Was Not Woke,"[97] received unexpected publicity. This happened after my essay elicited a heated response from popular controversialist and blogger extraordinaire, James Lindsay. My critic described me on Twitter as a deservedly "unknown" "idiot," who was clearly out of his depth writing about liberalism. Let me explain this complaint.

My essay was written partly in response to Yoram Hazony's identification of wokeness with Marxism in *Conservatism: A Rediscovery* (2022).[98] Although I disagreed with this linkage, I thought Hazony made a serious argument for his side. I also agreed with his description of "liberalism" as a spent force, which is no longer a match for woke totalitarians. This may have caused Lindsay to go after me, given his assumed role as a defender of liberalism against the anti-rational Left and a presumed ally of conservative establishmentarians.[99]

Lindsay's remarks about me produced, at last count, more than two hundred thousand electronic responses, and most of them focused on the inappropriateness of Lindsay's rude dismissal of my scholarly credentials. If I am "unknown" in those circles in which Lindsay moves, that is certainly not due to my ignorance of Marxism, cultural Marxism, wokeness, or Western liberalism. I have rattled people in power who prefer not to deal with me or with the controversies I've aroused.

But that hardly proves that I don't know what I'm talking about as a scholar. Some of the respondents were astonished that Lindsay seemed, at least implicitly, to question my knowledge of the Frankfurt School. After all, I had been a student of Herbert Marcuse, written for critical theory magazines in both English and German, and even produced entire chapters of books dealing with Marxism and what (for want of a better term) is called "cultural Marxism."

It would also have been hard to read the article that offended Lindsay without noticing that I knew something about the subject of my reflections. I also published a book with Princeton in 1999, *After Liberalism*, which should indicate that I know about liberalism as well as Marxism.[100] Liberalism, let us remember, is a cause that Lindsay claims to be championing; and I certainly treat it favorably in my book. We may therefore wonder why my essay offended Lindsay so profoundly that he responded to it with implausible insults.

It seems to me that the source of my offense can be found in the last two paragraphs of my essay, in which, like Hazony, I treat liberalism as a force that is no match for woke totalitarians. But Hazony is more sympathetic than I am to those cultural progressives who presume to call themselves "liberals." These would include Bari Weiss, Sam Harris, Douglas Murray, and presumably Lindsay, all celebrities who have been "canceled" by erstwhile friends on the woke Left. This, according to Hazony, underscores how frail the liberal tradition has become in relation to its mighty collectivist enemy. And this supposedly proves Hazony's premise that only conservative democratic nationalism can offer a collectivism that can compete with a woke rival.

My view about the authenticity of what now goes by the label "liberal" is markedly different from Hazony's. The liberal tradition I argue has been growing ever weaker since its heyday in the nineteenth century, when it found a home in a bourgeois civilization based on biblical morality, a strong nuclear family, and constitutional government. Later that tradition was significantly denatured as it became identified with alien substances like Progressivism, social democracy, feminism, and finally, wokeness. I find it exceedingly hard to identify robust liberalism with the social world of Lindsay and his comrades. The so-called Intellectual Dark Web, with which Lindsay was long associated, featured mostly moderate progressives complaining about their woke associates who unfriended them.[101]

Lindsay makes no secret about his sympathy for the woke Left, however he may label this persuasion. He claims to be strengthening that Left through his efforts to teach it rationality. His "liberal" critique of critical race theory, for example, may be little more than a charitable endeavor to bestow on the Left a methodological facelift. It is intended to protect kindred spirits against sloppy thinking that would "give power to anti-intellectual, anti-equality, illiberal currents on the Right."

Please note how Lindsay describes his moral mission in his co-authored book *Cynical Theories* (2020): "*Cynical Theories* is born of our commitment to gender, racial, and LGBT equality and our concern that the validity and importance of these are alarmingly undermined by Social Justice approaches."[102] Lindsay makes the LGBT cause and feminism nothing less than integral parts of his liberal tradition.

This occasions an obvious question for those of us who understand the liberal tradition differently: Is Lindsay's woke understanding of liberalism one that James Madison and other founders of America's constitutional order had in mind when they established the American republic? I think not. It may therefore be better to weep over the passing of real liberalism than to pretend that Lindsay is rushing to its defense.

Three Conceptions of Conservatism

Chronicles

JANUARY 2024

S OME OF the best studies I have read on conservatism as a historical phenomenon have come from authors who were not in any
conventional sense "conservative." In this venerable company I
would place the illustrious Harvard political scientist Samuel P. Huntington, whose essay "Conservatism as an Ideology" (1957) is one of the
most insightful, erudite studies on conservative thought from the
1950s.[103] That was a decade in which Russell Kirk published *The Conservative Mind* (1953), an Edmund Burke–revival was flourishing,
National Review and *Modern Age* were founded, and the Southern
Agrarians were still a significant cultural and artistic force.[104] In the
1950s conservative publishers Regnery Gateway and Arlington House
also came on the scene, as a conservative readership exploded.

It was also a decade in which English translations of Hungarian-
German sociologist Karl Mannheim's work became available. Although
not a self-identified man of the Right, Mannheim in his long essay "Conservative Thought" (1953) brilliantly explored the European counterrevolutionary worldview.[105] Much of what Mannheim published about
Burke, Louis de Bonald, and other seminal conservative thinkers was

reflected in the social theoretical writings of Robert Nisbet, who became an academic star in the same fateful decade. If Huntington explored the conservative phenomenon extensively in his essay, he was writing about what, in the 1950s, was a hugely popular topic.

Despite patrician lineage, Huntington was a self-described liberal Democrat throughout most of his long life. But that hardly mattered if one reads his essay about conservatism and notices its dispassionate tone. Clinton Rossiter, who published *Conservatism in America: The Thankless Persuasion* (1955) around the same time Huntington produced his essay, was a more left-leaning Democrat; yet Rossiter treated postwar conservatism with respect, if not with the same analytic rigor as Huntington.[106] Needless to say, political and cultural attitudes in the 1950s were light years more conservative than they are right now. Huntington called for "gradualism" in desegregating educational and other public institutions and extolled the conservatism of the Southern planter class, without ceasing to think of himself as a man of the moderate Left. Unlike our present era, self-described conservatives then would never dream of tearing down statues of the Founding Fathers or Robert E. Lee, celebrating gay marriage, or affirming various bizarre individualistic lifestyle choices.

Huntington examines his subject by way of "three broad and conflicting conceptions of the nature of conservatism as an ideology." These are "aristocratic" or tradition-based conservatism, "principles-based" conservatism, and "situational," or what we might think of as pragmatic or power-based conservatism. Although some might object to his use of "ideology" to characterize these conservative worldviews, Huntington does not mean any more by this usage than a political vision and the strategy for achieving it. He is not applying "ideology" in the sense in which Kirk rejected it, namely, as a total view of reality created to combat a hostile alternative.

Today, it is Huntington's second concept of conservatism based on principles that is now the most widespread understanding of conservatism. This strain, he wrote, "holds that conservatism is not necessarily connected with the interests of any particular group, nor, indeed, is its appearance dependent upon any specific historical configuration of historical forces."

It is Kirk who is often associated with principles-based conservatism, which he formulated as his case for as an expansion of the tradition-based conservatism established by Burke. Although Kirk saw the emergence of a conservative worldview as a response to the French Revolution, particularly in Edmund Burke's famed broadside, *Reflections on the Revolution in France* (1790), he did not want to limit conservatism to a particular historical situation or time period.[107] He and his followers therefore expounded a conservatism that "is relevant and desirable in contemporary America." This form of conservatism, which draws on enumerated "canons" or principles, may have been what Huntington had in mind when he referred to conservatism as "the preferable political philosophy under any historical circumstances."

Huntington contrasts principles-based conservatism to Burke's aristocratic version, which represented "the reaction of the feudal aristocratic-agrarian classes to the French Revolution." Following Karl Mannheim's notion of conservatism as the reaction of a displaced former ruling class to a "particular historical and sociological situation," Huntington regards this aristocratic conservatism as "indissolubly associated with feudalism, status, the *ancien régime*, landed interests, medievalism, and nobility." Since such conservatism was "irreconcilably opposed to the middle class, labor commercialism, industrialism, democracy, liberalism, and individualism," Huntington believed it was doomed to failure in an American society that lacked hereditary classes or an established national church.

Although Huntington recognizes aristocratic conservatism as the long prevalent form of conservatism in Europe, he believes it was foreign to America because of its clash with progressive ideas. Thus, Huntington repeats Louis Hartz's argument in *The Liberal Tradition in America* (1955) that because the United States was founded without a feudal aristocracy and with a liberal political tradition, any American conservatism based on aristocratic principles is a nonstarter.[108]

What Huntington overlooks in his comments on aristocratic conservatism is what Alfred Cobban argued in his book *Edmund Burke and the Revolt Against the Eighteenth Century* (1929).[109] By the late eighteenth century, there was a powerful reaction setting in throughout Western Europe against rationalism in politics and the tumultuous effects of the French Revolution. Aristocratic conservatism as espoused by Burke, Samuel Coleridge, and Robert Southey held a high place among Cobban's subjects, and was a critical influence for what became by the early nineteenth century the Romantic movement. In this cultural and literary reaction to the "Age of Reason," there was at least implicitly a glorification of the pre-Enlightenment and particularly the medieval past.

Contra Huntington, this aristocratic conservatism was relevant in America because it migrated to other classes, particularly the bourgeoisie. Literature stressing national antiquities and praising nobility and the lost age of chivalry flourished in the nineteenth-century homes of merchants and urban professionals, both in Europe and America.

Benjamin Disraeli, the scion of an Italian Jewish commercial family, became a leading light in the Tory Young England movement of the 1840s. In Disraeli's novel *Coningsby* (1844), the novel's protagonist is based on George Smythe, a founder of Young England and an aristocrat.[110] The aristocratic hero stands up for "the old England" before industrialization and bourgeois greed came to ruin what had been an agrarian country. The Young England movement, which Disraeli spearheaded with Smythe and the Marquess of Granby, saw the coming together of landed aristocrats with the rising bourgeoisie, who shared their idealization of a past golden age. This fellowship also aimed at preserving tariffs for British grain producers and lending support to the monarchy and England's national church.

The novels of Sir Walter Scott were steeped in this idealization of England's lost aristocratic age, read and reread by America's Southern planter class, as Rollin Osterweis shows in *Romanticism and Nationalism in the Old South* (1949).[111] Even the children of frontiersmen were quick to identify themselves with the European gentry after they acquired estates in the Antebellum South. Eugene D. Genovese underlines this point in *Roll, Jordan, Roll* (1974) and his other magisterial works on the Southern slave economy and the world that the Southern master class built.[112] Genovese focuses on the honor ethic and noblesse oblige this dominant class tried to personify, as it emulated European aristocratic standards of behavior.

The first families of Virginia, and more generally Southern conservatives, long identified themselves with the Cavaliers, who fought against the English Puritans in defense of King Charles I in the English Civil War. Whether these self-identified American aristocrats are in fact descended from the royalists may matter less than the monarchist legend they preserved, one that was very much alive in the years leading up to the American Civil War.

Moreover, conservatism has links to ideas that originated long before the French Revolution and Burke's *Reflections*. Greek-German intellectual historian Panajotis Kondylis in his 1986 magnum opus, *Konservativismus* ("Conservatism") sets out to prove that "aristocratic conservatism" was already taking form in the Middle Ages.[113] Kondylis offers as proof the detailed defenses of aristocratic privilege and decentralized government emerging from late medieval Europe. These defenses of aristocratic rule returned in a modified form during and after the French Revolution; and according to Kondylis, they acquired an appeal that extended beyond the aristocratic class in which they once incubated.

Arguments against political leveling and in favor of "tradition" penetrated bourgeois circles throughout the nineteenth century. Contrary to what Huntington suggests, aristocratic conservatism enjoyed a long life as a mutating form of discourse that fitted the need of various ruling classes struggling against upstart adversaries. It also imprinted itself in literary and even cinematic culture well into the twentieth century, such as in film adaptations of Anthony Hope's 1894 courtly adventure novel *Prisoner of Zenda* and, in Germany, films celebrating the Habsburg empire.

Huntington's third concept of conservatism is what he calls "situational." He writes that this concept:

> [A]rises out of a distinct but recurring type of historical situation in which a fundamental challenge is directed at established institutions and in which the supporters of those institutions employ their own conservative ideology defensively. Thus, conservatism is that system of ideas employed to justify any established social order, no matter when it exists, against any fundamental challenge to its nature, no matter from what quarter.

In his elaboration of this third concept, Huntington removes conservatism from any specific historical context and locates it wherever or whenever those holding power are challenged from below. Because it is a conservative strain of thought that is primarily concerned with how an elite defends its own power and privilege, its explicators in the twentieth century are the elite theorists inspired by Niccolò Machiavelli, whom James Burnham wrote about in his 1943 book, *The Machiavellians: Defenders of Freedom*.[114]

By this standard, it may be necessary to view woke Left administrators pushing back against their opposition as defenders of "conservative" interests. Since in this case it is the cultural leftists who are responding to their power being challenged by a populist Right, it is the left-wingers here who can be situationally described as "conservative." Please note that Huntington's third concept refers to a situation in which any group of defenders of established institutions are resisting those who challenge their control. If that is indeed the case, then it shouldn't matter what those institutions are advocating or imposing, in order to designate their defenders as conservatives.

Despite the vulnerability to contradiction inherent within Huntington's third concept, it does make a perfectly valid point that needs to be affirmed. Conservatism develops out of conflict, in which traditional ways of life and traditional loyalties come under attack and need to be defended. Mannheim notes that conservatives felt forced to defend their position only when what seemed "nonproblematic" suddenly fell under assault. Conservatives constructed their ideology in the course of protecting what had once been taken for granted as a permanent social order. Their defense was historically grounded and arose from a traditional ruling class going on the defensive. It had nothing to do with today's phenomenon of intellectuals putting together lists of preferred values, or college students discovering one day that they would rather vote Republican than Democratic. Conservatism is a position born of struggle, arising at a particular time in a particular civilization.

Aristocratic conservatism does refer to actual conflicts in which recognizable conservatives are united against a shared adversary. That form of conservatism was the template for its nineteenth-century manifestations and explains why we would consider Burke, who was an impassioned opponent of the French Revolution, a prototypically conservative thinker. Although Burke may have been more than a defender of Huntington's spurned aristocratic conservatism, he was unmistakably that as well.

All of Huntington's concepts of conservatism remain relevant for providing a comprehensive definition of the phenomenon under investigation. None of them can stand entirely on its own, however, in fulfilling that task. Moreover, if forced to pick from Huntington's list what seems furthest from the essence of conservatism, I would choose the type stressing autonomous principles. It may be fruitless to talk about political conservatism unless we can situate it historically. Value talk does not make a conservative movement.

The struggle on behalf of long-hallowed institutions, ideally led by traditional social elites, represents for me the conservative political tradition in its most complete form. Needless to say, we are not speaking here about cultural traditionalists, who may arise even when political conservatism is weak or nonexistent. These traditionalists are preserving a heritage, but it is one that only derivatively reveals a political nature. Pointing this out does not minimize the achievements of cultural conservatives. It only indicates what these worthy humanists and moralists are not.

We may, however, speak about a political right-wing that develops in place of a truer conservatism. That would involve a mass of activists who have mobilized against leftist domination but who would not meet all the requirements for what seems to me a full conservative movement. Unlike the advocates of mere value conservatism, however, a genuine right-wing grasps the existential threat that has called forth serious opposition. And this right-wing would certainly not modify its position to please friends and patrons on the Left.

In any case, I am not describing here an ideal conservative movement, which may not be possible in our present historical context. But that does not signify that no organized opposition to the Left is possible. Not every age can beget a full conservative movement, but an imperfect resistance against what is considered evil and perverse is better than pretending to resist forces to which one is surrendering by stages.

Finally, Hartz's notion that the United States never had a real conservative tradition because it never had a feudal aristocracy is open to question. In no way does the absence of such an institutionalized feudal beginning prove this country never had traditional hierarchies that approximated European aristocracies.

Such ruling classes did exist in early America, for example, in the Antebellum South, among Dutch landowners in the Hudson Valley, and in New England. One may doubt whether there was much difference between the political views of the High Federalists in New England during the 1790s and their European aristocratic counterparts; both deplored the demonic effects of the French Revolution, often in the same worried terms. Although class structure was not as formalized here as it was in Europe, Hartz may overstate the significance of egalitarianism and individualism as the key American traditions.

A patrician class living along the East Coast, from Massachusetts to Georgia, once definitely exhibited some of the same characteristics as European aristocracy. Digby Baltzell in his classic study *Puritan Boston and Quaker Philadelphia* (1979) minutely examines two once-influential elites in their Northeastern strongholds, one in Boston and the other in Philadelphia.[115] Baltzell leaves us with the impression that this once-established upper class exercised considerable influence in a previous age. In the eighteenth century, moreover, Eastern patricians held both indentured servants and, in some cases, slaves. Abolitionism and female suffrage, which often went together in early nineteenth century America, pointed ultimately in a leftist direction by highlighting the demand for greater equality. But neither was a notably strong force at the time that the United States became a constitutional republic.

Hartz's observation concerning America's liberal founding does offer a defensible position once it has been adequately qualified. The United States became gradually more egalitarian and more individualistic than those places from whence immigrants came. It also offered newcomers far more financial opportunity. But that does not mean the country they moved into did not include conservative communities and at least resid-ual hierarchical structures. This long remained the case, even if the American republic was born of a political revolution.

Although a "conservative rout" took place eventually in the United States—if we may cite the original title of Kirk's *The Conservative Mind*—conservative and even aristocratic conservative elements once prospered on these shores. Although that situation eventually ended, this hardly confirms Hartz's picture of our Lockean founding. Forces of change took over, and these would include an expanding frontier soci-ety, the ascendancy of an industrial capitalist elite, and in the twentieth century, a managerial takeover of government and society that has con-tinued to this day. Countries are internally transformed; and one would be hard-pressed to find much evidence of social or cultural continuity between the America of 1900 and the one we now inhabit.

Hartz at his most unconvincing tries to present the American welfare state as a natural progression of the atomistic individualist government that he ascribes to the American founders. This view is certainly open to question. Although the materialism and individualism that Hartz finds in America's origins may not please the traditional Right, it is different in its nature from the administrative collectivism that followed. The modern welfare state came partly out of a rejection of the "heartless," plundering capitalism that it was meant to replace or mitigate.

We may note that Hartz's view of an atomistic early America has not gone unchallenged. Barry Shain's *The Myth of American Individualism: The Protestant Origins of American Political Thought* (1994), which shows the dominance of the Calvinist clergy in early American commu-nal life, *The Basic Symbols of the American Political Tradition* (1970) by George Carey and Willmoore Kendall, and Kirk's *Roots of American Order* (1974) all exemplify correctives to Hartz's one-sided thesis about the American founding.[116] Although individualism, consumerism, and geographical restlessness have also been part of the American story, hierarchy, communitarianism, and European cultural and religious tra-ditions were also once integral to this country's identity.

Finally, those who notice that I've moved closer to Kirk's quest for a genuine American conservatism and further from Hartz's thesis than I was when I authored my last book on the conservative movement in 2007 (*Conservatism in America: Making Sense of the American Right*) are not deceiving themselves.[117] Kirk's exploration of American conser-vative traditions (please note the plural "traditions" here) continues to deserve our attention even seventy-one years after Kirk's publication of *The Conservative Mind*.

Our Grim Postliberal Future

Chronicles

A NY SERIOUS discussion of liberalism should begin by looking at
its historical context. The liberal worldview is not a collection of
abstract ideas that can be fitted into different situations and eras
at the user's convenience. Liberalism developed in the Western world in
a specific culture and time period, which was the early modern era.
While it incorporated principles and rhetoric taken from older traditions
of thought, including classical antiquity and the Bible, what was liberal
gained currency with the rise of the Western bourgeoisie.

One does not have to be a Marxist to recognize this connection, nor
does one have to deprecate or relativize liberalism's achievement to
acknowledge its distinctive cultural and social framework.

Liberalism at its height, which was the nineteenth-century Western
world, fostered certain identifiable political and moral developments.
They were, among other things:

- constitutional government
- a well-defined distinction between the state and civil society
- a generally free market economy
- and a high regard for private property.

It was a system that moved individuals "from status to contract," in the words of English jurist Henry Maine. That is, under pre-liberal systems, individuals had been tightly bound by their status, while under liberalism they were able to enter contractual relations regardless of social rank and to form associations with whomever they wished.

What liberalism, properly understood, did not require or necessarily encourage are the following:

* female suffrage redistribution of income
* tolerance of bizarre sexual practices
* replacement of nation-states by international organizations
* and the tolerance of clearly inflammatory speech intended to overthrow the government.

Although liberals in Catholic countries typically clashed with clerical authorities, very few were atheists. In Protestant countries, liberals were almost always churched. Both English Prime Minister William Gladstone and French Premier François Guizot, for example, were devout Protestant Christians. English historian Lord Acton was a fervent liberal but also a religious Catholic.

Providing such contextualization for liberalism, or so goes the argument of my book *After Liberalism* (1999), is essential for distinguishing the real article from the vagaries and eccentricities of those systems and people claiming to be liberal in this postliberal age.[118]

For instance, it's all fine and good if a homosexual atheist abandons some aspect of the LGBTQ cause. Indeed, given our present moral state, I commend anyone who has second thoughts about abandoning that practice, which is endorsed by modern America's unhinged state religion. But I'm not sure those second thoughts indicate that the person subject to them is either liberal or conservative in any true historical sense. That individual inhabits a world so vastly different from the one in which liberalism or conservatism flourished that the most we can say about his change of heart is that he's become slightly less radically leftist than his erstwhile friends.

The use of "liberal" becomes even less plausible when we are told that New York Representative Alexandria Ocasio-Cortez embodies the concept because she supports both a socialist economy and Black Lives Matter. Even allowing for the latitude that journalists take with language, I couldn't imagine a greater conceptual gulf than the one that exists between those whom our media characterize as "liberal" and those who answered to that label two hundred years ago. Does it make sense to apply the L-word to vastly different ideas in different ages by twisting it into utter meaninglessness? My answer is "no."

It seems to me that the liberal bourgeois age was followed by a postliberal one, which saw the rise of the modern administrative state and various post-Christian egalitarian ideologies. This postliberal age is not entirely divorced from its liberal predecessor but relates to it in the same manner as a Christian heresy does to Christian doctrine.

A theological deviation is, in ancient Greek, a *hairesis*, a "choice," meaning the choice of a particular doctrine from a larger set of beliefs, together with the rejection of other parts of the set. A similar process is at work when postliberals try to redefine liberalism by choosing and exaggerating one or more of its features out of the context of the historical whole.

For example, some but not all liberals believed, like John Locke, that individuals are endowed with a natural right to life and liberty. Today's progressives and cultural leftists calling themselves liberals have expanded Locke's list of inborn individual rights to include a right to income redistribution favoring clients of the state; a right to ensure gender equality; a right to have the acceptance of gay marriage inflicted on the unwilling; and a right to bestow special rights on members of racial minorities.

One may still discern bits of the older natural rights position in that expanded list. Nevertheless, under the progressive dispensation, rights are pushed in such a radical or opportunistic direction that they would be unrecognizable to long-dead authentic liberals.

Other examples come to mind. Liberals typically favored a popularly elected legislature, but that didn't mean they believed every resident of their society should be granted the franchise. Bourgeois liberals usually insisted that voting applicants establish longtime residence in the country, that those eligible to vote pay taxes at a certain rate, that they hold property, and that they be literate. Many self-professed liberals as well as conservatives opposed extending the vote to women, which they thought would have a ruinous effect on the family.

Voting was seen as a privilege, hardly a human right, and it was understood that extending it too far could deliver society into the hands of those who were unfit to rule and who might be a threat to life and property. It is clearly not the case that the loose way voting is now treated finds any precedent in the liberalism of an earlier age. Even John Stuart Mill, an early welfare-state democrat and feminist, wished to keep the illiterate and those who lived on the public dole from voting.[119]

Although liberals in the nineteenth century welcomed what was a minimal administrative state by modern standards, a striking difference between then and now should be apparent. In the nineteenth century, liberals applauded the public servant class, which, as Hegel famously described it in the 1820s, "stands above all particular interests" and served the common good. This reflected a widespread liberal approval of public administration, as long as it was limited to a few well-defined functions, such as delivering mail, looking after state property and public works, maintaining archives, and, in some places, providing relief for the poor.

Never was it imagined, except by some dreamers on the far left, that by the second half of the next century, state administrators would be put in charge of "family policy" and reconstructing social relations. That was not a small and inevitable step forward in the progress of the liberal idea, as is argued by those on the so-called postliberal Right, but a terrifying quantum leap into unknown territory.

One critical reaction against such developments has been to advocate for "classical liberalism." However, this represents not a return to the liberalism of the nineteenth century but the creation of a libertarian movement stressing individual autonomy. Libertarians have taken over traditions that have a genuine liberal provenance, such as Austrian economics,[120] constitutional originalism, and the defense of property rights.

But some libertarians have added to this mixture a focus on the individual resisting state power in pursuit of his own interests and pleasures. Moreover, in its extreme version, libertarianism has become associated with bohemian lifestyles, flouting bourgeois conventions, and reducing life to a series of economic choices. This is not true liberalism.

Indeed, much of what is now interpreted as a conservatism dating back to the 1930s combined the rejection of the administrative state, which was metastasizing under the New Deal, with the libertarian penchant for eccentric, individualist lifestyles.

Such responses to the postliberal order did not exemplify a return to anything "classical" but must be understood in their own context. These were postliberal reactions to a postliberal administrative state, which took over some of the features of nineteenth-century liberalism in an exaggerated form. Most liberal leaders throughout the nineteenth century favored protective tariffs (except in England, which was then the industrial pacesetter), were strongly nationalistic, and had no objections to a mutually profitable alliance with the state. In any case, these traditional liberals had a much broader view of the market than free-market purists now accept. Furthermore, on many moral questions and the defense of public decency, one would be hard-pressed to find common ground between them and most of today's self-described libertarians.

A predictable objection to my characterization of our postliberal age is that it ignores all the "liberal" assets that the postliberal age had been preserving, at least until quite recently. Didn't we enjoy, up until a few years ago when woke political and media elites decided to abolish them, all kinds of freedoms that came out of earlier times? For example, religious liberty, the right to an unhindered exchange of ideas, constitutionally limited governments, and protection of personal property? My answer to this objection is to concede the point, with one enormous reservation. What remained of the liberal tradition in the last hundred years was living on borrowed time; one should not be surprised that it gradually weakened and is now vanishing.

According to Aristotle, the creation and maintenance of regimes depend on *tropos*, a disposition and orientation that allows them to take root and flourish among particular populations.[121] Not every regime is suited to every culture; when the needed disposition disappears, the corresponding regime will disintegrate. As John Adams said of America, "Our Constitution was made only for a moral and religious people. It is wholly inadequate to the government of any other."

The historicist argument I would make is in some ways similar. A liberal regime with its accompanying principles and social arrangements prevailed in a situation that was favorable to its development. As those preconditions grew weaker, the regime gradually changed, although some of its founding ideas continued to flourish into the postliberal age, at least for a while.

I entirely agree with Carl Horowitz's critical comments about the postliberal Catholic Right, whose representatives often sound like New Deal social democrats with a changed label. It is hard for me to distinguish their plans for a larger welfare state from what has already been done to control us economically; and this may be why these supposed right-wing critics are not enduring a leftist backlash. They also seem to hate the Northern European Protestant culture that gave rise to our founding documents and its liberal institutions. In stark contrast to these detractors, I profoundly admire America's founding culture and what it produced. But I also doubt its political achievements have continued historical relevance, so I would apply here my favorite aphorism from Carl Schmitt: "An historical truth is true only once."[122]

At the present time in every major onetime Western country, there is an escalating confrontation between two warring groups: a self-conscious ruling class with globalist pretentions, and those "normies" whom the powerful are demeaning. While the former controls most vital political and educational institutions and most of the culture industry and media, the latter embraces most of the white working class and the population outside of metropolitan areas.

Divisions similar to what we see in the United States are characteristic of other Western countries. Everywhere in the West political elites are flooding their culturally divided countries with Third World migrants to increase the size of the administrative state's dependent class. Needless to say, the same elites are eager to play off the manipulable newcomers against the "deplorables," "fascists," or whatever else they call those rooted, patriotic families on whom they've made war.

Both these groups are locked in a struggle that is likely to go on for some time, and both belong to a postliberal world, which has less and less to do with a liberal one. Right now, the elites hold almost all the good cards; and their targets are on the defensive. But this can change in some limited ways. In the United States, unlike in more subjugated countries such as Canada and Germany, there are just too many on the populist Right for the Left to crush entirely. What's more, the resistance occupies large chunks of the continent. State governments in some regions are now acting to stem the floods of illegals that the ruling Left has worked to bring into the country.

Such resistance would be impossible, for example, in a country like Germany, where the population has been bullied into accepting the Third World resettlement of their land. As I write this essay, the local government of Augsburg, Germany, is encouraging mass demonstrations (which are likely to turn violent) against Germans who want tighter control of their borders. The officials doing this include the faux conservatives in the Christian Social Party.

Opponents of the woke regime in Germany have long been under investigation by government agencies as right-wing terrorists. Although such vindictive measures have been attempted by the ruling Left in this country, it has not had nearly the same level of success that such measures have attained elsewhere. High-handed action against dissenters has evoked a far more widespread backlash here than in other parts of what American neoconservatives still describe anachronistically as the "free world."

It seems highly unlikely that, if the populist resistance gains at least regional power in the United States, it would seek to return to the political culture of the nineteenth century or even embrace the milder form of postliberalism that once prevailed here. That ship has already sailed, as the cliché goes. The non-Left and the non-elites are now in survival mode, as the Left is swelling its numbers by opening borders to millions and millions of illegals. Opponents of this leftist takeover may survive but are unlikely ever to rule the entire country. The most they could hope for would be regional autonomy within a larger society that remained under globalist, woke leftist control.

In areas under their sway, these "normies" will preserve those values and beliefs that held them together in times of tribulation. These would consist of settled communal arrangements and a shared religious faith—but not necessarily what our strict constructionists understand as constitutional rights. Since these beleaguered outposts would have to protect themselves against infiltration, it is hard to imagine they would care about constitutional niceties or the fine points of a temporally distant bourgeois classical liberal society.

They would also be made up largely of those with little advanced education except in vocational fields. Most of those who have been influenced by academic culture now belong to the woke Left.

What I'm offering is a best-case outcome. If the present woke elites totally marginalize their opposition, a process that is already occurring elsewhere in first-world countries, we may soon be living in an anti-liberal hell. The victors would sooner jail the other side than allow it to gain influence. And if circumstances require this course, the ruling Left will unleash more violent riots and then, with media assistance, blame these disturbances on the Right, as they did after the death of George Floyd.[123]

For all these reasons, I am forced to conclude that liberalism, as it once flourished in the bourgeois West, may be a thing of the past. I say this without pleasure but with an understanding that those conditions and social underpinnings that permitted a liberal worldview and liberal sensibilities to flourish no longer exist. By now the remnants of that liberalism are vanishing in what may be the end phase of our late postliberal age.

CHAPTER FIVE

The Concept of Carl Schmitt

– ◆ ◆ –

Forgotten but Not Gone

American Outlook

FALL 2003

T HE RECENT, ambitious translation of *The Nomos of the Earth*, a work first published in 1950 by the great European legal thinker Carl Schmitt (1888–1985), turns out to be especially timely given the present situation in international affairs.[124] Both the translation and the accompanying commentary are by Schmitt's Anglophone disciple Gary L. Ulmen, who obviously labored over his task. The volume supplies a lucid translation of Schmitt's elegant German prose, clarification of concepts, a glossary of foreign terms, and a careful explanation of the Latin legal phrases.

Despite Schmitt's scholarly reputation in Europe and the fact that this English translation has received praise from the *Frankfurter Allgemeine Zeitung*, it is almost impossible (speaking as the author of an intellectual biography of Schmitt) to get Americans interested in his ideas. This may be due partly to Schmitt's decision to join the Nazi Party after Hitler's ascent to power. Yet the simple opportunism of Schmitt's initial decision, and his contempt for biological racism, were both apparent from 1933 on, and by 1934 Schmitt fell into disfavor with the Nazi government, which kept him under SS surveillance.

More to the point, Schmitt had little use for liberal constitutional regimes, which he thought had and would continue to give way to chaos or dictatorship. In fact, he believed that "democracy" went hand in hand with plebiscitary rule, and that twentieth-century parliamentary debates and party organizations were mere remnants of nineteenth-century liberalism.

Although I accept Schmitt's substantive distinction between nineteenth-century bourgeois liberalism and twentieth-century democracy, I do question whether pre-democratic liberals were as politically ineffective as he suggests. (Schmitt may have overgeneralized from the weaknesses of the Weimar Republic, which he ascribed to the legislative features of its constitution.) It may be asked, for instance, whether European liberal statesmen of the nineteenth century were not far stronger nationalists than modern democrats, who treat nation-states as relics and who prefer to fuss over universalistic human rights. Schmitt assumed incorrectly that egalitarian ideals travel best with nationalistic and communal ideologies. In our own time, to the contrary, we see democratic ideals linked to often abstract global identities. Moreover, it was European national liberals in the nineteenth century, such as François Guizot, Camillo Cavour, and Lord Palmerston, who built powerful states even as they accepted limits on what those states could do to change civil society.

What is undoubtedly galling to Schmitt's American readers, and was brought up by his hostile critic Mark Lilla in the *New York Review of Books* (May 15, 1997), was Schmitt's disdain for American political culture.[125] The US military occupants of Germany kept him in custody, as a possible war criminal, for more than a year. Although his investigators observed that there was "nothing in his career to de-Nazify," Schmitt's postwar correspondence and political commentaries show that he was miffed (another word comes more easily to mind) by his treatment. Schmitt presented the United States as a government that wielded great power but could never rise above being a soulless empire. Like much of the European Old Right, including the anti-Nazi Right, the aging German jurist could never overcome his revulsion for the rising transatlantic giant, which he nonetheless hoped might be persuaded to confine its activities to the Western hemisphere.

Despite this tick—which Ulmen, a pro–New Deal American nationalist, might downplay—Schmitt, in *The Nomos of the Earth*, throws light on our contemporary historical situation. Woven into his work is the premise that the European state system, which had arisen in the fifteenth and sixteenth centuries, had been broken by the two World Wars and was on its way to extinction. Although personally sympathetic to this order, which he believed had once restricted violence within and among states, Schmitt was convinced that something else would take its place in the postwar period. (Note that his book, though printed in 1950, was composed in large part during the war; still, it is not, with due respect to some of Schmitt's critics, a defense of Hitler's imperialism.)

Certain developments, Schmitt writes, had put off the inevitable reconfiguration of world politics—for example, World War II and the Cold War, which had left Europe at the mercy of the United States and the Soviet Union, two geographically and culturally peripheral powers. Nonetheless, Schmitt believed that in the long run, European states would be pulled into a polycentric international structure, a point that is made with particular force in the appendix to *Nomos* published in the late 1950s. Europe would survive as one of these "territorial spaces [Grossräume]" as an integrated political unit, since it was no longer possible to bring back the old order of nation-states. For Schmitt, this order had rested on certain preconditions, such as the association of European nations with particular territories (whence the Greek *nomos*, which refers to a distribution as well as an order and law), the establishment of sovereign states that became fused with particular peoples, and the treatment of power as a legal problem rather than as a theological or ideological one.

For Schmitt, the thought of legal scholar Francisco de Vitoria—the sixteenth-century Dominican and clerical descendant of Sephardic *convertidos*—exemplified a secularizing tendency among legal thinkers that coincided with the emergence of the nation-states. This tendency would become even more apparent in the English philosopher Thomas Hobbes, who worked to extricate political power from the control of ecclesiastical authorities. But it was Vitoria who began defining war, in this case between Spanish soldiers and Amerindians, as a relation between adversaries—as opposed to a struggle between Christians and their enemies. Schmitt believed that the subsequent transformation from an ethical standard of *bellum justum* (just war) to one of struggle against a *hostem justum* (an appropriate enemy) marked a critical stage in the taming of international tensions. By the eighteenth century, war in Europe would be understood not as a lofty moral crusade, as it had been in the age of religious wars, but as a violent dispute that was open to diplomatic negotiation. War was thereby stripped of ideological passions and relegated to the category of a recurrent nuisance.

What brought back the fury of war, according to Schmitt, was the age of democratic revolutions, particularly the upheavals wrought by

THE ESSENTIAL PAUL GOTTFRIED, ESSAYS FROM 1984–2024

the French Revolution and its Marxist sequel. The reattachment of violence to moral passion would result in nastier conflicts than had occurred in the eighteenth century. Moreover, the development of military technology, particularly naval and aerial power, would make the national borders that had existed in the old Europe a thing of the past. The wars of the twentieth century witnessed the fateful combination of rival ideologies and increasingly destructive weapons. The 1950s exemplify this pattern in the bipolar struggle between the United States and the Soviet Union, in which an already battered Europe was reduced to a spacious battlefield.

Reading Schmitt, one finds notions about international relations that crop up in later thinkers, such as the view of politics as the study of relations among nation-states presented in the textbook of Hans Morgenthau, or the polycentric clash of civilizations as conceptualized by Samuel Huntington. These conceptual connections are at least sometimes owing to the fact that the theorists in question, such as Morgenthau and Leo Strauss, were heavily influenced by Schmitt's thought while students in Germany. Even more important, however, is the fact that Schmitt preceded other thinkers in exploring the implications for international relations of both the former centrality and the later vanishing of the nation-state. In addition, beyond brilliant analytic studies, he offered a plausible picture of a post-national world divided into vast spheres of influence. The question is, how well did he predict the structure of power relations in the world we now live in? The answer is, despite his learning and theoretical inventiveness, not well at all. The bipolar division of the Cold War did not give way to a broader distribution of power. The United States went on to win against an economically mismanaged rival and establish a world hegemony that still staggers the mind. Regardless of whether this development is good or bad (and considering the nature of America's enemies since the 1930s, this outcome is at least arguably less bad than the alternatives that once existed), it seems that Schmitt was far less competent as a futurologist than he was as a legal historian.

Despite this shortcoming, *The Nomos of the Earth* is a political classic of our civilization, and we are indebted to Professor Ulmen for making it available and intelligible to Anglophone readers. Nonetheless, its author was a man of his time. In his shortsightedness, he calls to mind the Greek civic leaders at the beginning of the second century BC, described by Polybius, who failed to grasp the magnitude of Rome's rising power. They pretended that Rome was no more than a regional contender for territories, to be played off against the Illyrians and the

Macedonians. When the magnitude of Roman *dynasteia* became apparent, some Greeks capitulated and others went down in fruitless revolt. Despite his truckling to Roman patrons, Polybius showed intellectual integrity in setting out to investigate the cause of Rome's success. America's critics abroad would do well to follow his example.

The Concept of Carl Schmitt

The American Conservative

OCTOBER 16, 2015

R EINHARD MEHRING'S study of the long-lived German political and legal theorist Carl Schmitt (1888–1985) is the most exhaustive biography known to me of a deeply fascinating subject.[126] Given his opportunistic embrace of the Nazis in 1933, Schmitt does not fit the image that postwar Germans have worked to create for themselves. Yet Schmitt's *Dictatorship* (1921), *Political Theology* (1922), *Concept of the Political* (1932), *Legality and Legitimacy* (1932), and *The Nomos of the Earth* (1950) continue to be read because of their conceptual depth and stylistic brilliance.[127]

These elegantly phrased works cannot be reduced to the circumstances that inspired them—Weimar Germany, the Nazi regime, and the postwar American order—any more than Hobbes's masterpiece *Leviathan* (1651) can be seen purely as an artifact of the English Civil War. Indeed, aphorisms can be found in Schmitt's works that are so pregnant with meaning that they invariably fail in translation: "Sovereign is the one who determines the challenge of the exception," "All modern political teachings are secularized theological concepts," and "Historical truths are true only once."

Schmitt has always appealed to the political outliers, from the revolutionary Right to the anti-capitalist, anti-liberal Left. Geoffrey Barraclough's observation that the Hegelian Right and the Hegelian Left clashed at Stalingrad in 1943 might be applied even more appropriately to Schmitt, if we allow for a certain hyperbole. The Frankfurt School Marxist Walter Benjamin devoted one of his most famous essays to an elaboration of Schmitt's observations about Renaissance politics.[128] Otto Kirchheimer—who was Schmitt's graduate student at Bonn—and the young Jürgen Habermas were only two of the numerous German socialists who tried to adapt Schmitt's critical studies of Weimar German politics for leftist agendas. It was hardly accidental that Leo Strauss's first published work was a commentary on Schmitt's *Concept of the Political*, which Schmitt graciously appended to the second edition of his work.

In interwar Germany, Schmitt enjoyed indisputable renown. Leading jurists of the time like Hans Kelsen and Rudolf Smend, who had sharp disagreements with him, readily conceded his mental acuity and gift for language. It may have been almost incidental that Schmitt held a professorship in Bonn and eventually one in Berlin, or that he became the major legal adviser to the Catholic Center Party in the Reichstag during the Weimar era. As a literary and scholarly star he operated on a different level from the professional posts he held.

The details of his life of more than ninety-six years are truly staggering. Although the author of an intellectual biography of Schmitt, I learned from Mehring things about Schmitt's life I encountered nowhere else. Even longtime Schmitt researchers may be surprised, or shocked, by some of these revelations. Schmitt's first wife, for example, whom he divorced in 1922, was not, as is often believed, a Serb or Croatian from a prominent family but a thief and embezzler from Vienna who may have been involved in a prostitution ring.

The womanizing Schmitt became involved in an affair with an Australian teaching English, Kathleen Murray, while his divorce was still pending. At one point he promised to marry her, but she returned to Australia, having used Schmitt to complete her German-language dissertation. Later Schmitt plunged into other liaisons, perhaps most passionately with a certain "Magda" while he was still a professor in Bonn.

Teaching in Berlin while his second wife was in a sanitarium, he became so sexually promiscuous that Mehring refers to this period in his life as an "erotic state of the exception." Just as Schmitt argued that constitutional government required an awareness of "exceptional circumstances" in order to function even in normal times, so too did the survival of Schmitt's conjugal life depend on his liberty to plunge into serial affairs.

Perhaps curiously, given his sexual passion, Schmitt had chosen for his second wife a gravely ill, tubercular woman. The union brought Schmitt high medical expenses but minimal sexual satisfaction. This remarriage after a divorce also led to his excommunication. Mehring suggests that Schmitt's straying from his strict Catholic upbringing, a development hastened by his unsatisfied sexual desires, intensified his amoral careerism, culminating in his kowtowing to the Nazis. Although this causal connection is not provable, Schmitt's Catholic students and colleagues brought it up after 1933 when they attempted to explain their teacher's unexpected accommodation of the Third Reich.

Mehring confirms that Schmitt's devotion to the Catholic Church was mostly political. A Rhineland Catholic who grew up under Prussian Protestant rule, Schmitt resented the German imperial government as a foreign presence. He noticeably gravitated toward Latin cultures and seemed pleased with his mother's French ancestry, particularly since as a young man he managed to borrow money from his uncle in Lorraine. In his publications Schmitt defended the hierarchical structure and Roman law of the Catholic Church and became identified with Germany's (Catholic) Center Party. But theologically Schmitt was heavily influenced by the Danish existentialist Protestant Kierkegaard, and even when he defended the nineteenth-century Catholic counterrevolutionaries Joseph de Maistre and Juan Donoso Cortés, he habitually quoted his Protestant mentors Kierkegaard and Hobbes.

Mehring understandably questions whether Schmitt really believed in Catholic Christian doctrines. Here one should note Thomas Molnar's observation that Schmitt was a Catholic of sorts but certainly not a Christian. The inverse may also apply: Schmitt was intermittently some kind of a Christian but not a believing Catholic. In *Concept of the Political*—which interpreted the "political" as the most intense of human relations, characterized by friend-enemy relations—there is no underlying Catholic theme. Among the outraged critics of this work, as Mehring points out, were Catholic theologians. One surely discerns no Catholic leanings in Schmitt's praise for Hobbes as "the completer of the Protestant Reformation." Hobbes, as Schmitt reminds us, was the thinker who characterized papal influence over European sovereign states as "the kingdom of darkness." It is far from clear that Schmitt found this judgment to be objectionable.

Even more illuminating are the parts of Mehring's work dealing with Schmitt's attitude toward his Jewish connections. Attempts to find anti-Semitism in his writings and personal relations before his fateful decision to join the Nazi Party in May 1933 have turned up, as far as I can judge, nothing of consequence. Indeed, the Nazis had every reason to suspect Schmitt of dissembling in his anti-Semitic statements after 1933, given his longtime intimate association with Jewish mentors, benefactors, colleagues, and students.

Leo Strauss may have approached this academic luminary in the hope of obtaining a Rockefeller grant to do research in England precisely because Schmitt seemed especially friendly toward Jews. He also warned sternly against the Nazis before they came to power and had called on the German government in 1931 and 1932 to ban Hitler's party.

After 1933, however, Schmitt went out of his way to inject anti-Semitic remarks into his writings, while unceremoniously cutting off relations with his numerous Jewish acquaintances. Although the SS kept surveillance on him, as a suspect party member married to an ethnic Serb—his second wife—he nonetheless continued to flatter the regime. He even organized a conference of jurists in 1934 to discuss ways of removing Jewish influence from the German legal profession. Despite these gestures, Schmitt was upset that his onetime Jewish colleagues and students would not associate with him after the war. In letters and diaries he complained that he was being unfairly targeted for having decided to remain in Germany after 1933.

Schmitt was not the only amoral careerist who ever entered the academic world, but his character flaw was all the more shocking because of his greatness as a thinker and how he treated longtime friends. As a law student in Strasbourg he had been befriended by the son of a Jewish press magnate from Hamburg, Heinrich Eisler. Heinrich's son Fritz was his closest companion, and Fritz's soldier's death near the Marne in September 1914 left Schmitt bereaved. Almost ten years later he dedicated a book to his fallen comrade, and in the intervening time Fritz's brother Georg became Schmitt's bosom friend, particularly when the latter was between wives.

The elder Eisler had sent Schmitt, while he was an impoverished student and poorly paid legal clerk, regular gifts of money and had entertained him repeatedly at his sumptuous home in Hamburg. In his diaries Schmitt contrasted his admiration for the Eisler family, including the mother of Fritz and Georg, with his estimation of his own less generous and less well educated parents. But Schmitt suspended his relation with Georg in 1933, as well as cutting ties with Georg's sister, who had been his private secretary in Berlin.

There are two problems with Mehring's biography, other than the baffling absence of my writings on Schmitt in the extensive bibliography. One, the author provides such a mass of details that one sometimes loses sight of the forest for the trees. The chronological framework may not suffice to bear the crushing weight of all the data assembled. The author also shows a tendency to dart back and forth between discussions of Schmitt's writings and his personal and political life. In some chapters the result can be chaotic.

Two, Mehring never explains, certainly not to my satisfaction, why any of Schmitt's writings made such a profound impression on his contemporaries. Why would his Jewish editor Ludwig Feuchtwanger, who did not share Schmitt's political views, consider *Concept of the Political* a conceptual masterpiece? Mehring approaches Schmitt's work with painful reservations, as a "problem" in the history of German illiberalism. He dutifully quotes Schmitt's liberal and Catholic critics, but he never really explains why his subject's work bedazzled readers from across the political spectrum. As one of the bedazzled multitude, I would have appreciated a treatment of Schmitt's work that recognized more fully what made it so compelling. Although Schmitt was a morally flawed genius, one would have liked to find more in the biography about his genius and perhaps a bit less about the unmistakable moral defects.

But it may be hard for German academics, driven to engage "the burden of German history," to provide such perspective in writing about someone like Schmitt. We should therefore take what Mehring offers and attribute the resulting thematic imbalance to the burden of being a German academic historian.

Politics Is the New Religion

Chronicles

AUGUST 2021

T HE TERM "political religion" designates the infusion of political beliefs with religious significance. Political religions involve grand plans to transform society into a new sacral order unrelated to how humans have lived beforehand. Political religions also typically divide people into the righteous and the evil based on whether they conform to its transformational vision. They treat differences of opinion as heretical and call for suppressing dissenting views as a rejection of the Good. The priesthood of political religions demands that we punish those who express unsanctioned views as morally wicked—in the contemporary vernacular, these are "racists," "sexists," and "homophobes."

The concept of political religion is especially pressing because in the West, the struggle of intersectional, anti-white politics takes on the elements of religion. The now-dominant woke political religion has permeated Christian confessions, which often seem unable to resist ideological invasion. Complicating the matter is that the so-called liberal democratic opposition to the Left's political religion often resembles what it claims to be resisting.

Both sides exalt equality and universalism and view the end of human history in a similar fashion. Each sees history as culminating in triumph of their progressive doctrines, the effect of which will be the disappearance of human prejudice and the increasing indistinguishability or interchangeability of humankind.

Where today's political rivals differ is that one believes that designated victims of past injustices must be allowed to humiliate their supposed one-time oppressors at the present time. The other, supposedly more conservative, side wishes to dispense with such tribulations as we continue to overcome past sins on the way to a radiant future. Political religion has become so prevalent in our time that even what opposes the more dominant form often overlaps with what it claims to be combating.

My interest in political religion goes back to when I was writing a doctoral dissertation at Yale in the mid-1960s. The topic I chose to explore was the romantic revival in Southern Germany in the early nineteenth century. It was a development that reflected religious concerns, flowing from its connection to a Catholic renewal after the French Revolution and a reaction to the secularization of church property during the Napoleonic era. But this apparent return to religious tradition also incorporated romantic myths about the happy, socially integrated, and spiritually suffused Middle Ages, together with belief in an even older harmonious society from which primitive humankind had fallen away.

These mythic visions fueled a critical view of a then-incipient capitalist Europe, in which the cash nexus and profit motive were seen as weakening traditional hierarchical human relations. Although these romantics shared a conservative view of political and social organization, at least some of their critical perspective and appeal to an original human harmony poured over into early socialist attacks on economic modernization.

Not surprisingly, similar myths turn up in Benjamin Disraeli's novel *Sybil*, written in the 1840s, and in the Young England movement that Disraeli fashioned as a vehicle for Tory renewal.[129] One can discern in Disraeli's view of the past, which was also found in German and French romantics, a restatement of the biblical account of the Fall and the subsequent search for redemption.

While I was slaving away on my dissertation, which eventually became a book, I took out of the Yale Sterling Library the original 1938 German edition of Eric Voegelin's *Political Religions*. I came across the author while leafing through an early copy of the magazine *Modern Age*, which a friend in graduate school loaned me. *Political Religions*, published as Voegelin was fleeing Nazi-occupied Vienna, is by far his most compelling work. It shows how pre-Christian religious myths and images were poured into the cult-like veneration of Nazi leadership, and how a millennialist vision ran through the Nazi movement. I was impressed by Voegelin's evidence of the religious motifs that went into modern totalitarian politics.

The same emphasis on the mythical underpinnings of modern dictatorial movements can be found in Emilio Gentile's studies of Italian fascism as a political religion. Gentile explicitly identified the Italian fascist movement as an all-embracing form of substitute religion and affirmed his conceptual debt to Voegelin.[130]

The tie between the political and religious makes another appearance in a slightly different form in Leszek Kołakowski's *Main Currents of Marxism* (1978), which highlights the ecclesiological aspect of Marxism as a body of evolving theory with its own church doctors and sacred traditions.[131] In Kołakowski's case, a Catholic upbringing in Poland surrounded by a communist regime may have led him toward his view of Marxism as an accretion of holy doctrine, which generates both defenders and heretics.

My encounter with Carl Schmitt's *Political Theology*, first published in 1922, came decades after I had studied other works on this subject.[132] Although Voegelin was surely influenced by Schmitt's study, from all evidence he never mentioned that fact in print until he published his *Autobiographical Reflections* in 1989.[133]

Although an admirer and biographer of Schmitt, I believe Voegelin's *Political Religions* makes him the more provocative of the two. In comparison to Voegelin's troubled picture of ancient myths driving modern political disasters, Schmitt's study of the correlation between established Christian religions and concepts of sovereignty is tame stuff indeed. According to Schmitt, the Catholic worldview lends itself more to miracles and to a mystique of monarchy than does the Protestant one, while Protestants are better disposed than Catholics by their religious beliefs to republicanism and even a pantheistic worship of the "people." Such speculation makes for interesting debates but lacks the desperate sense of urgency that pervades Voegelin's analysis of Nazism as a political religion.

Schmitt does, however, raise in *Political Theology* and its 1970 sequel *Political Theology II* the critical question of whether Christianity carries political implications.[134] Schmitt underlines the point that Christian theology has led to different political dispositions and different forms of government, and this connection has not been accidental. We may therefore be justified in assuming a nexus between Christian religious beliefs and political theology.

Political theology, according to Schmitt, refers to the view that "theology served as the original basis for law, structure, and organization." It is the concept of divinity in various iterations of Christian theology that shapes the worshipper's view of sovereignty. Thus, Protestants who identify the operation of God in the world with a sacred text and its accompanying laws incline toward a legalistic and constitutional form of government. Catholics, by contrast, who view divine forces at work in their daily lives and who accept hierarchy in the state as well as in the Church, are more open to personal authority and exceptional political circumstances.

Schmitt famously argued that normal political life must always take into account the "state of emergency" that hovers over us even as our daily existence plays out. Schmitt believed Catholic societies were, all other things being equal, better able to live with this situation than Protestant ones, which placed greater confidence in legal procedures.

Although Schmitt was not speaking specifically about political religion, he did outline a relationship between politics and religion that would lead to Voegelin's more fully developed concept. He also, in my view, came closer to grasping the formative role of Christianity in producing modern political ideologies.

One need not return to ancient Gnostics to comprehend the rise of political religions. Ideologies of the Left, like communism and wokeism, recycle Christian elements, which even in their mangled or denatured state are still recognizable in terms of their point of origin. Indeed, it is impossible for me to imagine any leftist ideology that does not adapt such Christian principles as universalism and the spiritual equality of all people. The Left also recycles teachings about serving the poor and about the harmony of the messianic age, which are present in both the Old and New Testaments.

This is not to deny that what ideologues do with what they have taken denatures the borrowed principles and teachings. But it is unnecessary (*pace* Voegelin) to hunt among ancient pre-Christian cults to find material that modern ideologues can adapt to their purposes. They can easily extract their key themes from the religion they are working to destroy.

Needless to say, Schmitt's preferred political theology would support a traditional hierarchical society, which is not exactly what modern political religions promote. Our current ideologues are moving in the opposite direction, toward a leveled, homogenized, interchangeable humanity.

A point that Voegelin, Gentile, and other writers on political religion sometimes miss, or perhaps avoid confronting, is the relevance of their subject for the United States. These researchers have typically viewed Americans as immune to the danger they are describing. Their inability or unwillingness to notice the obvious may come from a misguided attempt to appeal to patriotic Americans or, in Voegelin's case, to personal circumstances: namely, that the United States offered him asylum from Nazi-occupied Austria, and he enjoyed living and studying in America in the 1920s.

As Jack Trotter and Grant Havers[135] both show in their contributions to this *Chronicles* number, any study of political religion is incomplete if it doesn't point to its specifically American manifestation. In America, political religion has masked itself as civil religion, which celebrates increasingly those who are viewed as progressive heroes. It also provides an at least implicit exaltation of consolidated managerial government and assigns a special place in its pantheon to Abraham Lincoln and Franklin Delano Roosevelt, both significant builders of the US administrative state.

In modern America's celebration of "who we are," the heroes sometimes change to fit an advancing political agenda. Thus such "racist" figures as General Robert E. Lee and John C. Calhoun have been desacralized, while the more politically useful Martin Luther King Jr. and Barack Obama have been added to the liberal democratic communion of saints. This manipulation of the pantheon of heroes by the state and, more recently, the media is different from the reverence for past rulers that one finds in traditional monarchical societies. It is not based on respect for a dynasty that is coextensive with the life of the nation and which expresses the continuity of a people. The heroes in America's changing civil religion are intended to reflect a revolutionary process.

Clearly the hagiography of the French and Russian Revolutions, both of which attempted to replace Christian saints with revolutionary ones, prefigured what is going on in our time and country. Like the cults associated with earlier revolutionaries, our American political religion acquired a powerful presence for patently political reasons, and this happened in the first part of the twentieth century, with the elevation of public heroes by the state and educators and with the growing emphasis on American exceptionalism. This adoption of an American political religion coincided with the Progressive Era and the centralization of an administered state and its unprecedented range of government-directed services.

Although there were earlier American cultic figures—for example, Lincoln in the North and in the South Lee and Andrew Jackson—and a shared veneration of Washington and other founders everywhere in the republic, a worship of American leaders chosen and promulgated from the top surfaced by the twentieth century.

The centrality of Lincoln in what Robert Bellah defines as this "American civil religion" was far from an accident.[136] Lincoln was an unabashed centralizer, who appealed to equality and America as the world's "last best hope." His cult was useful in eliciting approval for an expanding managerial regime and justifying foreign wars. Please note that I am not "bashing" Lincoln or his nationalism in noting this, but explaining why he was central to a state-sponsored American civil religion. The presidency of Woodrow Wilson, which combined a dramatic expansion of the modern welfare state with a bloody "Crusade for Democracy" in Europe, also exemplified the new political religion.

Attempts to see this development as an American adaptation of Prussian paternalism or English social democracy overlook the truly revolutionary nature of what occurred. It was a revolution in form that brought with it, as Walter McDougall and Robert Nisbet have maintained, the demand for an American crusader state together with ideological mobilization within the country.[137]

Solzhenitsyn and Burke understood the long-range danger of political religion better than Gentile or Voegelin. Political religion harks back to its leftist precursors in the French and Russian Revolutions. The Italian fascist "total state" or the Third Reich may be less relevant for grasping the continued appeal of political religion. While I am at a loss to think of current examples of fascist forms of political religion, leftist variants thrive everywhere in the West. The Left has been methodical in borrowing from Christian culture and using it to shape its own successor religion based on political control and continuous indoctrination.

Fascist political religions were much more ham-handed. There was always something farcical about Mussolini's grand design for the Italian state. Even when Nazi Germany took over the northern half of the country in the summer of 1943, they were more savage and aggressive than totalitarian. Once they had Nazified universities by kicking out Jewish professors and spreading Nazi propaganda, they proceeded to transform these institutions into army camps. Neither the Nazis nor the Italian fascists, moreover, undertook the massive economic reforms that the post–World War II English Labour government carried out.

Leftist political religions by contrast are entirely systematic in how they change society. They will not stop their work until every mind has been reshaped.

The Left does well in attracting adherents for a reason given by religious anthropologist Mircea Eliade: It wields myths that fit into a culture that has long been Christian.[138] The fascist vision of warrior nations locked in perpetual struggle pales next to the leftist dream of the suffering just triumphing in the fullness of time and creating Heaven on Earth. Unlike the Right, the Left has been able to harness moral guilt on behalf of its transformative vision. Even more significantly, it has weaponized hatred by recasting it as moral indignation in the face of injustice or prejudice.

The Left has even been able to maneuver its wannabe opposition into becoming a pale imitation of itself, a tendency illustrated by the conservative establishment's borrowing of the Left's rhetoric and positions. This indicates not only opportunism but also the difficulty that awaits those who wish to challenge the Left and its community of ideological faith.

These observations should not be read as an endorsement of what the Left is selling, which is dangerous totalitarianism that proceeds from a destructive vision of undoing human history and human nature. It also operates like a runaway train; conceding any ground to the Left will not cause it to stop roaring forward. Only a counterforce with equivalent power can halt its advance.

Like the ancient Gnostics, the Left sees itself as engaged in a struggle of Good against Evil in its own equivalent of the End Times. It therefore deals ruthlessly with its adversaries standing in the way of the long-sought victory over "prejudice" and "fascism." Misrepresenting reality, stealing elections, and allowing alleged "right-wing extremists" to rot in jail are small prices to pay for the prejudice-free age that they imagine awaits the righteous. This golden age will come more quickly if the opposition can be driven out of the public square and into fearful silence.

Although there is resistance, those on the Right are not armed with a vision even remotely as compelling as what drives the Left. Exposing the Left's double standards and glaring lies is fine up to a point, but opposing effectively what Burke recognized in the French Revolution as an "armed doctrine" can only be achieved with something equally compelling. Telling Americans, as I heard Fox News host Tammy Bruce do in early June, that racial relations "have never been better" will only convince those who have been secluded in their attics for several decades and haven't noticed the spasms of black racial hate.

Equally foolish is the conservative establishment's affirmation of the Left's egalitarian values. The conservative establishment insists that we've already realized those values but must stop before we reach "socialism," and that the Democrats are the real "racists" because they remain (at least in some Republican speechwriter's fevered imagination) the party of Calhoun.

Against the Left's contagious, militant political religion, one cannot win with such drivel.

Remembering Carl Schmitt

Chronicles

OCTOBER 2023

I T HAS been more than a hundred years since the German legal scholar Carl Schmitt (1888–1985) began publishing his legal and political studies. Unlike the fate of many of his contemporaries, Schmitt's thought is not forgotten.[139] In fact, it receives steady attention from young scholars, who find in his work much that is valuable.[140]

Schmitt was an advocate of relentless realism at a time of deep social and ideological division. This divisiveness is a key characteristic of both Weimar Germany and twenty-first-century America. Quite daringly, Schmitt questioned the worship of an elusive pluralism to which many Americans remain captive. He unequivocally endorsed cultural and moral unity as the precondition for any workable form of self-government. It is not diversity but homogeneity, Schmitt contended, that allowed such a regime to operate.

This versatile scholar wrote on many subjects over his lifetime of ninety-seven years, but three of his major themes are particularly well-known even in translation. The first is his exploration of the inherent conflicts among such systems of rule as parliamentary liberalism, democracy, and authoritarianism. This is the leitmotif of three of his books: *Political Romanticism* (1919), *Dictatorship* (1921), and *The Crisis of Parliamentary Democracy* (1923).[141] The second theme is his analysis of sovereignty, which is the core topic of his book *Political Theology* (1922).[142] The third theme is his consideration of how irresolvable political conflicts can be addressed while limiting existential enmity and avoiding total war. This last overarching theme shapes Schmitt's most famous work, *The Concept of the Political,* which exists in multiple translations and was first published in 1932.[143]

In the early 1900s Schmitt studied jurisprudence in Strasbourg, Munich, and Berlin; at that time the theory of positivism dominated German legal thinking. Schmitt's early writings expressed some doubt about this approach to legal and political theory. Such theories questioned whether real nations could operate within legal systems that had been constructed by "experts" on the basis of their own conceptual guidelines, a position that in the German-speaking world was identified with the Austrian-Jewish jurist Hans Kelsen. The emotional and physical upheaval of World War I and his own rootedness in a Rhineland Catholic culture set Schmitt on a very different path, which was opposition to artificial legal systems that had no roots in a particular people and culture.

After the German loss in World War I and postwar revolutionary disturbances, Germany's left-center parties produced the Weimar Constitution, which was promulgated in 1919. This document furnished Germany's governing framework until 1933, and it offered the occasion for the articulation of some of Schmitt's critical reflections on constitutional government. Schmitt saw the Weimar system as inadequate to the political challenges besetting his ideologically divided country, and so he attempted, as he explained, to "shift away from tactical and technical questions to intellectual principles and a starting point that does not lead to a dead end."

Curiously, Schmitt's first postwar study, *Political Romanticism,* which appeared in 1919, starts off as an aesthetic study before moving on to political questions. In this work, Schmitt took to task those who treated critical events through which they were living in an escapist fashion. These "romantics" manipulated words to create emotional effect while standing back from the real engagements of their time. Such self-absorbed fantasists could not look reality in the face. Instead, they indulged in "endless conversation," which never led to purposive action.

Demanding something more than conversation does not, however, indicate what that added requirement should be. Schmitt's works in the interwar period supplied this alternative in the form of "decisionism." This designated what Schmitt considered the proper exercise of power in a critical situation. According to Schmitt, because no system can contain within itself all the preconditions for successful governance, ultimately one supra-legal authority must decide questions that are not covered by existing law. "The decisionist enacts the proper law in a correctly recognized political situation by means of his personal decision," Schmitt wrote. Schmitt proposed decisionism as superior to the "endless conversation" that he found in Weimar-style parliamentarianism. This party system, argued Schmitt, had become an "empty apparatus" in the face of the political division that was convulsing Germany.

For Schmitt, all nations required someone who could make critical decisions when a political emergency, or what he called an "exception," arose. Such decisions and the decision-maker did not surge forth from a preexisting body of laws. Exceptions arise even where there is a legal government, but one that cannot meet an unexpected contingency. A gap therefore has occurred in the law and must be filled; and this task is inherently political. Someone must address the concrete situation that the law does not deal with in order to restore order. Thus, the opening line of Schmitt's *Political Theology* contains this memorable aphorism: "Sovereign is he who decides on the exception."

Schmitt rejects the definition of the state propounded by his teacher, renowned social theorist Max Weber. Weber famously defined the state as an entity that enjoys a monopoly of force. Rather, what defines sovereignty, and therefore ultimately the state, according to Schmitt, is the sole right to issue decisions that are not based on existing law. This is not an extra-legal arrangement. The sovereign issuing the decision is making law in an emergency situation and will necessarily reestablish an order as a set of norms, at some future point. Schmitt describes the irregular situation in this manner:

> The exception is more interesting than the rule. The rule proves nothing; the exception proves everything: It confirms not only the rule but also its existence, which derives from the exception.

(Note that presenting Schmitt's thought in the wooden translation above may be tantamount to sacrilege, seeing that he is among the most graceful stylists ever to write in German.)

In defining sovereignty, Schmitt also introduced the concept of "the Political" as a separate "endeavor of human thought and action" that requires drawing critical distinctions. "The specific political distinction to which political actions and motives can be reduced is that between friend and enemy," he wrote. The enemy "is, in an intense way, existentially different and alien." Therefore, "in the extreme case conflicts with him are possible. These can neither be decided by a previously determined general norm nor by the judgment of a disinterested and therefore neutral third party."

The antagonism that defines the Political is "the extreme case," and the participants enter a life-and-death conflict based on whether "the adversary intends to negate his opponent's way of life." The reasons for arriving at this decision may vary, but an unbridgeable line of division separates the two self-identified groups that are drawn into strife.

Schmitt's notion of the Political is still controversial and is most definitely not the friendly face of the caring-sharing welfare state. On the contrary, Schmitt wrote that "the Political is the most intense and extreme antagonism." In Schmitt's view, every concrete antagonism becomes an expression of the Political, and any antithesis that forces groups into the positions of friend and enemy fits the definition of the Political. The ultimate form of the Political understood as antagonism is combat, which may lead to the killing of other men. An underlying threat of violent conflict lay at the heart of every political disagreement. Schmitt wrote:

> War follows from enmity. War is the existential negation of the enemy. It is the most extreme consequence of enmity. It does not have to be common, normal, something ideal, or desirable. But it must nevertheless remain a real possibility for as long as the concept of the enemy endures.

Schmitt did not maintain that war is in itself desirable, and he praised the nation-state that developed in early modern Europe for restricting violence by setting up international rules for warfare. But Schmitt thought such strife would inevitably occur, no matter what the efforts to limit it. "War is neither the aim nor the purpose nor even the very content of politics," he wrote. "But it is an ever-present possibility which determines in a characteristic way human action and thinking and thereby creates a specifically political behavior."

According to Schmitt, the modern liberal state, which asserts the primacy of the individual and is focused on economic prosperity, may have trouble dealing with the reality of war. A state may justify killing to deal with "an existential threat to one's own way of life," but certainly not to achieve a higher gross domestic product. Schmitt wrote:

> To demand seriously of human beings that they kill others and be prepared to die themselves so that trade and industry may flourish for the survivors or that the purchasing power of grandchildren may grow is sinister and crazy.

Failure to understand the Political may even have the effect of ideologizing and totalizing war. Schmitt criticized the tendency in modern warfare to deny entirely the humanity of one's enemies. He maintained that such an attitude renders hostilities even more bitter:

> Such a war is necessarily unusually intense and inhuman because, by transcending the limits of the political framework, it simultaneously degrades the enemy into moral and other categories and is forced to make of him a monster that must not only be defeated but also utterly destroyed. In other words, he is an enemy who no longer must be compelled to retreat into his borders only.

Moreover, Schmitt viewed this demonization of one's foe as characteristic of liberal societies, which dwell on their moral superiority. Looking at America since the presidency of Woodrow Wilson, Schmitt might have found a confirmation for this intuition.

His study *Legality and Legitimacy* (1932)[144] may be the most relevant for grasping our own political and cultural situation. In this work, published just before the Nazi seizure of power, Schmitt asks whether a legislative state, one that is based on legislative supremacy, should determine the core norms of a constitution. By "norms," Schmitt meant expressions of the substantive values of a people, which preexist its constitution. For Schmitt, constitutions that are not merely expendable procedural guidelines should arise from the will of a people and their sovereign. They should not be the creations of imaginative intellectuals. "Norms are intended to be just and are the highest, decisive expression of the community will," he wrote. All else is subordinated to "this law of laws."

If such norms do exist, this implies that any law promulgated by a parliament which contradicts them should be invalid. This assumption would furthermore suggest that a legislature's power can be easily challenged if a crisis of authority results. Legislative state regimes are fragile, especially when they are constructed on the basis of procedural guidelines without reference to the will and traditions of a particular nation.

In the face of the challenge represented by the Nazi and communist parties in Germany, both of which swelled in membership in the wake of the Great Depression, Schmitt believed Germany's legislative state had shown itself to be inadequate. As an alternative he defended the act by which the aged German president, General Paul von Hindenburg, assumed emergency presidential powers to deal with the crisis at hand. Fortunately, the Weimar Constitution allowed for this assumption of presidential emergency power, and for Schmitt such a bold step seemed necessary for a legislative order that had become predictably impotent when challenged by internal breakdown.

Legality and Legitimacy also presents Schmitt's thoughts on "equal chance." Beyond ensuring that legislative acts are legal, what makes a legislative state legitimate must be its power to suspend the right of resistance. Although political movements in a parliamentary system should have the opportunity to win power, this should not include those who would actively deny an equal chance for their opposition. This meant in Schmitt's case the communists and national socialists, but we might extend his exceptions to Western political parties that weaponize administrative power against their designated enemies. This, too, has become a means of denying others the right to compete for power.

In Schmitt's analysis of equal chance, he also contends that majority rule, whether direct or indirect, can only work "when an essential similarity among the entire people can be assumed." In that case elections become not acts that suppress political minorities, but an affirmation of consensus by a self-conscious people.

Such a consensus most definitely did not obtain in Weimar, and it cannot be found in the United States today. Schmitt saw a fatal problem with a regime that empowers its sworn enemy, and he reminded his readers that self-government is not a suicide pact. A subversive majority may try to suppress any effective opposition because it is not "bipartisanship" but the quest for total power that drives its actions. This is a repudiation of the rule that Schmitt said allows a legislative system to function, which is that an "equal chance of achieving a majority really remains open."

A willful majority may choose to eliminate its opposition by pointing to an "emergency," Schmitt wrote. He saw this trick as likely to set off a reaction:

> Every critical moment endangers the principle of the equal chance because it reveals the inevitable opposition between the legal possession of power and the availability of an equal chance for the other side that also seeks to exercise political power.

It is therefore understandable that every call for "public security and order" by those at the helm of state will cause the other side to fear marginalization. It will then attack the majority party for denying it an equal chance. "The result is a condition without legality or a constitution," Schmitt concluded.

Much of this analysis would seem to apply to today's America, as we watch the administrative state and the majority party go after its battered opposition on charges of planning an insurrection. This action, it may be argued, is not taking place because of a recently invented legislative state of the kind that Schmitt critically examined in 1932. But it does bear out Schmitt's distinction between legality and legitimacy. Governments that do not rest on the will of an identifiable people and that lack a source of sovereignty (and one would be delusional to attribute this quality to Joseph Biden) are headed for disaster.

All that may save them in the end is someone assuming power who can grapple with the Schmittian "challenge of the exception." Like Germany in 1932, we are witnessing internal breakdown, and no appeal to the "constitution" (which is an expression of Schmitt's concept of legality) will save us in the absence of a regime that rests on a cohesive citizenry that recognizes its rulers and fellow citizens as legitimate.

On a personal level, more than anything else, Schmitt wanted to be recognized for his undeniable talents. He wanted great men to seek his counsel, and this led him to join the Nazi Party in May 1933. For a while, Schmitt maintained the pretense of being a Nazi true believer, but by 1936 his enemies pointed out his deviationist thinking and previous anti-Nazi statements. Schmitt showed other biographical oddities unbefitting an authentic Nazi. He boasted of his Latin Catholic roots, was married to a Serb (rather than a Nordic spouse), and had attracted as a teacher many Jewish students and admirers, including Leo Strauss. After the war, he was barred from teaching because of his associations with the Third Reich, which had been mostly a troubled one. Schmitt spent his last forty years living in relative obscurity, while continuing to publish brilliant legal and political works.

CHAPTER SIX

The World Wars

— ◆ ◆ ◆ —

Puritans or Habsburgs

Taki's Magazine

MAY 8, 2007

I N AUGUST 1966, while visiting Vienna as an ABD graduate student from Yale, I chanced upon the office of Aktion-Europa, a group that would soon change its name to the Paneuropabewegung. As I learned from going to its offices on the Prinz Eugen Strasse, Aktion-Europa was an organization that defended the Habsburg dynasty. As the nephew or in one case distant cousin of three junior officers who had served in the Austro-Hungarian Army in the Great War, and as the grandson of a *Proviantversorger* (a supplier of army provisions), a position that had once been filled at a higher level by the grandfather of my favorite Austrian man of letters, Hugo von Hofmannsthal (1874–1929), I sympathized with AE's evident but unannounced purpose, which was to refurbish the reputation of the deposed Austrian dynasty. After the First World War, the last Habsburg Emperor and King of Hungary, Charles I, had lost his throne, and he died in exile in April 1922, on the island of Madeira. This exile was the doing of Austria's Socialist-Marxist leaders, who first deposed the Habsburgs and then managed to keep its claimants to the throne out of their country for the next sixty years.

Charles was in no way to blame for the war, one that he had inherited from his aged predecessor, Franz Josef, who had passed on in 1916. The young emperor did his best to end the bloody struggle, and he lost no time after ascending the throne requesting the intervention of Pope

Benedict XV. Charles also appealed in 1917 to his wife's brother, Sixtus, Duke of Parma, as an intermediary, although the two were then on opposing sides. From his letters it is clear that Charles favored not only the removal of his own country from the war but also the arrangement of a just peace among all the belligerents. For his pious and honorable life, this emperor received the title of "blessed" from the Church in 2004, and he will soon likely be canonized.

Since the end of the monarchy in a country whose lands had once belonged to the Habsburgs, Charles's would-be successors, Otto von Habsburg and Otto's son, Karl, have distinguished themselves as scholars and spokesmen for European unity. For many years Otto has given lectures and written books in multiple languages on legal, historical, and diplomatic subjects. After the Second World War, in which he fought on the English side, he participated in the founding of the Mont Pelerin Society, an international organization of distinguished economists who were interested in the spread of (in the European sense) liberal market principles. For Otto, this interest was related to a more personal and more regional concern, which was his stated hope to reconstruct the tariff-free zone that the Habsburg Empire had provided for its subjects. It is often forgotten that Franz Josef had combined his medieval sense of monarchical responsibility with liberal economic ideas and a remarkable sense of religious tolerance. The Austrian School of Economics had flourished under the old order, and one of its chief economists, Eugen von Böhm-Bawerk, had been a tutor to the imperial children. The Austrian economist Ludwig von Mises, who was descended from a Rabbinic family from Galicia, had begun his rise to prominence under the Habsburgs; the dynasty had then bestowed upon Mises his title of nobility.

Since the Habsburg dynasty had been deposed in a war in which some of their own nationalities had taken up arms against them, its descendants have devoted themselves to the "European idea" rather than to any particular national cause. The role that Karl von Habsburg has assigned to Austria, especially while an EU Parliament Deputy between 1996 and 1999, is to be in the "vanguard (*Vorhut*) of Central and Eastern Europe in a European Union." As the victim of German and other nationalisms and as a target of Nazi hate propaganda in the 1930s, the Habsburgs and their devotees continue to keep their distance from nationalists of any kind. Their past and present allies have included the Catholic hierarchy, Jewish bankers, and religious and ethnic minorities that have attached themselves to this pre-national dynasty. A leftist critic, A. J. P. Taylor has described the family that had once ruled over much of Central Europe (and for a while the Spanish empire) as follows: "While other dynasties are episodes in the histories of nations, for the Habsburgs nations are episodes in a family history."

But this was not the whole of the story. The Habsburg Empire offered a highly adaptable form of government. Before it stumbled into a disastrous war, it was moving toward greater power-sharing within its realm, one that would have extended internal autonomy from the Germans and Hungarians to the Slavic minorities. The Hungarians, who had benefited from this arrangement with the establishment of the Dual Monarchy in 1867, had adamantly refused to extend the rights they enjoyed to other ethnic minorities. But the dynasty worked to break down this opposition, and it quite understandably viewed federalism as the only solution to its own problem as a multinational monarchy. Most importantly, the empire furnished its subjects with cultural vitality as well as economic unity. This could be seen particularly in the rich literary, artistic, musical, and academic accomplishments that poured out of Vienna and Budapest, and out of multiple smaller provincial cities— which were united by imperial rule, shared architecture, Viennese cuisine, and the use of Austrian-German.

That the Habsburgs in past decades actively supported the European Union, an organization that has promoted multicultural, anti-Christian transformation, seems in retrospect regrettable. But again it may be understandable that a dynasty that believes in Europe, without its nationalist enthusiasms, should seek alliances that, however defective, come closest to their aspirations. In any case the Habsburgs and their supporters have now drifted away from the present EU, and they may be hoping to find other, more useful embodiments of their purposes as presented in the Paneuropa program: "Commitment to a Europe united by its Christian-Western values," "the insertion of these value-conceptions into the daily lives of Europeans," and "the bringing to public attention of the goals of the movement."

In the interwar period, a Habsburg-led Europe found multiple advocates, from partisans of the "imperial idea" among German and Austrian journalists to such literary celebrities as Franz Werfel, Josef Roth, and Hugo von Hofmannsthal (all writers of Jewish descent). The father of psychology, Sigmund Freud, may have been a scoffer of religion who was preoccupied with sex, but he was also an ardent fan of the Habsburg Empire before its dissolution and regretted its passing afterward. It is also hard to mention other literary and intellectual lights such as Rainer Marie Rilke, Robert Musil, Karl Kraus, Heimito von Doderer, and Ludwig Wittgenstein without thinking of the imperial rule under which they had lived. All of these figures (with the possible exception of the essayist Kraus) felt a profound loyalty to Habsburg Austria.

Since the director of this website, who is named for the great emperor and king, has asked me to compare the *Habsburger Reichsidee* ("Habsburg imperial idea") to the neoconservative concept of a global democratic America, I shall begin by underlining the fact that these ideas operate in non-intersecting universes. Such a comparison may be likened to the task of looking for common characteristics in a Shakespearean drama and a Harlequin novel. If overlaps are ascertainable (and they may be from a structural perspective), they are far less significant than the differences to be noted. One chief difference between the concepts in question is that unlike neoconservatism, the "imperial idea" is a Western and European invention that comes out of the aristocratic and bourgeois past. It is rooted in the European civilization that extended from the late Middle Ages down to the early twentieth century; and while imperial rule shows the marks of a certain commendable political development, toward religious tolerance and a market economy, its history is baroque and imperial. It is in the truest sense Burkean, uniting monarchy and aristocracy to a modern liberal order, without damage being done to any of the parts of this civilizational synthesis.

It might be possible to suggest the difference between the imperial and neocon visions by looking at the postwar political concerns of Hugo von Hofmannsthal. After the First World War, this literary giant devoted the remainder of his short life to reviving a popular interest in medieval Austrian culture. His most famous contribution to this effort is the German version of Everyman (*Jedermann*), which he brought to the stage at Salzburg and which became an annual production there.[145] Despite his outspokenness as an Austrian patriot, Hofmannsthal called for a "new European ego" in an address in Berne in 1916. The problem of cultural and social dissolution that the war had unleashed seemed to the distinguished author to have affected the entire continent; and in the interwar period, Hofmannsthal contributed to Karl Anton Rohan's *Europäische Revue*, a leading advocacy publication for European unity, a process that the editor Rohan, an Austrian nobleman, hoped to see take place according to traditionalist and presumably pro-Habsburg principles. In a speech in Munich in January 1927, Hofmannsthal famously called for a "conservative revolution" aimed at bringing back a true European identity. This speech was specifically critical of the Germans for "their productive anarchy as a people." Hofmannsthal contrasted the sentimental outpouring to which his German cousins were prone to a "binding principle of form," which he thought necessary for the restoration of a Europe of nations. Unlike T. S. Eliot, Hofmannsthal wrote as a close friend of royalty as well as someone who was an aesthetic and cultural reactionary. He was also a scholar of romance languages; and he imitated the linguistic peculiarities of the Latin regions that had once been ruled by the Habsburgs in his literary work.

While Hofmannsthal pined for the lost Austro-Hungarian Empire, the neocons rejoiced at the toppling of the imperial governments of Central Europe. Francis Fukuyama, in *The Wall Street Journal* (December 31, 1999) expressed profound relief that the Central Powers had been stopped in World War I.[146] If the German Empire and its Austrian ally had won that struggle, Fukuyama explained, the result would have been to stunt our moral consciousness: "A German century may have been peaceful and prosperous but in the social sphere it would also have been stratified, corporatist, ultimately based on racial and ethnic hierarchy, a world made safe for [presumably pre-black-majoritarian] South Africa." A more savage attack on the Germanophone powers in the First World War, albeit one that does not mention the Habsburg Empire explicitly, was published by Fred Siegel in *The Weekly Standard* (January 30, 2002), an opinion piece that combines a tirade against H. L. Mencken for his "Nietzschean elitism and fondness for German authoritarians" with extended attacks on the "autocratic" Central Powers.[147] Siegel bashes Mencken for having expressed wartime sympathy for his ancestral land, since this neocon journalist assumes (undemonstrated) parallels between the Kaiser's and Hitler's Germany.

Better documented arguments about America's path toward war after 1914 and the events that were unfolding in Europe can be found in Walter Karp, Thomas J. Fleming, Arthur Ekirch, Ralph Raico, Hunt Tooley, and other historians who demonstrate how the government of Woodrow Wilson maneuvered the United States into the European conflagration. This involved dishonestly manipulating the alleged US peace initiatives in Christmas 1916 in such a way that the English side would not accept the terms offered. Such dishonesty is clearly shown in Arthur Link's generally complimentary five-volume biography of Woodrow Wilson, a work that treats among a multitude of subjects Wilson's instruction to American-controlled food relief agencies after the war not to feed those ethnic minorities that had fought for the Central Powers.[148] In Wilson's view, no less than in that of *The Weekly Standard*'s, the war had been fought between absolute democratic goodness and authoritarian monarchist evil. From this warped point of view, Kaiser Karl had fought on the evil side, as the authoritarian prison-keeper of nations that without exception should have been yearning to join the Allies.

Richard M. Gamble, in *The War for Righteousness* (2003), makes evident the connection between pro-Allied war fever among America's WASP population and the democratic millenarian thinking that had begun to affect mainline American Protestantism in the early twentieth century.[149] For almost three hundred pages Gamble offers up examples of Protestant ministers and theologians praising America's entry into the Great War as "the supreme act of public service." One of the most famous ministers of that era, Reverend William P. Merrill, prophesied that the outcome of a US crusade against the Central Powers would be "the future expansion of world-democracy and world-federation." Gamble stresses that Wilson came out of the same milieu as the global democratic Protestant crusaders who pushed him toward war. Among the most shocking illustrations of Wilson's imperialist arrogance can be found in his Flag Day 1914 speech at Arlington National Cemetery in which the president claimed that it was America's "duty" and "privilege" to "stand shoulder to shoulder to lift the burdens of mankind in the future and show the paths of freedom to all the world." In the oft-quoted peroration to this speech, Wilson expressed the grandiose hope that his country would make other nations realize that "Old Glory was the flag not only of America but of humanity." Gamble has pointed out in conversation with me that he became interested in his lifetime research project, studying the religious roots of democratic millenarianism, because of the unsettling fit between neocon global revolutionary rhetoric and Protestant Republican patriotism. Gamble believes that the roots of this unhappy connection may go all the way back to the American founding, a situation that makes it all that much harder to disconnect WASP America from neocon pied pipers.

Among its idiosyncrasies, the neocon imperial idea, which according to Gamble is especially tempting for Protestant Americans, assumes the inherent depravity of the Habsburg Empire, a regime that that paradigmatic neocon hero Woodrow Wilson had hated as authoritarian, and Teutonic. This hatred came to the fore in Wilson's letter sent to the Empire's "subject nationalities" on June 24, 1918, in which the American president looked forward to the "dismemberment" and "partition" of a structure that did not deserve to exist: "The Austro-Hungarian monarchy was organized on the principle of conquest and not on the principle of self-determination." Moreover, by fighting alongside the German Empire, the Habsburgs reduced themselves to mere "vassals" of the German ruling family. Needless to say, the "peace treaty" that Wilson signed on to denied "self-determination" to all the historical nationalities that had bet on the wrong horse in the war. It also typically placed those minorities, including my Central European relatives, under far more oppressive regimes than those nationalities who had lived under the Empire.

It is impossible to consider the neoconservative idea of an American empire (or, as the neocons would have it, "American non-imperial hegemony") without calling to mind its abstract and super-modernist quality. The neocon idea requires the imposition of an anti-traditionalist vision of America, one especially beloved to neocon urbanites, on the rest of humanity. It justifies itself as a heroic enterprise intended to spread "American values." While the imperial idea is formed around a cultural legacy growing out of the past and its former dynastic center, the neoconservative idea features military force and the subversion of foreign nations. What the two visions do share is an antipathy toward modern nationalism. Note that Hofmannsthal differentiated his own attachment to Austria from the glorification of a modern nation-state. Although Habsburg supporters have almost always spoken German, they tend not to be German nationalists (or German anti-nationalists in today's leftist society).

Neocons display an even deeper reservation than the bearers of the *Reichsidee* about the showcasing of national pride, unless it can be made to serve non-national ends. Thus neocons can be for the United States only to the extent that it is linked to a globalist project, and they typically favor porous borders for the country that they claim to represent. Their view of this country as a "proposition nation" is clearly aimed at divesting America's core population of any ethnic identity; at the same time, they urge the country whose heights of power they have scaled, as Allan Bloom reminds us in *The Closing of the American Mind*, to wage war against philosophically different societies as an "educational experience."[150]

Leon Trotsky, who not surprisingly has remained a neoconservative hero, spent several years before the First World War in Imperial Vienna; there the Habsburg government left him alone, as a harmless foreign noisemaker. From all accounts, the future revolutionary found Viennese life much to his liking, and he was often seen playing chess and gorging himself on strudel in coffeehouses. It is possible to see Trotsky's sojourn in *fin de siècle* Vienna as the overlap between two imperial ideas: the Habsburg and the neoconservative ones. For a brief while, the advocate of global revolutionary violence lived under the aegis of a gracious sovereign, but the sovereign and his empire vanished, and all sorts of noxious revolutionaries took their place. We are still living with the consequences of both catastrophes.

The Neocons and
Charles Maurras

Taki's Magazine

OCTOBER 7, 2007

AVING ALREADY finished most of a six-hundred-page biography about French man of letters and political thinker Charles Maurras (1868–1952) by Stéphane Giocanti, *Charles Maurras: Le chaos et l'ordre* (2006), I'd like to address a question that the managing editor of this site posed about Giocanti's subject.[151] Is there a useful comparison to be drawn between Maurras, a monarchist and religious skeptic who enlisted French Catholicism for political purposes, and the Straussian boosters of American global democracy? Are the Straussians, who appeal to a certain notion of transcendence in order to teach "democratic" virtue and to fuel foreign military incursions, replicating the exploitation of piety that French nationalists had committed a century earlier? Maurras and his movement (and newspaper) *Action Française* had clothed their nationalist agenda by appearing to be *plus catholique que le Pape*, e.g., by denouncing the French Christian Democrats of the early twentieth century who had sought an accommodation with the anticlerical French Third Republic, and even by disputing whether Protestants could be real Frenchmen.

But in the end it became apparent that Maurras, who might have been the most revered literary figure in France of his generation, and his almost equally brilliant collaborators Léon Daudet and Jacques Bainville, were demonstrable neo-pagans and philosophical skeptics. The ax fell on them on December 20, 1926, when Pope Pius XI issued an admonition to French Catholics "to keep their distance from *Action Française*. It is not permitted to Catholics to sustain, encourage, or read published newspapers by men whose writings depart from our dogmas and morals." Three days later, the Congregation for the Holy Office condemned by decree literary works that had been published by Maurras going back into the 1890s; these were writings that showed an explicitly anti-Christian or materialist bias. Curiously, the second condemnation had been prepared in 1914 but because of political events and the Papacy's attempt to hold on to Catholic royalists in France, the dissemination of the document had been delayed twice. When it was finally promulgated at the end of 1926, the Pope and his advisers may have decided to throw in their lot with French Catholics seeking a rapprochement with secular republicanism. At the same time, in Italy early Christian Democrats, led by the anti-fascist priest Luigi Sturzo, were pointing the way toward a new political possibility for the Church, the building of a Catholic, pro-welfare-state parliamentary party. Maurras and his followers by the end of 1926 seemed to belong to the past and therefore the anti-Christian or neo-pagan baggage that they brought with them was no longer an acceptable price to be paid by Rome for an alliance with French royalist religious skeptics.

Without delving further into this break, the question remains whether the appeal to religious faith among the Straussians and, more broadly, among the neoconservatives into whose camp they fall, offers an historical parallel to the French royalist Right of the 1920s. My answer would be for the most part no, although certain overlaps are too obvious to be ignored. Both groups have appealed to traditional religious sentiments in their societies, Maurras to *catholiques confits*, devout Catholics with a strong dislike for the Third Republic, and the Straussians and neocons to Zionist Jews and Evangelical Christians. Neither group of manipulators has been particularly God-fearing but each has been willing to manipulate a particular religious sensibility for political ends.

Another similarity to be noted is the Teutonophobia that has animated both groups. The neocons and the Straussians continue to associate the Germans, whenever the opportunity is presented, with the Holocaust and anti-Semitic fascism. Because of his passionate identification as a Provençal and as a classicist with Latinity and because of his repugnance for the Germans as the upstart enemy of the ancient French nation, Maurras was equally obsessive about Teutonic evils. Because of this shared antipathy, certain similarities seem undeniable. Allan Bloom's invectives against the "German connection" in *The Closing of the American Mind* look as if they had been drawn from Maurras's editorials in *Action Française* against the snares of German thought.[152] Maurras's book *Devant l'Allemagne éternelle, chronique d'une résistance* (1937) might indeed have come from a neoconservative or Straussian, if such a hypothetical author could have mastered the appropriate French forms of expression.[153] Teutonophobic passions often take the same expressions, no matter what the source.

Despite Maurras's attachment to what he called "political anti-Semitism," his writings on Germany throughout the 1930s attack the Germans as a whole, and not only Hitler, for anti-Jewish prejudice. Maurras looked into the distant German past for the origins of the "*antisémitisme de peau*" (anti-Semitism of the flesh) that was characteristic of the Nazis; and like the later Straussians and neocons, he never ceased to blame the Germans for World War I. In his defense, however, it might be noted that German armies did devastate about a quarter of France's territory after they overran it in 1914.

One might also note the shared political modernism of the groups being compared. Despite their talk about antiquity, the Straussians, as a neoconservative subspecies, are riveted on a presentist ideology, their own version of liberal democracy, which they would like to impose globally. What Straussians call "the modern enterprise" is their parochial political experience, from which they generalize about the Good, and it is this Straussian-neoconservative ideal, supposedly personified by contemporary America, which defines the missionary politics of, say, *The Wall Street Journal* or *The Weekly Standard*. Maurras was equally focused on the present moment, and most of his defenses of monarchy have nothing to do with traditional notions of royalty as being divinely ordained or in sync with a natural order. His monarchism was based on his view about what was necessary for the France of his time to function as a political entity. Having a king, and indeed a descendant of the bourgeois king, Louis Philippe of the House of Orléans, was seen as beneficial for a modern French state, and particularly in view of its troublesome neighbor to the east. The Third Republic, under which France labored in the 1930s with revolving door governments, would never provide, according to the French royalists, an adequate sense of French political unity.

Although critical of both Jews and Protestants, Maurras attacked neither for theological reasons. Protestants were seen as an extension of the specifically German Reformation, and as a people who were spreading a doctrine of religious individualism. They were therefore dangerous to French national cohesion. Although not every Jew was seen by Maurras as a threat to France, to whatever extent this group placed their own ethnic interest before that of the French *patrie*, they were unsuited to be French citizens or subjects. Maurras assumed that most Jews fell into the second category, and this was certainly his position during the Dreyfus Affair in the 1890s when he insisted on the presumed guilt of Captain Dreyfus, a French officer of German Jewish lineage. But there were some Jews whom Maurras held up as model Frenchmen (*bien pétris*), and one such presumed patriot Daniel Halévy was his longtime friend and collaborator. While Maurras certainly had his quirks, he usually defended them for what he imagined to be "empirical" reasons. His favorite social thinker was the nineteenth-century father of positivism, Auguste Comte, and Maurras never abandoned the belief that he too was applying a "science of society."

Having pointed out the similarities between Maurras and his movement and the bête noire of this website, it might be a good idea to underline their even more obvious discrepancies. The first difference concerns the disparity in analytic intelligence and cultural erudition between the groups under consideration. Maurras was a major European humanistic figure who even if he had never addressed European politics would still be remembered as a prolific and influential poet (in Provençal as well as French), a literary critic of the first water, and a commentator on ancient and medieval thought. Maurras is still regarded as a gifted French stylist, and the range of his knowledge in comparative literature and in ancient and modern history was truly phenomenal.

Aside from his partisan journalism and his essays written to flatter the Orléanist pretenders to the French throne, with whom he remained on intimate personal terms until the late 1930s, Maurras's political tracts *Enquête sur la monarchie* (1900), *L'Avenir de l'intelligence* (1905), and his five-volume *Dictionnaire politique et critique* (1931–34) are full of unsurpassed insight.[154] Even French Jewish readers with political opinions that have differed sharply from his, such as Raymond Aron and Élisabeth Lévy, have nonetheless considered Maurras's investigations of intellectuals in contemporary politics to be ground-breaking, indispensable reading. Maurras's royalist, decentralist politics and admonitions against the German threat were passions that he indulged on the side, when he was not becoming the French role model for T. S. Eliot (a figure about whom Giocanti has already written a massive biography) and for other literary giants.

Having read neocon and Straussian tracts, it does not seem to me that these printed opinions show the depth of thought or elegance of Maurras's political writing. (Even Maurras's worst ravings are far better crafted than the denunciations of Islamofascism or European anti-Semitism that regularly appear in the neocon press.) Bloom's *Closing of the American Mind* reads like a civics textbook designed for New Deal Democrats. It might appeal especially to those who dislike Germans, pop culture, and ill-mannered hippies and who are trying to relate all three to each other. Moreover, Bloom's onetime bestseller is composed in a style that is fully worthy of its movement conservative readers. It shares in the mediocrity of other Straussian writers on contemporary politics. The global democratic preaching that one hears coming from the Straussian Harry Jaffa and his acolytes at the Claremont Institute differs from Bloom's bromides to the extent that it claims to be rooted in Judeo-Christianity. But all of this boils down to the preaching of a democratic creed that we are told it would be good for Americans to embrace. Jaffaite Straussians wish us to believe that Moses, Jesus, Saint Paul, Aquinas, etc., were all precursors of Abraham Lincoln, as read through the lenses of Harry Jaffa.

The Church may well have been justified in fearing Maurras, an author who combined argumentative brilliance and Thomistic scholarship with pseudo-Catholic convictions. But I'm not sure who in the neocon or Straussian fold resembles Maurras as a seducer of once faithful Christians. The only one here who might approach his intelligence would be the father of the Straussian persuasion, Leo Strauss. And even here the fit doesn't quite work. Unlike Maurras, Strauss is a ponderous, tedious writer in either English or German, and unlike his students, he does not explicitly manipulate religion for ideological purposes.

Strauss's channeling of religious energies for Jewish national ends does not mean from a Jewish perspective what it did for Pius X when he responded to French nationalist Catholics. The Jewish kingdom is precisely of this world, and it centers on the land of Israel. All Jewish groups, save for a small sectarian fragment of the Hasidim, the Satmar sect from Eastern Hungary, and the totally marginalized Reform Jews in the American Council for Judaism, would implicitly agree with the above statement. The former Archbishop of Paris, Cardinal Lustiger, made no secret of his Jewish nationalism—which he claimed was natural for someone who, like himself, belonged to the "Jewish people," even if he was a Catholic convert and an otherwise traditional Catholic clergyman. Strauss was forthright about his Jewish national commitment, and he was notorious for his intolerance toward those who did not share his position. But there was nothing dishonest when Strauss appealed to other Jews as a Zionist; although by no means an unequivocal theist, he did perform the Jewish commandment of *ohavas yisrael*, loving his ethnic nation.

Where his disciples have been dishonest is in denying Western Christian nations the ethnic solidarity that they have claimed for Jews. Why are Jews, it might be asked, allowed to be an ethnic people—but according to the Zionists and Straussians, American Christians must see themselves as belonging to a propositional "universal nation"? Or so the Straussian and Orthodox Jew Douglas Feith asserted in a speech at the Hebrew University in 2002. But even if one must balk at this double standard, it does reflect a certain underlying truth. There is an unbridgeable theological difference between Christian universalism and a Jewish national community, as the foundation for Jewish ritual practice and a Jewish relation to the Divine. Christianity and Judaism do not have equivalent views on the connection of religion to ethnic identity. And while it is possible to fault Strauss's disciples for hiding their ethnic loyalty, they are not being irreligious in a Jewish sense by expressing such a sentiment. Note that even those Hasidic Jews who reject the present Jewish state of Israel are not opposed to Jewish nationalism. They simply insist that the Jewish Messiah must first come and take over the Jewish homeland before Jews will be allowed to become a political nation. These ultra-Orthodox Jews question the timetable but not the concept of Jewish national rebirth and political dominion. Dispensationalist Christians and their leftward drifting Evangelical counterparts both seem to share the same Zionist focus of most religious and secular Jews, and so from a theological perspective, they are not being "unchristian" when they advance Jewish nationalist ends.

Far from constituting a value judgment, this is an attempt to show why neoconservative or Evangelical Zionism does not constitute the same theological error as a religion of French nationalism would for the Catholic Church or French Calvinists. Arguably most neoconservatives disguise their Jewish nationalism by identifying it with global, nonsectarian democracy. While this pretense may look odd, it does not justify the hasty conclusion that neoconservatives or more specifically Straussians are bad Jews or defective Evangelicals because they are zealous Jewish nationalists.

A not so obvious difference between Maurras and his movement and those to whom we are comparing them is the disparity in power and influence. Unlike the neoconservatives who have swarmed all over the Bush presidency and control tens of billions of dollars in propaganda resources, *Action Française* was a rather modest enterprise. Maurras's newspaper issues drew about one hundred thousand readers at the very most, and the corresponding organization managed to enlist about thirty thousand members at the supposed height of its influence in the 1930s. In the same decade the right-republican organization Croix-de-Feu had almost three hundred thousand members, and various French fascist organizations reached a comparable size in the same period. This, mind you, was during a time when France was being rocked by economic disaster, a series of government scandals, and the meteoric growth of a Communist Party that numbered more supporters than the entire French nationalist Right together. Giocanti makes clear that Maurras's followers, including the youth organization Camelots du Roi, which hawked newspapers and occasionally engaged in scuffles, had only marginal impact on the bloody confrontations between Right and Left that erupted in Paris in the mid-1930s. Maurras and his followers had important friends in government only during the presidency of Raymond Poincaré (1913–20), the right-republican French nationalist who had presided over the French state during World War I. In the 1930s the *Maurrassiens* were typically harassed by the Paris authorities for outbreaks of violence and political subversion that they were in no position to incite.

The trial of Maurras and his longtime associate Maurice Pujo as Nazi collaborators, in Lyons in January 1945 by the triumphant French Resistance, was further proof of Maurras's powerlessness. Although he had been unwisely associated with the collaborationist government of Marshall Pétain and although he had made indiscreet remarks about Jews during the Occupation, in a less hysterical situation, certain facts would have been apparent. No one in France had warned against Nazi Germany as persistently and forcefully as Maurras. He had called for a French attack on Germany when Hitler occupied the Rhineland in 1936, and unlike the French Communists, who stood in judgment of him in 1945, Maurras had been against Hitler, and not allied to him, when the fall of France had occurred in 1940. Among those who should have been held responsible for Nazi crimes, Maurras was less guilty than all of the members of the French Communist Party and all of the left-wing French advocates of disarmament and appeasement in the 1930s.

The reason this aged poet was forced to spend five years in prison after having been found guilty of treason is not that he was worse than many of his accusers. He suffered this fate because History had dealt him a weaker hand. He had identified himself with the monarchist Right in a war in which the communists went from being Nazi allies to the leaders of bloody reprisals taken against "fascist sympathizers." Maurras had in fact never been a fascist sympathizer, and he had lost droves of supporters in the interwar years, including the revolutionary nationalist Georges Valois, because of his impassioned attacks on fascism. He viewed Mussolini and his imitators as successors to the French Jacobins, and he preached a form of national identity that would be mediated through regional loyalties and the moral influence of a well-educated monarch.

During the Vichy regime, Maurras was particularly isolated and embittered, as a despiser of the Germans, the French Left, and those French fascists who seemed overly comfortable with the Nazis. The deafness he had had to endure from his youth on may have made this marginalization seem even more severe, but in any case, it was real enough. Many of his most prominent admirers—Charles de Gaulle and much of de Gaulle's staff, and leader of the Resistance spy network within occupied France Colonel Gilbert Renault (aka Colonel Rémy), and finally Maurras's own family members—were on the Allied side. In a desperate act of faith, Maurras talked himself into believing that Pétain and another general who had initially supported Vichy, Maxime Weygand, were actually building an army within France to drive the German occupiers out. By 1937 the Orléanist pretender, the Count of Paris, had broken with Maurras and his followers because they were viewed as too powerless to help the monarchist cause. But isolation has not been the fate of the subjects of my latest book. Unlike Maurras, the neoconservatives and their Straussian mentors have been anything but consigned to the historical dustbin. As powerbrokers, they have fared far better than the stormy, deaf Provençal.

The last difference between Maurras and those to whom he is being compared is so great that, for me it is almost too obvious to be mentioned. Unlike most of the Straussians and all of the neoconservatives, Maurras was not a leftist but a man of the Right. Nothing more need be said on this matter.

Buchanan, Kennan, and the "Good War"

Taki's Magazine

JUNE 2, 2008

The following is the first installment in a three-part critical symposium on Patrick Buchanan's Churchill, Hitler, and the "Unnecessary War" (2008).[155]

I T IS not surprising that Pat Buchanan's new book, exploring the collapse of the British Empire and the connection of that disaster to England's involvement in two world wars, should have received a strong endorsement from George F. Kennan, written (it might be surmised) shortly before this luminary's death at the age of a hundred and one. Although Kennan praises Pat specifically for taking over and developing his argument that "the British guaranty to Poland [in 1939] was neither necessary nor wise," there is little in Pat's work that is not traceable to this once-celebrated American exponent of political realism. There are other historians whom Pat cites, such as Giles MacDonogh, Thomas Fleming, John Charmley, and my close friend Ralph Raico, all of whom have written critically about Churchill. But his main guide to enlightenment is Kennan. Moreover, the work by this author and one-time American ambassador to Russia that fuels Pat's "revisionist" arguments, concerning the misuse of British power, the overly close connection between the United States and Britain, and the overextension of English participation in continental European conflicts, is Kennan's *American Diplomacy, 1900–1950*, a work that was first published in 1951.[156]

When I was in college and later graduate school in the 1960s, this book was regularly assigned to undergraduates as an authoritative introduction to America's role in international affairs in the twentieth century. As Lee Congdon will surely explain in his forthcoming monograph, Kennan then enjoyed a certain cachet on the academic Left as a critic of Cold War hawks, and he was even allowed to publish in the "anti-anti-communist" *New York Review of Books* a tribute to the Prussian aristocracy that had tried to overthrow Hitler in 1944.[157] By the 1980s Kennan had predictably come to rattle the neocons as someone who had never been particularly favorable to Israel and who had even shown the effrontery to warn against weakening the white minority government in South Africa. Despite Kennan's mostly accidental association with the Left, the neocons, led by the sociologist Paul Hollander, correctly reminded us that Kennan was a "reactionary" and certainly no friend of progressive democracy.

I bring this up because Pat's discovery of Kennan indicates a union that was perhaps inevitable. Once their differences over the Cold War had begun to recede, paleoconservatives were bound to rediscover Kennan as a thinker of choice. How many true conservatives would disagree with these lines from his *American Diplomacy*:

> Today if one were offered the chance of having back again the Germany of 1913, a Germany run by conservative but relatively moderate people, no Nazis and no communists, a vigorous Germany, united and unoccupied, full of energy and confidence, able to play a part again in the balancing-off of Russian power in Europe, well, there would be objections to it from many quarters, and it wouldn't make everyone happy, but in many ways it wouldn't sound so bad, in comparison with our problems today.

Although Kennan's wistful observation is essentially sound, one could not imagine a "respectable" publication these days that would allow it to be printed on its pages. (Try for example the raging Teutonophobic *Weekly Standard*!) In the immaculately anti-fascist democracy that we bestowed on the Germans in 1947, moreover, anyone expressing Kennan's views in print could conceivably face criminal prosecution for "right-wing extremist" verbal assaults on the "German liberal democratic order." Indeed, German journalists and scholars have been hounded by the "democratic" German government for saying far less than what Kennan and Buchanan have written.

On the less positive side, I am not particularly impressed by the arguments offered against England's decision to guarantee the security of Poland. According to this view, stated by Buchanan and at least intimated by Kennan, without the empty British guarantee, which England was in no position to uphold militarily when Nazi Germany invaded Poland in September 1939, the war would not have turned out in such a way as to ruin the British as a world power. The Soviets would have had to take the "brunt" of the German attack earlier, since a Soviet–Nazi pact would not likely have come about in 1939, setting up the division of Eastern Europe between two mass-murdering regimes.

But it is hard to see why such an alliance would not have come about, no matter what the British did by guaranteeing Poland's territorial integrity. It was to the advantage of both the Soviet and German tyrants in 1939 to make a pact for territorial gain. And there is no reason to believe that Hitler would not have moved his armies westward after bringing down Poland, with or without a British guarantee to the then-beleaguered Poles. A wealth of evidence, including broad hints in the *Hossbach Denkschrift* (November 1937), in which Hitler had revealed his plans for territorial acquisition to his generals, indicate that German westward expansion was in the cards even before the *Anschluss* with Austria in March 1938.

Another detail gets in the way of Buchanan's imaginative reconsideration of the outbreak of World War II. Nazi Germany failed over the long term to control European Russia, because it was fighting a two-front war. Buchanan's wish for a great war between Russia and Germany that would have spared "tens of millions" in Western Europe is not based on convincing evidence. The only way Hitler was driven from power was in a two-front war, and tens of millions necessarily died to achieve that end. Although actions might have been taken to end that war sooner, and in a less unconditional and more humane fashion, without conceding Eastern Europe to Stalin, England could not have gotten rid of the Nazi government without taking up arms. Certainly the United States could not have afforded that luxury.

I am also not convinced by Buchanan's suggestion that since Stalin exterminated more people than Hitler that Churchill made the wrong decision, in effect, using Stalin to deal with Hitler. In terms of England's geopolitical interests, Nazi Germany represented a much greater threat than Soviet Russia, particularly after Hitler had launched Operation

Barbarossa. Furthermore, once Hitler had sent armies into Russia, the Soviet Union and England, which had been at war with Germany since September 1939, were on the same side militarily. Pointing this out, however, is not to justify what Churchill later did, in order to remain in good odor with the Soviets or such brutal acts as Operation Keelhaul, in which the British and American governments actively assisted Soviet crimes against refugees who had fled Stalin's tyranny. Such misdeeds, including the firebombing of defenseless German civilians, were certainly reprehensible but they were not necessitated by the fact that both the British and the Soviets had fought Nazi Germany at the same time.

Having noted my areas of disagreement with Buchanan (or Buchanan/Kennan), it also seems necessary to note that generally I agree with almost everything else in this book. Whether the theme is Churchill's critical role in unleashing the First World War, the disastrous consequences of England's entry into that struggle (which helped to widen it into a World War), the folly of the Congress of Versailles, or the mistake of the British in exchanging their naval alliance with Japan for one with the United States in the 1920s, Buchanan's book is on the mark. Although not likely to influence our neo-Wilsonian political class, his reassessment should cause some intelligent Americans somewhere to rethink our country's role in the world. Moreover, unlike his questionable interpretations about the Second World War, his conclusions about World War I are so self-evidently correct that one must wonder why they are not more widely represented. The passages about World War I from Kissinger and other diplomatic historians whom Buchanan cites sound like the most hysterical propaganda manufactured by Wilson's Department of Information. There is little to no evidence known to me that would justify this one-sided interpretation of Germany's sole responsibility for the war or the soundness of the Treaty of Versailles. Although Buchanan, for the sake of comprehensiveness, should have gone into the now fashionable theories about exclusive German blame for the War, what Buchanan does present is enough to show us the dubious nature of all such anti-German views about the events of July and August 1914.

Was Wilhelm Just Another "W"?

Taki's Magazine

JULY 31, 2008

T HE LATEST issue of *The American Conservative* (July 14) includes a provocative symposium on whether World War II should be considered "the good war" and, no less significant, whether Winston Churchill deserves the adulation that the media have accorded him as "man of the century."[158] The contributions are all well-documented and boldly framed, and it would be hard to find a passage in any of them that seems stereotypical or not worth stating. Of the published commentators I personally learned the most from Christopher Layne and Michael Vlahos. Both make useful observations that Churchill's most lasting achievements have yielded dubious benefits. These results include by now outmoded rules of statecraft that have sometimes been applied indiscriminately, and what became the authorized narrative for *The Second World War* (1948–53), Churchill's multi-volume text which continues to shape the popular perception of the last European war.[159] The conclusion that Layne, Vlahos, and several of the other contributors suggest, is that for all his talents and his willingness to stand up to Hitler, Churchill might have left behind a troubling

legacy, and particularly for those who are unwilling to assess his catastrophic mistakes and self-interested historiography.

More troubling for me than these commentaries are Scott
McConnell's introduction, or, to be more accurate, his concluding
remarks. There McConnell expresses the probable views of his esteemed
former professor Fritz Stern. For those who don't know, Stern is *The
New York Times*'s favorite German historian and his intellectual historical study *The Politics of Cultural Despair* (1961) remains a classic for
politically correct, anti-national Germans.[160] In line with his mentor's
spirit, McConnell offers this portentous lesson from the German imperial past:

> Look instead [of to the Munich meeting in 1938] to German
> conduct in the prelude to the First World War, when the Reich,
> the most powerful state in the world, felt itself encircled, while
> its military and diplomatic leaders grotesquely exaggerated the
> threats they faced. If Germany didn't confront tsarist Russia
> then, the opportunity would be lost: preventive war was the
> much-discussed option. Learned men in the thrall of worst-case
> thinking were blind to the ways Germany's outward thrusts of
> power were perceived by others.

McConnell ends his somber reflection by expressing this pious
wish: "We might pray that analogies to Wilhelmine Germany never fit
too well."

The problem with these warnings is they have no real connection to
the present American situation. Moreover, they don't even offer an accurate picture of Germany's political and military history a hundred years
ago. The United States is far more powerful economically and militarily
than any other world power, and it was on the verge of becoming this
by 1914, as British historian Niall Ferguson reminds us in several of his
books. Incidentally, in 1914 Germany was not the "most powerful state
in the world." The United States was already overtaking it industrially
and had a far greater military potential, and because of its navy and
overseas empire, England enjoyed a power comparable to that of Wilhelmine Germany, which had only recently forged ahead of England
industrially. Until the eve of the Great War, when the Germans worked
to increase the size of their army, France had a land force that was
numerically comparable to Germany's. Because of the foolish distraction
of its naval buildup, which intensified the anti-German animosity of

Churchill without allowing the German Empire to get ahead of England as a naval leader, Imperial Germany thrust itself into harm's way.

The German government's fear of being encircled was anything but "grotesquely exaggerated." Since the 1890s France and Russia had built an alliance that was aimed at the Germans and Austrians; and as late as the summer of 1914, the Russians and English, as German historian Egmont Zechlin has documented in detail, were negotiating a naval alliance that was emphatically directed at the Germans.

No one is claiming that the last German emperor was a skilled or prudent diplomat. His intermittent bluster, maladroit attempts at playing off the British against continental powers, and his naval build-up, which Wilhelm presented as a defensive measure but one that understandably unsettled the English, all serve to underscore his lack of diplomatic finesse. But the Germans were not alone in that department. Most of Europe's prominent statesmen in the years preceding World War I seem to have been almost equally tactless. Wilhelm exemplified the political style of Europe's major powers in his age, a widespread flaw that contributed to the Old World's undoing. While the German emperor did his share of mischief, given the location of his country and the recentness of Germany's rise to world power, there is abundant evidence of hasty, bombastic speech among his opposite numbers elsewhere in Europe.

Anti-German German historians Fritz Fischer, Imanuel Geiss, Hans-Ulrich Wehler, Wolfgang Mommsen, and Fritz Stern have all focused specifically on German diplomatic faux pas in the early twentieth century. These critics then undertake to link these real but exaggerated blunders to some peculiarly Teutonic "culture of illiberalism." Because of its undemocratic, sexist, patriarchal, and nationalist culture, we are told, Germany's bid for power in the twentieth century became an inevitable development. This perspective assumes a causal link between an ominously depicted social culture and exclusive responsibility for the disastrous conflict in 1914. But it is not clear why the Germans' failure to move toward a currently enshrined liberal model would create the necessary conditions for a German bid for world conquest in 1914 or the atrocities of the Third Reich. It is even hard to show that the Germans in 1914 were more anti-Jewish than most of their European neighbors, a contention that most German Jews of the time would have vigorously disputed.

Indeed this view of a German "special path" into modernity is based on a special German provincialism, one that has caused anti-German historians to treat as peculiarly and dangerously Teutonic what were

European-wide values a hundred years ago. German society in 1900 looked much more like French or English society than like our own late modern one. Moreover, there was nothing peculiarly German about the lack of measure shown by the Germans in dealing with other European powers. Churchill was at least as truculent in his statecraft as the German executive before the First World War, and he represented a country that has been generally spared the critical responsibility its leaders had for the magnitude of the war that broke out in 1914.

Of course, we are talking here about the war that no one wanted, that is to say, not in the destructive form in which it came. Most European statesmen of the time had nothing against some limited hostilities to achieve their geopolitical ends, and since they could not imagine the possibility of the bloodbath unleashed, they were willing to pursue their parochial advantage through military means. The French were more than open to a struggle against Germany during the two Balkan Wars, but they expected the Russians to do the fighting for them. Once the Germans and Russians had proceeded to take up arms against each other in the east, or so went the desired scenario of French ambassador to Russia, Maurice Paléologue, French troops could then enter the struggle from the west, by occupying Alsace and Lorraine, the two provinces that France had lost to Germany after the Franco-Prussian War in 1871.

Despite their impetuousness, however, early twentieth-century European leaders might have been less, not more, prone to rhetorical excess than the present US leadership. With due respect to McConnell, it does not seem that the United States is now inching slowly toward the noisy boastful example of Imperial Germany. The Kaiser's speeches about Germany's right to "a place in the sun," meaning a few colonies in Africa, sound almost schoolmarmish, when compared to W's sweeping references to an American imperial mission, as set forth in his Second Inaugural and fifth State of the Union addresses. In these elocution exercises, our president explained that we could only be a moral nation by bestowing our form of government on the rest of the world. W's would-be successors Senators McCain and Obama are planning to bestow on the world more of the same, McCain by creating a Union of Democracies, which, for all we know, may be the neocon equivalent of the Warsaw Pact, and Obama by sending our inspectors across the globe to make sure that elections in foreign countries occur "democratically."

In Germany the Kaiser received from the Reichstag sharp reprimands in 1908 for saying stupid things about the German Navy to the British *Daily Telegraph*, in an interview in which the German ruler asserted that his navy was being expanded to counter Japanese expansion in the Far East. German elected officials thought that Wilhelm, who was then ineptly trying to appease British public opinion, had spoken indiscreetly, and his subjects didn't hesitate to let him know. In our country, by contrast, the president receives congressional applause when he rhapsodizes about universal crusades for democracy.

I wish that someone could explain to me why our leaders are thought to sound more prudent when they talk about *Weltpolitik* than did the architects of Imperial German foreign policy. Moreover, if one reads the collected speeches of American religious leaders about our providential role on the eve of America's entry into World War I, speeches that are cited at length in Richard Gamble's *The War for Righteousness* (2003), European jingoist rhetoric produced by Wilhelm or Churchill pales by comparison.[161] None of this Old-World bluster even approximates the millenarian lunacies exhibited by Wilson's clerical cheering gallery.

But the difference is the United States can afford to be righteous and arrogant without having to pay the price that Europeans did in 1914. Our economic and military strength, our isolation from other lesser powers, and by now the clear disparity between our menacing moralizing and the limits of what we can actually accomplish by force all protect us against our folly. We are fortunate not to have to operate in the narrow spaces and almost claustrophobic diplomatic circles in which European tensions festered at the beginning of the last century. Our present leaders can afford to sound obnoxious in a way that Europe's political actors in 1914 could not. That having been said, it does seem a bit much to dwell on the verbal intemperateness of a particular German ruler a hundred years ago. What does the New Testament say about the beam in one's own eye as compared to the mote in someone else's?

How England Helped Start the Great War

Taki's Magazine

MARCH 1, 2012

A VASTLY underexplored topic is the British government's role in greasing the skids for World War I. Until recently it was hard to find scholars who would dispute the culturally comfortable judgment that "authoritarian Germany" unleashed the Great War out of militaristic arrogance. Supposedly the British only got involved after the Germans recklessly violated Belgian neutrality on their way to conquering "democratic" France.

But British Foreign Secretary Sir Edward Grey had done everything in his power to isolate the Germans and their Austro-Hungarian allies, who were justified in their concern about being surrounded by enemies. The Triple Entente, largely constructed by Grey's government and which drew the French and Russians into a far-reaching alliance, encircled Germany and Austria with warlike foes. In July 1914, German leaders felt forced to back their Austrian allies in a war against the Serbs, who were then a Russian client state. It was clear by then that this conflict would require the Germans to fight both Russia and France.

The German military fatalistically accepted the possibility of England entering the struggle against them. This might have happened even if the Germans had not violated Belgian soil in order to knock out the French before sending their armies eastward to deal with a massive Russian invasion. The English were anything but neutral. In the summer of 1914, their government was about to sign a military alliance with Russia calling for a joint operation against German Pomerania in case of a general war. The British had also given assurances to French Foreign Minister Théophile Delcassé that they would back the French and the Russians (who had been allied since 1891) if war broke out with Germany. Grey spurned attempts by German Chancellor Theobald von Bethmann-Hollweg to woo his government away from their commitments to Germany's enemies.

German concessions in 1912 included:

- the acceptance of British dominance in constructing railroads and accessing oil reserves in what is now Iraq
- investments in central African ventures that would clearly benefit the English more than the Germans
- meekly following England's lead in two Balkan Wars where Austria's enemy Serbia nearly doubled its territory

The Russians and French were also vastly expanding their conscription to outnumber the German and Austrian forces, but neither German concessions nor the saber-rattling of England's continental allies caused the British government to change direction. Lord Grey, who remained Foreign Secretary until 1916, never swerved from his view that Germany was England's most dangerous enemy.

A book that makes this clear is Konrad Canis's study of German foreign policy from 1902 to 1914. A massive volume of more than seven hundred pages, Canis's *Der Weg in den Abgrund* ("The Road Into the Abyss"), published in 2011, is a groundbreaking revisionist account of the entanglements leading up to the war.[162]

Canis makes several points one is not likely to encounter in ordinary historical scholarship:

1. The German Second Empire's foreign policy was largely passive. This was true not only of Bismarck after German unification in 1871 but almost equally true of German foreign policy from 1902 onward.

2. The British were more hostile to the Germans than vice versa. They viewed Germany as an upstart economic competitor which

had established itself as the continent's dominant military power. Both German public opinion and German leaders were strongly Anglophilic; the Chancellor Bethmann-Hollweg considered English friendship to be something worth striving for even at the cost of German interests.

3. The German government and most of the German press made a sharp distinction between hoping to see their country become a world power and aspiring for dominance over all other countries. Canis's sources suggest that influential Germans were hoping to become a power "on the scale of England," a country they respected and had no interest in fighting.

In 1914 Russia posed more of a threat to England than either Germany or Austria did. England was struggling with Russia for dominance in Central Asia. Instead of reassessing his country's geopolitical priorities, Sir Edward Grey offered Russia a third front against the Germans by promising to make British ships available for a landing in northern Germany. This was how the British government tried to settle its conflicts with Russia, as both of them were expanding into the same region. In these British commitments, it is unclear whether a distinction was still being drawn between offensive and defensive wars.

And then there's the United States. When the German ambassador approached Teddy Roosevelt to join the Germans in upholding open trade in China's Yangtze River Valley and other regions then being closed off by the British and French, TR refused. He said he could not sign such a document before first consulting the British. This may be further proof for those who believe the United States was a vassal state of England's before the First World War.

The autocratic Russian government, which entered the war from the east, was not quite as "democratic" in 1914, but by the time Woodrow Wilson pulled us into the European cauldron, Russia had undergone the first of two revolutions, this one a democratic revolutionary change in March 1917. Thus, the United States could ally itself with Russia's morally acceptable provisional government when it took up arms against putative German warmongers.

George Kennan's *The Fateful Alliance* (1984) and Sean McMeekin's *The Russian Origin of the First World War* (2011) both document the role the aggressively expansionist Russian government played in bringing about the Great War.[163] But such revelations are no longer surprising.

What is more of a discovery is England's role in creating this catastrophe. This oversight may be attributed to certain obvious causes: the mistaken view that England only entered the war because of the violation of Belgian neutrality (this confounds a pretext with a cause); the Anglophilic disposition of American political and academic elites; and more recently, the tendentious notion that "democracies never fight each other." Unfortunately for this generalization, the governments of Germany and England (and certainly their societies) in 1914 looked much more like each other than either would resemble the present American or Canadian regime.

Canis does not defend Germany's ultimately disastrous decision in 1914. The Germans should have restrained the Austrians even after Serb agents killed Austria's Archduke Ferdinand. The ensuing war wrecked the Old Europe. The war industries that Grey, Churchill, and others of their kidney were lavishly funding were not what the populace wanted. The war hawks were diverting revenues from social reforms. Although I am hardly in favor of the welfare state, creating one in England in 1910 may have been less ruinous than Grey's foreign policy.

Sleepwalk to Suicide

The American Conservative

JANUARY 21, 2014

PERHAPS NO war has been treated more tendentiously—and in recent decades more inappropriately—than World War I. Since the 1960s, a fixed view of that conflict has developed in academic and journalistic circles that places the blame almost entirely on one side. The German government, led by an evil, authoritarian emperor and his bellicose general staff, unleashed a struggle that cost more than thirty million lives and wrought untold destruction on the European continent.

According to the scholar Fritz Fischer—who became the German Left's darling, despite his background as a loyal Nazi—the war was planned and initiated by a Germany bent on world domination.[164] What other belligerents did to get the ball rolling in 1914, Fischer suggests, was inconsequential. The rest of Europe was pulled into a struggle that Germany had planned for decades, a conflagration its anti-democratic ruling class and ultranationalist public happily initiated.

Defenses of the Fischer thesis and other versions of the outbreak of the Great War stressing exclusive German or Austro-German responsibility have been driven by moral and ideological considerations. Unfortunately, there are facts that historians until recently tried studiously to avoid. As critics of Fischer's position were already showing in the early 1960s, his singling out of his own country, already burdened with Nazi

217

crimes, for starting an earlier European war was based on questionable investigative methods.

Fischer and his followers ignored what other European countries did to provoke the Great War, unfairly blackened the reputation of German Chancellor Theobald von Bethmann-Hollweg—who tried earnestly to iron out differences between England and his country for at least three years before the war started—and misquoted key German actors in the conflict, such as the Kaiser and the chief of the German general staff.

In recent decades those who write non-prescribed histories dealing with the outbreak of the First World War typically ignore Fischer and like-minded interpreters. Niall Ferguson in *The Pity of War* (1999), Konrad Canis in *Der Weg in den Abgrund* (2011), his massive three-volume work on the failures of German diplomacy leading to the "abyss" in 1914, Christopher Clark in *The Sleepwalkers* (2013), and Sean McMeekin in *The Russian Origins of World War One* (2013) have all produced estimable studies about the Great War that are clearly incompatible with Fischer's stress on exclusive German guilt.[165]

All the Great Powers behaved rashly, and to their credit the most scrupulous historians do not spare any of the actors on the Allied side. The avoidable disaster of 1914 teaches us, according to Christopher Clark, how the Great Powers "sleepwalked" their way into a war from which European civilization never recovered. Russia in its drive to dismantle Turkey and control the Dardanelles; Britain in its efforts to reduce a rival's power even at the risk of encircling the German Empire with hostile alliances; Serbia in its attempts to split apart the Habsburg Empire; and France in its desperate desire to punish the Germans for defeat in the Franco-Prussian War all helped stir the pot.

Canis has shown in staggering detail how German foreign policy after the fall of Bismarck floundered for decades. The German Naval Program designed to achieve a 3:5 ratio in relation to the British Navy, which was then the world's largest, was an irritant to British political leaders. It allowed firebrands like Winston Churchill—who became First Lord of the Admiralty in 1911—to exaggerate German hatred for England, which in fact was never particularly great, as Canis documents by looking at the German press.

The German government naively thought it could create a large enough navy to force the British to make an alliance with its fellow Northern European power. The royal families of the two countries were closely related, and the Kaiser believed his British cousins would never go to war with him—indeed, they would seek his friendship—if they couldn't blockade his coastline.

The Kaiser was wrong. Although Bethmann-Hollweg managed to halt the German naval buildup by 1912, the British government still plowed on and plunged their country into further entangling alliances with Russia against the Germans. The British managed to bottle up the Germans even before the war began and then imposed what was probably an illegal starvation blockade until 1919.

Niall Ferguson argues convincingly that if Britain and the United States never entered the war—and even if the Central Powers prevailed after a long, bloody conflict—Britain would have remained Europe's premier power, blessed with an enormous navy, an extensive empire, and an economic lead over other European countries. No matter the outcome of the war, the United States would eventually have become the greatest world power on the basis of its industrial and agricultural wealth.

As it was, American intervention on the Allied (read British) side was always a matter of time. The US government, as historians Thomas Fleming and Walter Karp have demonstrated, was never really neutral. Any crisis that put the Central Powers in a bad light was played up by America's fervently Anglophile political class. The sinking of the *Lusitania* by a German submarine in 1915 was not a belligerent act directed against the United States: the ship was loaded with arms and other contrabands that were earmarked for the British. The German government had warned Americans and other neutrals not to board the ship because it was a fair war target—as indeed it was.

Already in 1914 the American ambassador to London and a close friend of President Wilson, Walter Hines Page, had announced to British leaders that he would do all he could to bring the United States into the war on England's side as soon as an appropriate pretext could be arranged. No similar assurance was given by Page's counterpart in Berlin in talking with German leaders.

But Woodrow Wilson and his party were not the major backers of getting the United States involved in the bloodbath. Wilson delayed in the face of Republican hysteria about not moving fast enough to stand with England for "democracy." Today's neoconservatives are not the first to talk up the "Anglosphere." Onetime Republican celebrities like Theodore Roosevelt, Elihu Root, and Henry Cabot Lodge were demanding in 1914 that we get into a European war we would have done well to stay out of. The GOP's horrid habits go back a very long way.

President George W. Bush exceeded in his calls for America to liberate the rest of the world any expression of chauvinism from a major European leader on the eve of World War I. But tactless behavior has not produced the consequences for us that it did for the "sleepwalking" subjects of Christopher Clark's history. We are lucky about where our country is located and how much wealthier and stronger we are relative to other states. What did Bismarck say about God looking after fools, drunkards, and the United States of America?

The Myth of Nazi Inevitability

Chronicles

MARCH 2020

L ATELY, I'VE been studying a segment of German history about which I knew little as compared with the period before World War I or the great German cultural awakening between 1770 and 1820, sometimes characterized as *Die Goethezeit*. Germany's failure to stave off a Nazi takeover, which was well on its way to happening when Hitler became Chancellor on January 30, 1933, has been considered proof positive of a bad national character.

Supposedly, Germans were always following a "special path" toward a Nazi regime, which just took several centuries to reach its explosive end. This is the view currently propounded by German educators and the leaders of all German parties, except for the patriotic, right-of-center Alternative für Deutschland. But it may be argued that the Weimar Republic faced so many difficulties that it would have taken years of economic prosperity for the interwar German state to have won legitimacy in the eyes of the German people. Instead, it had to labor under the Depression that befell every Western country in the fall of 1929.

The Republic's parliamentary organizers, who represented the Socialist, the Democratic, and the (Catholic) Center Parties, were compelled to sign a vindictive peace agreement inflicted on them by the victorious Allies. They were also, not incidentally, made to endorse this document under the threat of invasion without a prior right to negotiate. The defeated side had to pay an unspecified amount in reparations, swallow the loss of about a fifth of its territory, and accept a home defense force limited to one hundred thousand soldiers. Also, in Articles 227 through 232 of the Treaty of Versailles, they had to acknowledge "war guilt and sole responsibility" for all the human losses and property damage caused by the war.

The Weimar Republic also started out with French forces occupying the coal- and iron-producing Saar region, as well as a large chunk of the Rhineland, which the French vacated only in 1930. Germany's former eastern borders barely existed after the war since most of what had been West Prussia and Silesia was given to France's protégé, the newly established Polish Republic. Although Germans held on to a piece of East Prussia and at least indirectly the Free City of Danzig, which had a near majority German population, the Poles were left in a position to close off Danzig and to isolate East Prussia.

Given some of these political and geopolitical problems, and Germany's perpetually feuding parliamentary parties, it is a wonder that the Weimar Republic survived for as long as it did. That this was possible was owing to the dedicated, patriotic statesmen who served the "German fatherland." Several of these stand out as especially commendable political leaders: the first president of the Republic, Friedrich Ebert; a later Chancellor and Foreign Minister, Gustav Stresemann; the Minister of Defense and later Minister of the Interior, Wilhelm Groener; and the Chancellor between 1930 and 1932, Heinrich Brüning. All but the Republic's first president, Ebert, who was a moderate socialist, were by disposition monarchists who rallied to the postwar regime as *Vernunftrepublikaner*, or sensible rather than sentimental republicans.

The last Kaiser, Wilhelm II, had in any case become useless to his country once he had been talked into abdicating and obligingly went into exile on November 9, 1918, at the urging of Groener, who was then a member of the German High Command. The Kaiser took this fateful step principally to please the American president, Woodrow Wilson, who refused to negotiate with the defeated Germans unless they first unseated their ruler. The French, who pushed for the hardest peace against their German rivals, seem to have been utterly indifferent as to which head of the German government they would inflict their terms on. But once the Kaiser had left to take up residence in Holland, not even the explicitly monarchist German National People's Party (DNVP) did much to bring him back. The German war commander, Paul von Hindenburg, who became the Republic's president in 1925 and was then reelected in 1932 in an election against Hitler, was known as a staunch monarchist. But not even this venerable Prussian officer, who had led the Kaiser's forces during the war, seemed concerned about a monarchical restoration.

In *Alternativen zu Hitler: Wilhelm Groener* (2008) Klaus Hornung, a onetime professor of political science at the University of Hohenheim in Stuttgart, puts into relief Groener's struggle as a military officer and minister to preserve the Weimar Republic.[166] Although a member of the German High Command who enjoyed exemplary relations with his superior, Hindenburg, Groener became known for his political flexibility. At the war's end he developed close ties to Friedrich Ebert, upon whose cooperation he depended to put down radical leftist uprisings after the war. The majority socialists, the *Mehrheitssozialisten*, backed Ebert and his Defense Minister Gustav Noske, despite defections on the Socialist Party's left, in dealing with what Ebert as well as Groener condemned as a violent threat to Germany's constitutional republic. Later in the 1920s as Defense Minister, and from 1931 to 1932 as Interior Minister, Groener tried to cooperate with the democratic Left in building a workable parliamentary coalition that would exclude both the Nazis and the communists.

In the German election of September 1930, which came at the height of the Great Depression, the Nazis and the communists together won enough seats in the Reichstag to create a near obstructionist majority, a *Sperrmehrheit*. The Nazi deputies in Germany's parliament shot up from 12 to 110, although the Chancellor at the time, Heinrich Brüning of the Center Party, commented in his memoirs that he expected an even more resounding victory for Hitler's party.[167]

Groener made multiple enemies on the German nationalist Right, for understandable reasons. He talked the Kaiser into abdicating, then induced parliamentary leaders to sign the Treaty of Versailles, including its "shame paragraphs" blaming Germany for the war. Although Groener considered the treaty to be outrageously unjust, he also believed Germany's armed forces were in no condition to resist an Allied invasion if one were undertaken. Later as Interior Minister he persuaded Hindenburg to ban Nazi paramilitary groups, and in his persistent effort to place the Reichswehr "above parties," Groener prosecuted young soldiers who distributed inflammatory Nazi literature in their barracks.

In the summer of 1930 Hindenburg established "a presidential regime" under Article 48 of the Weimar Constitution, which allowed the aged executive to govern "under emergency powers." Groener supported this move as necessary to protect Germany's republic and, with Brüning, became a leading figure of the "emergency cabinet." Like Hindenburg, Groener and Brüning were convinced that this assertion of constitutionally guaranteed presidential power was necessary to save their country from the Nazi and communist dangers.

During Groener's political service to the Weimar Republic, he tried persistently to win over American Republican administrations. Wishing to free his country from onerous reparations and to rebuild the German Army, he recognized that American leaders had no interest in further humiliating the Germans or keeping them in an economically weak position. By the 1920s, moreover, second thoughts had set in across the ocean about America's involvement in World War I, and certainly about the harshness of the Treaty of Versailles. Both Groener and Brüning thought they could link plans for disarmament among the major powers to Germany's own interests.

If Germany's former enemies cut their military expenses and reduced the sizes of their armies, the resulting situation might lead to a revision of the status quo for the war's losers. The Germans might then have been allowed to achieve military parity and have their reparations costs shrunk. But this would not happen. The British and French were unwilling to accept a revision of the Versailles Treaty that would have permitted the Germans to create a serious military force. Additionally, the Depression put the French in a financially precarious position, rendering them more dependent on German reparations. Note that much of the money paid in reparations came from American banks, which provided the Germans and other Europeans with generous loans.

Groener lost his cabinet posts in June 1932, at which point his former assistant, General Kurt von Schleicher, formed a new government with the devious Center Party politician Franz von Papen. This successor cabinet moved toward the position of allowing Hitler into the government, supposedly on the government's own terms, a move that Groener and Brüning doggedly resisted. By 1932 Hindenburg had become a decrepit shadow of his former self, and he was finally persuaded to bring the Nazis to power by his son Oskar, whose financial irregularities enabled Hitler's henchmen to blackmail him. In 1934 Hitler rewarded Schleicher's assistance by having him murdered during the Night of the Long Knives. Von Papen barely escaped this bloodbath, which was carried out by the Brownshirts against Hitler's internal targets.

Perhaps because of both his moral stature and his retirement from political life, Groener was left untouched. In 1933 this forcibly retired statesman pointed out the obvious: As late as May 1932 it was possible to work with an anti-Nazi coalition in the Reichtstag. And, while the fall of Brüning's government had actually resulted in a crisis that added to the Nazis' electoral strength, it had begun to ebb by the end of 1932. Further, if Hindenburg had not agreed to make Hitler Chancellor when he did, the Nazis' appeal, which correlated with the intensity of the Depression, would have declined by 1934, when an economic upswing occurred.

A naive observer might think that the German Federal Republic would be celebrating Groener as an anti-Nazi warrior allied to the moderate socialists. Guess again! The only reason that Hornung's matter-of-fact biography was published at all is that a very conservative Austrian press, Leopold Stocker Verlag, agreed to do so.

By current German anti-fascist standards, Groener was a highly suspect figure. He opposed a radical leftist revolutionary takeover of Germany in 1919—a revolution that would have been a good thing according to the current German intelligentsia. And, behind the backs of Germany's "democratic" enemies, he built up the Reichswehr above the one hundred thousand limit stipulated by the Treaty of Versailles. Groener was also an avowed German patriot, who did not express the now obligatory loathing for his country that characterizes today's successful German politicians and intellectuals.

Oh, and lest we forget: He coordinated Germany's military transportation system in World War I and failed to defect to the other side. Recently the city of Dresden fired a bus driver for daring to write in German that he was a "German driver," presumably to indicate that unlike other drivers he could speak to passengers *auf Deutsch*. It's highly unlikely this would have befallen a Muslim immigrant bus driver who chose to advertise his non-German nationality.

The Red Butcher

Chronicles

NOVEMBER 2021

S EAN MCMEEKIN'S massive tome *Stalin's War: A New History of World War II* (2021) is more than a new history of World War II. It is above all a depressing confirmation that the crimes against humanity committed by Stalin's regime, including during the war, were comparable to those of Hitler. Moreover, McMeekin reveals that the Nazi regime could have been removed from power without the disastrous territorial concessions in Eastern Europe that FDR and Churchill granted to Stalin and his underlings.

McMeekin shows there were defensible limits on wartime help that American congressmen and most of the American public wished to impose on the Soviets after their former Nazi allies invaded Russia. In Congress in the summer of 1941, Hamilton Fish III, Robert M. La Follette Jr., Robert Taft, and Harry Truman all reminded listeners of Stalin's crimes when Lend-Lease aid to Russia came up for discussion.

Throughout the period of Soviet–Nazi cooperation between September 1939 and June 1941, the Soviets swallowed up as many onetime independent countries as did Hitler's armies. After German and Soviet armies invaded Poland in 1939, the Soviets murdered in just two years four to five times as many civilians as did the Germans. During their accord with Nazi Germany, the Soviets grabbed even more foreign territory than Hitler appropriated. Stalin's regime spread aggressively into

Eastern European countries and threatened the mineral and fuel resources on which Nazi Germany was dependent, e.g., the Ploieşti oil fields in Romania. Although there is no conclusive indication that Stalin planned to attack Nazi Germany before being attacked on June 22, 1941, what happened should not have been shocking. The attack on the Soviet Union came after relations between the two partners in crime deteriorated into squabbling over their ill-gotten conquests.

The slowness and inefficiency with which the Soviets responded was more surprising, although it was they who enjoyed an initial overwhelming superiority in manpower and in many categories of weaponry. German soldiers fought better and were more capably led than their adversaries. If the German armies managed to control most of European Russia and laid siege to Leningrad for two-and-a-half years starting in September 1941, the main reason for this success was that the invaders were far better trained.

During Russia's occupation by Germany, the rate of loss between the two sides stood at 14-to-1; even after the loss of hundreds of thousands of troops at Stalingrad in January 1943 the Germans almost managed to defeat the blundering Soviets around Prokhorovka, to the west of Stalingrad, in July. Hitler handed the Soviets an unexpected gift by transferring German divisions to southern Italy where Allied armies were then on the offensive. It allowed Stalin to turn what was an imminent disastrous defeat into a "second Stalingrad."

Between October 1941 and the end of the war, the Americans showered Lend-Lease gifts on the Soviet regime, which demanded, not requested, aid from its "capitalist" allies. This mass of weapons, planes, trucks, and foodstuffs totaled more than $180 billion in today's currency and enabled the Soviets to continue fighting against the Germans and their allies. At least initially this aid could have been justified, since the German invasion had devastated Soviet war production. But the assistance went on and on and became ever more extravagant.

The Lend-Lease policy had some peculiarities. The Soviets would not allow American planes to land on their soil except at designated spots like Murmansk and Arkhangelsk near the Arctic Circle and later Vladivostok in the North Pacific. Stalin entirely controlled the conditions under which American aid was to reach his armies. He made steady demands concerning his country's putative needs, and contrary to the conditions of the agreement, almost none of the cost of the aid was ever paid back.

Worse, after the Soviets went on the offensive by the summer of 1943, they deployed American Lend-Lease supplies to aid them in, among other things, wiping out non- or anti-communist resistance. In other words, the United States' policy aided the imposition of communist regimes in Eastern Europe.

These targets of Soviet brutality included the Polish Home Army resistance,[168] which had fought valiantly against Hitler's armies but also opposed the Soviet takeover of Poland and the imposition on their nation of the Soviet "Lublin Provisional Government."[169] In August 1944, when the population of Warsaw revolted against the German occupation, the Red Army—parked across the Vistula—did not offer the help that the insurgents expected. Instead, Soviet commanders waited until the German occupiers suppressed the revolt, killing more than two hundred thousand Poles, and then the Soviets wiped out isolated Home Army forces that were connected to the uprising. The Soviets had already murdered about fifteen thousand Polish officers in the Katyn Woods in White Russia during their alliance with Hitler.

Despite compelling evidence of Soviet misdeeds, Stalin bullied FDR and Churchill into blaming murders of the Poles improbably on the Germans. The allies went along for the sake of wartime amity. This compliance was entirely in keeping with the usual servility shown by FDR and Churchill in the face of outrageous Soviet demands. As McMeekin heavily documents, this relationship worked steadily and consistently in favor of Stalin's interests.

There are three obvious reasons for Western leaders' extraordinary tractability. One was their concern that the Soviets might enter a new Soviet–Nazi pact by patching up relations with the German enemy. This was also the kind of deal that Stalin and his Foreign Minister Vyacheslav Molotov suggested that FDR and Churchill might try to negotiate with the Germans. Any perceived or imagined attempt to "deal softly" with the Germans would cause Stalin and his henchmen to complain that the Western "capitalists" were seeking a reconciliation with Hitler and planned to unite their combined forces against "socialist Russia." While German armies were occupying large masses of Russian territory, the renewal of a Soviet–Nazi pact was certainly unlikely. Afterward, as the Red Army was sweeping across Eastern Europe on its way to Berlin, there was no reason that Stalin would try to cut a deal with a soon-to-be-decimated enemy.

Another reason for American compliance with Stalin was the pervasiveness of Soviet assets within the Roosevelt administration. FDR's rabidly anti-German Secretary of the Treasury, Henry Morgenthau Jr., who was relentless in advocating a vindictive, even genocidal campaign against the Germans, was a natural target for Stalin's agents. Although

Morgenthau's Germanophobia was a reaction to evidence that the Nazis were engaged in the mass killing of European Jewry, those around him who encouraged him were working for the Soviets and merely serving Stalin's purposes. Morgenthau repeatedly allowed himself to be duped by Soviet agents such as his chief adviser, Harry Dexter White, who took orders from NKVD agent Vitaly Pavlov.

Even more useful to the Soviet regime was FDR's closest confidant Harry Hopkins, who virtually never left the president's side. Hopkins, as McMeekin documents, was exuberantly pro-Soviet. He not only took Stalin's side in every major war conference; he also persuaded his boss to remove from the presidential cabinet anyone known to be even slightly critical of Soviet intentions, starting with the only mildly anti-Stalinist Secretary of State Cordell Hull, who was replaced by the more amenable Edward Stettinius Jr. The pro-Soviet presence within the American government helps explain its willingness to give Stalin just about anything he demanded in Eastern Europe without even the threat of reducing aid.

The pro-Soviet infiltration of the American government also clarifies why a postwar program for Germany as lunatic as the Morgenthau Plan was presented as something definitive and doable at the Second Quebec Conference in September 1944. Morgenthau's misconceived plan called for the almost total deindustrialization of a defeated Germany, the removal of at least part of its population, and the reduction of German agriculture to a bare subsistence level. Other ideas that Morgenthau tried to get FDR to accept were the shooting of fifty thousand German officers—a proposal that Stalin was then pushing on allied leaders—and even the castration of German males.

To his credit, Churchill was appalled by such final solutions for the German problem but at the Second Quebec Conference he lacked the military independence to make much of a stink. The Soviet agents, who regarded Morgenthau and Hopkins as useful idiots, were not really interested in depopulating Germany, let alone castrating its males. But they would have been delighted to have German industry relocated to the Soviet Union and to other areas under Soviet control. Further, Stalin was obviously eager to remove any German obstacle to Soviet expansion into Eastern Europe. Mercifully, due to how the war ended and the rapid deterioration of Western-Soviet relations, only pieces of the Morgenthau Plan were ever put into operation.

Another reason the Western allies were willing to give the Soviets as much as they took, even at the expense of those nations they claimed to be liberating from Nazi control, was the desire to see Germany totally wrecked. Both Churchill and FDR had been strong anti-German interventionists in World War I, and FDR complained that the Germans had been let off too lightly after losing that war. The demand for Germany's unconditional surrender, the Anglo-American use of saturation bombing against defenseless German civilians during the last year of World War II, and the consideration given to even the most vindictive elements of Morgenthau's plan were all indicative of the vengeful mood that substituted for statecraft in the closing period of the war.

But one shouldn't rule out other factors in trying to explain why "Stalin's war" yielded certain unfortunate results, like placing Eastern and Central Europe under oppressive Soviet domination, advanced by a Red Army that had murdered and raped its way across the continent. The British government, for example, made an inexcusably stupid decision to support Stalin's agent Tito and his communist partisans against the leader of the Chetnik royalist resistance, Draža Mihailović, in German-occupied Yugoslavia. This disastrous decision did not follow from any attempt to appease the Soviet tyrant; the British government just didn't care for Mihailovic and ignored or falsified the effectiveness of his resistance forces in destabilizing the German occupation.

By March 1943, Tito announced to his communist partisans that exterminating the Chetniks rather than driving out the German armies would be their most important task. By war's end, the Titoists succeeded in wiping out hundreds of thousands of non-communist resistance fighters.[170] The obliging Western press would present this achievement as the rooting out of Nazi collaborators and treated Tito almost as obsequiously as it did his boss in the Kremlin.

Another moral outrage was the action of the Anglo-Americans in returning to Soviet lands millions of people who had fled to the West to escape from Stalin's clutches immediately after the war. These unfortunate refugees were destined to be killed or dragged off to labor camps. Not a few of them committed or attempted suicide to avoid that fate. But this despicable act of appeasement, as far as I can tell, was not driven by communist agents. It was simply one more cringing effort to appease Stalin.

One should also not leave out of the picture the near-death condition of FDR, by the time he won his fourth term as US president in November 1944. The president who made a twenty-one-hour flight from Washington to Yalta to confer with Stalin in February 1945 showed a blood pressure reading of 250 over 100 after his arrival. It was remarkable that he could be kept alive and sentient, but hardly surprising that the Soviet leader, who insisted on meeting in his own backyard, easily dominated him at the conference.

This reader is grateful to Sean McMeekin for having produced his exhaustively researched study. It richly confirms what I long suspected about Soviet treachery and brutality, characteristics that Stalin did not abandon to fight "fascism." The book also strengthened my conviction that the post–World War II reaction against communists in the American government was totally justified and long overdue.

Finally, the work has made me furious in remembering my many hours spent as a graduate student in the mid-1960s listening to my Sovietophile professors and fashionably radical classmates defend Stalin as a postwar victim of American anti-communism. There is a veritable gulf between the factual truth and what these arrogantly pro-communist intellectuals wished me and many other Americans to believe.

Some critics of McMeekin's book have falsely alleged that in detailing Stalin's crimes, he has somehow whitewashed Hitler's role as an aggressor or murderer. This is nonsense. McMeekin is merely shining a light on aspects of World War II that many of its panegyrists and certainly its Soviet apologists chose to ignore.

The Hitler of Legend

Chronicles

MAY 2023

I N 1997, John Lukacs published *The Hitler of History*, a book that presents a provocative but also reasonable argument: Contrary to the standard view of historians, Hitler was not a conservative who embodied the values of the pre–World War I German ruling class.[171] He was in fact a radical revolutionary who felt nothing but contempt for the political and social order of Imperial Germany and who rejoiced at its abolition after Germany's defeat in 1918. According to Lukacs, Hitler was not a German patriot or old-fashioned monarchist but an expansionist nationalist who appealed to the masses directly, over the heads of traditional German elites.

Lukacs's perspective challenged what has been known as the "continuity thesis," dominant among postwar historians. English historian A. J. P. Taylor previewed the continuity thesis in his World War II propaganda tract, *The Course of German History* (1945).[172] According to Taylor's brief, which I heard restated ad nauseam as a graduate student, German history exhibits a reactionary, anti-democratic pattern that inescapably culminated in Hitler's dictatorship and its ensuing catastrophes. Particularly since the "anti-liberal" unification of Germany in the nineteenth century, Taylor saw Germany's journey toward a reactionary abyss as preordained.

THE HITLER OF LEGEND

Lukacs's reinterpretation of Hitler as a revolutionary, not a German reactionary, was entirely correct. It is a reading that receives exhaustive treatment in the books of German historian Rainer Zitelmann, whom Lukacs consulted in doing his research.[173] Zitelmann provides striking quotations—from Hitler's speeches, correspondence, and "Table Talk" remarks recorded by his subordinates—that prove how radically anti-traditional Hitler really was. Zitelmann also produced works documenting the palpably anti-traditional nature of Hitler's iconoclastic world-view, including statements in which Hitler deplored the fact that the overthrow of the last Kaiser in November 1918 did not go far enough in revolutionizing Germany.

Unfortunately for Zitelmann, his work didn't fit the politically motivated anti-fascist German narrative prevalent in his native country. Germans, and now Americans, are supposed to believe that Hitler was a German ultraconservative, pursuing the policies of the founders of the German Second Empire, proclaimed in January 1871. He was supposedly a backward-looking fanatic, who believed in invented racial theories and Nordic myths but not in the "scientific progress" characteristic of the Left. Zitelmann demonstrates something very different: that, like leftists of his age, Hitler was a scientific materialist who worshiped "science."

Lukacs adopted Zitelmann's depiction of Hitler both because it clarified the historical picture and because a revolutionary Hitler was a useful foil for his all-time hero, Winston Churchill, with whom Lukacs contrasted the Austro-German tyrant in several of his books. Whereas Lukacs portrayed Churchill as a true patriot and admirable reactionary, he depicted Hitler as a crude populist and unbridled revolutionary. Lukacs was deeply suspicious of nationalism and populism, and he viewed Hitler as an ominous prototype of the populist demagogue who might one day capture the American political imagination.

Although Lukacs did not live to see the rise of Donald Trump, the latter might have been considered by Lukacs to be the kind of dangerous populist whom Hitler exemplified in a more extreme form. Lukacs shared at least some of the sensibilities of the liberal establishment of his day, which may be why that establishment relished his books. But he came to his establishment position as a Central European of gentry stock (on his father's side) who felt misgivings about popular rule, like his aristocratic Austrian friend, Erik von Kuehnelt-Leddihn (whose position Lukacs took at Chestnut Hill College after Kuehnelt-Leddihn went back to Austria).

Anti-egalitarian sentiment in Kuehnelt-Leddihn's case led to explicit contempt for the Left, and he therefore had no trouble viewing Hitler, Robespierre, and Mao as all being cut from the same evil cloth. Lukacs's case, however, was more complicated. He longed for an "establishment" that would protect polite society from democratic demagoguery, something he almost always associated with the Right. Lukacs's admiration for the American patrician George F. Kennan, who managed to be both socially reactionary and bitterly critical of America's anti-communist Right, suited well Lukacs's complicated ideological disposition.

Not surprisingly, Zitelmann left his original field of study to become a real estate broker in Berlin, a vocation in which he did quite well. He is now producing books once again, but not in his original area of research. Rather, he is writing in defense of the free market, as a disciple of Austrian School economist Ludwig von Mises.

To say that Zitelmann felt unwelcome in his country as an historian of Hitler and the Third Reich would be an understatement. Although a gifted stylist and diligent researcher, he violated the continuity thesis embraced by German journalists and politicians.

The continuity thesis also complemented the Western postwar liberal democratic platform. In this view, because the German Constitution, enacted after German unification in 1871, vested too much power in the emperor and his Chancellor and too little power (outside of controlling the purse) in the popular assembly (the Reichstag), and because the German military and administration remained largely in aristocratic hands, a "democracy deficit" put the Germans on a dangerous historic path that ended in the Third Reich.

Jonathan Steinberg, an American biographer of the first Imperial Chancellor, Otto von Bismarck, expressed this continuity thesis with admirable concision: "Bismarck's legacy passed through [World War I German General and later President Paul von] Hindenburg, to the last genius statesman that Germany produced, Adolf Hitler, and the legacy is thus linear and direct between Bismarck and Hitler."

Lest anyone doubt Steinberg's portentous narrative, the very anti-fascist, anti-nationalist German president, Frank-Walter Steinmeier, has repeated its main points with monotonous regularity. Steinmeier presents the entire German past as necessarily pointing toward Auschwitz. The German president has also made a habit of visiting foreign capitals, like Warsaw and Jerusalem, to express regret for German history and even for the fact that he speaks in his native language, given the enormous guilt that has accrued to his people.

Such a now-authorized view of the German past draws from a particular interpretation of Hitler's life and personality. Not accepting this interpretation can exact a heavy price for a scholar. Zitelmann's portrait of Hitler as a modern revolutionary clearly clashes with the teachings of Germany's state-of-the-art "democracy," which requires that the depiction of Hitler and his rule be presented as the fruits of a specifically German reactionary past. The playing out of that past, we are told, preceded the Allied "liberation" of the Germans in 1945, a step that led to the repression, if not total extirpation, of the German authoritarian character and to Germany's now perpetual role as repentant sinner. This role has necessitated a faithful imitation of whatever is considered to be "Western," most recently accomplished by enacting the rituals of the American woke Left. Being "democratic" in Germany also now means a continuing denunciation of the present Russian and Hungarian governments as "authoritarian" for their rejection of the LGBT agenda.

According to this received "democratic" teaching, Hitler was a typical anti-Semitic, anti-democratic German or Austrian nurtured by an anti-democratic society. He grew up in the provincial Austrian town of Braunau am Inn surrounded by Jew-hating German nationalists, and his authoritarian father, unlike his sorely browbeaten mother, bullied him mercilessly. Here we may note that this psychological profile gets its inspiration from the influential book *The Authoritarian Personality*, published by members of the Frankfurt School in 1950, which portrays right-wing thought as the result of mental illness induced by childhood trauma.[174]

It is a matter of record that Hitler left Linz, in Upper Austria, in 1909 to pursue studies as an artist and settled in Vienna, where he remained until 1913. While in this supposed hotbed of bigotry, he allegedly became imbued with the anti-Semitic and anti-Slavic passions that infected the Austrian capital. Of course, by the time Hitler slipped over the border and settled in Munich in 1913, he was already scarred, as we have been made to believe, by the mentality of the Germano-Austrian political and social world of the early twentieth century. That pernicious mentality was just waiting to express itself in the future German dictator, and when he joined the German National Socialist Workers' Party after World War I, he was already eager to carry out his quintessentially German mission, which involves mass murder and genocide as a matter of course.

Significantly, the description of the English translation of Brigitte Hamann's monograph, *Hitler's Vienna: A Portrait of the Tyrant as a Young Man*, which was published in German in 1996, includes these details:

> Hitler's was not the modern, artistic *"fin-de-siècle Vienna"* we associate with Freud, Mahler, Schnitzler, and Wittgenstein. Instead, it was a cauldron of fear and ethnic rivalry, a metropolis teeming with "little people" who rejected Viennese modernity as too international, too libertine, and too Jewish. It was a breeding ground for racist political theories, where one leading member of parliament said, to the cheers of his colleagues, "I would like to see all Jews ground to artificial fertilizer."[175]

Brigitte Hamann vividly depicts the undercurrent of disturbing ideologies that flowed beneath the glitter of the Habsburg capital. Against this background, Hamann tells the story of the moody, curious, intense, painfully shy young man from the provinces, Adolf Hitler.

The groundbreaking argument in Hamann's work is exactly the opposite of what this English summary states. According to the actual book, the young Hitler was very much part of the *"fin-de-siècle"* Vienna that we associate with Mahler and other Jewish or quasi-Jewish cultural figures. He hung out with the cultural avant-garde during his Vienna years and even demonstrated against the putatively anti-Semitic opponents of Mahler's music. (Although a Catholic, Mahler was of Jewish ancestry.) There was in fact nothing in Hamann's treatment of "the apprenticeship of a dictator," that suggests the vicious behavior of the later Hitler, who, in Vienna, was an unsuccessful painter of local scenes but hardly a raving bigot.

There was furthermore nothing ominous about Hitler's upbringing. From available records, we learn that his parents were by no means fanatically intolerant Catholics, despite the claims made by the "new atheists" Christopher Hitchens, Sam Harris, and Richard Dawkins. Such crusading non-deists imagined that the Christian theism they ascribe to Hitler drove him into religious bigotry and mass murder. In point of fact, Alois and Klara Hitler were conventional Austrian Catholic churchgoers, and one of their close family friends was the local Jewish physician, Eduard Bloch, who looked after Hitler's widowed mother after she became fatally ill with cancer. Hitler also had a sister who grew up in similar domestic circumstances but who never exhibited the nasty qualities associated with her brother after his rise to power.

Another German historian who, like Zitelmann and Hamann, doesn't stick to prescribed narratives is Ralf Georg Reuth. In his book *Hitlers Judenhass: Klischee und Wirklichkeit* ("Hitler's Hatred of Jews: Cliche and Reality," 2009), Reuth shows exhaustively that Hitler's ferocious hatred of Jews resulted from his being present during the communist takeover of Munich in 1919.[176] According to Reuth, there is exceedingly little evidence of Hitler's genocidal anti-Semitism until he reacted to the brutal communist dictatorship established in Munich in the wake of the German defeat in World War I.

The Communist Council Republic (*Räterepublik*), which took control of Munich in early April 1919, was led by Russian Jewish Bolsheviks, most importantly Eugen Leviné, who was killed after the counterrevolutionaries took back the city in May. The earlier radical government that established itself in Munich (but not uniformly in the rest of Bavaria) after the collapse of the German Empire and Bavarian monarchy in early November 1918 had also featured Jewish radicals Kurt Eisner, Gustav Landauer, and Ernst Toller. Jewish overrepresentation in postwar revolutionary activity fed a wave of anti-Semitism in Germany, Austria, and Hungary. (In significant contrast to the widespread impression at the time, most Jews in Central Europe had no noticeable sympathy for the communists. Many, in fact, sympathized with the counterrevolutionaries.)

Hitler did make "Jewish Bolshevism" the keystone of his politics, but he came to this position in a strange way. From all indications, he supported the revolution in Munich and even had himself elected to a "Council of Soldiers." After Leviné and other foreign Bolsheviks who had taken over the Bavarian revolution were driven from power and their revolutionary government crushed, Hitler changed sides quite opportunistically. He not only abandoned his many Jewish friends, some of whom were leftist revolutionaries, but also became fixated on a pervasive Jewish threat to Germany's existence.

Reuth attributes this behavior, at least partly, to self-defense. Hitler was trying to hide his own association with the Munich revolution by expressing, in an extreme form, the anti-Semitism that was then surging throughout Europe in the wake of postwar communist uprisings. He jumped on this issue and made it his own in an obsessive way. In any case, Hitler attributed both the punitive peace treaty suffered by Germany as a defeated power and communist internationalism to a pervasive Jewish influence. He also included Jewish capitalists in this web of evil, which came together in his mind as he watched events unfold in Munich. Finally, Hitler came to view himself as the savior of his country and thought his theatrical oratorical skills, which he had already been honing, would allow him to play a "providential role" in the resurrection of his country.

What is certainly not demonstrable, according to Reuth, is that Hitler's anti-Semitic fixation can be traced back to his youth in Braunau or to the years that he struggled financially in Vienna. It is only fair to point out that other biographers of Hitler, most notably Joachim Fest, also underline the transformative nature of Hitler's experience in post-war Munich.[177] But unlike other biographers, Reuth demonstrates that Hitler changed his political direction in response to the suppression of a revolution that he had actually welcomed.

Not surprisingly, Hitler's partly autobiographical *Mein Kampf*, which was published in July 1925, includes details about his life in Vienna and his military service that correspond to the accounts given by Fest, Ian Kershaw, and other Hitler biographers.[178] But these accounts, as Reuth points out, were produced after Hitler's opportunistic embrace of anti-Semitism and do not jibe with certain documentable facts, such as Hitler's friendship with Jews, including revolutionary leftist ones, and his active support of revolutionary events in Munich in 1919. One might also ask why ferocious critics of Hitler have been so willing to accept at face value Hitler's politically colored narratives about his early life, which he produced to advance his career as an anti-Semitic politician. Reuth is correct to ask why curiosity had not impelled these biographers to probe more deeply into their subject's fixation.

In conclusion, I am not suggesting that Hitler was not a brutal tyrant, nor am I saying that there were no circumstances in post–World War I or in earlier German society that allowed him to take power more easily than might have been the case elsewhere. In England, for example, which had stronger parliamentary traditions, a totalitarian takeover would have been less likely, even if the English, instead of the Germans, had suffered defeat in World War I. The Germans, it may be conceded, lacked the constitutional and civic resources to withstand the totalitarian nightmare that descended on their country in the 1930s.

But none of this suggests that German society was moving inexorably from the nineteenth or early twentieth century toward the grim end that it reached with Hitler's accession to power in January 1933. Nor can it be shown that Hitler became a maniacal despot because he was steeped from earliest childhood in an evil German culture. The attempt to depict his life in this manner is ideologically driven. It is an effort to paint the German past in such a way as to justify the anti-fascist social control of the present German government.

This received account of Hitler's life also is meant to legitimize a government that is busy rooting out the remnants of the German past, an enterprise that is entirely compatible with the Hitler of legend. This strenuous attempt to reconstruct society and politics in the name of overcoming an evil past is, of course, no longer exclusively German. It has become the shared destiny of both the defeated powers and the

Western victors in the World Wars. What the Germans call a *Schicksals-gemeinschaft*, or a "community of fate," now links the two.

CHAPTER SEVEN

Germany, Harbinger of the Abyss

$-\blacklozenge\ \blacklozenge\ \blacklozenge-$

Where Have All the Nazis Gone?

Chronicles

OCTOBER 2004

B ACK IN the 1960s, as a graduate student at Yale, I kept hearing that the Germans had still not confronted their past. They would do so only when they understood that Hitler, as explained by German leftist historian Fritz Fischer, was not a *Betriebsunfall* (operational accident) but emerged from Germany's history, which went in a straight line from Bismarck to Auschwitz. Fischer, a Nordic-looking Hamburg historian who died in 1999 at age ninety-one, had set out to prove, from archival sources supposedly made available to him in East Germany, that the German imperial government had launched World War I in a quest for world hegemony.[179] Despite his argument having been largely refuted by the 1970s, Fischer's view of the Germans bearing exclusive guilt for World War I carried the day at home and abroad. Anglophone conservatives Paul Johnson and Donald Kagan have been as enthusiastic as the German Left in embracing this thesis. Last year, German Chancellor Gerhard Schröder expressed shock when German literary historian Martin Walser stated the obvious: Believing in Fischer was intended as an act of German contrition for the Holocaust and had nothing to do with scholarship.

Fischer's critics, starting with the estimable historians Gerhard Ritter, Joachim Remak, and Golo Mann, had all been anti-Nazis. The SS arrested Ritter in November 1944 for participating in the plot to overthrow the Nazi government. These anti-Fischerites were not unqualified defenders of the Imperial German government but made the once-conventional (and correct) case that both sides had behaved recklessly in 1914. It is also methodologically questionable, as Niall Ferguson has pointed out, to blame the Central Powers exclusively for plans of territorial expansion or nationalist hysteria found among all the major belligerents.[180] Significantly, the memorandum in which Chancellor Theobald von Bethmann-Hollweg set out provisional German war aims in September 1914 came from his confidant, Kurt Riezler (as German historian Karl Dietrich Erdmann proved from Riezler's diaries over forty years ago). Far from being a proto-Nazi, this author of Fischer's key evidence for German expansionism was an Anglophile classicist and the son-in-law of a Jewish expressionist artist. Riezler, who subsequently fled from the Nazis, helped to script Hollywood films and, in the early 1950s, became a cofounder of the New School for Social Research. Among his protégés was Leo Strauss, whose disciples would evolve into outspoken Fischerites. Even so, the Straussians would never acknowledge the responsibility of Strauss's patron for the September 1914 program so savagely denounced by Fischer.

Equally important, as one discovers from Klaus Grosse Kracht's sprawling 2003 essay in the *Zeitschrift für Neuere Theologie-Geschichte*, Fischer became an honored Teutonophobe after having spent his youth as a Nazi booster.[181] Before the Nazi seizure of power, and contrary to his later autobiographical cover-up, the youthful Fischer was involved in Nazi-like nationalist organizations. In 1933, he went to work as an SA propagandist and, in 1937, joined the Nazi Party outright. By then, he had joined his dissertation director at Berlin—an undisguised Nazi ideologue, Erich Seeberg—as an advocate for the Reichsbewegung der Deutschen Christen, an unsavory body of Hitlerian theologians who were planning a National Socialist Christian church. Fischer took pains in 1939 in his study of the Prussian Church reformer Ludwig Nicolovius to add conspicuously anti-Semitic comments. According to Grosse Kracht, his subject hoped to advance his academic career on the coattails of party loyalists, a policy that resulted in his being named to a chair in Hamburg in 1942. (After the war, he would get back that chair as a darling of the German Left.) The Americans imprisoned Fischer after the war, like the more talented Carl Schmitt, as an influential Nazi thinker; like Schmitt, however, he was never brought to trial. By the late 1940s, Fischer had exchanged worldviews and, unlike Schmitt, spent the rest of his life pot-shooting dead Germans— starting with the Evangelical Church in nineteenth-century Germany, now criticized as overly nationalist.

It is mind-boggling that so little light has been shed on Fischer's checkered past. Even Grosse Kracht treats his Nazism the way American liberals have usually interpreted the Stalinist backgrounds of their favorite progressives, as something that only boorish reactionaries would bring up. The dirty secret is that the post-Marxist Left does not care about real Nazi pedigrees but simply about whom they can accuse of being a Nazi or a fascist, while trashing their country and its culture. Thus, they excuse Jürgen Habermas and Walter Jens, two anti-German leftist intellectuals, for their extensive activities in the Hitler Youth. They also jolly along former German President Richard von Weizsäcker, who covered up his father's work in greasing the skids for the Holocaust, as Hitler's ambassador to the Vatican. In the mid-1980s, Weizsäcker made himself into a *Gutmensch* (a leftist Goody Two-shoes) by speaking publicly on the need for perpetual, collective German atonement for the Nazi past. Meanwhile, those who excuse the genuine Nazis throw dirt at heroic German martyrs Claus von Stauffenberg and Carl Friedrich Goerdeler, who died trying to overthrow Hitler, for being insufficiently philosemitic and persistently patriotic.

In the postwar American occupation, anti-leftist anti-Nazis were considered politically dangerous. For several years, certifiable opponents of Hitler who disliked the communists or exhibited patriotic feelings were denied the right to publish newspapers or books. Former Nazis who changed sides, unlike conservatives who had opposed Hitler, were considered "educable." This continued to be the rule for Fischer and those of his ilk. By tacking leftward and doing so as despisers of the German past, they have been turned into the public "conscience" for a hated and self-hating country. Perhaps it is time to notice the swastika lurking beneath this artificial conscience.

How European Nations End

Orbis

SUMMARM 2005

T HE BOOKS on contemporary German history under review here
reveal several overarching themes: the possibility of what the
Germans call "constitutional patriotism"—that is, basing the
country's national identity on commitment to what are supposed to be
universal legal norms and rights; the future of the European nation; and
the level of self-government required for genuine democracy. How has
this postwar undertaking to manufacture a German identity independent of ethnicity and historical pride worked after almost sixty years?
While some of the trends that now prevail in Germany can be found
elsewhere in Western and Central Europe—particularly state-sponsored
moves to replace national with supranational administrations and loyalties—the German case stands out as an exceptionally vivid illustration
of this.

Germans call their situation a *Sonderfall* (special case). The German
people lost two devastating world wars in the twentieth century, and
after the defeat of Hitler's iniquitous regime in World War II, Germany
was occupied and "reeducated" by the victors. The Allied occupiers in
West Germany guided the rewriting of Germany's history texts to under-

score a total break from its national past, using all possible means to drive home the magnitude of Nazi atrocities under the Third Reich. The occupation also left behind a Basic Law (*Grundgesetz*) under which the then-only-partially rehabilitated (and still territorially divided) Germans would govern themselves. Although this Law, which was promulgated on May 23, 1949, was technically the work of German jurists—most of them associated with the Center-Left—it is hard to miss here the fingerprints of the American occupation government. The first nineteen articles—particularly the first, which dwells on the "unassailability of human dignity"—safeguard "human rights," which include, significantly, a "right to asylum" for the politically persecuted. Article 23 provides for the eventuality of a European Union, toward the creation of which the German republic would presumably work and to which sovereignty would be transferred, with the support of the upper house (*Bundesrat*) of the federal assembly. If the fervent hope of America and Britain were fulfilled, Germany would soon sink into an EU founded on "democratic principles" but allowing the Germans only limited room for regional autonomy.

Other measures were also imposed to make sure that the once-rogue nation stayed out of right-wing mischief. Articles 20 and 21 provide the means to prosecute individuals or political parties that threaten what Article 21 identifies as the "freedom-oriented, democratic basic order." Moreover, Article 21 refers to a "federal constitutional court" (*Bundesverfassungsgericht*) that would be authorized to decide whether a party was acting "against the Constitution" (*verfassungswidrig*). Thus there emerged in the Federal Republic a Teutonic counterpart to the American Supreme Court, albeit one that not only judges whether legislation conforms to the Basic Law but also whether certain parties, whatever the size of their popular base, pose a threat to German "democracy." As a backup, the Allied High Command made the Germans accept a *Verfassungsschutz* (intelligence agency) that was put in place on both the federal and provincial levels.[182] This agency both gathers evidence and keeps records, which it routinely hands over to courts and public administration, about the "extremist tendencies" it finds in individuals and groups.

Although the *Verfassungsschutz* cannot try or detain suspects, it is allowed to infiltrate organizations and make public its judgments. Unlike the American FBI, the *Verfassungsschutz* is authorized to deal with only one form of public threat: ideologically driven attacks on the German democratic, constitutional order. As historian Claus Nordbruch demonstrated in his 1999 work on the subject, such powers have been turned repeatedly to partisan use, and in the largest German state, Nordrheinland-Westfalen, the *Verfassungsschutz* has served as an instrument of intimidation against the center Right.[183] When groups have been thought to stray in the direction of the nationalist Right, the Socialists, through their political appointees, have pursued them as a threat to the German democratic order. This agency's largely uncontested right to infiltrate has made it an even greater threat to what Anglo Saxons understand as ordinary liberties. In a 2001 investigation of the right-wing National Democrats, the *Verfassungsschutzmänner*—those put in charge of protecting the constitution against extremists—planted incriminating evidence on members of the group that they were trying to have banned. Although the exposure of this stunt kept the National Democrats, who have done well in elections in the former East German states, from losing their right to organize and campaign, it did not result in any restraints being put on the transgressing agency. Moreover, the center Right CDU-CSU (Christian Democratic Union/Christian Social Union) continues to goad the *Verfassungsschutz* to find evidence of "extremism" in its electoral opponents on the Right, in order to avoid being forced to compete with an "extreme Right" party for the votes of German nationalists.

The *Verfassungsschutz* continues to be a bull in the china shop of German constitutional freedoms. An address given in 1985 by Germany's then Minister of the Interior, Friedrich Zimmermann, illustrates the obstacles encountered by all politically incorrect critics of German democracy. Zimmermann stated that he "who challenges the mission of the *Verfassungsschutz* calls into question the constitutional principle of militant democracy established by our constitution."[184] Nordbruch underlines the self-serving definition of "democratic parties" that now prevails in Germany, by which those parties that control parliamentary institutions are by definition "democratic" and those they hope to exclude are "extremist" and therefore subject to investigation. For example, the recycled communists who organized the Party of Democratic Socialists (PDS) have been *reingewaschen* (washed clean) by the usually left-leaning *Verfassungsschutz*; at the same time, the Republikaner, formed in 1983 by breakaway CDU-CSU officials, has been kept under steady investigation. Although Nordbruch found nothing to suggest that the anti-immigrationist Republikaner would suspend democratic government, or in fact would not practice it more fully than the current party rule, the *Verfassungsschutz* kept the Republikaner under a cloud of suspicion on the grounds that some members "in all probability represent right-extremist positions."[185] The same *Verfassungsschutz* office in Cologne, however, refused to investigate the PDS with the same thoroughness, claiming that only individual members but not the entire group held "left-wing extremist views."

In *Demokratie-Sonderweg Bundesrepublik* (2004), a sprawling inquiry on the Basic Law, Josef Schüsslburner, a Bavarian jurist formerly attached to the UN and then to the EU, asserts that German democracy has abandoned the exercise of popular self-government.[186] The term now refers to something that Ralf Dahrendorf, Jürgen Habermas, and other celebrated defenders of constitutional patriotism call *wehrhafte Demokratie* (militant democracy), a concept rooted in the Jacobin ascendancy of the French Revolution and, more recently, in the American occupation of Germany. Germans rule themselves democratically when they make electoral decisions that reflect authorized democratic attitudes. Hence, those who oppose diversity or gay rights cannot possibly be speaking or acting democratically, because what they express is both undemocratic and extremist. Nor should Germans value their national solidarity or any specifically German heritage if they wish to be truly democratic. For their history largely exemplified illiberalism up until the Allied occupation, and thus the Germans must strive to overcome their past by becoming global citizens in a world community held together by human rights. Schüsslburner easily demonstrates how widespread such views are among German elites and traces this thinking back to the construction of the Basic Law.

Schüsslburner does not claim that the entire document—particularly after additions such as Articles 79 and 146, which deal with substantive changes or the possibility of replacing the document in case of reunification—is all of a piece. He is also aware of the intrinsic tensions between the guarantee to express one's opinions freely in Article 4 and the powers that the Basic Law bestows on judges to suppress political opposition. Article 21 defends the free formation of parties as necessary to "mold the popular will," but then creates a court authorized to close down parties that "threaten" the order that the free flowering of parties is supposed to foster. Schüsslburner asks whether judges may stifle as constitutionally prohibited threats to Germany's ordered freedom parties that call for radical change in the current parliamentary system. For the view that has won out in the German press and government—that the state is free to crush opinions, particularly on the anti-immigrationist Right, that do not meet "democratic" criteria—may not have been what Article 16, Paragraph 2 originally intended. Schüsslburner points out that the Basic Law may not be mandating the German government to treat civil liberties as cavalierly as do the present federal regimes and at least some of the provincial governments. He observes that academic and press freedoms were far better protected in Germany under the now-despised Second Empire than under the present version of "militant democracy."[187]

But having conceded that the Basic Law has been tendentiously interpreted for decades to destroy freedom and real self-government, Schüsslburner also emphasizes that the Basic Law greased the skids for this development. It was inflicted on a people who were not allowed to express a collective self that did not derive from universal rights and from certain technical governing procedures. Although provisions were added permitting drastic revision and even replacement of the Basic Law, the heart of the founding document in 1949 lay elsewhere. That document was integral to an effort to denationalize the Germans, the results of which are still abundantly in evidence. In December 2004, the speaker for the CDU-CSU delegation in the Bundestag, Wolfgang Bosbach, proposed a motion that the nation recognize that Germans have a *Leitkultur* (dominant culture) consisting of "liberal democracy," the advocates of which "demand integration and oppose with determination all forms of extremism." This motion, which would only be controversial in a country embarrassed about its national identity, stems from the fact that Germany currently is home to about seven million Turks, of whom many know little German and seem drawn to the Islamist movement that is rising in German cities. If Chancellor Schröder gets his way on this point and Turkey—whose per capita income is some fifteen to twenty-one percent of Germany's, according to German economist Paul J. J. Welfens—enters the EU, then by 2010 at least four million additional Turks will have likely joined their compatriots already in Germany. Earlier, Christian Democratic critic Friedbert Pflüger observed that his party seemed to be having cold feet about "overcoming the radical '68ers" who turned self-hate into the only acceptable German identity. Unless Germans learn to like themselves better as a people, noted Pflüger, they will not only fail to address their immigration problem but also cease to exist as a recognizable nation.[188]

The Left opposition, which until now had equated *Leitkultur* with disguised neo-Nazism, this time responded to the Union with amused perplexity. There seemed no reason, they argued, to designate as peculiarly German what the Left had already advocated: "living together on the basis of shared values" of diversity and loyalty to existing constitutional processes.

Social Democrats Helmut Schmidt, Chancellor from 1974 to 1982, and Egon Bahr, a journalist and former Bundestag delegate, have taken exactly the same stand. Both now express the opinion that Germans spend too much time feeling guilty and denying *Vaterlandsliebe* (love of country). Thus Germans cannot deal emotionally with the cultural and social problems produced by the arrival of large numbers of non-European Muslims; they look at European integration as a cure-all for a national identity that they are trying to disown. Bahr, foreign minister under Willy Brandt in the early 1970s, has remarked, "There is no recipe by which our peaceful and peace-loving country in the middle of Europe can celebrate the end of History. Germany must develop a politics of its own, as a sovereign state that can no longer hide behind the back of its elders."[189] Tony Judt, an American moderate liberal, has made a similar argument about the false expectations that some Europeans have for a eurocracy that has yet to prove itself a suitable replacement for the nation-state.[190] Judt urges Europeans to think clearly before yielding their sovereignty to commissars in Brussels and Strasbourg.[191] In Germany this monumental cession of democratic power is occurring without a popular vote: Even in this land of uninterrupted politically correct conformity, the present left-of-center coalition is afraid that their fellow citizens might revert to being Germans.

CONTINUING REEDUCATION

SCHÜSSLBURNER SUGGESTS THAT the increasing self-abnegation that has overtaken the Germans as a people is partly a legacy of the radicalism that took off during the 1960s. This is the narrative favored by both the German Left and the German Right, despite the fact that they apply to this story diametrically opposed value judgments. Thus for leftist anti-nationalist Habermas, the entire Cold War was an unhappy interruption in the process of ripping Germans away from their past, which began with the postwar occupation in 1945. Morally contrite Germans therefore needed to start the ball rolling again, which they did in the 1960s, by refusing to be diverted by anti-communism and by backing out of the Cold War.

The best conservative treatment of this approach to coercive reeducation has been done by Caspar von Schrenck-Notzing, former editor of the German quarterly *Criticón* (1970–97) and since then director of a Munich-based educational foundation.[192] His *Charakterwäsche* has now been published in an expanded edition. A superb German stylist, Schrenck-Notzing tells his story with elegance and interpretive cogency. His work plots the reeducation efforts that were made in postwar Germany, how the American struggle with the Soviets altered American-

German relations, and the anti-national reeducation resumed by the Germans themselves. *Charakterwäsche* divides this process of "denazification" into two distinct, although occasionally overlapping, phases. The first was the postwar phase, characterized by military occupation; far-reaching censorship that favored the Left, including the communist Left; intimidation to achieve certain desired social psychological ends; and a new official history stressing the German's culpability for all recent wars involving their country. Phase Two, which goes back to the mid- and late 1960s, involved a selective resumption, minus the pressure of occupation forces, of Phase One. Since Schrenck-Notzing's work was first published in 1965, what he predicted through a glass darkly has come to pass with a vengeance. We now see what German critics call a specifically German "cult of guilt," which public administrators, educators, and journalists have all worked to keep going.

What separated the two phases was the onset of the Cold War and America's need to rehabilitate the Germans as Christian and/or democratic allies against the Soviets. Further hastening this transformation was the resounding victory of the anti-communist center Right in the American congressional elections of 1946 and the subsequent repudiation of the pro-Soviet policies pursued by the wartime Democratic administration. By 1947 the US government was losing interest in prosecuting suspected Nazis or applying psychological methods drawn from radical German émigrés to reconstruct formerly fascist societies. What the Germans produced was the ideological counterpart of this American anti-communism—namely, an intellectually fortified campaign against totalitarianism. This campaign was anchored in a prewar, liberal bourgeois outlook, and its representatives, who often came out of the academy, focused on the overlaps between Nazi and communist practices. The anti-totalitarians thought they were defending a constitutional order that incorporates Christian moral teachings and maintains non-state-controlled spheres of individual autonomy and corporate authority. And while they accepted those Allied-imposed agencies intended to restrict threats to the political order, they viewed them initially as playing only a very limited political role. In time, however, this view would change, as the revolutionary Left in the 1960s became more violent and the non-revolutionary Left more willing to dig up and divulge classified information; thereupon the liberal conservative establishment responded by pushing for extraordinary measures to contain perceived threats to the constitutional order. This tendency could be seen in 1962, when German Minister of Defense Franz Josef Strauss impounded the press and put several editors under temporary custody in order to show his displeasure with *Der Spiegel* for leaking classified military documents. Self-described German constitutional liberals rallied to the defense of Strauss, a fiercely anti-communist Bavarian, though the anti-anti-communist and anti-nationalist elements of the German Left played the incident up in order to discredit the "authoritarian Right."

The leader who from 1949 until 1963 presided over the new Germany and inspired the anti-totalitarian consensus was Chancellor Konrad Adenauer (1876–1967), a onetime Rhineland separatist, a Catholic anti-Nazi, and a loyal ally of the Eisenhower administration. In his steady control of the helm of state, Adenauer dwarfed all his predecessors since Bismarck.[193] Curiously, Adenauer, an anti-Prussian Catholic, may well have loathed Bismarck almost as much as he loathed Hitler, and his pronounced Francophilia reflected the regional culture from whence he came. The elderly Adenauer gave form to the postwar CDU, expanding it from the exclusively Catholic Zentrumspartei of the Weimar era, in which Adenauer had once served, and building bridges to both Protestants and the Bavarian regionalists grouped in the CSU.

While Adenauer was a bridge-builder, he wore the mantle of German patriotism uneasily. He was willing to offer Germans expelled from Eastern Europe both rhetorical sympathy and subsidies. And he went along with the Hallstein Doctrine, which refused recognition to any country that recognized East Germany. (Although this practice remained in force from 1955 until 1969, it was contradicted by West Germany's establishing diplomatic relations with the Soviet Union within months of its introduction.)

But while the anti-German Left attacked Adenauer and his circle for being insufficiently contrite about the Nazi past (it is hard to see how Adenauer, given his hunted status under the Nazis, could have felt any personal contrition), it is impossible to portray this figure as a German nationalist. It was his adversary Kurt Schumacher, on the Left, who happily wore that label, before the Socialists in the late 1960s under Willy Brandt swerved in the opposite direction. Although from the standpoint of the present Social Democrats, as indicated by party historian Franz Walter, Schumacher "sent the wrong signals," there can be no doubt about his patriotic feelings.[194] Despite having spent the war years in a concentration camp in harrowing conditions (from which he never recovered), this Socialist academic pined for the lost independence of eastern Germany and accused Adenauer of closing the door on the possibility of negotiating German reunification. Contrary to the American view of the 1940s, that Schumacher was simply soft on the Soviets, he was actually brutally upfront about his welfare-state German nationalism, particularly in his diatribes against "the American prefects" in his own party and on Adenauer's side.

Until the Brandt takeover in 1969, Adenauer and his successors were decidedly internationalist, launching the EU, signing the Treaties of Rome, and subordinating German reunification to an American-led struggle against communism. What they were not, and what their successors would become, were single-mindedly "anti-fascist," fixed on destroying any moral justification for German patriotism and blindly pursuing internationalist projects as a moral imperative. For these undertakings, the 1970s left-of-center found a legal foundation in the Basic Law, which, as noted by Schüsslburner and Schrenck-Notzing, had an anti-national purport and whose authors were concerned chiefly with right-wing threats to the new constitutional order. The left-of-center German establishment had a readymade document for its work, without having to replicate the American judicial invention of a "living constitution."

THE CRISES OF DEMOCRACY

THE FACT THAT the Basic Law excludes referenda (or direct election of presidents) throws light on how the Socialist-Green coalition now in power can impose the EU constitution on their fellow Germans without having to consult the popular will. In Die Krisen der Demokratie (2002), Ralf Dahrendorf, a German sociologist who changed residence and now sits in the English House of Lords, notes how haunted the architects of the Grundgesetz were by the populist aspects of the Weimar constitution, which supposedly helped the Nazis find public endorsement for their work.[195] But Dahrendorf then observes that "Weimar is already in the distant past . . . Now many, including many liberal thinking people, believe that there are subjects about which one ought to ask the voters." Alas, these "fears" were overblown to start with. In Germany's last direct presidential race, in 1932, Hindenburg beat Hitler handily. Once in the driver's seat, the Nazis manipulated referenda (Volksentscheide), but such manipulation does not discredit a democratic practice that continues to be applied in American states (notably California) and in nations (such as Switzerland) without creating a Nazi dictatorship. Equally unconvincing, Schüsslburner explains, is the creation of a five-percent-of-the-vote "hurdle" that parties must reach in order to enter provincial or federal legislative bodies. Schüsslburner further notes that the actual hurdle may be closer to seven percent, since parties need at least that percentage in order for their candidates to look electable.

Many political scientists have assumed that the more proportionate representation for parties that existed under the Weimar constitution made it easier for the Nazis to increase their share of delegates. But a proportionate system without hurdles has operated elsewhere without this untoward effect. According to Schüsslburner, the Basic Law has moved Germany toward neither anarchy nor personal dictatorship, but the rotating rule of two monopolistic blocs, a lock hold that is protected by encouraging judges and Schützmänner to go after potential competitor parties as "extremist."

I read Dahrendorf's book, an extended conversation held with the Italian journalist Antonio Polito, in a highly fluent German translation. Despite the self-importance that comes through in Dahrendorf's references to his high-placed British friends, his membership in the House of Lords, and his self-attributed "liberal" *bien-pensance*, he does raise timely issues about the EU, the European nation-state, and judicially run government. He notes that there is a democracy deficit in the Union and that the European Parliament does not represent the interests and views of Europeans to the same degree as do traditional parliamentary representatives. There is a point of remoteness from the voter at which elected officials cease to speak for them, particularly when the Union's commissars, judges, and functionaries wield most of the actual power. Dahrendorf distinguishes between "liberalism" and "democracy" and acknowledges that nineteenth-century Prussia met the requirements of a "state under law." Despite its admittedly restricted practice of popular government, it was equipped with a generally impartial judiciary. He also grasps the fact that parliamentary blocs in today's Europe can establish a ruling monopoly that is almost impossible to break. And it is questionable whether this monopoly can be accurately described as democratic.

SOVEREIGN NATION-STATES

DAHRENDORF MIGHT HAVE done better in his interview not to work so hard as a spokesman for today's regnant form of liberal democracy. He views America's as possibly the best of all regimes "because it has functioned for over two centuries" as a responsive popular government. Clearly he misses the dramatic changes in the American government over the last century, particularly the steady progress toward administrative and judicial centralization. Dahrendorf quotes John Stuart Mill on the need for cultural and geographic dimensions in a nation-state, but then quickly reminds us that culture has nothing to do with ethnicity.

Rather it reflects "an unwritten value consensus among people living within a delimited space." He also questions Mill's assertion about "the mutual sympathy leading to cooperation" that defines nations, a predisposition often strengthened by a shared language: "The Swiss can contest this thesis with good reason. And the United States today is a greater land now than two hundred years ago, while Spanish has established itself as a second language."

In fact, most of those living in Switzerland speak German or Swiss-German as their first language; and except for the Muslim newcomers, who have added disproportionately to crime and welfare rolls,[196] almost all of the Swiss are Catholics or Calvinists—and therefore Christian. Moreover, before the Swiss Republic achieved its present degree of unity, which is now being politically challenged by anti-immigrationists, its cantons fought wars against each other for centuries. And the comment that America is a "greater land now" because of Hispanic immigration is too vague to mean anything. "Greater in what way?" might have been Polito's follow-up question.

Dahrendorf then inveighs against European regionalists, specifically Jörg Haider and Umberto Bossi, who "aim at ethnic homogeneity" and claim "rights of sovereignty for those living within particular borders in order to exclude minorities." Such behavior, "which has created havoc in Europe," causes states "to become intolerant of its minorities and to practice aggression against neighbors belonging to a different ethnic group." It is hard to see how Bossi's or Haider's attempt to limit immigration into their region, particularly in the case of uneducated third-worlders, will incite aggression against their neighbors. And why is it less "democratic" for a region to decide on who will be allowed to enter as new residents and eventually citizens than to consign such decisions to federal or international administrators and judges?

Equally unsettling is Dahrendorf's lack of historical understanding of nation-states. What distinguished the nation-state from the governing artifice that was Thomas Hobbes's new sovereign state was its ethnic, cultural, and religious specificity. Unlike a mere governing instrument, a nation-state has internal cohesion that sovereigns once favored in building stable relations among their subjects. Sovereign states in early modern Europe, and those that imitated their examples, featured established churches, national languages, and, if possible, ethnic homogeneity. One does not have to be an anti-immigration populist to grasp these historical facts. In the nineteenth century, the rising European bourgeoisie worked to establish parliamentary governments and liberal freedoms, particularly religious liberty, but also embraced nationalist ideas and promoted national literatures. Dahrendorf deplores any return to an ethnically related political identity and expresses fear that such a course would bring about "wars of conquest and suppression." Still, it is unclear that he is interested in nation-states or in actual democratic self-determination. As a self-exiled member of a humiliated and self-debased people, Dahrendorf wants heterogeneity and enforced tolerance for ideologically reconstructed European nation-states. Whether he is describing or denaturing these entities is another matter.

Others have deplored as a straitjacket what he celebrates. Thus Gianfranco Miglio (1918–2001), the famous jurist at the Catholic University of Milan and occasional adviser to the Northern League, explained that the national liberal aspirations of Italy's unifiers had not borne fruit either under Mussolini or in the bureaucratically suffocating *partitocrazia* in which Italy existed before and after fascism.[197] Miglio proposed a regional division of Italy, which allowed his fellow North Italian burghers to develop their own culture and economy and, above all, to control access to citizenship. Such an arrangement, he stressed, was consistent with the bourgeois nation-state that his progenitors had worked to bring about.[198] For Dahrendorf, such critical thinking has no place in a discussion about European governments but must lead to "the fragmentation of the world into aggressive and brutal ministates." One may be justified in raising doubts about this gloom-and-doom prediction.

The German Disease

Taki's Magazine

JULY 11, 2007

A DEBATE in the French weekly *Courrier International* (December 21, 2006) held between Polish political scientist Marek Cichocki and Claus Leggewie, a widely respected German professor at the University of Giessen, points to two diverging paths into the European future.[199] Both commentators explain how their views about the end of the Second World War have affected their visions of Europe. For Cichocki, a relatively young Pole of forty, his national identity and the memory of Soviet oppression are the shaping factors in his understanding of the history of his region. He also stresses the unbridgeable difference between Western Europeans who fret over fascist dangers and the historical consciousness of his own country. (Cichocki's most recent book, *Wladza I Pamiec* ["Power and Memory," 2005] deals precisely with this theme.)

While in Western Europe, particularly among obsessively guilt-ridden Germans, "European integration would be a systematic form of institutionalized security to prevent Nazi recidivism," Eastern Europeans, who had to contend with Soviet deportations and Stalinist concentration camps, have a less dated picture of the postwar past: "Since the countries on the other side of the Iron Curtain have been joining the European Union, this vision of integration as a response to Nazism does not suffice to create a sentiment of European cohesion." Indeed Eastern

Europeans are shocked by how little attention the politically correct leaders of the present European Union have bestowed on communist atrocities. "When in 2004 the Latvian Foreign Minister affirmed on German soil that communism was as criminal as Nazism, she aroused cries of indignation throughout Germany. It is undoubtedly for the same reason that when some Euro-deputies proposed in 2005 that the hammer and sickle should be treated the same way as the Swastika, their remarks elicited widespread jeers." Perhaps because of their sharper memories of the recent past, concludes Cichocki, Eastern Europeans, unlike their Western counterparts, have a high regard for national traditions, and they do not embrace the multicultural imperative of Western intellectuals and politicians. And "while the memory of the Eastern Europeans has been shaped by Nazi tyranny" (more than two and a half million Poles were killed by the Nazis during World War II), their history was also disastrously impacted by the more recent communist occupation. Any vision of Europe that "excludes" this experience and focuses on the imminent return of the now largely irrelevant Nazi enemy cannot make room for Eastern Europeans.

Leggewie's views, which contrast starkly to those of his Polish co-commentator, are in Germany so common that one would have to look there to what is imagined to be the "extreme Right" to find contrary opinions. As the former German Foreign Minister, Joschka Fischer, has stated multiple times, "Auschwitz is the founding myth of our German democracy." And in line with this morbid obsession, German Chancellor Angela Merkel, who in the international press is deceptively characterized as a "conservative," wants to use Germany's succession to the EU's presidency to impose on its members the speech controls that are the proud accomplishment of her country's managed democracy. (Pleading their nation's shame as an aggressor people, German politicians will not allow their countrymen to vote on the EU Constitution that would surrender what remains of German national sovereignty to the Union.) In Merkel's peculiar understanding of "democracy" as a way of life, any European "trivializing" the Holocaust will have to face criminal charges before an international tribunal. For those who celebrate our success in bringing the defeated Germans a "democratic political culture," it may be necessary to point out the difference between citizens of a republic and PC laboratory mice.

Leggewie seems taken aback that any right-thinking person would not be hot to trot for anti-fascist multiculturalism. Although admittedly "certain regions of Eastern Europe were occupied by Soviet troops even before the Nazi invasion as a result of the Soviet–Nazi pact," and while some might "minimize Stalinist terrorism by appealing to communism's objectives and humanitarian arguments," Leggewie is profoundly disturbed by the view that Nazi and communist genocides were equally evil. He brings up the charge that "those who wish to play on the memories of the Gulag overlook the conscious and unconscious acts of collaboration with national socialism committed by Stalin's victims." Moreover, the Spanish communist Jorge Semprún, a former inmate at Buchenwald, has wisely insisted that "European unity will only succeed on the existential and cultural level if we share and unify our memories." One can guess which set of memories Semprún would like to establish as the authorized ones for the EU. Furthermore, while communist misdeeds only affected "parts of Europe," "the use of the Holocaust as a negative founding myth for Europeans is plausible to the extent that anti-Semitism and fascism have been phenomena that have affected all of Europe." Once this tool is properly applied, "at the national and international levels, the Holocaust can provide an invaluable basis for European integration."

Leggewie's observations can only be justified by referring to the professional situation in his country: No one can obtain or hold a position at a major German university these days, and particularly in political science or history, who does not sound as outrageously stupid as he does. The depiction of Stalin's victims as Nazi collaborators, including "unconscious" ones, goes back to the Soviet propaganda of the 1930s, when those whom Stalin decided to kill, including Jewish Trotskyists, were routinely accused of being Hitler's collaborators. Does Leggewie believe (perhaps he does) that the Poles who fought the German invasion and were then occupied and brutalized by Stalin deserved what they got, because they had really supported Hitler? Or did the Balts deserve to lose at least a third of their population to death or deportation under Stalin because a minority of them might have collaborated with the Germans after their occupation by Hitler's Soviet allies in 1940? Only a robotized product of postwar German reeducation, often conducted by Stalinists, could say anything quite so repulsive.

And what kind of silly assertion is it that only isolated parts of Europe were affected by communist abuses? The same mystifying assertion, incidentally, was cited against my book *The Strange Death of Marxism* by a reviewer last year for the neo-Stalinist *Political Science Quarterly*.[200] In my right-wing zeal, I had apparently failed to notice that, in contrast to (an all-encompassing, mind-snatching) "fascism," Stalin's willing executioners were only found in certain carefully demarcated areas on the European mainland. This overlooks obvious facts.

West Germany in the 1950s and 1960s teemed with refugees who had fled or were driven from their homes by communist tyrants or by mobs whom these tyrants incited; the communists in France and Italy had gone on a rampage of murder and looting after the German Wehrmacht had been pushed out of their countries.

Finally, the Second World War, rather than ending with a "day of liberation" for Germans and everyone else but Nazi fanatics, as Leggewie announces, came in the midst of an orgy of killing and rapes, many committed by Soviet troops. The notion that communist atrocities were somehow more restricted in their scope or effect than those committed by the Nazis or generic "fascists" is sheer moonshine. But in German public life this concoction is to be found everywhere. In 2005, German Social Democratic Chancellor Gerhard Schröder had insisted on being invited to a celebration of VE Day, together with Germany's former enemies. There he belabored his listeners with counterfactual gushing expressions of gratitude for how the Allies "had won a victory for the Germans, and not against them." Leggewie no doubt would have applauded Schröder's masochistic performance if he had been on hand.

It is never made clear why normal people would gravitate toward Leggewie's "negative founding myth," which is also Merkel's and Fischer's. In Germany such mythologizing has worked because freedom and nationhood have been sacrificed on the altar of anti-national indoctrination; nonetheless, as Cichocki strongly suggests, not everyone in Europe wants to be like lobotomized Germans. Not all European nations would celebrate being told that they were historically and emotionally predisposed toward exterminating European Jewry, or would bestow honors on Daniel Goldhagen, Dan Diner, and other "Holocaust historians" for demanding their "unconditional atonement" and the dissolution of their national identity. For all the corruptness and rhetorical extravagance of their current conservative nationalist government, the Poles seem a mentally healthy people, unlike the new "sick man of Europe," which is no longer Turkey, as it was in the nineteenth century, but Germany.

A point that Cichocki and Leggewie both make is that "because of their different experience with communism" and their relative indifference to the cult of anti-fascism, Eastern Europeans have rallied to the Americans. Their observation is correct but has more to do with our role as an alternative to EU control than it does with our government's appeal to Eastern European identities. Our policies have in fact been to encourage the formation and strengthening of the EU and the use of public education in both Eastern and East Central Europe to foster anti-fascist, internationalist attitudes. The support of these liberated Eastern Europeans may be far more than we deserve, but we should make the most of the situation by teaching our allies to respect their national distinctiveness and above all, not to hand over their country to Islamic militants. Everything being equal, countries that respect their national identity and ancestral religion will outstrip the vanishing Germans in population replacement. (Germany's demographic replacement level, at 1.3, is one of the lowest in the world; and by 2025, if current trends continue, sixty-five out of every one hundred children born in Germany will have foreign, which means overwhelmingly Muslim, parents.) Although the Poles, who are now barely replacing themselves, could do better demographically, their self-respect as a nation would seem to be a positive factor in preparing them for their collective future. In any case Poles have not "enriched" themselves, to use the multiculti lingo, by importing an Islamic Third World population. The Bush administration may have it right for the wrong reasons when they describe Eastern Europe as the "New Europe." What makes this Europe, typified by the Poles "new," is not its dedication to "American democratic values" but the reemergence of its historic nations following the Soviet occupation. To the extent that these mostly Slavic peoples have not caught up with Western Europe, and particularly with Germany's experimental democracy, we should consider them fortunate.

The Eternal German Guilt Trip

Taki's Magazine

JANUARY 11, 2012

P OLITICAL CORRECTNESS has permeated the historian's craft to such a degree that honest historians must reinvent the wheel. PC has infected German history in particular. The doctrine of German "collective guilt" is often held as a precondition for German good behavior. Established historians in the United States, England, and especially Germany must assume their subjects' general wickedness since at least the 1871 unification. The German Republic's leading social theorist, Jürgen Habermas, has argued repeatedly that viewing Germans as less than responsible for all of modern European history's major catastrophes is "pedagogically dangerous."

Habermas seems unconcerned with what the father of modern technical history, Leopold von Ranke, gave as the historian's true function: describing the past "as it actually occurred." He is quite happy that Germans learn half-truths and even total fabrications, provided these make them aware of their sinfulness and therefore willing to atone. Such self-loathing will also make Germans eager to give up their tainted national identity and become members of a world community (whether or not one really exists). Certain untruths have an apparently salutary character, and all the major German political parties now accept Germany's sole responsibility for both World Wars and the positive role of Stalin's armies in "liberating" their country from "fascism."

Basic to this self-flagellation is having Auschwitz serve, in a former German Foreign Minister's words, as the "founding myth for the German Federal Republic." One must believe that not only did the Third Reich murder millions of Jews, but that Germans of all classes and regions happily cooperated. The most extreme form of this accusation is found in Daniel Jonah Goldhagen's *Hitler's Willing Executioners* (1997), released in Germany as *Hitlers Willige Vollstrecker* (1996). The book was a German bestseller despite its insubstantial or invented evidence, a fraud methodically dissected by Jewish critics Norman Finkelstein and Ruth Bettina Birn in *A Nation on Trial: The Goldhagen Thesis and Historical Truth* (1998). Still, Goldhagen conducted book tours among the descendants of those he indiscriminately trashed, bringing mass displays of smarmily repentant German sinners.

Not all books about what Germans supposedly knew about the Holocaust and what they did to assist it are as tacky as Goldhagen's work. The more respectable formulation of his thesis goes like this: The Nazi extermination of the Jews was an "open secret." No German administrator or military officer was supposed to know "state secrets" unless they pertained to his assigned function. While any violation of this restriction would be met with severe punishment, the secret was not as well kept as Germans would have their conquerors believe. Jews could not have been removed, we are told, without their non-Jewish neighbors knowing they would suffer a horrendous fate wherever they were taken.

The now received view preaches that there was anti-Semitism in Germany going back many centuries. It notes that in the interwar period, nationalist parties urging the exclusion of Jewish citizens received many votes. There is something else that anti-German historians now emphasize but which they may exaggerate: the occasional breakdown of the distinction between the Waffen SS Einsatzgruppen—which rounded up and murdered Jews, Poles, and Russians—and Wehrmacht soldiers who were simply fighting a war.

Just about every Anglophone historian writing on the Third Reich is now arguing that the Holocaust was mostly the work of regular German soldiers. The complaint of "Holocaust minimizers"—that the numbers of prisoners killed in death camps has been inflated—now seems acceptable. But historians such as Tim Snyder and Richard J. Evans have turned the argument around: It wasn't necessary to transport Jews to death camps to kill them because so many soldiers were rushing to do the dirty work. They depict the Holocaust as a public-works project, fueled by sympathy for Hitler's "Final Solution."

This view has become so prevalent among anti-fascist Germans (there is no other kind now permitted) that in public demonstrations and lavish exhibitions the average Wehrmacht soldier has been turned into the major perpetrator of Nazi murders. On these occasions young people come forth to tell us that their grandfathers or great-grandfathers were most certainly mass murderers. These penitent descendants seem to hope their ancestral nation will soon disappear.

It is against this background of lunacy that Alfred de Zayas, a retired high official from the UN Commission for Human Rights, has released *Völkermord als Staatsgeheimnis* ("Genocide as a State Secret," 2011). Zayas has authored other controversial works that go against the prevalent leftist grain. Among his earlier studies are heavily documented examinations of Eastern Europeans' organized murders of *Volksdeutsche* (ethnic Germans) after the Second World War, as well as the postwar agreements that greased the skids for these crimes. Zayas's works are all painstakingly documented, and his latest study is based on thirty-five years of interviews and a laborious sifting of sources. The author fine-combed the records and testimonies of the Nuremberg Trials in 1946–47 and interviewed surviving "war criminals" including Albert Speer and Admiral Karl Dönitz, the Nuremberg prosecutors, and former war prisoners of the Nazis.

Records from the Wehrmacht Office for the Investigation of Violations of International Law indicate an official willingness to investigate reported crimes against civilians. There is nothing to suggest that these investigators knew about Hitler's Final Solution. When they received reports about "unwarranted" shootings of civilians in occupied areas, they prosecuted the offenders. Even the judges assigned to the Waffen SS were often in the dark about the Einsatzgruppen's mission, and sometimes they launched inquiries into reports about mass murders taking place in the east. Even the regime's enemies—ranging from anti-Nazi aristocrats associated with the Resistance, to persecuted Social Democrats (such as the partly Jewish family of former Chancellor Helmut Schmidt), and even former concentration-camp inmates—had no idea of the Final Solution. According to the official story, Jews were being "relocated" and would be employed in "work divisions" outside Germany. Although this forced evacuation caused some concern among friends and neighbors, what was happening did not look like the beginning of genocide.

The most obvious reason for this is that secrecy was strictly observed. The Holocaust was planned by a small circle meeting outside Berlin in January 1942. In addressing his SS subordinates in Posen in 1943, Himmler boasted about how well their secret was being kept. Other factors worked to keep the secret from getting out: The death camps, as opposed to generic concentration camps, were located in the east, not in Germany. Then from 1943 on, German civilians were subject to Allied bombing and had to protect themselves while enemy forces overran them. In this situation it was unlikely that a war-weary German would wonder about a "relocated" Jewish neighbor's fate.

Even foreign sources, which were mostly available as radio transmissions, had little to say about the murdered Jews, and being caught using these sources could land the offender in a concentration camp. Germans who found out about the murders couldn't do much to stop them, since divulging the secret to a government official could be deadly.

Ironically, Zayas confirms findings about the Holocaust that came out of the Nuremberg Trials. Although these trials were planned to make Germans feel ashamed of their country, the judges did not declare all Germans to be complicit in the Holocaust. It was assumed that the mass extermination of Jews was a carefully guarded secret. Very few of those put on trial were sentenced to death or to long imprisonment for planning to murder Jews. Even the prosecutors believed what Zayas tells us concerning knowledge of the Final Solution. Admittedly there were isolated instances of Wehrmacht units participating in the shooting of Jews and other civilians, particularly in Kharkov and elsewhere in the Ukraine. But those were treated as special cases and not seen as typical of Wehrmacht behavior.

It speaks volumes that Zayas—who echoes the postwar, Nuremberg Trial view of who knew what about the Holocaust—is now regarded in some circles as a German apologist. From the warped perspective of today's German intelligentsia, their country's postwar humiliation can never go far enough.

Germany, Harbinger of the Abyss

Chronicles

MARCH 2022

INIS GERMANIA (2017) is a posthumous collection of melancholy writing by German ecologist and sometime academic Rolf Peter Sieferle, who took his own life in despair in 2016.[201] Sieferle regretted the disappearance of a recognizably Western civilization and deplored the likely ecological effects of a European continent thrown open to almost unrestricted Third World immigration.

The book's publisher, Götz Kubitschek, has been recently declared a "right-wing extremist" by Germany's internal secret police service, the Bundesamt für Verfassungsschutz (BfV) (Federal Office for the Protection of the Constitution), and his publishing house, Antaios, has been smeared as a far-right propaganda publisher. Kubitschek's heroic efforts to reach the German public with Sieferle's work produced an underground bestseller, despite the decision of Germany's anti-fascist government and its even more anti-fascist national media to tar *Finis Germania* with a fascist brush.

There is nothing fascist or neo-Nazi about Sieferle's writings or his thoughts about Germany's immigration problems. In fact, in assessing

Germany's situation, Sieferle shows a more advanced example of the same trend that is going on here in America.

The enthusiastic reception of millions of barely identified "migrants" into Germany was the established practice under the government of Angela Merkel. Unfortunately, the recent replacement of Merkel's rule by an even more woke Green Social Democracy coalition will undoubtedly accelerate immigration trends. It will also result in the BfV going on a binge of investigating lots more German citizens as extremists and threats to the country's democratic system. Of course, the present German regime is only technically "democratic." In reality, it is a grotesque anti-fascist dictatorship that is explicitly and unapologetically anti-German.

Germany's president, Frank-Walter Steinmeier, was recently elected to a second term by the German parliament. Steinmeier's forte, as far as I can determine, is trashing his country and its people everywhere on the planet. In his speeches, Steinmeier heaps attacks on his countrymen for having unilaterally unleashed every major European war during the last 150 years. It also seems, according to Steinmeier, that anti-Semitism is as much a threat now in Germany as it was when the Nazis were sending Jews to concentration camps. If Germans do suffer from *Sündenstolz* (a tendency to revel in listing their sins), Steinmeier embodies that masochistic spirit, even if he habitually places himself above his sinful nation.

Recently this crusader for democracy gave an inauguration address in which he declared himself the friend of all democrats, not someone who will tolerate the enemies of democracy. From the context, it was clear that Steinmeier was designating as his anti-democratic foe whoever opposed the COVID mandates and mask-wearing imposed on Germany's population. Any disagreement with this self-appointed custodian of the cult of democracy, it would appear, constitutes an anti-democratic act.

On the 150th anniversary of the founding of Germany as a unified nation-state, Steinmeier made a sharp distinction between Germany and other European nations. While other countries presumably enjoy peaceful founding rituals, the Germans forged their nationhood through conflict (*Kriegsgründung*). This made Germany's founding something we should not be celebrating but loudly lamenting as a catastrophe.

One wonders whether *Herr Präsident* ever studied the history of any country but his own and whether he undertook the study of German history with anyone but raging Germanophobes. Almost every nation-state, including the American republic, was established through a clash of arms. In that respect, Germany's founding was no different from that of other European countries; and it was quite similar to that of Italy, which was formed about the same time after a series of military actions.

The kind of tirades that Canadian Prime Minister Justin Trudeau recently unleashed on striking Canadian truckers is the everyday rhetoric employed by German government leaders as they tear into those who disagree with them. Those who object to what the leftist German regime is doing may end up being more than just a rhetorical punching bag. They may also be spied on by the BfV and then prosecuted as a danger to the German democratic order.

If the critic is a public employee, he may also lose his post. A German former public servant, Martin Wagener, fired for his undemocratic candor, wrote a detailed account of how the BfV has gone rogue in the last quarter of the twentieth century. In *Kulturkampf um das Volk* ("The People's Culture War," 2021), Wagener writes how BfV President Thomas Haldenwang has corrupted the bureau into a political instrument in the hands of the woke Left.[202] Although the BfV has followed the same general path as American surveillance agencies, it is even better positioned to defame and professionally destroy those whom government leaders target.

Ever since Merkel's accession to power, a continuing objective in Germany has been the "struggle against the right," a crusade which the federal government generously finances and which Haldenwang in his politically slanted investigations steadily assists. Wagener shows how this crusade can count on the combined assistance of the BfV, multiple LGBT organizations, pro-immigration pressure groups, and the national media. Not surprisingly, this campaign rarely confronts right-wing terrorists. The mission is weaponized, rather, against any group or political leader who is more patriotic than Germany's anti-national political leaders and/or whose presence annoys them. Any German who describes himself as wanting to preserve his nation, expresses reservations about gay marriage, fails to support COVID restrictions, or questions the official anti-German narrative about its national past may run into the government's crosshairs.

The only party that has frontally challenged this arrangement is the Alternative für Deutschland (AfD). An outcast party, the AfD has positioned itself programmatically where the Christian Democrats used to be, about fifty years ago. Anyone known to belong to this party or suspected of voting for it may be removed from an academic post or from the state bureaucracy. The BfV investigates members of the AfD as extremists, with far more thoroughness than it typically uses in cases of

Islamist violence. No other national party will even deal with the ostracized AfD.

The situation in Germany is far more hopeless than that of North America, which still has a large vocal opposition to the leftist ruling class; the Germans don't. Sieferle might have been correct when he concluded there was no way back from the abyss toward which Germany was rushing. His somber predictions include a scene from Berlin as he pictured the German capital two hundred years hence. Indigenous Germans are no longer found there because they failed to reproduce. Instead, rival Muslim gangs, whose ancestors had been Third World migrants, fight over war zones. Friend-enemy relations survived but no longer include white Europeans, who have disappeared, leaving the field open to more virile and prolific ethnicities. Berlin and the rest of Germany have sunk into ecological ruin, since their new inhabitants don't care about preserving the environment.

No wonder these frightening pictures of what lay ahead for his country and the rest of Western Europe drove Sieferle to despair.

For two obvious reasons the Germans will have problems avoiding the future Sieferle envisions. One, anti-fascist indoctrination is more ingrained among Germans than among the citizens of most other Western countries. This mindset began with the Allied occupation after World War II and was advanced through strenuous efforts to reconstruct the national psyche. During the early phases of the Cold War, particularly under the guidance of Germany's first postwar Chancellor, Konrad Adenauer, the theme of "overcoming the German past"—which meant the Nazi, or fascist, past—was broadened to include "totalitarian" threats to the democratic constitutional order.

Under German Basic Law, introduced in 1949 and written under close Allied supervision, it became the duty of German citizens, once they were democratically reeducated, to protect human rights for the sake of humanity, while special agencies like the BfV were created to oppose threats to German democracy.

In the early years of the Federal Republic, the designated enemy was totalitarianism, which pertained to Soviet agents and pro-communist "anti-fascists" as well as neo-Nazis. After the Sixty-Eighters rose to power, and after the German government's leftward lurch in the early 1970s, anti-fascism replaced anti-totalitarianism as the German state religion. This designation of the universal enemy has remained since then. By the time Merkel, a former East German communist with fervent communist parents, arrived at the chancellorship as a Christian Democrat, significant opposition to the government's leftward march was waning. Already in 1998, onetime anti-fascist terrorist leader Joschka Fischer became German Foreign Minister and later Vice-Chancellor. Fischer's past career as a bomb-throwing radical hardly caused waves in Germany or in the international media.

More recently, the current woke coalition appointed as Minister of the Interior Nancy Faeser, who, just before her appointment, published an incendiary tear in the appropriately named magazine *Antifa*. Quite predictably, the international media attributed this "rumor" to the "far right weekly" *Junge Freiheit*, which broke the story. In an interview with the newspaper's editor, I made the point that after Joschka Fischer turned his bomb-throwing past into political success, there was no way that Faeser would not benefit from her far-left association. Germans have moved beyond the double standard that we complain about in this country. There is only one standard among them. Violence and terrorism are fine, providing they come from self-described anti-fascists.

The second reason the Germans will have problems avoiding the future Sieferle envisions is that the German anti-fascist Left, which has moved into a particularly self-destructive form of wokeness, has not encountered critical resistance because most Germans happily embrace it. And this may be the main difference between what we're seeing in America, or even in Canada, and what is occurring in Germany. In the recent German federal elections, most of the votes went to the woke, anti-fascist Left. The only parties that even by our present minimal standards could be regarded as conservative, the Freidemokraten and the AfD, gained less than twenty-two percent of the vote. And since the last federal election in 2017, Merkel's CDU-CSU union lost 8.8 percentage points to parties further to the Left.

Even though it was clear at the time that government agencies were bearing down hard on groups that were perceived as "nationalist" or vocally unhappy about the extensive lockdowns, when the election came, the Germans voted for more of the same, served up by a more extreme anti-fascist Left. It's not as if the voters had no choice. In the privacy of the voting booth, they could have opted for the only party that would have tried to end the drift into leftist totalitarianism. They also could have voted to approach the abyss more slowly, at the speed of the previous administration.

But most Germans, being Germans, are profoundly conformist, and chose to put themselves even more closely in sync with woke opinion. Although Germany's intellectual Right, whose members have suffered grievously for their convictions, does possess a more serious and more principled conservatism than that now prevalent in America, it also has no power and its influence is severely restricted.

Only last week I discovered an illuminating book on anti-fascism by the distinguished German historian Antonia Grunenberg, *Antifaschismus: ein deutscher Mythos* ("Antifascism: A German Myth," 1993).[203] Her book clarifies the links between the invention of the word "anti-fascism" and the history of postwar Germany. She traces how the present concept developed from the East German communist manipulation of the operative term, underscoring how deeply German thinking was marked by the communist Left.

I'm relieved to learn that another historian writing in the early 1990s was as struck as I still am by this morbid German fixation. Still, no matter how much an earlier anti-fascism was made to serve an unpleasant dictatorship, anti-fascism's woke version may be socially even more pernicious. It combines Marxist-Leninist coercion with a war on human nature. What's more, it's now arrived in our living space here in America.

CHAPTER EIGHT

The Death of the WASP

– ◆ ◆ ◆ –

Sinful WASPs

National Observer

2008

M Y TOPIC for this article is the relevance of secularism for understanding our political situation, which is the one that is now dominant in Canada, the United States, and much of the Western world. Underlying this investigation are two assumptions about what secularism is or is not. One, it is not clear that secularism in the contemporary West is an entirely post-Christian phenomenon. Although secularists are committed to removing traditional Christian icons and phraseology from public life, e.g., substituting neutered "Happy Holidays" or the black festival of Kwanzaa for any mention of Christmas, the secularist alternatives nonetheless incorporate discernible Christian residues. What my books describe as the "politics of shame," that is, the public and often state-sponsored attachment of a special stigma to one's nation or race for past discrimination against other groups, is by no means a worldwide development. It is mostly limited to Northern European Protestant societies. In England, Germany, and Canada, the administrative and cultural elites impose the politics of outreach on the majority populations. They require their citizens to exhibit toward exotic and even threatening designated minorities a degree of sensitivity they need not and perhaps should not extend to their own tribe.

An enthusiastic Protestant of the political Left, Jimmy Carter, may be overstating the appeal of his ideas when in the foreword to *The*

Great Awakening (2008), authored by another Christian of the social Left, Jim Wallis, he writes that this book is helping us to "tap the power of the revival of faith in order to inspire and encourage the secular social reforms espoused in all the great religions."[204] The "secular social reforms" that Carter has in mind sprang from a Western religious tradition, and the mindset that marks him and Wallis is recognizably Protestant.

While Western Christians in their societies are typically punished for sexist and religious discrimination, incoming Muslims are usually allowed to do what Christians are forbidden to do. There is a willingness on the part of English, German, and Canadian authorities to be indulgent about Islamic abuse of women, and this has gone so far that there is talk at the highest levels of government in some predominantly Protestant countries of institutionalizing Islamic social practices, as the accepted legal framework for Muslim communities. The reason for this double standard, I would argue, is not that Christians have ceased to be religious in any sense. Their religion has mutated into social guilt and acts of public confession focusing on the supposedly ultimate evil of prejudice. In the United States this kind of behavior has taken clear forms. While the plainly Christian festival of Christmas is giving way in universities and public administration to a generic holiday season, the birthday of the black civil rights advocate, Martin Luther King, on January 21, is now the only national holiday in the United States dedicated to a national hero.

King's birthday has also become invested with Christological associations. Our national media and our politicians stress his martyr's death (at the hands of an assassin while leading a garbage-worker's strike in Memphis, Tennessee); and while it is considered in *The New York Times* a form of art, worthy of public financing, to depict Christ suspended in urine, anyone who would portray MLK with less than iconic reverence, reminiscent of medieval depictions of Christ, would be ruined professionally and socially. Recently, *US News and World Report* noted that, for Americans between the ages of eighteen and twenty-eight, Martin Luther King is viewed as "the most respected person in human history." Oprah Winfrey places fifth, well ahead of Jesus. In his best-selling collection of political sermons, *God's Politics* (2006), Jim Wallis rejoices that his son Luke attends a school where "the teacher made so much of black history month in February. Luke is now getting the same things in school that we teach him at home—books about Martin Luther King and the civil rights movement . . . At the end of black history month, Luke announced to his parents, 'I am going to be just like Dr. Martin

Luther King Jr., except I will have a different name and a different skin.' Of course, nothing could have pleased his mom and dad more." Not surprisingly, there is nothing in Wallis's book to suggest that Luke had ever been exposed to the Bible, except possibly in the context of his father's advocacy of particular social programs. Nor can one say that Christianity's founder receives in *God's Politics* the same degree of awe as the assassinated King. Jesus seems to move through this work like an errant social worker or like a blogger on an anti-war, anti-Bush website.

King's birthday comes at the beginning of another key event in our new liturgical calendar, black history month, which is followed by another monthlong showcasing of what is presented as an epic struggle against prejudice, this one dedicated to women. Needless to say, women's month does not center on motherhood, a condition that earlier revolutionary liturgical calendars, such as the one in communist Russia, paid honor to. Instead, we are urged to praise such women as Betty Friedan and Susan B. Anthony, both feminists who prepared women for the gender revolution that our current public administration continues to promote.

A sign on the Pennsylvania Turnpike put up by the National Organization of Women explains that many women had to give their lives for the right to vote. Contrary to this false assertion intended to build a postmodern church on the bones of martyrs, no American woman, as far as I know, ever gave her life to extend to other women the right to vote. The extension of the franchise was the work of men; furthermore, in the American South and in the Midwest, it enjoyed the support of nativist men, who favored extending the suffrage to their Anglo-Saxon wives to offset the political influence of Latin and Slavic immigrants.

We are also occasionally made to celebrate civic saints who perform double duty, such as Harriet Tubman, a black woman who smuggled slaves from Southern plantations into Northern states in the Antebellum era. (Ms. Tubman, by the way, is rated in second place in the survey results in *US News and World Report*.) Another Christian-post-Christian saint is Eleanor Roosevelt, who had the advantage of far-left political affiliations and who was once an advocate of "women's rights." Mrs. Roosevelt is someone who enjoys considerable attention during women's month. But her hagiography ignores the fact that she tirelessly campaigned for a single-family wage, one that would keep women out of the workplace and which would allow husbands to provide food and housing for the mothers of their children. This single-family wage, which feminists in the United States have attacked as a male sexist creation, was the paramount goal of American feminists through the early twentieth century. It was long seen by such champions of women as Mrs. Roosevelt and Frances Perkins as necessary for the protection of women who wished to be mothers and homemakers.

Although I am in no sense an apologist for the horrible crimes committed by the Nazi regime, a wave of terror that claimed members of my family, there is something noteworthy and not entirely pleasing about how Germans obsess over their unequalled historical nastiness. This Teutonic fixation has taken two forms, frenetically extending Nazi-like behavior or portents of the Third Reich to the entire course of German history and taking inordinate delight in any threat to a continued German national existence. Only Germans would organize large mass demonstrations to applaud the firebombing of helpless German civilians in Hamburg and Dresden during the closing months of World War II. Furthermore, one could not imagine any other nation that would create "anti-national" movements in the tens of thousands devoted to destroying, as soon and thoroughly as possible, the remnants of their already battered identity as a people. The proud observation by Germany's past Foreign Minister Joschka Fischer that "Auschwitz ist der Gründungsmythos der BRD" is only the preliminary first step for German political officials and educators playing up their country's special burden. This collective self-abasement, which requires among other things that German historical studies always blame Germans for all international strife, even when both sides seem to have been responsible, is so pronounced that one has to be non-sighted not to notice this eccentricity.

But here too we are dealing with something that is culturally specific. Shintoist Japanese do not beat their breasts because Japanese soldiers in the 1930s committed murder and mayhem against the Chinese and other Southeast Asians. Nor does the Eastern Orthodox Church exhort the Russian people to ask the world's forgiveness for Soviet Russian crimes. After all, it was the former Russian government that murdered even more people than the Nazis. Moreover, when the Poles were charged with having killed more than a million Germans and having expelled at least that number from those territories they occupied after World War II, their leaders explained that the Germans had it coming because they were all Nazis.

When the descendants of Polish Jews in America complained that the Poles had actively cooperated with the Nazis to get rid of Poland's Jewish population, Polish historians insisted these charges were overblown. Indeed, the Polish-American historian Marek Chodakiewicz, who works at the World Institute of Politics, produced a hefty monograph on this very topic, *After the Holocaust: Polish-Jewish*

Relations in the Wake of World War II (2003). Chodakiewicz, whose work has been translated and widely distributed in Poland, demonstrates that the Polish situation in the years he treats was far more complicated than Poland's critics would recognize. Germans and Russians had invaded Poland simultaneously, and while some of the Jewish population fought with the Polish resistance, other Jews offered their support to the Soviets. In the subsequent struggle between Stalin and the Polish freedom-fighters, those Jews and others who backed the Eastern invader were looked upon as enemies. Chodakiewicz also notes that an infamous attack on the Jewish population in Kiele in 1946 was probably the work of Soviet agents. When the Soviets took over postwar Poland, they stirred up incidents in order to marginalize their Polish opponents as "Nazis."

But an equally suspect occurrence, the defacing of Jewish tombstones in Cologne in 1959, an act that had Stasi East German fingerprints all over it and which came during a delicate crisis in East-West relations, was not viewed with comparable doubt. German intellectuals, journalists, and educators used the occasion to condemn the German people for not having faced their past. This act of desecration unleashed a series of laws and demonstrations that went on for decades, and whose effects are reflected in German public discourse, about the "unsubdued German past."

But here too a distinction must be drawn between German Protestants and German Catholics. The prolonged fits of guilt and masochistic confessions that go with the politics of shame are far more characteristic of German Protestants than of their Catholic fellow citizens. Ever since the Evangelical Church of Germany issued its first Declaration of Guilt in October 1945, its spokespersons have been taking responsibility on behalf of their people for every political misfortune in which a German government was involved. These self-condemnations now extend from Nazism back to the First World War, and from there to Bismarck and Frederick the Great, all the way back to Luther's unkind references to Jews in his *Table Talk* (1566). And even before the Germans became a recognizable nation, there were the Crusades that contemporary Germans are still gnashing their teeth over. These periodic bloodbaths during the Middle Ages are blamed exclusively on the West, and this one-sided blame is heard now in Western Europe as well as the Muslim world. Since the 1990s, moreover, the self-accusations of the German Evangelical Church have been ample enough to encompass the now widely mentioned problem of xenophobia. The lack of a welcoming attitude toward Third World immigrants, German Protestants are told, is a sickness of the soul, indeed a very grave one that the bishop of Berlin-Brandenburg attributes to the residual toxin of German nationalism. Presumably, his congregants will have to work harder not to notice the soaring crime rate among Muslim youth in the Berlin suburbs.

Such self-incrimination is far less obvious among Catholic dignitaries even in Germany. For example, Karl Cardinal Lehmann of Mainz has scolded the Muslims in his country for their intolerance of Christians and their deplorable treatment of their wives and daughters. Unlike the Evangelical bishop of Berlin, Wolfgang Huber, and his fellow Protestant churchman, the Archbishop of Canterbury, Lehmann, like other German and Austrian Catholic dignitaries, has opposed bringing Islamic law to onetime Christian countries. Another critical distinction may be called for before proceeding further: although American Catholics often favor Latin American immigration and vote for left-of-center political parties more typically than American Protestants, their clergy are less inclined than mainline Protestants to dwell on Political Correctness. This is a point that Thomas C. Reeves has little trouble showing in his book *Empty Church* (1996).

And, even more relevant, it is hard to find in Catholics the religious motivation for social guilt that has become increasingly characteristic of Protestants. It might be said that while Catholics more frequently than Protestants support the Left in the United States, Canada, and England, they do not do so because they are religiously driven. They are embracing their position because they believe themselves (or their ancestors) to have suffered under a Protestant majority. Equally important, they do not view themselves in most cases as applying religious principles, and certainly not Christian ones, to public life. It is not unusual to encounter young or even middle-aged Catholics, who say that they personally believe that "abortion is homicide"; still these respondents don't want to force their views (or at least not those particular views) on anyone else. Such a stand is so laden with contradiction (presumably such bearers of tolerance would have no trouble sticking down someone else's throat the latest wrinkle of feminist dogma) that one is forced to infer that those things that do not really matter to the speaker are precisely the ones to be tolerated and even state-subsidized. What is irrelevant here in any case is a traditional religious conscience, which does not usually explain why Catholics are to be found on the cultural or multicultural Left.

But the Protestant case is different. Protestant teachings and habits have played a crucial role in creating and popularizing the politics of shame. Meditations on one's fallen state, attempts to distinguish the righteous from the sinful, and public declarations of collective remorse as signs of one's election are, in the United States, the traits of a traditional Protestant culture, and all of these traits can be found in our mainline churches. These are institutions whose leadership has been sliding for decades toward the multicultural Left, and a vast literature, including studies by Thomas E. Reeves, Wade Clark Roof, Stanley Hauerwas, and Paul Wilkes, underscore how far-reaching the effects of this tendency have been. The most damning study of it (which I sedulously consulted for my book on multiculturalism) is a work by Barry A. Kosmin and Seymour P. Lachman, *One Nation Under God* (1993). In this book the theological disintegration of the American Protestant mainline is related to other unsettling developments, and most especially to the continuing economic and professional decline among establishment Protestant church members relative to members of other confessions. One leaves *One Nation Under God* with a strong sense that its Protestant subjects have not done well by any socioeconomic measure since they espoused their present beliefs.

A process similar to the one described in these books went on among Protestant leaders and spokesmen in the early and mid-twentieth century. Back then it took the forms of bewailing imperialism and engaging in Communist fellow-traveling. Thus we had the spectacles of such Protestant clergyman as Hewlett Johnson, Dean of Canterbury in the 1940s, and the Congregationalist chaplain at Yale, William Sloane Coffin, in the 1960s making jubilant pilgrimages to Communist states or extolling African socialist dictators. Now we find another version of Western self-rejection, in forms that are at least partly motivated by religious impulses. For evidence of this new Protestant fashion the reader is referred to Jim Wallis's books, which provide a certain theological justification for the latest "secular social reforms."

But Wallis and his clerical devotees reject the idea of pushing radical politics as an explicitly Christian public activity. They are more than willing to hail secularism as the fulfillment of Christian piety. Wallis also extends an invitation to impoverished Third World populations to "enrich" our own geographical space. No longer do supposedly enlightened Protestants expiate their collective sins by visiting and praising left-wing dictatorships across the globe. Instead they try to rebuild their society by "welcoming" foreigners. If the American working class recoils from this Christian imperative, Wallis explains in *The Great Awakening*, the reason is "economic insecurity." But this is not the fault of illegal immigrants but of "national economic policy, the morally flawed budgets, and the lack of living wages from huge corporations." Apparently,

Wallis has never discovered that "huge corporations" and their defenders at *The Wall Street Journal* have been in the forefront of those demanding amnesty for illegal residents in the United States. Cheap labor in the case of big business easily trumps "xenophobia."

Note the term "one's group" is not an entirely accurate description of what the Protestant secularists wish to free the Western world from. His or her group also includes the once invisible saints, who are now making their presence known through public contrition and outpourings of social guilt. The majority Christian population that does not stand in this saintly company belongs to an unredeemed xenophobic world, one that deserves to perish as the final age of global citizenship is imagined to be approaching. The solemn renunciation by the saints of public recognition of Christianity, a habit that is thought to "make the other feel uncomfortable," is viewed as a very modest step in the war against Western small-mindedness. No reciprocity is, of course, demanded from the other side, which "enriches" by merely being present on one's soil.

Let me point out that what I have sketched is the set of religious attitudes that I encounter in my daily workplace. Every day I meet there the people I have just evoked, as a professor at a German Pietist college, which still bears the imprint of its founding. Not surprisingly, the Christian core of this college has given way to a "Center for Global Citizenship," and the pronouncements coming from the president's office celebrate diversity and internationalism as expressive of the "school's traditional religious mission." When the remaining clergy on campus are asked whether this secularist mission really embodies their beliefs, my question never fails to occasion wonder. It seems foolish that I would even be asking.

In a certain sense, I am witnessing the fulfillment of the prophecy found in a book that created a splash when I was in graduate school in the mid-1960s, Harvey Cox's *The Secular City* (1965). This widely read analysis of Protestant outreach, which was also a statement of the deepest conviction of the author, a Harvard professor of theology, viewed the alleged secularization of his confession as a sign of its triumph. Cox's view is that secularists are on the right track when they try to wean Americans away from their "unhealthy reliance" on a God figure. In order to achieve the kind of social progress that the Bible "hints at," we must first become "true humans," and this means that we must abandon the childish doctrines taught by organized religion over the centuries.

Such opinions are not only widespread in today's theology departments, as a profusion of critical literature and the testimony of many divinity schools would reveal. They also point to a specifically Protestant path into secularism, which must be distinguished from other paths leading away from traditional religious beliefs. Although these paths leading to secularism occasionally intertwine, they are nonetheless different from each other. Muslim religious sceptics are more likely to become Arab nationalists than they are to become advocates of massive immigration and cultural mixing. It is also inconceivable that Third World secularists would expend energy apologizing to other nations and national minorities whom their peoples once hurt or offended. As far as I can ascertain, there is no Buddhist or Hindu politics of guilt, and to the extent that such flora has taken root among Christians, it generally thrives best, although not exclusively, in secularizing Protestant societies.

Let me close by calling attention to what I am not saying. I do not mean to suggest that Northern European Protestants and their North American counterparts have never acted badly in their history. Demonstrably they have, as have other groups to at least the same extent. Moreover, Western Protestant societies have expressed deep remorse over their misdeeds, including exaggerated or invented ones, against other groups. And unlike most of the rest of the world, they have tried to make amends for past wrongs. They have also made available to the rest of humanity the fruits of their economic productivity, high health standards, educational institutions, and aid to underdeveloped areas. But in addition to doing nice things, they have made a fetish out of beating up on their ancestors and viewing their civilization as more sinful than the rest of the human race. And this tic has become more noticeable the farther one moves historically from what is being deplored. The self-incrimination is always expanding in content; and it now includes even such normal human practices as drawing gender distinctions or preferring heterosexual to homosexual family units.

Finally, I am not condemning the fathers of the Protestant Reformation or traditional Protestant theology for the derailments I have focused on. Luther, Zwingli, Cranmer, and Calvin had nothing to do with what others did to their ideas hundreds of years later, for reasons that no one in the sixteenth or seventeenth century could have possibly foreseen. What we are dealing with is a twisting of what my friend Grant Havers calls the obligation of "charity" into something very different, and the appeal to a distinctly non-metaphysical guilt in order to generate a total commitment on the part of the believer to a faith substitute. What allows this development to occur are forces that did not exist until well into the modern era, e.g., the identification of justice and charity with equality and the treatment of any historic inequality permitted by Western Christian societies as evidence of their wickedness. Because of their stress on the equality of all believers, their heightened sense of individuality, and their tendency to brood on sin as an existential condition, Protestants have been at special risk to succumb to certain modern political temptations. But the emphasis here should be placed on the word "modern," lest we anachronistically ascribe the weakness discussed to those in the distant past. My interest is in showing how old habits of thinking can be made to serve current ideological practices. This should be distinguished from indulging in the now-widespread practice of sitting in perpetual judgment over the past.

The Politics of Guilt

Taki's Magazine

AUGUST 27, 2009

R ECENTLY WHILE talking to a "moderate" conservative and faithful *National Review* reader, I was struck by this person's profoundly negative view of the past, including the recent past. When I mentioned research by Thomas Sowell in the late 1970s proving that American blacks had made greater economic strides in the 1930s and 1940s than in the 1960s or 1970s, my acquaintance responded by saying that no economic gain is as important as the fact that blacks can now vote in large numbers. When I then proceeded to cite a study that suggested that women were happier in the 1950s than they seem to be now, the retort was that women in the 1950s had no right to be happy. They were forced to be homemakers and were still restricted in their career opportunities. This reminded me of a column of George Will's that appeared in *Newsweek* during the presidential primaries in 1992. It was an attack on Pat Buchanan for having said that he was happy to have grown up during the Eisenhower era. Such a statement, according to Will, indicated gross insensitivity to blacks, who were then being segregated and kept from voting in many parts of America.

There are two observations that I would like to make about what is now the established view of the past, including the age in which Buchanan, Will, and I all grew up.

One, talking about politics and history is rarely "scientific" and less so in our frenetically progressive and anti-traditional age than in the older bourgeois age that preceded it. It was once possible for the devoutly Lutheran German historian Leopold von Ranke to write about the Renaissance Papacy with detachment and even sympathy, because historians in nineteenth-century Europe were expected to write that way. (Of course, in practice not all historians met such a demanding standard, but at least they knew what the standard was.) In our age, by contrast, any failure to dwell on sexism, racism, anti-Semitism, and homophobia in one's account of the past will likely result in the kind of career that I and other academic mavericks of my acquaintance have had to endure.

Curiously, as cultural Marxist fixations have taken over universities and commercial presses, the word "scientific" continues to be attached to all things good and sensitive. For twenty years I have taught in a "political science" department, in which "science" is rarely taught. Most of my colleagues are intent on pointing out how far we have progressed, thanks to a benevolent government, from the poisonous prejudices of a less enlightened past. They also stress how much more still must be done before we can truly practice "fairness." Other "political scientists" try to counter this argument by getting their students to vote Republican. These "scientific" classes often have nothing to do with the kind of exercise that one might have to pursue in a study about how rapid oxidation results in fire.

But there is no need to single out political scientists for blame, and especially since one of my female colleagues, who teaches statistics, works hard to hide from her students her strong libertarian views. Unlike ninety-nine percent of her colleagues, this young lady is not an ideological missionary. In any case my experience with Poli Sci teachers has never been as bad as what I've endured from my colleagues in the humanities. This is a field that at our college and elsewhere now includes such attractions for the cognitively challenged as "women's studies" and "diversity" minors. And for those who teach in these areas, being "scientific" and "objective" means being unswervingly politically correct (PC).

Two, it is a puzzle to me, which can only be explained by the hegemonic PC ideology, that a multiplicity of views about the value of historical change is no longer permitted. There was a time when the "conservative" response to the Voting Rights Act of 1965 was "This could radicalize American politics!" and when conservatives responded to the argument that Castro had increased literacy in Cuba with statements about "how this means that the masses will be reading the government's communist propaganda." In a similar vein, an earlier conservative movement, and even many people then on the Left, attacked feminists in the 1960s for wishing to displace domestic life as the primary sphere of activities for women. If one, for example, cared deeply about the perpetuation of a Euro-American population with at least average Western intelligence, why would one be in favor of pushing women into the job market and away from a maternal role as the preferred way of life for them? Moreover, simply saying women can have it all, while belittling those who stay at home, will likely have no other effect than the one it is now having, namely, contributing to a sub-replacement reproduction level for indigenous Western populations and the transformation of heterosexual marriages, together with children, into multiple "family arrangements," including group marriages in Holland.

Given how things have turned out, a traditionalist may well sympathize with the advocacy by Eleanor Roosevelt (who was hardly a conservative in her age) of a "single-family wage," one that would allow working men to support their families without having to send their wives out to work. In this arrangement, with restricted job possibilities for women, wives would stay home (like my eldest daughter) and look after the rising generation. Note that I'm not glorifying the world I grew up in. I am simply pointing out that it was reasonably constructed, given what it valued.

It should also be possible to view other recent historical changes without ritualized fits of guilt or transports of joy about overcoming the past. The civil rights movement was, at least for me, a profoundly problematic development. Although I personally find little moral justification for denying access to educational institutions to worthy candidates of all races, the civil rights movement was about a lot more. Out of this cataclysm came certain changes of a kind that William F. Buckley in the 1960s suggested would undermine surviving constitutional restraints on the American managerial state. It is dishonest to separate things like the politics of guilt among American whites generated by the media, churches, and public education, and black misrule in American cities, the radical course that both the American republic and American culture have taken since the 1960s, from the "civil rights revolution," the Voting Rights Act of 1965, and other spin-offs of the drive for black "equality."

When Charles Krauthammer attacked Trent Lott in 2005 for praising the states-rightist and onetime segregationist Strom Thurmond on his one hundredth birthday as someone who is "deaf" to the greatest American triumph in Krauthammer's life, this neocon guru was not giving us the entire story. For the sake of honesty, Krauthammer should also have acknowledged the underbelly of that historical process he exultantly celebrates. Is there really no connection between the growing black dependence on government, corrupt black urban politics, and the leftward swing in our national politics and political culture and the object of Krauthammer's veneration?

To draw an apt comparison: One might admire the French Revolution for abolishing the remnants of serfdom in France. But full disclosure requires that historians call attention to the Jacobin terror and the Vendée massacres as well as to those sides of the Revolution they might happen to like. It is also necessary to ask in the case of our most recent revolution whether a greater good might have been accomplished if certain changes had occurred in a more piecemeal fashion, that is, without having the government mobilize black voters, whose weight would be felt entirely on the Left or without having courts micromanage social change in race relations and eventually in everything else in American life. Have we really benefited as a constitutional republic with a onetime limited government because blacks who were once discouraged from voting now do so in large enough numbers to tip our two parties and politicians in a radically statist direction?

One need not be a Klansman to notice this effect. And it is quite possible to see it as an inescapable result of the United States becoming a more egalitarian society in the post–World War II years. But why should we all be required to celebrate this fact? As the English classical liberal James Fitzjames Stephen said about the inevitability of universal suffrage in the late nineteenth century: there is a difference between observing a rising tide "and singing 'hosanna' to the river god." As a critical historian, I think that it may be a good idea to discuss revolutionary developments from all sides, without shutting up those who point to the hole in the donut. Needless to say, the aforesaid hole is not only about the injustices once inflicted on a growing list of designated minorities. An open historical discussion about race and gender relations would also address such currently forbidden topics as the high rates of violence in almost all black societies, the critical role of black Africans in the slave trade, the accumulating evidence about socially significant gender differences, and, above all, the professional sanctions leveled against those who engage politically incorrect questions.

The final related point I would make is that there is nothing admirable or even reasonable about such former elites as American WASPs reveling in their disappearance as a ruling culture. There is now a debate within the unauthorized Right between zealous critics of Jewish influence in Western countries and those who, like myself, believe that WASPdom has destroyed itself. To put my cards on the table: I've never heard American Jews or American blacks pour as much contempt on white Protestant America as I hear coming from white Protestant intellectuals and clergypersons. Like the Germans, repentant WASPs delight in *Sündenstolz*, being morally arrogant while lamenting the bigotry of their ancestors.

When a younger colleague of mine recently published a book on the Progressive historians at the University of Wisconsin, he dutifully devoted several pages to the "nativist" and "sexist" mindset of his WASP subjects. And he cited with apparent approval a New York Jewish Marxist, who had quarreled with Merle Curti and then attacked this Wisconsin Progressive historian as a prejudiced white Protestant. The evidence given by my friend, who is himself a Midwestern WASP, for Curti's lapse into atavistic gentile behavior was less than convincing. All he seemed to show was that his generally leftist subjects did not always conform to the most updated edition of the PC catechism.

My friend also brought up the putative dark side of historian Frederick Jackson Turner, who, when he encountered a recently arrived Russian Jew, in side-locks and a black caftan, in Boston in 1909, observed that it would take a long time to assimilate such people. I wonder whether my friend has any idea about how a non-WASP society, except for the one that this stranger had come from, would have reacted to the same sight. Most Israeli Jews of my acquaintance would have been even less tolerant than Turner of that exotic person whom the Wisconsin-born historian once chanced upon. It was a mark of Turner's tolerance that he hoped to absorb this stranger into his own culture, in the fullness of time.

One of my most vivid graduate school memories was listening to a speech given by Yale President Kingman Brewster expressing unqualified support for the Black Panthers. I recall being shocked to hear this direct lineal descendant of two founders of the Massachusetts Bay Colony behave like such a jerk. But Brewster was certainly not a more extreme anti-racist than his fellow-patrician and Yale chaplain, William Sloane Coffin. This Congregationalist chaplain had trouble even finishing a sentence without deploring the slave trade in which his ancestors had once been implicated. And if I think back hard enough, most of the WASP patricians whom I met at Yale as a graduate student were almost as wacky as Brewster and Coffin. Their pompous self-debasement had progressed so far that they didn't need Alan Dershowitz or Cornel West to come scourge them.

The tirades against WASP nativism and close-mindedness, often produced by their tribe, have caused me to wonder by what ethereal standard these critics are judging their past. What other group in world history has been more "tolerant" or less hostile to outsiders than were white Protestants? Although some of their progenitors had engaged in the slave trade, so had the rest of the human race, and particularly blacks for a far longer time. And only WASPs feel guilty about social institutions that most other groups have taken for granted. Needless to say, these other groups are all too happy to browbeat masochistic Westerners about doing what everyone else has done. And for all I know, this browbeating may be serving psychological needs on both sides.

I once listened to an Ashanti cab driver in Washington boasting about how his tribe had sold the black slaves who would be used to construct the US capital. Whether it was true or not, I found this boast to be refreshing. The African cab driver did not suffer from the choking sense of guilt I encounter in American WASPs. Enemies of their own putative prejudices, they have come to remind me of the elderly Irish spinster, who would drive the village priest batty by confessing to trivial and often imaginary sins. There is something unseemly and even profoundly pathological about such a perpetually overburdened conscience. The question that occurs to me as I observe such politics of guilt is "What would Nietzsche say?"

The Death of the WASP

Taki's Magazine

JUNE 20, 2010

A REMARK by Richard Brookhiser in May in a syndicated column in *The New York Post* about how "we are all Protestants now" made me realize that Brookhiser's statement taken in context does not prove what he thinks he's saying. A journeyman author, long associated with *National Review*, Brookhiser, to all appearances, is an upper-class WASP endowed with all the proper manners and tics. Nonetheless, for decades he's been in the employ of the neocons, people who would hardly qualify as *le gratin*.

A scene involving one of their leaders, John Podhoretz, sticks vividly in my mind. While in the employ of *The Washington Times*, where Arnaud de Borchgrave entertained him lavishly as a favor to his parents, the present editor of *Commentary* was known for his crude table manners and general loutishness. I recall seeing him in Borchgrave's office slouched over his chair and (dare I be so frank) picking his nose while in conversation with the apparent boss. (Actually it was Norm and Midge, John's parents, who called the shots at the *WT* then.) But people like John Podhoretz are precisely the ones whom Brookhiser and other WASPs, and particularly those at *The New Criterion*, have been kissing up to for years.

This subordinate position certainly does not demonstrate the assertion that "we are all Protestants [that is, WASPs] now." The fact is members of our onetime dominant ethnicity and its onetime social elite are down on their luck. They've been reduced to menials serving at the beck and call of other groups, and in the journalistic and media world, this means working for Jewish liberals and Jewish neocons.

Such a situation should distress the new class of menials (perhaps it does!), but as I've indicated in more scholarly venues, their fate is entirely deserved. Elites that melt into spasms of guilt or niceness and which fail to continue to produce figures of the caliber of George Kennan, the Tafts, Robert E. Lee, Henry Adams, etc., are not going to continue to be around as social, political, and cultural leaders. In doing research for my book on multiculturalism, I encountered statistical information that showed the decline of WASPdom since the middle of the last century in just about every area of human endeavor. The exception here (and it's nothing to be proud of) is the disproportionate white Protestant representation at the public trough, and particularly in the ranks of the GOP. The last significant WASP patrician in public service was our recent, unmissed president, George W. Bush, someone whose ancestry is almost as noteworthy as the evidence of his verbal ineptitude. Needless to say, W took orders, whether or not he understood them, from neocon control-persons.

Clearly we're not all WASPs now; and in my book *Encounters* (2009) I described in detail how differently the WASP gentry behaved when I was at Yale in the 1960s as compared to the Jews and even Irish Catholics. The WASP gentry were noticeable for their lack of élan and for their overpowering desire to be non-controversial. The Jews, by contrast, were conspicuously nasty. They had chips on their shoulders, and profoundly loathed the group they were destined to replace. Once they took over academic and journalistic posts these parvenus left no doubt who was in charge. They behaved with an ideological and sociological intolerance that was truly breathtaking.

Even that over-the-top critic of Jewish power, Kevin MacDonald, has hardly scratched the surface in delineating the nastiness with which the children and grandchildren of Eastern European Jewish immigrants clawed their way to the top of the academic-media industry, on the backs of those they often despised. And all the while they appealed with brilliant success to a guilty WASP conscience.

This tactic worked like a charm because of the ruthlessness and hypocrisy of those doing the climbing and because of the mentality of those they supplanted. Apparently WASPs suffer from an onerous sense of guilt toward others whom their ancestors excluded or were alleged to have discriminated against. Other groups, particularly Jews, blacks,

Irish Catholics, and Latinos, consider themselves to have been the victims of discrimination, and they therefore happily associate with the Democratic Party as an in gathering of victimized ethnicities.

One may attribute the WASP's far deeper sense of social guilt to any number of causes, but his ancestors were hardly worse than those of the groups whom he now worships as designated victims. Did African blacks treat their slaves better than did American slave owners? What about the Muslims who dragged captured blacks eastward, to Arab countries, well into the twentieth century, when they weren't enslaving European Christians, whom they captured in naval raids? When one of my students, who himself is predictably WASP, noted in class that his ethnic group lost influence in the United States "because they practiced discrimination against other people," I asked somewhat impatiently: "How the hell did everyone else get into the country?"

Certainly many other groups have been more oppressive than American WASPs. Human history is full of them. But no other group, except for their pathological German cousins, seems to enjoy quite as much as WASPs the ecstasy of wallowing in guilt. And no other group seems quite as easily swayed to engage in moral crusades, perhaps to atone for their past sins as racists, sexists, or whatever. Unfortunately these crusades show our WASP population at their worst, trying to save the rest of the world with confected "human rights" after laying waste to their countries. If there's anything WASPs should feel inexpressibly guilty about, it is this Jacobin fervor that causes them to unleash wars on other societies in order to bring them the gift of American democracy. But for some reason my Republican WASP neighbors think such devastation is alright and may be redemptive for its victims. After all, blowing up non-democrats is not reprehensible in the same way as refusing to let other ethnicities into WASP country clubs or being against affirmative action for Australoid transvestites.

Although I've loads of respect for their Protestant antecedents, I can't say that I like or respect this present generation of WASPs. And least of all can I understand why their elites, by the time I was in my teens and early twenties, began to feel guilt toward those who hated their guts. As the great Italian thinker Vilfredo Pareto pointed out about a hundred years ago, ruling classes fall not so much because of opposition from below as they do from disintegration from above. Or as the Russians put it, the fish rots from the head on down.

Antecedents of Neoconservative Foreign Policy

Historically Speaking

JANUARY 2011

A FREQUENTLY heard complaint on the Old Right is that American foreign policy has changed for the worse since the neoconservatives have become a dominant force in our political life. Neoconservative influence, which was particularly evident during the Bush II administration, has linked American foreign policy to certain problematic visionary ends. These ends are no secrets but have been stated repeatedly in *The Wall Street Journal*, *Commentary*, *Weekly Standard*, *National Review*, and other publications in which neoconservative philanthropists and advocates have made their weight felt. We are also speaking here about those foreign policy ideals that the Heritage Foundation, the American Enterprise Institute, and other predominantly neoconservative think tanks have propounded for decades.

Among those aims that the neoconservatives wish to promote is making as much of the world as they can teach bear a close resemblance to Anglo-American democracy. Although other favored countries such as Israel are given high political grades, neoconservatives stress the shared democratic inheritance of the English-speaking world, as illustrated by the statesmanship of such heroes as Winston Churchill and Woodrow Wilson. Although critics of this Anglo-American democratic world order, such as Andrew J. Bacevich, James Kurth, and Claes Ryn, have certainly not been anti-British, they have tried to turn the discussion of international affairs away from making the world safe for democracy—in conjunction with the rest of the English-speaking world and often by force of arms—to a more limited, realistic policy line.[205]

Some of these critics have been conspicuously unhappy with Andrew Roberts, James Bennett, Max Boot, and other glorifiers of the "Anglosphere." This supposed cultural-political entity has been praised by its advocates for having worked to advance "democratic values." The Anglosphere is thought to have been preeminently at work in the Anglo-American struggle against the undemocratic enemy in the two "German wars."[206]

And one would have to be truly obtuse not to notice the anti-German theme present in neoconservative Anglophilia. This Teutonophobia has arisen in all probability out of memories of the Holocaust, the past that will not pass, and it has taken an identifiable narrative form in neoconservative publications. In the now-authorized neoconservative version of the early twentieth century, one accepts at face value the anti-German propaganda released by the American government after the US entry into the First World War. One also strains to find continuities between Imperial Germany and Nazi Germany, typically by citing the controversial accusations against Imperial German war aims associated with now-deceased German leftist historian Fritz Fischer. This Teutonophobic source is usually brought up to confirm a preconceived notion, but without much knowledge being exhibited about Fischer's thesis or its demonstrated multiple weaknesses. The anti-German Atlanticist Paul Johnson, who writes frequently for the neoconservative press, tells us in *Modern Times* (1983) that "the case for German war guilt in 1914 is established beyond doubt."[207] But what Johnson declares to be axiomatic is never shown to be plausible, let alone "established beyond doubt."

Those who have deplored such bias have sometimes assumed that there was a time when truly dispassionate people oversaw American foreign policy. Then, sober, white Anglo-Saxon Protestants and other staid types were able to supervise our foreign policy establishment. These embodiments of prudence, fortified by a belief in original sin, warned our heads of government against ideological fanaticism. Whether these advisers were like the subject of Lee Congdon's admiring biography of

George F. Kennan or the "wise men" described by Walter Isaacson and Evan Thomas in their celebratory study of the blue bloods who became presidential advisers in the 1940s and 1950s, we are made to believe that foreign policy advisers were not always like Madeleine Albright, Paul Wolfowitz, Douglas Feith, and Michael Ledeen.[208]

At one time, perhaps fifty or eighty years ago, there were patricians, or so some would like to think, imbued with a sense of limited national interest and with a desire to stay out of entangling alliances, unless American survival was at stake. In the good old days, secretaries of state and presidential confidants did not rant against the nondemocratic world or call for foreign crusades to impose the American way of life.

Such an age of sobriety has not existed for a very long time. The sober realist Kennan was an isolated dinosaur by the end of the Second World War; and it is hard to think of many struggles that the United States has engaged in since the First World War that were not sold as a crusade for democracy and universal rights. The late Hans Morgenthau, who claimed to be a foreign policy realist, argued that it was okay for the United States to wage foreign wars for universal ideals, as long as our leaders understood that it was all for show.

But that dichotomy has never worked. All crusades for democracy, from the time they are launched, have to be defended and prosecuted as struggles with global moral significance. In the two World Wars this ideological zeal resulted in demonizing the enemy. Particularly in the last two years of the Second World War, a governmentally incited demonization of the absolute foe justified the mass bombing of the "undemocratic" civilian population on the other side. The United States also insisted on unconditional surrender in both Europe and Asia, and it engaged in expensive efforts to either kill or imprison the leaders of its erstwhile enemies and then to reeducate the surviving civilian population, until they became more or less like us. That's how democratic crusades undertaken for universal ideals are likely to end, particularly if they involve large standing armies and continue to be fought with considerable bloodshed until the other side has been totally defeated. Such crusades were not pursued while global democratic ideologues or super-Zionist hawks were controlling American foreign policy. Rather they took place on the watch of WASP patricians like FDR, who espoused a drastic course of action by totally destroying anti-democratic enemies in a way that FDR believed that Americans had failed to do during an earlier crusade for democracy.

That earlier struggle was the one that Wilson, a southern patrician, pulled his country into in 1917. Other gratin between 1914 and 1917, beginning with Theodore Roosevelt, Elihu Root, and Henry Cabot Lodge, expressed disgust that Wilson had taken so long to throw us into the European meat grinder. Yet many of these patricians balked at American adhesion to the League of Nations. They did not want armies being sent to Europe to aid the French and those successor states created by the victorious Allies in Central Europe against a return of the vanquished. It was widely known at the time that the League was intended to hold down through collective security arrangements the war's losers, namely the Germans, Austrians, and Hungarians, together with Soviet Russia. But these patricians should have shown greater care about embroiling us in a massive war in the first place, one in which we became complicit in mass killing and in the unjust treaty that ended that struggle. Far better if the United States had taken the advice of Wilson's first Secretary of State, the decidedly unpatrician prairie populist William Jennings Bryan, someone who had been serious about being neutral and about working to reconcile the European belligerents.[209]

The WASP patrician pressure to push this country into the war to end all wars was far more consequential than anything that anyone in the Bush administration did by invading Iraq. Although neocons applaud in retrospect what WASP patricians did to spread democracy by force of arms, there was nothing they themselves achieved that was quite as devastating as what our social elite did to this country and to Europe during the First World War. We sacrificed American lives to bring about an unjust peace, when we had untaken opportunities to act as an honest peace broker in the European conflict.[210]

Needless to say, the appeal to the universal or universally applicable ideal of democracy played a role in greasing the skids; and whether it was our ambassador to England Walter Hines Page, Secretary of State Robert Lansing, or President Wilson, the war in Europe was always characterized as a global struggle between world democracy and military autocracy. Presumably by fighting for the British and the Japanese empires against the Habsburg and the Hohenzollern empires, we were making the world safer for democracy. Pursuing this position required us to ignore certain injustices committed against the anti-British side, starting with the hunger blockade that Churchill and the British Navy imposed on the Germans in August 1914. The blockade involved the laying of mines in the open sea and classifying food destined for civilians as contraband for the first time in modern warfare.[211]

Now it is possible to look back at nineteenth-century American framers of foreign policy, such as John Quincy Adams, James Buchanan, or even Lincoln's Secretary of State William Seward, and notice their avoidance of democratic missionary tropes. And though the Spanish-American War in 1898 featured rhetoric about America's progressive republic opposing Spain's decadent Catholic monarchy, the United States did not claim to be waging war then in order to spread democracy or obliterate its enemies. It was fighting for a time-bound nineteenth-century cause, for a vigorous Germanic Protestant world against Latin Catholic decadence. And once we got the colonies we wanted, no American in his right mind spoke about occupying Spain and then converting its inhabitants to global democratic values—or even to Protestantism.

The real shift in attitude came around World War I, which was the source of much evil, save for those European successor states formed out of fallen empires that had been mostly on the losing side. Trying to explain why American social and ethnic elites embraced a democratic world mission before and during the war, historian Richard Gamble in *The War for Righteousness* (2003) stresses the transformation of American Protestant culture in the early twentieth century.[212] According to Gamble, the liberalization of Protestant doctrine and the beginnings of the Social Gospel movement produced two characteristic attitudes among those affected by these trends. First, Protestant democratic missionaries believed it was their mission to bring moral uplift to the entire world, and such improvement was often associated with the transmission of American political ideals, ideals that liberal Protestants like George W. Bush and Michael Gerson have also touted as universally applicable. Second, the nontraditional Protestants who Gamble cites held to an increasingly secularized postmillennialism, one in which Christ's Kingdom would be prepared by changing social and political structures to conform to the believer's vision of the Good. Indeed every change these Protestants approved of would be given cosmic significance in terms of the end times, understood as democratic political perfection.

When war came to Europe, the liberal Protestants, exemplified by Woodrow Wilson, who had ceased to be an orthodox Calvinist, believed they were living through a struggle between democratic Good and autocratic Evil. Once the partisans came to identify their English kinsmen as the progressive side, it became a moral and millenarian imperative for the United States to enter the European war on behalf of the Allies. Anything less would have been a dereliction of religious duty and would have prevented God's Kingdom from being rapidly established. And those who at home failed to take their side in the war deserved to be treated as enemies of the Good. Such liberal Protestants were totally intolerant of the neutralists or pacifists, and they continued to rage against the Central Powers long after the war was over.

Although Gamble documents his arguments, one point that he never addresses to my satisfaction is why liberal Protestants held such strong views about the war from its outset. Why did they view Germany and Austria so negatively and England so positively? England had a more robust tradition of parliamentary government, but German workers had a higher standard of living, were better educated, and were far less subject to social prejudice than were the English lower orders. If the Germans invaded Belgium on their way to fighting France, the British Navy was starving German civilians possibly in violation of international law. What I'm suggesting is that there would have been good reason for Gamble's Protestants to have taken the same position as other Protestants, including some very liberal ones, who wanted to keep the United States out of the European war.

The reason these figures didn't take this neutral course is that most of them were Anglophiles of English descent, like Henry Sloane Coffin, Lyman Abbott, and most of the editorial board of the *Christian Century*. Gamble ignores certain cultural shifts that began before the war and that expressed or resulted in changed allegiances. From the 1890s on, England and Germany were competing European powers; and of the two, Germany was outpacing England economically and educationally. Germany would also challenge Britain's and France's pursuit of African colonies and insist on being given her share as a rising colonial power. And although Germany was behind England and several other countries as a naval power, by the 1890s the Germans were producing state-of-the-art battleships, which the British government considered a threat to British naval supremacy. The naval race was not really a race, since the Germans were not likely to catch up to the British; and in the end it provided grist for the mills of British politicians, and particularly Churchill, who targeted the German Empire as a continental menace.

This rivalry necessitated a change in perspective on the part of American patricians. In the nineteenth century they had adored the British and the Germans with almost equal enthusiasm. New Englanders had gone off to study in England and Germany; they considered both of these countries to be a Protestant, Germanic land that had contributed to the growth of liberty. This view, however, had come about in a tortuous fashion, since Liberty had traveled far, from the dense forests of Germania to Westminster Abbey and from there, to the American frontier by way of Boston and Philadelphia. But this legacy of constitutional freedom in any case had come from the Saxons, who had settled Central

Germany and England; and it was also the Saxon Martin Luther who had freed the Germanic world from Latin religious bondage by spearheading the Protestant Reformation.

As a plaque from the early twentieth century on the Conrad Weiser estate near Reading, Pennsylvania, reminds the visitor even now, the German Lutheran clergyman who settled this land in the mid-eighteenth century "represented Germanic Protestant civilization against Latin Catholic civilization." That was how many Pennsylvanians once interpreted the Anglo-French rivalry that eventually burst into the French and Indian War. Even more importantly, the phrase also indicates that Protestant Americans in the early twentieth century viewed themselves as Germanic rather than strictly English. The First World War and the Anglo-German competition preceding it made it harder to accept that Germanic identity; and what took its place, as the German historian Heinz Gollwitzer points out, is a fractured Germanism, splitting into English and continental German types.[213] This fracturing had begun to occur even before the war, but the struggle that broke out among Germanic kinsmen made it much sharper.

The Imperial school of American history, inaugurated by Charles McLean Andrews at Yale and George Louis Beer at Harvard shortly before the war, focused on early America as a part of British civilization. Although a famous revolution severed the American colonies from their mother country, this occurred, according to Andrews and his friend Woodrow Wilson, after a permanent British Protestant identity had been imparted. Note that this corresponds to Francis Parkman's history of the French and Indian War, which had been written two generations earlier. Parkman, too, had presented the victory of Protestant Anglo-Saxon institutions over French Catholic ones in the New World as the defining American experience. Any subsequent break of the American colonies from England according to Parkman became therefore anticlimactic.

In 1914 WASP patricians had a full set of arguments for why they were part of a British cultural and political orbit as opposed to a competing German one. They were heirs to the English language and literature, English common law, and English parliamentary democracy. This last point was particularly useful for the pro-British side. British parliamentary institutions were better established than their German counterpart, despite the fact that Germans seemed more advanced in other ways. But WASP patrician loyalties were formed on the basis of ethnic identity—and not because of any mystical belief in the unchanging democratic nature of English society or the British Empire.

The leftist opponents of America's entry into the war saw through this democratic phraseology, and especially when it came from racial segregationists and condescending social elites. John Lukacs observes that the typical Anglophile interventionist in the United States in 1916 was not less but usually more conservative than the American neutralists.[214] But the interventionists adopted a cosmopolitan, progressive tone in pursuing their ends. And to some extent, they may have believed what they said, although it remained ancillary to their main concern, which was helping the English motherland win a gruesome war. In the process, they invented a global democratic rhetoric that became integral to American thinking about the rest of the world.

Still, as Erich Kaufmann shows in *The Rise and Fall of Anglo-America* (2004), WASP patricians continued to mix their liberal internationalism, which was often a code term for Anglophilia and an Open Door policy in China, with ethnic national attitudes.[215] This ethnic consciousness quickly surfaced once the crusade for democracy was over. A look at the membership list of the liberal internationalist Council for Foreign Policy, formed in 1919 under the guidance of former Secretary of State Elihu Root, would reveal not a few of the members of the Immigration Restriction League. Henry Cabot Lodge was both a chastened liberal internationalist and an outspoken opponent of the de-WASPification of the United States, starting in Boston as viewed from Beacon Hill.

Lodge's close friend A. Lawrence Lowell, president of Harvard since 1909, combined his liberal internationalist politics and wartime Anglophilia with deep concern over a threatened WASP America. When Lowell was not campaigning for American membership in the League of Nations, a matter that he and Lodge thought differently about, he worked to keep non–Northern European immigrants from coming to the United States. Lowell was a fervent advocate of the Johnson-Reed (immigration reform) Act of 1924; and as president of Harvard, he expressed alarm over his institution being reshaped by ethnic newcomers. Above all, he feared the arrival of Latin Catholics and Eastern European Jews at his Brahmin institution, a concern that never hindered him from embracing the aggressive democratic internationalism of his presidential predecessor at Harvard, Charles W. Eliot.

These observations are by no means a protest against hypocritical xenophobes. I am describing the way an ethnically and socially dominant group reacted when threatened, and WASP patricians generally reacted less inhumanely than other groups have in similar situations. The relevant point, however, is that WASP patricians conceived of the British Isles as their ancestral land. As late as 1965 the conservative

Democratic Senator Sam Ervin of North Carolina, in arguing against an Immigration Reform bill that eventually passed, complained that such legislation would eclipse the English character of the United States: "You take the English-speaking people, they gave us our common law, they gave us a part of our political philosophy." If the projected bill were passed, according to Ervin, it would put the people of England "on the same plane as the people of Ethiopia."[216] Although Ervin's Anglophilia would not bother liberal internationalists and neoconservatives in the least, his opposition to Third World immigration would not sit well with either group. But to Anglophiles of an earlier generation, English ethnicity and international values were thought to be compatible. And within this mix, ethnicity was dominant.

Part of the WASP establishment began to defect from liberal internationalism between the wars. Onetime enthusiasts for the war to end all wars, such as Robert McCormick, Robert Taft, and Herbert Hoover, joined midwestern and western isolationist Progressives in scolding FDR for plunging the United States into a second European war. Such gentlemen expressed second thoughts about the crusading spirit shown by the Eastern establishment in 1917 and 1918. And though Anglophile interventionists before America's entry into the Second World War included some of the same people who had stirred the pot during the Great War, the number of prominent WASP interventionists was shrinking by 1940. As the historian of American anti-interventionism Justus Doenecke has demonstrated, the overwhelming majority of those associated with the America First Committee in 1940 had Protestant ancestors from the British Isles.[217] Still and all, people of the same ethnic strain were also highly represented in the pro-interventionist Fight for Freedom Committee, organized in April 1941.[218]

In sum, ethnic loyalty had a great deal to do with WASP liberal internationalism. That is why this particular stance attracted southern politicians, who although not liberal in their cultural views, came from a region that viewed itself as Anglo-Saxon. It also explains why members of the Immigration Restriction League saw no contradiction between international crusades for democracy and favoring ethnic nationalism at home.

Clearly this patrician political outlook did not coincide entirely with the world vision that has come from neoconservatives and neo-liberals. Henry Cabot Lodge, A. Lawrence Lowell, Carter Glass, and Richard Byrd of Virginia were not the predecessors of Michael Ledeen or of other neocon advocates of cosmic democratic reconstruction. They were WASP nativists. One could never imagine any of these figures sounding like Robert Kagan, who in *The Washington Post* (November 3, 2002) stated that "American bullying" is a good thing but that the United States is, unfortunately, an "underachiever in the bullying business." Nor could one imagine Root, Lodge, or Lowell anticipating Michael Ledeen's boast in *The Washington Times* (January 20, 1989) that "creative destruction is our middle name, both within our society and abroad." WASP patricians were not democratic globalists or apostles of our contemporary American lifestyle. And unlike the neoconservatives, they were not dedicated Zionists, which is another obvious difference between WASP interventionists of an earlier generation and later neoconservative and neo-liberal policy advisers.

But these differences should not overshadow the continuities between these groups. Anglophile internationalism and its rhetorical justification paved the way for neoconservative values and emphases in the framing of American foreign policy. One served as a bridge to the other. Neoconservative internationalism could not have prevailed had it not been for the WASP internationalism that became an American staple by the early twentieth century. Here then may be an example of what historians characterize as the law of unintended consequences.

The Puritan Legacy Birthed the American Creed

Chronicles

SEPTEMBER 2020

R IGHT-WING critics of Christianity often quote from *The Hour of Decision*, the last work of a once widely read German historian of philosophy, Oswald Spengler.[219] This short, graphically composed book was published in 1933, the year Adolf Hitler took power in Germany. Although it has never been proven, there is a suspicion that the Nazi government disposed of this onetime hero of the Right, who did not hide his contempt for Hitler or his "plebeian" followers. Spengler supposedly referred to Christianity as the "Bolshevism of antiquity," and today's neo-pagan Alt-Right has picked up his description to justify its contempt for Christianity as a proto-socialist religion of slaves.

Having found the original statement in the German text, which I own, I am not sure the Alt-Right has interpreted Spengler's drift correctly. The author is not expressing contempt for the primitive church but rather viewing it as a prototype for revolutionary movements. Spengler correctly suggests that Marx, Engels, and the Bolsheviks, despite their pretension to being "scientific socialists," viewed the early church as a model for their own movement; as did the French anarchist Georges Sorel, who thought his labor-class revolutionary movement needed a "redemptive myth" as powerful as the one that animated early Christians.

In Christianity, Spengler and Sorel saw a religion of the downtrodden—though they may have exaggerated the predominance of slaves and the poor in early Christianity—one that practiced communal ownership as it awaited the end of human history. Moreover, after an initial persecution and the killing of martyrs, this religious community managed to become the official religion of the Roman Empire. All other revolutionaries on the Left, as opposed to revolutionary nationalists on the Right (who were heavily influenced by neo-paganism), found lessons in the ascent of the early church from its humble beginnings.

Christians themselves later looked back at how their church rose from these blood-stained, painful beginnings to become a dominant world religion. They ascribed this course of events to divine Providence. Sometimes, as in the writings of Saint Augustine, the trials would have to be endured by the faithful until the end of secular history. But there was an upward course in which the founding of the church presaged the end times, when Christ would return.

The centrality of this founding and its institutional arrangements played an even larger role for radical Protestants. Sects like the German Anabaptists in the sixteenth century and the Fifth Monarchy Men during the English Civil War in the seventeenth century believed they were living in a final historical age and that their attempted return to the primitive church was being undertaken in preparation for Christ's Second Coming. Among such sectarians, of whom there were many in early modern Europe, going back to the early church was essential to their plans.

Indeed, much of the Protestant Reformation was about returning to a purer form of Christianity before papal councils and institutions borrowed from the pagan world were thought to have corrupted the true faith. Significantly for Luther and other earlier Reformers, the "fall of the church" was not seen to have occurred in the early centuries. This fall was mostly identified with the High Middle Ages and papal monarchical pretensions. But for the more radical Anabaptists, Christendom had already fallen into grievous error when the church leaders gave power over its deliberations and decisions to Roman emperors. The early church had remained uncorrupted because it was separated from political power.

A different model, however, became prevalent in Puritanism, especially after this religious movement traveled to the New World. Perry

Miller's classic study *Errand into the Wilderness* (1956) leaves no doubt about the overshadowing presence of the ancient Hebrews on Puritan society and religion.[220] The New Israelites—which is how the Puritans envisioned themselves—were bound by a covenant, just as the ancient Jews had been under the covenant of Abraham and Moses. Just as the Hebrews had gone forth from bondage to settle the Holy Land, so too were their Puritan successors summoned into the North American wilderness to carry out a divine mandate. They were to establish their own community of believers where they would build the godly city on the hill as the New Jerusalem. Puritan sermons and political ordinances are so permeated with Hebrew and Old Testament images and phrases that their borrowings from an earlier chosen people are unmistakable. Harvard, Yale, and other originally Puritan institutions encouraged the study of biblical Hebrew, and the most common Christian names given to both sexes were taken from Hebrew Scripture.

In considering why these early American settlers were so mesmerized by the example of the ancient Hebrews, we might look at the European Calvinists from whom they were theologically descended. Like the American Puritans, Protestant followers of John Calvin strongly rejected the tradition of Roman authority they found in the Catholic Church. For them, the Catholics were too heavily influenced in their authority structure and canon law by Roman paganism. The early Protestants felt it necessary to return to the Bible as a guide for building a Christian society.

Calvinists also believed that salvation came through unmerited divine election. Since all humans had fallen away from God with the sin of Adam, no mortal could earn grace through his own efforts. Indeed, any sense that humans earned grace was mere vanity on our parts, for outside of God's will, which was inscrutable to man, there could be no salvation. Yet those who were elected had a sense of being saved and lived in a manner that comported with the undeserved grace that had been ascribed to them by an all-knowing and all-powerful Deity.

Particularly revealing for the Calvinists in general were the passages in Deuteronomy, in which the Israelites are shown two paths, either obedience to divine commandments, which will result in blessings for the people, or falling away, which will bring collective curses. In this narrative, the Puritans and other Calvinists saw the paths that were laid out for their own lives. If they grasped the signs of divine election and acted accordingly, they would prosper; if they were among the sinners, they would suffer in this life and in the next.

Like their ancient model, the Calvinists strongly focused on signs of divine favor or divine disfavor in this life. Preparing for the next life was not a particularly rewarding task for those who never knew for sure whether they belonged "in that number when the saints go marching in." No matter how hard the Puritans tried to believe they were in "that number," some doubt probably lingered in their minds. That black spiritual about the saints marching in, which first began to be sung about a hundred years ago, refers to the end times, not to the afterlife.

Millenarianism, which refers to a preoccupation with the thousand-year kingdom that would usher in Christ's rule, became a recognizable part of American Protestant culture. Although tonier Calvinist denominations, like Congregationalists and Presbyterians, moved away from such speculative points, less upper-class denominations like Southern Baptists absorbed them. Such speculation about the end times drew from the Hebrew prophets and the Book of Daniel, as well as from the Book of Revelation in the New Testament. It also became strongly associated with an American brand of Protestantism. It was one in which fevered debates took place between Pre- and Post-Millenarians, those who believed that Christ would return before the end of secular history and those who believed that humanity would first have to endure "the tribulations" before Christ returned.

A Calvinist legacy, with a strong Old Testament orientation, and various forms of millenarianism shaped American culture and politics. A once deeply embedded Protestant work ethic, which originated in Calvinist moral theology; an emphasis on public morality, the content of which went back to the Mosaic law; and a view of religion as above all an individual commitment, have roots in America's Calvinist founding. The willingness to tolerate religious dissenters, which by the late eighteenth century had become a more-or-less prevalent American view, also went back to the Protestant idea that religion depended on the individual's experience of faith, independent of priestly mediation or hierarchical structures.

Finally, republican government fit with the Calvinist-Puritan historical experience. In Europe, Catholic and High Church Anglican monarchs had opposed the proliferation of Protestant sects and had often been at war with the Calvinists. When James I tried to unite the Anglican and Presbyterian confessions in the late sixteenth century, the deal breaker was the Scottish Calvinist refusal to accept the office of bishop. To which James famously and presciently responded, "No bishop, no king." The political and ecclesiastical chain of command understandably went together in the king's mind.

These Protestant traditions have served the American people well. Religious freedom but not indifferentism, the enforcement of strong communal moral standards, and the expectation that the young will apply themselves diligently to their work and study as a religious act, have all benefited our country. So have the Calvinist Protestant suspicion of power in the hands of earthly princes and an awareness of the need to rein in such political actors. One need not denigrate other political or religious traditions that suit other societies to recognize the strengths of what has worked well in this country. It is also the case that the Puritan-Calvinist value of teaching the young to study biblical and classical languages was a spur to education and the founding of great universities in early America.

Still, the Protestant legacy has had its problematic side, much of which is related to the idea of divine election. At least in American politics, it has expressed itself in a moral arrogance that has nurtured a missionary foreign policy from which our country cannot seem to break free. Martin E. Marty, a Lutheran scholar, entitled his history of American Protestantism *Righteous Empire* (1970). The American government's relation with other countries has usually meant trying to export our "democratic values" and "human rights" while making others more like ourselves. That means stressing whatever our dominant values are at any given time, be it traditional Judeo-Christian morality or LGBT self-expression. But whatever those rights and values are, they are supposedly universally valid because they come from an "exceptional nation" (read: Calvin's ingathering of the elect); and it has been America's destiny to become "a city on a hill," albeit not in the manner intended by Governor Winthrop of Massachusetts who constructed that phrase in the seventeenth century. We end wars against the wicked with demands for unconditional surrender and then we hold war trials so that our virtues can stand out more brightly in relation to those reprobates whom we have just defeated.

Calvinist scholar James Kurth once defined "the American Creed" that dominated American views of international relations in the twentieth century as a degraded form of American Protestant theology:

> The elements of the American Creed were free markets and equal opportunity, free elections and liberal democracy, and constitutionalism and the rule of law. The American Creed definitely did not include as elements hierarchy, community, tradition, and custom. Although the American Creed was not itself Protestant, it was clearly the product of a Protestant culture—a sort of secularized version of Protestantism . . .

Although Kurth views this American missionary politics as peculiarly American and as a "declension of the Reformation," he also stresses its rootedness in the individualism and repugnance for hierarchy that came out of older Protestant thinking. This creed is intolerant of societies and countries that display traditional ways of life. It requires redeemed Americans to raise the less fortunate or perverse out of their degraded conditions. According to Kurth, one has yet to figure out how to keep the Protestant baby while disposing of the unwanted bathwater. But as the American Creed has become more widespread, much of its original Protestant character has eroded. Today, Protestants are far from the only ones boasting about American exceptionalism and an American mission.

CHAPTER NINE

A Race Apart

– ◆ ◆ ◆ –

Toughs, Softs, and Jewish Masculinity

Chronicles

FEBRUARY 1, 1994

J EWISH STEREOTYPING is an activity in which Jews and their enemies have both engaged. Among the self-images that Jews have popularized is that of the bookish Jewish male. The medieval biblical commentator Rashi depicts the patriarch Jacob as a scholar and homebody, "in the tradition of Shem and Eber," Jacob's two Semitic ancestors to whom his qualities are also ascribed. Jacob's brother Esau was a "cunning hunter and man of the field," and he came to represent for rabbinic commentators the hostile Gentile whose way of life was decidedly non-Jewish. The contrast between Jacob and Esau was already critical for the later prophets: Malachi, for example, states that God "loved Jacob but despised Esau," who received desolation as his inheritance. The impetuous, bloodthirsty Esau became a symbol of what the descendants of Jacob were to fear, and the rabbis saw that enemy as variously incarnated in Israel's Edomite neighbors to the South (supposedly descended from Esau), the Roman Empire, and the medieval Church. All of these groups were identified with the color red, going back to Esau's association with the pot of lentils in return for which he sold his birthright to Jacob. (The Hebrew word for lentil, *adom*, can also mean red.) All of

Israel's political foes, moreover, were seen as sanguinary and unreflective, in contrast to Jacob's scions, who were shown cultivating sedentary, domestic virtues.

The Jewish self-image is, of course, tied to the stifling of Jewish masculinity that was evident by the Middle Ages. The received view, which the Zionist movement has stressed, is that Jewish manhood was stunted by the restrictions that a hostile Christian world placed on Jewish society. This view is partly correct. The prohibitions imposed on Jews in medieval Europe—against owning land and bearing arms—prevented Jewish men from tilling the soil, practicing self-defense, and engaging in other manly pursuits. In the proverbial Jewish family of the Eastern European ghetto, the wife ran a business and the husband pored over Talmudic texts. This division of labor was both the product of prolonged social discrimination and a creative adaptation to an unfriendly environment.

But that family pattern, as Jacob Neusner demonstrates, was already there, at least embryonically, centuries before, in the Talmudic reconstruction of Jewish culture. In the face of successive defeats—the destruction of the Second Temple and of the Jewish Commonwealth and the rise of an ungrateful daughter religion—the authors and redactors of the rabbinic texts shifted the emphasis in Jewish life from national resurrection to the study and performance of detailed rituals. As this became the focus of Jewish life, it was also necessary to recreate biblical role models: thus the warrior King David is depicted as a proto-Talmudist, like the son of Noah, Shem, and Shem's grandson, Eber. Anything orienting Jewish life toward military affairs is kept out of the Talmudic prescriptions: King Messiah, for example, is exalted as a future respondent to legal conundrums but never as a warrior.

These interpretive traditions are critical for understanding modern stereotypes (and self-stereotypes) of Jewish masculinity. The polarity constructed between Jacob and Esau returns in a provocative fashion in Nietzsche, for whom Jews became the destined priests of slave morality. Unlike the joyous warrior who innocently and instinctively vents hostility, Jews, Nietzsche explains, have learned to fight by cunning. They manipulate the "bad conscience" of others, which they have shaped by introducing "guilt," "sin," and other servile concepts. Jews are accused of making the West ashamed of the Hellenic worship of physical beauty and of supplanting a virile civilization with the ideal of self-mortification. With due respect to Nietzsche's "liberal" interpreters, these criticisms are not directed at Christians first and at Jews secondarily. True, Nietzsche deplored anti-Semitism, but he also leveled numerous attacks, particularly in his correspondence, on Judaism as the source of Christian self-debasement. He also mocked Jewish cunning and lack of aristocratic virtue.

As a recently published French anthology of essays, *De Sils-Maria à Jérusalem: Nietzsche et le judaïsme* (1991), edited by Dominique Bourel and Jacques Le Rider, makes clear, Nietzsche's ridicule of the Jews made a deep impression on early Zionists, who were drawn to Nietzsche for his lyrical style and anti-Christian neo-paganism.[221] For these Zionists it was important to meet Nietzsche's criticism by reconstructing Jewish identity in a Jewish homeland. Even the socialists among these Zionists thought Nietzsche had made valid observations about the unnatural mentality of their fellow Jews, even if he had also rejected socialism and liberalism.

It is not surprising that the candidly self-hating Jew Otto Weininger, in *Sex and Character* (1903), should dwell turgidly and splenetically on the problem of feminized Jewish men.[222] More interesting, in 1905 the father of what later became the Zionist Right, Zev Jabotinsky, proposed as basic to his nationalist movement the achievement of Jewish remasculinization:

> Our starting point is to take the typical Yid of today and to imagine his diametric opposite. Because the Yid is ugly, sickly, and lacks decorum, we shall endow the ideal image of the Hebrew with masculine beauty. The Yid is downtrodden and easily frightened, and, therefore, the Hebrew ought to be proud and independent.

Freud also read Nietzsche on the Jews and believed what he read, to the point that he sought physiological explanations for the "feminization" of Jewish males. According to Sander L. Gilman *in Freud, Race, and Gender* (1993), the father of modern psychology long agonized over the "proneness to hysteria" and other "female qualities" that he thought typical of Jewish men. He found these qualities, which he identified with his own father, embarrassing, and he speculated on how they might be removed provided they were not part of an "immutable biological construction."

In recent years this issue of feminized Jewish males has reemerged in a different context: an intramural Jewish dispute over contemporary Jewish identity. Neither side in this dispute is particularly pro-Western: both view Western Christian society as a continuing fount of anti-Jewish sentiment. But for one side Western Christian hostility is responsible for Jewish feminization, while for the other it produced the forced masculinization of a once "sensitive" Jewish culture. The sides are presented (or present themselves) as "tough" vs. "soft," or in Yiddish, "starke" vs. "schwache." Meir Kahane's *Never Again!* (1971) and Ruth Wisse's *If I Am Not for Myself: The Liberal Betrayal of the Jews* (1992) are representative of the "tough" Jews; Paul Breines's *Tough Jews: Political Fantasies and the Moral Dilemma of American Jewry* (1990) and the writings of Jewish feminist Letty C. Pogrebin exemplify the "soft" thinking.

Having forced myself to read such polemics, I am struck more by the similarities than by the differences between the two sides. Both are fixated on the insidious presence of anti-Semitism and express Jewish alienation from Gentile society, but both also reveal no positive religious elements. Wisse and Kahane, though residing in North America, scold other Jews for not recognizing Israel as their only homeland. For both of these toughs, Arab opposition to Israel is derivative from Christian anti-Semitism, which also informed the Nazi movement. As Wisse, a frequent *Commentary* contributor, puts it:

> The Arab charge that the creation of Israel is a crime against an Arab people has much in common with the earlier Christian charge that the Jews denied the son of God, or that of the Nazis that the Jews polluted the Aryan race. These charges are unanswerable except through dissolution of the Jewish religion, the Jewish people, the Jewish state.

Though the softs seem to like what Wisse condemns, a "Jewish civilization of self-blame," and what Kahane presents as the "victory of Hellenism over the Jewish people," clearly the two sides agree on other matters. For toughs and softs, the victory of the Left throughout the West would not be a bad thing, as long as leftist anti-Semitism were controlled. For the softs, conservative movements are inevitably unkind, anti-feminist, and anti-Jewish. In Breines's words: "A critique of tough Jews ought, then, to begin and end with a summons gently to abolish the conditions that generate toughness." A continued alliance with international socialism and feminism, argue the softs, helps Jews and other oppressed minorities. It weakens traditionalist cultures in which Jews have been disadvantaged, and so Zionists should aim at cooperation with social and cultural progressives everywhere. Though Breines is more sympathetic to "feminized" Jewish males than Wisse or Kahane, his reasoning is also anchored in an appeal to Jewish self-interest. Like the toughs, Breines thinks Jewish interests are best protected where Gentiles are not allowed to be their unruly selves.

In a perceptive review of Wisse's book, Allan C. Brownfeld makes the point that "for an academician of note, Wisse's discussion of liberalism is largely superficial. She does not properly differentiate between the classical liberalism of the nineteenth century . . . and the statist liberalism of the twentieth century." Moreover, "what seems to disturb Wisse most is the classical liberalism which ended the theocratic exclusion of Jews from the life and culture of Western Europe. She seems to long to restore the ghetto walls, which maintained the kind of artificial Jewish unity she would like once again to impose." What Brownfeld might have added is that Wisse and other Jewish toughs are producing their own Jewish counterpart to black separatism: presenting Jews as Western victims, who are to be indulged no matter what they demand, whether it is the right to view themselves as embattled anti-Westerners condemning their loss of collective identity or only a universal attention to their concerns. Brownfeld is right that Wisse has fewer reservations about contemporary than about classical liberalism. The old liberalism brought Jews into a European middle-class civilization that she wishes to have them forget. The new liberalism, though sometimes allied with the Palestinians, features the kind of victimology in which Wisse feels most at home.

As for the debate about the feminization of Jewish males, it might be best to pursue it under different auspices. Toughs and softs are both Jewish victimologists wearing interchangeable masks, like feminists and men's rights groups. One even finds the same Jewish figures combining soft and tough stances, e.g., Alan Dershowitz, Abe Rosenthal, and Martin Peretz, all social liberals who are Zionist hawks. Here the affinities to Afro-American nationalism are all too plain. In both cases the most militant and easily offended nationalists feel a natural pull in America toward the victimological Left. That pull is subject to change only when the Left favors some other victim group at the expense of one's own. But as soon as that sense of slight passes, the militant, alienated majority again aligns itself with the Left.

Thus Jewish toughs and black power advocates typically identify themselves with the same political side as gays and feminists. Alienation is a stronger theme in both instances than the cult of masculinity. Both Wisse and Kahane rebuke Jewish liberals for not being sufficiently suspicious of Gentiles. Liberalism, for these toughs, would be fine, so long as it incorporated enough Jewish suspicion of Arabs and their Western Christian apologists. This tough position is entirely consistent with the liberalism it never gets around to criticizing. It is in fact parasitic on that liberalism, like black separatists and Irish American supporters of both the IRA and Ted Kennedy. Behind all these shows of masculine toughness is the same whining by self-designated victims, much of it intended for guilt-obsessed WASPs. And the point of this whining is always the same: certain victims are not getting enough attention and refuse to be Uncle Toms. This may exemplify the proneness to hysteria that Freud believed afflicted only Jewish males.

I close this essay with one critical observation about the best of the works studied in the course of my research: Paul Breines's *Tough Jews* (1990).[223] In a detailed discussion of American Jewish schlock, Breines notes the continuing popularity of tough Zionist novelists like Leon Uris, Gloria Goldreich, Chayym Zeldis, and Joel Gross (the most prototypical of these authors, Ben Hecht, belonged to an older generation). Such novelists appeal to aggressive Jewish nationalists in America, who are always criticizing fellow Jews as "self-hating." Breines observes the cultural resentment abounding in some Zionist novels, which invariably treat German Jews as Uncle Toms and the old Protestantized American Jewish elite as even worse. The aesthetic and moral judgments here are certainly sound, but Breines ascribes too much of a consistent rightist gestalt to his subjects. Are they psychological "fascists," as he seems to suggest, or just too contradictory and too trivial to be assigned ideological labels?

And was that ardent Europeanist and despiser of communism, Zev Jabotinsky, the spiritual ancestor of the tough Jews who read and write hyper-Zionist schlock? The pre–World War I generation of tough Jews whom Breines cites faced real existential and cultural problems: their identification with Western thought in a society that was largely non-Westernized and the task of transforming that society, to which they felt morally and ancestrally bound, into something that they could admire and that also would survive its enemies. In no sense did Jabotinsky, a multilingual novelist who felt at home in most of Europe, foreshadow the American ghettoized schlepp who reads Goldreich, Zeldis, and perhaps Ruth Wisse: i.e., one who gets macho kicks out of accounts about how Israelis shoot Arabs or capture Nazi scientists but also allows himself to be dominated by his opinionated, bleached-blonde spouse. Breines's genealogy is wrong for at least two reasons: first, he goes too far in demonizing Jabotinsky's and Freud's Jewish self-criticism, and then he assigns too much theoretical importance to those who are better left to satirists. As one Austro-German Jew to another, I would urge Breines to lighten up and take schlepps less seriously.

A Race Apart

Chronicles

JUNE 2000

A people still, whose
common ties are gone;
Who, mixed with every race,
are lost in none.
　　　—George Crabbe

K EVIN MACDONALD'S THE *Culture of Critique* (1998), a study of
the Jewish people in sociobiological perspective, will not likely
help his career for reasons having nothing to do with the
author's scholarship or his accumulation of pertinent evidence. While
treating his subjects respectfully, attributing to Ashkenazic Jews a mean
IQ one standard deviation higher than that of white gentiles, he commits
the indiscretion of describing Jewish behavioral characteristics noted as
well by anti-Semites: for example, an aggressive demeanor toward the
core cultures of host peoples in combination with the practice of ritually
and socially prescribed separation from gentiles, which he ascribes to a
form of collective consciousness that may be inborn as well as culturally
acquired. MacDonald presents this consciousness as endemic to a group
that has worked strenuously to preserve its genotypal identity.

MacDonald's argument is based on two presuppositions. One, Mac-
Donald regards the Jews not as a succession of self-identified peoples

revealing genetic and cultural overlap, but as a single nation existing from antiquity to the present. Since Jews view themselves in this fashion and because they have been at pains, until recently, to refrain from inter-marriage, his assumption may be defensible. Two, MacDonald main-tains that contemporary Jews, particularly in the United States, oppose and protest even the remnants of the Christian host culture not because of any threat they face but simply in order to displace what they view as alien. Their distinctive culture, group dynamics, and jealously guarded genetic inheritance explain why organized Jewry resists any public man-ifestation of a non-Jewish American identity. Related to this stance of relentless opposition, which finds academic expression in the "culture of critique," is a Jewish characteristic that MacDonald views as invariably present: a drive to compete for social and material resources with those perceived as outsiders.

Since Jews supposedly have acquired a cognitive advantage over most other groups through careful eugenic practices, competition yields them remarkable success. In the past, their group performance was hin-dered by the host peoples' possession of a degree of ethnic consciousness comparable to their own. In these circumstances—medieval Europe, say, or twentieth-century Russia—Jews have been limited in their collective and individual ambitions. As MacDonald explains in the second two volumes of his trilogy, such obstacles forced them to adopt daring strate-gies, most fatefully the embrace of revolutionary ideologies and programs. As an embattled out-group, Jews supported and led revolu-tionary movements in vast disproportion to their numbers. And while tensions have existed over the last two hundred years between Rabbinic and revolutionary Jews, MacDonald is correct in suggesting that the conflict has not been as sharp as is commonly believed. Many observant Jews have been on the political Left, and today Orthodox Jews feel no compunction about voting for left-liberal politicians such as Barbara Boxer and Charles Schumer. (The same observation would apply to Catholic minorities in England and Canada.)

Like most speculative studies, MacDonald's work is open to ques-tion. Its emphasis on the continuities between ancient and modern Jews assumes more sameness than may exist, while exaggerating the degree to which Jewish theism was an invention intended to intensify ethnic solidarity. A huge historiographic literature presents the opposite view: namely, that Jewish national consciousness began as a by-product of Jewish monotheism. And in pre-Rabbinic Judaism, intermarriage did occur frequently between Jewish and non-Jewish elites—Moses, Solomon, and the rulers of the two post-Solomonic Jewish kingdoms and of the Hasmoneans at the end of the Second Commonwealth all were married to gentile wives.

Generalizations about prohibitions against intermarriage derived from the restrictions imposed on the Kohanim (the Jewish priestly class) can be dangerous. As explained in Leviticus and by the priestly historian Josephus, the priesthood represented a "pure race" by virtue of having kept itself from certain forms of intermarriage. Among the forbidden unions in question, however, were those between priests and widows or divorcees, while priestly families were expected (and continue to be expected, especially among Sephardim) to marry within their caste. Exogamy for non-priestly Jews is an overstepping of social boundaries. Moreover, the most outspoken of the Jewish separatists at the time of Jesus were the Essenes. According to Josephus's *History of the Jews*, no other Jewish sect, including the eventually triumphant Pharisees, went so far to avoid contact with alien peoples. But Essenes were also self-isolated monks, whose members shunned contact with women as much as they did with gentiles.

MacDonald also infers too much from current Jewish social behavior. Granting that present-day Jews and Jewish organizations deny to host nations the ethnic solidarity they claim for themselves, what historical generalizations can be drawn from that fact? MacDonald leaves the impression that Jews in exile have always operated in this fashion, but the gaps in historical evidence are too large to justify the inference. As he himself acknowledges, Jews a thousand years ago viewed life among gentiles as a penalty for their sins, a penalty that they would continue to suffer until a national savior returned them to their ancestral land. Before the last two centuries, Jews were in no position to dispossess gentiles, but coexisted with them in a situation of disparity. Even had they wanted to take over a Christian society, such a goal would have seemed beyond reach. And given their exclusion from professional and many commercial activities, premodern Jews could not successfully compete for resources. But is the Jews' present attempt at reconstructing gentile societies a recurrent aspect of Jewish-gentile relations? Or is MacDonald dealing with a unique cultural context, in which Jews and gentiles play historically conditioned roles?

Over the last hundred years or so, Jews have moved out of a traditional Talmudic society to assume commanding positions in an increasingly secularized and morally confused Christian world; they have done so most dramatically in anglophone societies, whose Protestantism represents Christianity in its least anti-Semitic form and whose prevalent political traditions are the most individualistic. From these favorable circumstances, according to MacDonald, two developments have emerged: Jews have made disproportionate contributions to science, the professions, and commerce; they have also contributed to the breakdown of traditional gentile culture.

MacDonald has devoted an entire volume to the latter activity, treating it as illustrating a Jewish double standard. While celebrating internationalism, socially critical individualism, and antiseptically secular public squares, Jews are forever making exceptions for themselves. Those who fail to recognize and exalt this exception earn the censure of Jewish spokesmen, who condemn them either as anti-Semites or as Jewish self-haters. MacDonald offers so many instances of this double standard that he belabors the obvious as he reaches back to the late nineteenth century for examples of Jewish civic leaders taking stands simultaneously on behalf of a supposed Jewish right to ethnic cohesion and a heterogeneous American nation. According to MacDonald, this inconsistency was typical of the relatively assimilated German Jews in the United States, even before the arrival of their Eastern European coreligionists.

The Jews' current view of the United States as a culturally evolving "global democracy" goes back a long way in the history of American Jewish organizations. Their preachments, far from having been inspired by the Holocaust, were being propagated even before the Eastern European Jewish immigration of the early twentieth century. And the wedding of these views to the justification of Jewish ethnic particularity, MacDonald convincingly demonstrates, contributed to pluralist agendas drawn up in the early part of the century. German Jewish humanist and socialist Horace Kallen expressed both a call for political internationalism and the hope that the United States would be filled with ethnic enclaves; MacDonald speculates that Kallen's Jewish identity and his sense of marginality in a gentile society contributed to his pluralist politics.

MacDonald notes the overlap between contemporary Jewish polemics against immigration restrictionists and those produced by Jewish organizations in the 1920s. Well before midcentury, Jews were savaging critics of liberal immigration policies as "un-American" and "Nordic supremacists." These invectives, coming from the opponents of the McCarran-Walter Act of 1952, had also been directed against supporters of the naturalization acts of the 1920s. In both cases, public advocates for restriction emphasized cultural and economic, not biological, considerations in suggesting immigration policy for the United States. MacDonald shows how persistent the issue of open borders has been for his subjects. Jews have combined intervention on behalf of immigration and the demonization of immigration restrictionists with the promotion of "diversity education." The Anti-Defamation League has introduced and sponsored "A World of Difference Together," a program for public education that it is now exporting to Germany, Russia, and South Africa.

MacDonald does not present such advocacy as the misguided humanitarian design of those whose ancestors suffered dispersion and who are therefore receptive to later strangers. Instead, he locates Jewish support for multiculturalism in the context of an already venerable strategy: "de-ethnicizing" the once majority population while insisting on the right of Jews as righteous victims to persist as an ethnic cluster. Although the interpretive perspective seems correct, at least for the United States, two questions nevertheless go begging. Was Jewish intervention decisive for the immigration revolution of the mid-1960s? If not, were other factors and circumstances critical to the success of that revolution—in which Jewish bullying and complaining played a secondary role? My guess from reading Chilton Williamson, Peter Brimelow, and Lawrence Auster is that the reassessment of immigration, especially from the Third World, was part of a general cultural change that beset Western societies and was pushed by the managerial state. While Jews contributed to cultural change and immigrationism energetically and disproportionately, they were far from constituting a sufficient cause. In countries without a conspicuous Jewish presence (say, Scandinavia and Germany), the same general cultural-political trends can be observed.

Two observations are in order regarding Jewish-American tendencies highlighted in MacDonald's third volume. First, assaults by American Jewish leaders against a Judeo-Christian core culture do not advance any rational Jewish interest. It is hard to see how Jews benefit from awarding preferential treatment to blacks and Hispanics, insisting that the Ten Commandments be removed from public schools, or denigrating the heritage of America's white majority; they would seem to have a greater interest in supporting a Western Christian society in the United States than in helping to subvert the remnants of one. Why should they wish to replace a world that amply rewards their talents with one that will likely be less tolerant of them? Or in the words of my friend Rabbi Meyer Schiller, "Do American Jews honestly believe that multicultural majorities will give them bigger Holocaust monuments?"

The second observation concerns the present state of Western Protestant societies. The "culture of critique" has done best among those whom James Kurth (himself a Presbyterian) calls "progressively deformed" Protestant peoples. Starting with the theologically based individualistic and anti-hierarchical bias of classical Protestantism, this deformation of Reformationist thought has expressed itself in various late-modernist obsessions, most of them linked to Protestant sources but without the sobering notions of Original Sin and divine redemption, these Protestant variants emphasize moral subjectivity and self-esteem, while replacing the concept of sin with that of social guilt.

Fits of self-rejection are also characteristic of deformed Protestants, and in the United States, Canada, Germany, and England, Protestant clergy have been in the forefront of those demanding atonement for racism, anti-Semitism, sexism, and homophobia. Ray Honeyford and Claus Nordbruch have documented the growing role of the English and German governments in pushing victimological agendas, and that of Protestant churches in conspicuously goading them on: In the United States, even the Religious Right is not immune to this mentality. For neoconservative philosopher Sidney Hook, MacDonald observes, "ethnic diversity" was a code word for democracy. He sees Hook's sleight of hand as yet another example of the Jewish attempt to destabilize out-groups, but in fact it represents something more significant: This is the way gentile conservatives, almost all professing Christians, wish to see their national and religious heritage. Hook took his place within the American conservative movement as a spokesman for American values.

No assessment of this multivolume work would be complete without commenting on MacDonald's assertions concerning Jewish cognitive superiority. His assumptions on the subject coincide with those of respected scholars, among them Hans Eysenck, who (shortly before his death in 1995) approved the presuppositions upon which MacDonald's first volume rests. Noting Jewish ascendancy in the financial and professional worlds, Ashkenazic Jewish overrepresentation among chess champions and Nobel Prize recipients, and the continuing standard deviation between Ashkenazic Jewish and white gentile IQ scores, MacDonald and Eysenck attribute Jewish accomplishments to successful reproductive strategy. Other explanations, however, are available. According to researcher J.R. Flynn, mean IQ across ethnic groups has risen by approximately 0.2 percent each year. This steady rise can be linked to environmental factors, particularly the frequency of test-taking and exposure to test materials among the young. The Flynn effect may also point to environmental reasons for displays of Jewish intelligence during the last several generations. Jewish urbanization, professional aggressiveness, and the repeated exposure of Jewish children to test-taking may all be leading to the prize-gathering coups noted by Eysenck and MacDonald. Those who push themselves forward, whether on research teams, in business organizations, or as applicants for professional schools, will do better, *ceteris paribus*, than those who (like my Pennsylvania Dutch neighbors) have been taught not to stand out in a crowd.

Within the same civilization, moreover, ethnic groups and subgroups have been culturally productive for a time, and then declined. The Lowland Scots, Northern Italians, Swabian Germans, and American WASPs have all waned culturally, and in other ways, after making remarkable contributions to learning and the arts. The theory put forth by Arnold Toynbee—that peoples rise to greatness by responding to particular challenges—may shed light here. Furthermore, Jewish cooperation and Jewish competitive strategies as explained by MacDonald obviously account, at least in part, for present Jewish successes.

For me, the most engrossing part of MacDonald's trilogy is a long, learned section in the third volume entitled, "The Frankfurt School and Pathologization." *The Authoritarian Personality*, published in 1950 by the American Jewish Committee, bore the marks of the Frankfurt School.[224] Its editors and contributors, particularly Theodor Adorno and Max Horkheimer, were the fathers of the school's Critical Theory, and it is hard to study that turgid exploration of "fascist" and "pseudo-democratic" personality types without noticing its social point of reference: Adorno, Horkheimer, Else Frenkel, and Paul Lazarsfeld were all Frankfurt groupies before they contributed to this collective enterprise. So were Erich Fromm and Herbert Marcuse, who wrote supporting puff pieces. The pivotal themes in *The Authoritarian Personality*, as emphasized by MacDonald, were nothing new to those who assisted in the project; rather, they represented the same complaints directed against Western—not only German—society by the youthful radicals grouped around Adorno at the University of Frankfurt in the early 1930s. From Frankfurt, these "anti-Nazis" emigrated to the United States; later, they reestablished their ideas in postwar Germany in the context of Allied denazification. Little attention was paid to the fact that the proposed antidotes for Nazism were not exactly disease-specific: They targeted anything that gave cohesion to middle-class families and societies.

MacDonald argues that the "pathologization" of normal gentile society in *The Authoritarian Personality* foreshadows today's coerced political correctness. The social criticism of the Frankfurt School implies the need for a powerful regime of socialist administrators to level inequalities and resocialize reactionary personalities. MacDonald links this call for massive social engineering to characteristically Jewish concerns and anxieties shared by its overwhelmingly Jewish formulators: The gentile Other would remain—or so it was assumed—a prowling presence absent reconstruction of the surrounding society. The plea for resocialization in 1950 continued to resonate among Jewish "social scientists" who shared Adorno's fears; both it and the rhetoric in which it was couched live on in the efforts of some Jewish organizations to identify traditional Christian values with incipient "fascism."

Mopping Up
the Israel Lobby

Taki's Magazine

NOVEMBER 11, 2007

T HE LIVRE *de scandale* of John J. Mearsheimer and Stephen M.
Walt, *The Israel Lobby and US Foreign Policy* (2007), was for
me a mostly disappointing read. Having seen the earlier article
by these two illustrious academics, one at Chicago and the other at Harvard, "The Israel Lobby," in the *London Review of Books* (May 2006),
I found nothing particularly original about the expanded version. Their
five-hundred-page book is noticeably repetitious and by the time one
reaches the conclusion, one has heard it all before. The ecstatic reaction
by Michael Massing in that *Pravda* of East Coast Jewish liberalism, the
New York Review of Books, is full of overstatement. What "detonates
with force" for the Eastern establishment reacted on me far less dramatically. Unlike the hysteria at the *New York Review* occasioned by a real
iconoclast, Norman Finkelstein, who pulls no punches when going after
the German-haters and the Holocaust-exploiters, the explications of
Mearsheimer and Walt are so soporific that it may be hard for anyone
but an AIPAC fanatic to get really mad at them. "Respectable" critics of
the Israeli lobby are, for the authors, certifiable leftists such as Jimmy
Carter, the homosexual activist playwright Tony Kushner, and the ultra-

liberal leaders of American Reform Judaism. To their credit, Walt and Mearsheimer do make respectful references to Pat Buchanan, Robert Novak, and Georgie Anne Geyer as critics of the first Iraq War, who pointed the finger at AIPAC for fomenting the invasion of Kuwait.

But the illustrious authors, both pillars of the foreign policy journalistic establishment, have conspicuous liberal blind spots. For example, they seem to believe that support for the Iraq War comes entirely from "the very extreme Right," as I heard Professor Mearsheimer emphasize in a panel discussion at Swarthmore in 2005. Moreover, there is insufficient recognition in the book that some of the strongest criticism of the Israeli lobby has emanated from the paleo Right. This is one reason that liberal commentators, most recently in the *New Statesman*, have presented paleos as "anti-Semitic," a charge that is also habitually made by the same sources in noting the Old Right's opposition to the neoconservative-inspired war in Iraq.

The authors' knowledge about religious matters is so embarrassingly limited that one has to blush whenever they touch on things ecclesiastical. "Christian Zionists" is for them a synonym for "Dispensationalists," who are imagined to be a Svengalian presence hovering over our otherwise progressive land. But many "Christian Zionists" are not people fixed on a peculiar reading of the Book of Revelation but garden-variety, misguided Philosemites. Moreover, Evangelical is not synonymous with Dispensationalist or Fundamentalist, as the authors might have learned from reading Darryl Hart, George Marsden, Mark Shibley, or any one of a few hundred other American religious historians. Unlike the Fundamentalists, the Evangelicals, who make up much of Rudolph Giuliani's support base, have been sliding leftward on theological and social issues for decades. But like George W. Bush, Michael Gerson, Cal Thomas, and Ralph Reed, they are embattled Zionists and advocates of an American mission to spread "human rights," even at the point of a bayonet.

The authors also take an overly optimistic view of both normal American international relations and the possibility for ending Middle Eastern tensions by showing the Israeli government tough love. On this last point I am closer to Harvey Sicherman and James Kurth of the Foreign Policy Research Institute than I am to my friends on the paleo Right. The religious and cultural hatreds that inflame the Muslim world would likely be there even if the Israelis managed to cut a deal with the Palestinians. And significantly, the Israeli "new historians," whom the authors quote for recognizing the obvious fact that Zionists engaged in ethnic cleansing against Palestinians, typically do not come down on the Mearsheimer-Walt side in terms of how to deal with the Palestinians at the present time. While one might readily concede that American Indians were expelled from their tribal territories in the nineteenth century, why would anyone but a self-hating white Christian call for allowing Indian tribes to take back sizable chunks of the United States? And it would seem even more foolhardy to welcome back into one's land those who have repeatedly called for killing or expelling the present settlers. Mearsheimer and Walt note that Israelis seem willing to create a separate state for West Bankers, while continuing to treat as citizens the one-million-plus Palestinians living in Israel proper. But Israelis polled on these matters would not try to absorb hundreds of thousands of Palestinian refugees, many of them from camps in Lebanon and Jordan, into their already multinational and Palestinian-laden population.

It might also be asked why the Israelis, who run a Western-type constitutional government, should trust the Palestinians politically—even if admittedly Israeli military forces have sometimes taken brutal revenge on the Palestinians after Hamas-incited terror bombings. There is nothing in the Palestinian, or for that matter the Arab Muslim, past that would suggest the likelihood that they would honor and enforce treaties or control violent minorities that might seek to wipe out the Israelis. I am always amazed when my friends on the Right who, although justly skeptical of the belief that Arab Muslims could develop Western-type regimes, express every confidence that the Palestinians are closet-moderates. All that is needed for the unexpected to happen is for the Israelis to give the West Bankers a chance by clearing out of the West Bank and by giving the Arabs control of East Jerusalem.

If I were an Israeli, I would not support these concessions, and certainly not at this time, even if the American government cut its six billion dollars in annual direct aid. Nor has the special relation with Israel always been as one-sided as the authors suggest. It is highly unlikely that certain delicate missions, e.g., bombing Iraqi nuclear installations in 1978 or the Israeli strike on Syrian territory last month to test its radar system, took place without bi-national cooperation.

Mearsheimer and Walt are correct to stress that the American government, as in the Pollard Affair, has put up with outrageous behavior from the Israelis that it would not likely have accepted from most other (Western) countries. Moreover, the amount of money that is transferred each year from the United States to Israel, in private Zionist donations and military equipment as well as public aid, is in the tens of billions of dollars—and this payoff cannot be fully explained in terms of "American national interest." But what can be questioned is whether the United States has come out of this relation entirely empty-handed. And despite the long chapter about how AIPAC mucks up our dealings with Iran, I am not convinced that Mahmoud Ahmadinejad and his mullah advisers would not be bulls in the china shop of international relations even without the disinformation provided by the Israeli lobby. The Iranian government would remain a problem for us even if Israeli Prime Minister Ehud Olmert, in a speech on May 24, 2006, had not tried to goad the US Congress into taking military action against Ahmadinejad.

Equally challengeable is the unstated but strongly suggested notion that our relation with Israel has derailed what might otherwise be a rational foreign policy. *Pace* the authors, our ties to Israel are characteristic of how American foreign policy is conducted, on the basis of internal ideological and ethnic pressures. AIPAC is simply better at doing what the Black Caucus, gay and feminist groups, Armenian and Greek Americans, American supporters of the IRA and other special pleaders have tried to achieve for many decades—influencing American foreign policy. The problem is that in a mass, pluralistic democracy this situation is all too normal. It would be happening even if the Israeli lobby were not around.

But what makes this lobby especially obnoxious, and this is the one valuable series of revelations in the book, is not only its money and power. It is also the lobby's arrogance and sheer viciousness, which extends to issues going beyond Israeli security, and which is manifested in its close ties to such shrieking gentile-haters as Abe Foxman and Alan Dershowitz. AIPAC enjoys and cultivates the support of some very unpleasant types, who specialize in maligning those they disagree with. On page after page, the authors document AIPAC's defaming of politicians such as Charles Percy and Paul Findlay (both from Illinois) who dared to question our "special relation" with Israel. These and other politicians were routinely smeared as "anti-Semites," and most of them were brought down by the charge. Incidentally, the authors, to their credit, don't bother to distinguish between AIPAC and its numerous slanderous front organizations, such as the Anti-Defamation League. These groups act in unison not only by backing what the Israeli government, and especially the Israeli nationalist Right, wants but also by wielding what Pat Buchanan has called "the branding iron of the charge of anti-Semitism."

What is frequently omitted from the larger picture, but something that the authors notice, is that such charges as Jew-baiting or being a "self-hating Jew" are often leveled at unlikely targets. For example, the Anti-Defamation League in 1998 tried very hard to keep Metropolitan Books from publishing Norman Finkelstein and Ruth Bettina Birn's

A Nation on Trial (1998), a closely researched refutation of Daniel Goldhagen's *Hitler's Willing Executioners* (1997). The work has nothing to do with endangering Israeli security, it simply discredits Goldhagen's preposterous thesis, that "the Holocaust was not simply the product of Nazi beliefs and Hitler's own madness but was rooted in a pervasive 'eliminationist ideology' rooted in German society that predated the Nazi period." AIPAC and its affiliates, and the Central Committee for Jews in Germany, worked overtime trying to keep this refutation, by honorable Jewish authors, from being published and circulated. The reason for this zeal was not that Finkelstein and Birn were defending Israel's interests but that their would-be censors hated Germans.

My tribulations ten years earlier when I was trying to obtain a graduate professorship at Catholic University of America indicated the same thought patterns among my enemies as those of Finkelstein's. Those who blocked my appointment complained to administrators that I was "not entirely reliable on Israel." But at the time I had expressed no views about Israel that were different from those of my accusers. What made them attack me at least in one demonstrable case was that my writings had questioned Germany's "sole responsibility" for the origins of World War I. The subject had nothing to do with Israel but everything to do with certain tribal prejudices that those associated with AIPAC hoped to keep alive.

In the end it didn't matter whether my accusers were the employees of AIPAC, of the ADA, or of the American Jewish Committee, or in this case merely misguided Zionist neoconservatives. Making such distinctions among all of these interlocking groups is about as useful as trying to distinguish in the 1940s between the Lawyers' Guild or the Soviet-American Friendship League and the American Communist Party. Further, as Peter Novick has shown in *The Holocaust in American Life* (1999), a book on the reactions to the Holocaust in America, American (and even more opportunistically European) Zionists have been eager to highlight the collective guilt of Christians for the killing of European Jewry because the resulting guilt feelings are thought to help the Israeli cause. Although obviously true, another reason for this invidious focus is that those who apply it are expressing a gut reaction to Christians. This may be even more critical for their behavior than the desire to exploit Christian guilt for Zionist ends. The blown-up charges against Christianity as the *fons et origo* of Nazi anti-Semitism and the generally meek reactions that these accusations elicit, as my book *Multiculturalism and the Politics of Guilt* (2002) suggests, illustrate a quintessential sadomasochistic relation, which AIPAC has not hesitated to exploit.

This brings me to a final observation, which much of the material in the Mearsheimer-Walt volume can be cited to underscore. For many Americans, and particularly those on the Old Right, it is difficult to distinguish the Israelis from their partisans in this country. The fault is not entirely that of the Israelis. Being a vulnerable, beleaguered small country, they will take aid where they can, and particularly from generous overseas patrons who have the ear of politicians. And these patrons have come through time and again, shutting up Israel's critics and making sure that the foreign aid and military equipment keep rolling in. But this has been achieved at a high price—part of which in this country has been allowing the neoconservatives to lord it over a cowardly and fearful American Right, whose members live in fear of being called "racists" or "anti-Semites."

But even within the existing sadomasochistic relation that the Israeli lobby has heretofore milked, there are other possible developments that may not favor the Israelis in the long run. Weakening Christian institutions, while opening the Western world to Islamic and other Third World influences, does not help the Jews here or in Israel. It might also be helpful for the Israelis if the United States had a more deeply Christian character and more secure borders. Admittedly, pushing for a less Western West may satisfy particular inveterate hates—which cause their bearers to exaggerate Christian anti-Semitism and to encourage the resettling of Western countries by non-Western populations (a policy that in Europe means Muslims). But such policies destroy what remains of the substance of the only civilization that is likely to assist the Israelis out of genuine affection.

Moreover, the victimized pets of the guilt-ridden, often culturally illiterate Christians do not have to remain Jewish victims. In Europe the victim card is already going over to the Muslim immigrants, who usually dislike Jews even more than they do Christians. No matter how strenuously European Zionists may blame Christians for Muslim vandalism against Jewish targets, the truth might be more important than the pleasures of goy-bashing. These are facts that the Israelis themselves should take into consideration. Their supporters in other lands show defective long-term political judgment because their heads are not screwed on straight. And if the gentiles ever awaken from their stupefying, self-inflicted politics of guilt, God help those who have tried to use it!

Jews Against Israel

The American Conservative

JUNE 17, 2012

A N ANTI-war libertarian and a principled critic of Jewish nation-alism, Jack Ross seems the ideal author to have undertaken a biography of Elmer Berger (1908–96), the Reform rabbi who pursued a rearguard action against the Zionist movement for more than fifty years. An increasingly marginalized figure after the birth of the Jewish state in 1948, Berger spent the remainder of his life fighting through various organizations—particularly the American Council of Judaism, which he co-founded in 1942—against the inevitable victory of his enemies. It is now almost impossible to recall that there was a time when a large, influential body of Jewish leaders vehemently opposed the creation of a Jewish national state. Indeed, there was a time when most of Reform Jewry took that stand, and when Berger's book *The Jewish Dilemma* would not have occasioned the widespread Jewish indignation that it did when it was published in 1945.[225]

Berger's position in that work and in other polemical writings is clearly stated. If Jews insist on their ethnic uniqueness and define them-selves as a separate people entitled to their own country, then they are admitting that their adversaries have been right all along: Jews cannot be citizens of the countries in which they live, except in a purely techni-cal sense. They have their real country in the Middle East. Moreover, argued Berger, if the Zionist project succeeded, it would declare all Jews, no matter where they lived, to be first and foremost members of a purely Jewish state. The Zionists would therefore raise questions about the loyalty of Jewish citizens to the countries in which they lived, and the Zionists would do so in a way that would keep non-Israeli Jews permanently on the defensive.

Even more significantly for Berger, and for such other kindred spirits as State Department hands Alfred Lilienthal and George Levison, Rabbi Morris Lazaron of Baltimore, and Irving Reichert of Temple Emanu-El in San Francisco, Zionism was incompatible with a universalist understanding of Judaism based on prophetic ethics and not excluding the "Jewish" teachings of Jesus. Such ideas belonged to a Reform tradition that came from Germany in the mid-nineteenth century. Reform leaders such as the long-lived German-born Rabbi Isaac Mayer Wise, and such educational institutions as Hebrew Union College, founded in 1883, and the Union of American Hebrew Congregations, organized ten years earlier, showed the shaping influence of German Jews in the United States.

These formative ideas about universal ethics and social concern as the basis for religious practice were also reflected in the Pittsburgh Platform, which two of Wise's students, Kaufmann Kohler and Emil Hirsch, drafted in 1885. This authoritative platform for Reform congregations for half a century was unequivocally anti-Zionist and regarded most established Jewish ritual practices as coming out of an age that was "under the influence of ideas altogether foreign to our present moral and spiritual state." What Jews were expected to draw from the "Mosaic law"—and by implication, its later Rabbinic glosses—was the "God-idea as the central religious truth for the human race."

One might wonder how the adherents of this platform, who for all intents and purposes were German Jewish Unitarians, remained united through their rhetoric about moral progress. The answer is social cohesion, good manners, and the habit of attending the same congregation week after week. There was also nothing in their creed that stood in the way of their assimilation into the WASP upper crust, save for non-acceptance on the part of those they were coming to resemble through conscious imitation.

It is usually argued that the victory of the Zionist cause came about because of the anti-Jewish persecutions of the Nazi period. Undoubtedly the growth and importance of such groups as the World Jewish Congress and the fact that longtime critics of Zionism such as Berger's mentor Rabbi Louis Wolsey (who was originally associated with the Euclid Avenue Temple in Cleveland) went over to the Zionists in 1945 may be attributed to historic pressures: after World War II and the Holocaust, the establishment of a Jewish state seemed both necessary and just. (The Palestinians were peripheral to this decision; many Americans believed Palestine was largely unsettled before European Jews went there to live.)

But a far more critical explanation to which Ross's book may lead the reader—although that is not necessarily the author's intention—is social. The anti-Zionists were largely the upper-crust German Jews, while the Zionists were overwhelmingly the *Ostjuden* who arrived in the United States a few generations later and who seemed less clubbable. Some spokesmen for the anti-Zionists, like Wolsey and Reichert, were originally from Eastern Europe but worked hard to fit in. Berger, who grew up in an affluent home in Cleveland, was the son of a Hungarian Jewish railroad engineer, but his mother's family were German and had lived for generations in Texas before Elmer's mother, Selma Turk, moved to Ohio after her marriage. Elmer's association with the tony Reform Temple on Euclid Avenue was a socially desirable connection, and his decision to study for the Reform Rabbinate, without knowing a word of Hebrew, may have been the Jewish equivalent of becoming an Episcopal minister, when such a career move still counted for something.

As the struggle went against Berger's side, the American Council for Judaism had to look for new allies, most of whom would not have pleased its original membership. At first Berger's efforts against the Zionist project attracted people of high standing, such as the conservative isolationist senator Karl Mundt, Teddy Roosevelt's son Kermit, and the president of Union Theological Seminary, Henry Sloane Coffin. By the end of his life, however, Berger had to settle for radically leftist allies who shared, if nothing else, his negative attitude about Jewish nationalism. In the 1970s he built bridges to an ordained Conservative Rabbi, Everett Gendler, who combined disapproval of Israel with ties to the counterculture. Gendler was a close friend of both Abbie Hoffman and Todd Gitlin.

Despite recent attempts to treat Berger's cause as a leftist one, it certainly did not begin as such. One notices reading Ross's work how many of Berger's early associates were linked to the Republican Party and in some cases the America First movement that opposed US entry into World War II; they were located in places like Galveston, Texas; Shreveport, Louisiana; and San Francisco; that is, just about anywhere outside the Northeast. By contrast, one of the most prominent Zionists in America, the Reform Rabbi Stephen Wise, combined Jewish nationalism with communist fellow-traveling. At the same time Wise was defending Jewish political and ethnic identity, he was denouncing Churchill for

THE ESSENTIAL PAUL GOTTFRIED, ESSAYS FROM 1984–2024

daring to criticize communist oppression in his "Iron Curtain" speech of 1946. The leading Yiddish newspaper *Forward* in New York upheld Zionism and socialism with equal zeal.

Generally, the German Jews were politically well to the right of their Eastern European coreligionists. But most of the Eastern Europeans with congregational affiliations were Orthodox, while the German Jews sounded and acted like liberal mainline Protestants. It was also the case that as the ethnic and social composition of Reform Judaism changed, so did its politics. It moved to the left in American affairs while becoming more emphatically Zionist.

Other factors worked to the advantage of the Zionists, beside superior numbers and sympathy from Christians reacting to the persecution of European Jewry. They had an informed understanding of the core Jewish tradition, as opposed to the imaginative reconstruction devised by nineteenth-century German or German-American Jews. Jewish ethnic nationalists could find a multitude of Biblical texts to support their position, many of which Evangelicals have also noticed and taken seriously. The Prophets, who were beloved to the authors of the Pittsburgh Platform, were not silent when it came to foretelling the restoration and enlargement of the Jewish kingdom. (See for example Ezekiel's detailed sketch of the rebuilt Temple.) Perhaps the most famous medieval Jewish biblical commentator, the eleventh-century French Rabbi Solomon the son of Isaac, insisted that the story of Creation comes at the beginning of Genesis to confirm the right of the Jewish nation to repossess its homeland. No less than the Creator of the Universe, according to this commentator, guaranteed the Jewish claim to their ancestral territory.

Listening to the present members of the ACJ explain that the "Jewish tradition" categorically excludes a Jewish national identity, one has to wonder on what planet these advocates are living. It is certainly possible to challenge Jewish nationalism from a different religious perspective, but it's foolish to pretend that the Jewish tradition, about which the anti-Zionists usually seem to know little, rejects what it obviously and repeatedly affirms. The statement that Berger was fond of making that the Zionists were defending a form of Judaism "that is about fifty years old" is true only in a limited sense. Jews became modern nationalists only at the end of the nineteenth century. But it was a piece of cake for them to move from their traditional view of themselves as a "people" to modern political and ethnic nationalism.

Having offered these critical remarks about Berger's cause and Ross's valorous defense of the "Rabbi Outcast," let me also express my irrepressible sympathy for those who rallied to the anti-Zionist side. They comported themselves with dignity in a fight in which they were invariably outnumbered—and in a struggle in which their loudmouthed, bullying opponents behaved with predictable boorishness. It is even hard to notice any effect that the American Council for Judaism had on America's relations with Israel. The one time it exercised some clout, through its members in the State Department after World War II, the council seems to have advocated an anodyne policy of trying to maintain peace between Arabs and the growing Jewish settlement in Palestine. Even this policy, to whatever extent it was applied, had no effect on anything.

Ross cites the truly vicious attacks against Berger launched by his enemies when this aged gentleman was in no position to hurt AIPAC. Berger's adversaries continued to assault him even when he was frail and beaten. One would expect no better from such graceless winners.

Anti-Semitism in Antiquity: The Case of Apion

Chronicles

JULY 2020

I HAVE a passing interest in a first-century rhetorician and Hellenized Egyptian named Apion, who is the target of a famous polemic by Flavius Josephus, a member of the Jewish priestly class who became the court historian of the Flavian emperors. Published in Greek but known by its Latin name *Contra Apionem*, Josephus's diatribe faults Apion for siding with the local Greek population in Alexandria in their quarrels with their Hellenized Jewish neighbors.

While *Contra Apionem* is not perhaps Josephus's most admirable text, it provides insight into the personality of its author, whose historical writings are our most important source, after the New Testament, for understanding the Palestinian emergence of Christianity. It is also likely the first attempt in history to undermine an opponent through the charge of anti-Semitism: Josephus charged Apion with disrespecting the Jews by invidiously comparing them with the ancient Greeks. Given the present power of calling someone an anti-Semite, it is a polemic worth examining.

Apion argued that local Jews were seizing power from the descendants of a much more illustrious race—the ancient Greeks. The altercation resulted in a Jewish delegation traveling to Rome from Alexandria in AD 38 to appeal to the emperor, Caligula. Of course, Apion was not himself Greek, but he worked energetically as an upstart to associate himself with Hellenic culture, even writing a lexicon on Homeric Greek and producing well-chiseled Greek epigrams.

Apion's accusations against the Jews remain open to investigation. We are forced to rely mostly on his accuser for the list of charges, most of which Josephus probably culled from Apion's *Aegyptiaka*, which survives only in fragmentary form. As Josephus tells the story, Apion claimed that the Hebrew nation was not as glorious or as ancient a race as the Greeks, citing as proof the fact that Greek historians hardly ever mentioned the Jews in referring to historic nations and their cultural accomplishments. Josephus also states that Apion accused the Jews of engaging in strange religious rituals, including occasional cannibalism.

This chilling vice was certainly not exclusively ascribed to Jews. Two Greek historians, Herodotus and Diodorus Siculus, attribute cannibalism to various non-Greek peoples. Yet the Oedipus cycle is full of portentous references to the curse on the House of Atreus and its descendants, such as King Agamemnon. This series of disasters memorialized in Greek tragedy starts with two cannibalistic outrages, one committed by a distant ancestor, Tantalus, who tried to feed his son to the gods at a feast, and the other committed by Tantalus's grandson, Atreus, King of Mycenae, who fed his nephews to his brother Thyestes.

What we know about Apion comes mostly from Josephus's unfriendly account written about sixty years after Apion's death. Millennia later, the attacks continue. A 2016 article in the *Jerusalem Post* depicts Apion as the quintessential anti-Semite, who pioneered both the blood libel charge thrown at medieval Jews and the denigration of the same ethnic group by educated Nazis. The author, Eli Kavon, turns Apion into the precursor of his people's eternal enemy. One might think that Kavon had poured over Apion's words and perhaps had even gone beyond Josephus in looking for evidence of his subject's baseness. If so, then he might have revealed his special sources unknown to classical historians.

Kavon assures us that Josephus's charges must be true, because the author of *Contra Apionem* was a misunderstood Jewish patriot. Kavon even vouches for Josephus's supposedly honorable relationship with the Romans, who were then brutally mopping up a Jewish rebellion. During the Roman siege of Jotapata in the North of Palestine, Josephus, who was commanding Galilean forces, surrendered himself to the enemy.

Considerable debate has taken place about whether Josephus was, as he claimed, a war captive or a deserter. In any case, he was with the Roman legions when they besieged and then devastated Jerusalem.

A member of the Jewish nobility who had initially opposed the revolt, Josephus subsequently wrote a *History of the Jewish War* (AD 75–79), and did so under Roman imperial supervision. In that work, as well as in his *Vita* and in *Contra Apionem*, Josephus is "conveniently taken captive" and then placed in the care of the Roman emperor and his son Titus. Eventually, the erstwhile captive finds himself living in opulence at the imperial court.

Aside from Josephus's account of his falling under Roman "captivity," there are certain questionable statements that punctuate the opening section of *Contra Apionem*. Josephus stresses the care with which the Jewish high priests preserved intact all the sacred books of Hebrew scripture. Moreover, this "transmission" of Jewish antiquities was assisted by the Jewish prophets, who, on Josephus's telling, also assured the literal transmission of biblical texts.

In point of fact, neither group was assigned that particular task. But the high priests were charged with maintaining genealogical registers, something that Josephus does point out, though he confuses keepers and transmitters of sacred documents with historians. He segues from an enumeration of the tasks of the priestly classes among the Jews, Babylonians, and Egyptians to noting the failure of Greek historians to accurately preserve historical accounts. This comparison falls flat, since the activities that Josephus describes are not the same in the two cases.

He then explains that the priesthood that preserved the relevant documents was "an aristocratic class whose very function was to guard holy books as a sacred obligation." Moreover, they "were established as a class of priests that would remain unmixed and pure." Careful genealogical records were kept concerning which spouses Jewish priests were allowed to wed; and these spouses came unfailingly from their own *genos* (*shevet* in Hebrew). Even when driven into exile, members of the priestly class would work to preserve their pure lineage, the tainting of which would result in their removal from their customary functions.

One may wonder how any genetic requirement was necessary for keeping documents intact. Conceivably, an archivist could do this work, whether married to the daughter of a priest or to a commoner. However, Josephus is probably trying to answer a specific charge by Apion, perhaps that Jews were ethnically mixed with some particularly despised group of foreigners. But if that were the case, Josephus does not show that the charge is uniformly untrue. What he demonstrates is that this hypothetical charge wouldn't apply to his own caste.

Perhaps the most egregious error in the opening pages of the *Contra Apionem*, and one that is repeated intermittently in this polemic, is the denigration of Greek historiography. Because Greek chroniclers were "ignorant or feigned ignorance of our antiquities," we are led to assume that they were not serious about their craft.

Not surprisingly, those whom Josephus cites as idle dabblers are mostly minor figures who produced forgettable histories of the Athenians or Argives, or those writing in Greek who presumed to challenge his account of the Jewish uprising against Rome. He characterizes these writers as lacking any high purpose: The Greeks put together words "in an offhanded fashion in accordance with their whims."

Even when Greek historians write about events that actually occurred, "they seek fame without inquiring very deeply on the basis of their conceptions." Still worse, these dabblers were equally neglectful in depicting the Jewish War, "having never ventured into the places affected nor proceeding anywhere even close to the events, but preparing their exiguous accounts from hearsay and confusing their shameless drunken revelry with history."

One must ask whether Josephus ever heard of Thucydides, Polybius, and other Greek historians, who scrupulously examined sources and often wrote about events at which they had been present. According to Charles Norris Cochrane in his *Thucydides and the Science of History* (1929), Thucydides and those Greek historians who adopted his method of inquiry, devised an approach to studying human events that foreshadowed modern research techniques.[226]

Given Josephus's thorough classical education, we may assume that he knew something about the advances of Greek historiography, which had begun several centuries before his birth. Moreover, Josephus's identification of true historical writing with the investigation of "events" (*pragmata*) follows the definitions that had come down from Thucydides and Polybius. Josephus clearly had some idea of this Greek endeavor to separate the study of history from myth and to apply carefully constructed concepts of historical causation.

His snide remarks about the low quality of Greek historiography did not likely arise from ignorance. Rather, Josephus was irritated by the unwillingness of Greek historians to acknowledge the antiquity of the Jewish nation. He had dwelt on this subject in *The Antiquities of the Jews*, a treatise completed in AD 93, just before he settled scores with the long-dead Apion. Much of *Contra Apionem* is in fact devoted to demonstrating from Egyptian, Phoenician, and Chaldean sources how far back in time the Jewish people went.

Like other Greek writers, Apion had committed the cardinal sin of treating dismissively Josephus's ancestral nation. As a member of the Jewish aristocracy—a fact that he never lets us forget—Josephus probably found this anti-Semitic snub particularly offensive.

Driving Miss Racial Activist

Chronicles

FEBRUARY 2022

A T FIRST blush, the 1989 film *Driving Miss Daisy* seems innocuous. Its plot centers around the relationship of an aging Jewish matron, Daisy Werthan (Jessica Tandy), and her black chauffeur Hoke Colburn (Morgan Freeman). Yet a recent rewatch caused me to notice irksome elements of the plot I missed the first time around. This has to do with the injection of the producer's politics in an otherwise pleasant movie.

As is often the case with films today, *Driving Miss Daisy*'s political message doesn't correspond with true history, particularly the history of Jews and race relations in the American South.

The story begins as Miss Daisy's son, Boolie (Dan Aykroyd), hires Hoke to drive his aging mother, whose reflexes are declining, around on her daily tasks. Boolie, a wealthy businessman who dutifully runs an industry inherited from his grandfather and father, cares deeply about his mother and is grateful that the widowed Hoke looks in on Miss Daisy after doing her driving. Boolie and his wife—to whom he is equally devoted—have no children, and I found myself feeling sorry for this kind son and indulgent husband.

Set in 1950s Atlanta, the movie highlights the increasingly close relationship between two senior citizens of obviously different social backgrounds. Over time Miss Daisy comes to view Hoke less as a black house servant and more as her closest friend, a truth she states at the end of the movie as she is being cared for in a diminished state in an upscale nursing home.

The movie would have done well sticking to character development. Instead, nearly every scene reminds us that segregation existed in Atlanta, as it did in other places in the South in the 1950s, as well as Washington, DC. The film also belabors us with the message that anti-Semitism was raging in Dixie back then. In one example, we are shown some nasty Southern bumpkins sneering at the Jewish Miss Daisy and black Hoke as they ride together on a trip from Atlanta to Mobile, Alabama.

This outbreak of bigotry makes no dramatic or logical sense. Why would anyone care that a black chauffeur was driving an elderly white woman? Moreover, why would this sneering bigot even think that Tandy's Miss Daisy is Jewish? She certainly doesn't look Semitic, and the character that Tandy was playing was someone descended from German Jewish settlers who came to the South in the nineteenth century. People of that background and class would have been hard to distinguish physically or behaviorally from Southern Christians. Indeed, Southern Creoles would look more different from Germanic-looking Southerners than Miss Daisy does from her Christian neighbors.

An event that is shown to have transformed Miss Daisy—and which unfortunately did occur—was the 1958 bombing of the oldest Reform Temple in Atlanta by a crazed segregationist. Miss Daisy is so moved by the pervasiveness of Southern bigotry, from which she suddenly realizes that her fellow Jews as well as blacks were suffering, that she becomes an ardent supporter of Martin Luther King Jr.

One of the later scenes in the film shows Miss Daisy attending a speech by King, whom she now ardently supports. King's voice is projected, just like the voice of Christ in *Ben-Hur*, as an ethereal, divine presence whose physical form may be too sacred to be viewed. Significantly, the apolitical Hoke, who drives her to the event, is not even aware of who King is.

In any case, the bombing is supposed to have changed Miss Daisy to such a degree that she obviously disapproves of her insensitive daughter-in-law, Florine (Patti LuPone), going to San Francisco as a Goldwater delegate in 1964. This was somehow a betrayal of the struggle against Southern bigotry, in which all of us should be passionately engaged by the end of the film.

All this talk of Southern bigotry reminded me of an occasion last summer when I was interviewed by R. Michael Givens, a Georgian filmmaker working on a documentary about Southern Jewry until 1877. Givens was inspired to undertake this project after reading Robert Rosen's informative work *The Jewish Confederates* (2001). Rosen documents how thoroughly pro-Confederate Southern Jews became during and after the Civil War.

Out of the twenty five thousand Jews who settled in the American South by 1861, two thousand volunteered to fight for the Cause. Secretary of War, and later the Confederate Secretary of State, Judah Benjamin, was a Sephardic Jew (of Spanish or Portuguese origin), as was one member of the Confederate Senate. One of the first houses of worship in Charleston that declared for secession was Temple Bethel, the congregation to which Judah Benjamin's parents had belonged.

Moreover, even after the South's defeat, synagogues throughout the region were decorated with pictures of General Robert E. Lee, General Stonewall Jackson, and Confederate President Jefferson Davis. The graves of Jews who fell in the war were accorded special veneration by their coreligionists, the latter of whom, Rosen notes, were among the most fervent celebrants of the Lost Cause.

Although only a few hundred slaves were in the hands of Jewish owners, Jews in the South had no interest in the abolitionist cause, as the Israeli leftist newspaper *Haaretz* noted reproachfully in a June 2021 article, "The Uncomfortable Truths of Jewish Life in the US South." Indeed, many of the Sephardic Jews residing in the American South came from families that ran plantations in the West Indies. Although German Jews came to be numerically the larger Jewish group by 1861, the Sephardim set the tone for Southern Jewish culture and political attitudes.

By the early twentieth century, the relationship between Southern Jews and Southern Christians was undergoing a change for the worse, one reason why Givens is wise to end his documentary of Southern Jewry around the 1870s mark. Sephardic and German Jewish dominance in the South and elsewhere in the United States gave way to a far less assimilable Jewish majority from Eastern Europe. The newcomers were politically more radical or else lived apart in culturally alien Orthodox communities. Their presence aroused deep concern and even distaste among members of the Jewish establishment, who did not take kindly to their newly arrived fellow Jews. But even more ominously, this uncongenial addition gave rise to an anti-Semitism that had hardly existed in the South before.

It made itself felt in the revived Ku Klux Klan of the early twentieth century, and it showed its face in the 1913 Leo Frank case in Atlanta following the murder of thirteen-year-old Mary Phagan, an employee in the pencil factory partially owned by Frank's uncle. Frank came from an old-line affluent Jewish family, rather than a recently arrived Eastern European immigrant family. Although Frank's guilt now seems almost indisputably established, the fact that he was lynched by a mob after his death sentence was commuted was a horrifying development. And there were certainly anti-Semitic tones that ran through the rants of Frank's accusers. The reaction of the Jewish old settlers to this shocking event was generally to remain in their social space, while continuing to mingle with the Christian upper class.

The temple Miss Daisy is shown attending—the Hebrew Benevolent Congregation, Atlanta's oldest and most prestigious Jewish house of worship—was under the spiritual direction of Rabbi David Marx for more than fifty years, overlapping the time of the Frank case, but ending in 1946 before the bombing.

Marx was born in the Deep South, and his family arrived there from Germany well before the Civil War. Always intent on maintaining collegial relations with his Christian—particularly mainline Protestant—clergymen friends, Marx recoiled from the Zionist movement, which he believed ascribed to all Jews (including his congregation) a foreign ethnic identity. Like most representatives of the classical Reform movement, which was brought over from Germany, Marx and his worshippers defined Judaism as a universal religion, related to biblical Christianity and stressing ethical monotheism.

His successor, Jacob Rothschild, was of a different disposition and acted as a social activist and strong Zionist, something that the changing composition of his congregation following World War II made possible. The German Jewish old guard was dying off and being replaced by Eastern European Jews, who were not interested in joining polite Southern society and who often felt quite estranged from it. Hailing from Poland, Lithuania, and Russia, these Jews certainly did not have the deep roots in the Old South that the older Jewish community did; and when Rabbi Rothschild became an outspoken civil rights activist, his newer congregants welcomed the move.

Author David Verbeeten documents the conflicts, mostly in Northern urban centers, between German and Eastern European Jewish communities from the late nineteenth century on in a well-researched monograph, *The Politics of Nonassimilation: The American Jewish Left in the Twentieth Century* (2017). Verbeeten throws light on this matter by underscoring the blending of radicalism and Jewish identitarianism among the newcomers. The Jews who poured in from Eastern Europe resented the remote Jewish elites for two reasons: for not being sufficiently self-assertive about their ethnic identity and for timidly allying with the Christian upper class.

The response of the newcomers, which marked Jewish leftists thereafter, was to embrace political radicalism as a form of Jewish self-assertion. A long-standing objection that they expressed in Atlanta against Rabbi Marx was that he didn't push back hard enough against bigoted Gentiles and that he failed to unite with black activists against the ruling class. Verbeeten might have added to his convincing argument that Eastern European Jews were not alone in the course that they took. Blacks and many others have done exactly the same, namely, express their ethnic nationalism by taking radical leftist stances.

The bombing of the Hebrew Benevolent Congregation on October 12, 1958, came as a likely consequence of Rothschild's activism, and the Atlanta government and Atlanta civic organizations donated huge amounts to repair the damages. This generosity occasioned complaints from black leaders that Atlanta whites cared more about their local Jews than the blacks they had kept down for centuries. *Driving Miss Daisy* tells us nothing about the ethnic tensions that roiled the congregation. The new political course was a symptom and result of cultural battles that were already unfolding. In this environment, someone of Miss Daisy's background and lineage would be more likely to repine about the troublemakers who had caused the temple's problems, rather than becoming a fangirl of MLK.

Atlanta's Jewish community thereafter continued to move to the left, but the bombing was less a cause than a result of political changes that were already taking place. The "Jewish Confederates" and their descendants whom Rosen depicts were no longer a critical factor in Southern Jewish society by the 1950s. One would not have expected Miss Daisy, as a survivor of what was an older Southern Jewry, to move so quickly in the direction that she did.

It is also hard to imagine Boolie telling Miss Daisy shamefacedly about Florine's support for Goldwater, as the movie suggests. Perhaps in a sequel, we might see a Boolie-like character "growing" even further— or, perhaps, the phrase that would be used in a modern sequel would be "getting woke." He would join the black-Jewish coalition in Atlanta that promoted the Senate campaigns of Raphael Warnock and Jon Ossoff in January 2021.

Note that I am aware of obvious exceptions to the generalizations about the history of Jews in the American South I've offered in this commentary. German Jews who fled to the United States in the wake of the Nazi accession to power were often on the far left, for example; this is illustrated by the Frankfurt School in exile, whose members were often communist sympathizers. This essay focuses on older German and Central European Jewish settlements in the United States going back into the early nineteenth century. Nazi refugees (like my own family) were another matter.

There have also been descendants of Eastern European Jews in the United States who do not fit my generalization, like members of the American Jewish League against Communism in the 1950s, or the movie mogul Samuel Goldwyn, or the Annenberg family in Philadelphia, or Hasidic Jews in Brooklyn. But exceptions do not negate the possibility of generalizing about dominant ideological preferences among particular groups.

The cultural conflict to which this commentary refers played out in a historically distant fashion, when a *New York Post* columnist in 2015 proposed that a tile in the New York City subway depicting a Confederate battle flag be torn out. The tile, which shocked the paper's neoconservative sensibilities, was the gift of the German Jewish owner of *The New York Times*, Adolph Ochs. Ochs's family had fought for the Confederacy, and his mother Bertha was a proud charter member of the United Daughters of the Confederacy. The tile in the subway was intended to honor a cause to which Ochs's family had been passionately devoted.

CHAPTER TEN

Neoconservatism

– ◆ ◆ ◆ –

Equality, Left and Right

Chronicles

JANUARY 1999

A MONG THE significant changes on the American intellectual Right in the last fifty years is the growing emphasis on equality. From the speeches of Jack Kemp and the collected works of Professor Harry V. Jaffa to the arguments advanced for Proposition 209 in California, it seems that equality is not only a principle worthy of our attention: It is now the highest principle and one that Jack Kemp calls the "conservative principle" *par excellence*. Although such tributes to equality predictably come from neoconservative politicians and Straussian "political philosophers," they do indicate what is becoming a characteristic of the conservative mainstream.

According to this recently revealed conservative dogma, the United States was founded as a "proposition nation," and its germinal creed is "All men are created equal." Abraham Lincoln, by destroying the states, helped give flesh to that creed, and the federal government waged war on foreign powers in this century to advance it. (This was Allan Bloom's argument in *The Closing of the American Mind*.) Moreover, the American crusade for equality continued as the "good" civil rights movement, exemplified by Martin Luther King Jr., and Bayard Rustin, and in "moderate" as opposed to "radical" feminism. Since respectable conservatives do not want the egalitarian ox to get close enough to gore them, the march of equality is conveniently brought to rest in the mid-1960s with the emergence of an American immigration-expansionist and anti-discrimination welfare state.

Considerable sophistic energy has gone into explaining why we should not push a splendid principle too far, e.g., by treating "equality of opportunity" as "equality of result" or, as minicon Bill Kristol argued in *The New York Times* (February 12, 1995), by threatening the "political progress on equal rights for women" by asking too much from the state.

The multimillion-dollar neoconservative project of promoting "moderate" versions of welfare-statism and social engineering is a manipulative rather than philosophical enterprise, and it depends, for its justification, on a series of philosopher-kings who, like Lincoln and Roosevelt, seize executive power with both hands. The achievement of Lincoln as depicted by Harry Jaffa or that of FDR as presented in Harvey Mansfield Jr.'s *Taming the Prince* (1989) was to have twisted and suppressed constitutional liberty for a universal ideal. As Jaffa himself pointed out in *National Review* (September 21, 1965), "no American statesman ever violated the ordinary maxims of civil liberty more than did Lincoln." But these violations of American liberty were entirely justifiable because, as Lincoln knew, "civil liberties are the liberties of men in civil society," and those liberties are tied to higher principles and duties. As Jaffa explains in *Equality and Liberty* (1965), constitutional liberty for us was intended to be subordinate to the "principles of the Declaration of Independence," understood as political equality. In the name of that equality, Lincoln had a right to sacrifice "bodies whose souls remained dedicated" to foundational American principles.

Jaffa and other neoconservatives and Straussians apply the same justification to later presidents who entangled their countrymen in ennobling struggles, from the punishment of Southern slave-owners to the "crusade for democracy" waged against Kaiser Bill to the Gulf War. Those conflicts provide, as Allan Bloom suggests, "educational experience," and that experience involves teaching our people and those whose brains we knock out about "human rights," especially about "democratic equality." These educational experiences usually entail fighting ethnic groups that neoconservatives dislike—Germans, Slavs, Arabs, and reactionary Southerners—and on the side of those they like—upper-class Englishmen, Israelis, and progressive Yankee millionaires. The pursuit of moderate egalitarianism results inevitably in a slow drift leftward that they and their friends can presumably control and that will not empower minority leaders to a point that is intolerable.

The obvious problem with conservative egalitarianism is that there is nothing historically conservative or even classically liberal about the glorification of political equality. This new conservative principle is in fact the ideal of social democrats and Jacobins. As Clyde Wilson observes, "What they say is not unusual but certainly not conservative." And, so far from being conservative, it is not even defensible on rational grounds. In a still unpublished manuscript, analytic philosopher David Gordon has gone through the works of Harry Jaffa and his disciples to expose their perpetually ragged reasoning. Treating as apodictic what is never demonstrated, ascribing disagreement with their ideas to racist and anti-Semitic attitudes, and ignoring historical contexts are all essential to the arguments defending these "universal" positions. Gordon notes how little concerned his targets are with the circumstances surrounding their texts of choice. Though Lincoln intermittently may have opposed slavery, his remarks during (though not exclusively during) his debates with Senator Douglas indicate that he did not believe that blacks could or should enjoy political equality with white Americans.

There is in fact nothing in Lincoln's words or biography up until 1856 to show that he ever held anything like Jaffa's opinions on race and politics. Even leading Abolitionists like Ralph Waldo Emerson disliked slavery for, among other reasons, introducing into an otherwise Northern European people black Africans whom Emerson thought unsuited for citizenship. Similar nonegalitarian objections to slavery could be found in the writings of Thomas Jefferson and of other signers of the Declaration who owned slaves. Though these Southern planters signed a document with a borrowed phrase from John Locke about natural equality, it is a long leap from there to the modern politics of equality. He who says "yes" to the Declaration as a statement of national independence need not be endorsing the idea of political equality for all races, as both leftist historian Richard Hofstadter and Southern conservative M. E. Bradford have pointed out.

There is no compelling reason to assume that the Declaration (mostly a list of grievances like the 1629 English Petition of Rights) stands behind the Constitution, which nowhere invokes the "principles" of 1776. There is no reason to assign pivotal importance to the Declaration's phrase about equality, even if Lincoln pointed back to it as the "sheet anchor" of our founding. After all, the equal right of all people not to be enslaved, to which Lincoln does refer, does not imply other more radical forms of equality.

But there is another observation to be made. Those who now prate about equality believe even less in it than does the reactionary Right. Democratic ideals in the past were identitarian ones, assuming the kind of unity among citizens that Aristotle, Rousseau, and Jefferson thought indispensable for democratic polities. *Homoiotes* (likeness, or parity), which the Greeks saw as the essence of democratic regimes, meant something entirely different from such late twentieth-century democratic litmus tests as the availability of entitlements or adherence to a "universal proposition." It signified membership in a community held together by shared ancestry, gods, and customs. As Aristotle notes in the *Athenian Constitution*, Pericles rose in the esteem of the demos when he struck from the list of Athenian citizens those who were not descended from Athenian parents on both sides. As ancient historian Paul Veyne observes, open citizenship is the mark of an empire, not of a democracy. To carry the analogy with antiquity one step further, modern global democracy creates imperial subjects, not democratic citizens.

While the American founders were not trying to replicate a claustrophobic ancient democracy, they did assume that their own extended, representative republic would require sharp cultural and ethnic boundaries. Whether one quotes from Jefferson's *Notes on the State of Virginia* (1785) or from *Federalist*, no. 2 (on the good fortune of culturally and ancestrally homogeneous republics), it is clear that the founding generation did not believe their country could survive as a proposition nation. Citizenship would require a high degree of *homoiotes* (which was more necessary for republics than monarchies) if the federal union was to be maintained. In this respect the advocacy of ethnic unity, combined with Protestant-tinged civic culture, was consistent with American ideas of democratic homogeneity.

Most early Americans presumably believed there were social and cultural preconditions for citizenship. They believed that a democratic society could not function without an (at least residually) homogeneous population. Such a concern, however embarrassing to neoconservatives and other liberals, is quintessentially democratic. In a regime dependent on an active popular will, as opposed to our current system of electronic manipulation, a deep sense of community is vital.

Significantly, the appeal to equality made by Ward Connerly and other supporters of Proposition 209 suggests the same misunderstanding about democracy encountered among neoconservatives. Connerly crisscrossed the country speaking about returning to true American equality. Allowing commercial and educational enterprises to engage in discrimination, for the purpose of rectifying past injustices against blacks, Hispanics, and women, goes against the "vision of equality" preached by Lincoln and Martin Luther King. It also contradicts the 1964 Civil Rights Act, which tried to implement that vision by creating a "colorblind" society. Not surprisingly, Proposition 209 drew on the language of that act.

But the Civil Rights Act promoted neither conservatism nor democratic government. It empowered a federal commission, overlapping the congressional and executive branches, which monitors all sorts of social and commercial relations. While supposedly designed to fight discrimination, that oversight commission, in alliance with the courts, has been inflicting minority quotas and mandating minority set-asides since the 1960s. Whether or not this was supposed to happen, the fact is that it did, and for an obvious reason: Vast discretionary power was conferred on the central state to alter social behavior. How could anyone have expected a different outcome?

In taking sides on a false issue such as Proposition 209, potential critics of the managerial state are distracted from the real question that is important for a democracy. Is the incursion by federal engineers into communal relations across the United States compatible with self-government and with the civic life necessary to generate and preserve it? Unfortunately, this question was never addressed in the debates over Proposition 209. Partisans on both sides agreed about the central role of the managerial state as the source and instrument of socialization. A ritualistic debate took place, appealing to the fictitious visions of Lincoln and Martin Luther King and to variant strategies for democratically enforcing "true" equality. For genuine democrats and for those of the Right, however, it is not worth fighting over whether public administrators create a color-blind, gender-neutral society with or without explicit quotas. Yielding such power in the first place is entirely unacceptable.

Though I'm not writing a plea for democracy as the only legitimate form of governance, such a regime does feature distinctive strengths and ways of life. But our "democratists," as Claes Ryn calls them, have no interest in fostering these characteristics, and they attack those who would restore popular government as right-wing extremists. By now, it is clear that this talk about democratic equality is not the profession of a philosophic creed, but the self-justification of careerists attached to a post-democratic and post-conservative American empire. The pampered defenders of a generous regime have little interest in philosophy and still less in meeting the objections of anyone to their right.

The New Face of
National Review

Taki's Magazine

APRIL 17, 2007

I N ONE of the more grotesque episodes in the ongoing slide of "conservative" opinion into nonsense and ideology, Stephen Schwartz, in a commentary for National Review Online, offered a flattering depiction of onetime Soviet communist leader Leon Trotsky (1879–1940). The loser in a power struggle with Stalin after the death of Lenin in 1924, Trotsky in exile, first in Norway and later in Mexico, had warned against the rise and spread of "fascism." According to Schwartz, who has made a career denouncing the danger of "Islamofascism," the democracies should have heeded the admonitions of the "anti-fascist" communist revolutionary Trotsky. Our own society, contends Schwartz, has had trouble mobilizing against Muslim fascists, because we have been weakened by "neo-fascists" at home. So-called anti-democrats typified by Pat Buchanan, consider every war against "fascism" the work of Trotsky's disciples. Hateful rightists are supposedly still blaming Trotsky for a Soviet dictatorship, to which, according to Schwartz, he had contributed only minimally. Were Trotsky still alive, we are told, he would be lending his considerable talents to fighting Islamicists and other right-wing extremists. Schwartz ends his commentary by declaiming:

> To my last breath, I will defend Trotsky who alone and pursued from country to country and finally laid low in his own blood in a hideously hot house in Mexico City, said no to Soviet coddling to Hitlerism, to the Moscow purges, and to the betrayal of the Spanish Republic, and who had the capacity to admit that he had been wrong about the imposition of a single-party state as well as about the fate of the Jewish people. To my last breath, and without apology. Let the neo-fascists and Stalinists in their second childhood make of it what they will.

There are several observations occasioned by this fevered peroration. The least important of them, from the standpoint of my comments, is that Schwartz grossly understates Trotsky's complicity in the mass murders carried out by his associate, the communist dictator, Lenin. In the gulags that Lenin and Trotsky, who then headed the Red Army, set up and in the prisons run by the Soviet secret police, alleged enemies of the communist regime were routinely butchered; and this killing went on even before Stalin had bested Trotsky as Lenin's successor in the late 1920s. Noticing Trotsky's "anti-fascism" is a bit like praising Hitler for defending Western Christian civilization against Bolshevism or for criticizing the unjust Treaty of Versailles. In both cases relevant parts of the story are left out. As for Trotsky as an opponent of anti-Semitism, his sympathetic Jewish biographer, Isaac Deutscher, admits that he advocated the jailing of Russian Zionists as counterrevolutionaries both before and after his exile from Russia in 1929. Nor is it clear that Ramón Mercader, the Belgian radical and longtime confidant of Trotsky, who murdered him in Mexico City in August 1940 was acting upon orders from Stalin. Even less certain is that his assassin was punishing his host for not supporting the alliance concluded in the summer of 1939 between Soviet Russia and Nazi Germany.

But far more noteworthy than Schwartz's laundered history of Lenin's accomplice is the fact that *National Review* published his ode to Trotsky and to the fallen communist's anti-fascist militancy. It is for me hard to believe that such a piece dropped by accident from the sky or that the editors were not looking very carefully at what they posted on June 3, 2003. For decades now, almost all paleoconservative and paleolibertarian authors have been kept from publishing in *National Review*; nor have they been allowed to appear on its online extension, as far as I can determine. The only time that one encounters such reprobates there is when *National Review*'s gatekeepers pull out the names of evil people in campaigns against putative anti-Semites and Arab appeasers. Even a quick survey of *National Review* and the rest of the neoconservative press will reveal that T. S. Eliot, H. L. Mencken, and other heroes of the Old Right have been assigned to eternal perdition, as anti-Semites, Teutonophiles, and/or racists. One might therefore conclude that Trotsky is less offensive than other, more conservative personalities to the editorial boards of *National Review*, *The Weekly Standard*, and *The New Criterion*, despite the fact that neither Eliot nor Mencken was involved in murdering counterrevolutionaries.

One reason for these judgments is the closer correspondence in beliefs between Trotsky and the neoconservatives than between them and Mencken, T. S. Eliot, or anyone else revered on the Old Right. What is being suggested is not a total agreement but an overlap between the way the neoconservatives understand politics and history and certain recurrent themes in Trotsky's view of the human condition. A leftist critic of the neoconservatives, Michael Massing, observed in 1987 in *The New Republic* how "Trotsky's orphans" had moved into the camp of Ronald Reagan as the sworn enemies of Soviet "Stalinism." What had driven them toward the anti-Soviet Republicans was not an imaginary conversion to the Right, but rather hatred for the Soviet government, a regime that had betrayed their vision of revolution. Internationalism, the call for a world upheaval that would transform pre-modern, anti-egalitarian societies, and the continuing struggle against "fascism," linked to anti-Semitic, anti-modern regimes, were the ideals that "Trotsky's orphans" had hoped that Russian socialist revolutionaries would pursue. Since they did not, the incipient neoconservatives became anti-communists of the Left; and in due course they took over a moribund and highly corruptible "conservative movement." (My forthcoming book on this movement, *Conservatism in America*, goes into exactly how this happened.) The fact that Trotsky and the neoconservatives were Eastern European Jews, who had been touched by socialist thinking and who identified traditional nationalism with anti-Semitism, rendered this affinity even more probable.

Among the neoconservative first generation the attraction to Trotskyism had taken concrete form: Irving Kristol had begun his journalistic activities as a Trotskyist; while CUNY professor of philosophy Sidney Hook had spent years trying to vindicate Trotsky's reputation as a "democratic revolutionary." Many of the older generation of neoconservatives were members of or very close to the Fourth International that Trotsky had set up as an exile in Mexico. Basic to this rallying of non-Stalinist communists were the rejection of Stalin's notion of "socialism in one country" and the insistence that revolutionary socialism must be international and should not be identified with any one nation and its interests.

One of the prices that neoconservatives have sometimes had to pay as directors of the "movement" has been to tone down their revolutionary language. But these efforts have not been very successful, and abundant evidence exists that many neoconservatives have never stopped sounding like Marxist revolutionaries. My friend Claes Ryn and I have laced our recent books with quotations from Michael Ledeen, Joshua Muravchik, Allan Bloom, William Kristol, and Robert Kagan. All of the passages in question read as if they came from Trotsky's Soviet Comintern, the institution that he founded to foment international Marxist revolution. Although I would not deny the presence of other components in what one eulogist calls "the neoconservative vision," the Trotskyist aspect has never been abandoned completely. The zeal for revolutionary upheaval, summed up by the boast of Michael Ledeen while speaking to the American Enterprise Institute, that "Destruction is our [America's] middle name" goes well beyond the parameters of the vision proclaimed by Woodrow Wilson and his followers for a "world made safe for democracy." Because of Wilson's declaration of war against the hated Germans and his extension of the welfare state at the federal level, neocons are happy to identify with him. But their vision includes more than Wilson's Anglophile policies and his hopes for Anglo-American hegemony. Neocons yearn for a world democratic revolution, a term that one does not find in Wilson or even in FDR. American "national greatness" is measured by Kagan, Kristol, and other neoconservative policymakers as the willingness to deploy American armies and to lavish revenues on a continuing crusade to remake the world.

Such journalists are also no more nationalist than was Trotsky, who saw Russian soldiers simply as a means toward a modernizing revolution that had to be exported to other countries. The talk by the neocons and their dependents that the United States was founded as a "propositional nation" is a Trotskyist ploy, to deny the country in which they find themselves and which they have come close to taking over propagandistically a true national character. Like Soviet Russia, the United States is a means toward a universalist end, which can only be advanced through revolutionary violence. It is a measure of the utter worthlessness of the American establishment Right that it mistakes such radical Left lunacy for a conservative teaching consistent with our national traditions.

Two final observations seem in order. One, it is possible to have adapted Trotsky's thought without having taken away what neoconservatives now believe. One Catholic of English descent, James Burnham, had been Trotsky's leading disciple in the United States in the 1930s. Although Burnham had drifted away from Marxist-Leninism, even before Trotsky's assassination, he continued to write on the Trotskyist theme of how the Soviet experiment had been "derailed bureaucratically." From Burnham's Trotskyist phase came his continuing interest, which he eventually carried over to the Right, in the managerial transformations of democracy and socialism. Both of these themes informed Burnham's classic *The Managerial Revolution* (1941), a work that decisively shaped the thinking of his later right-leaning disciple Sam Francis.[227] But the Trotskyist imprint on the neoconservatives is of another kind. It reflects their passion for universal revolution and an instinctive repugnance for things as they are, unless neoconservative revolutionaries are causing things to happen. This vision is also distrustful of national identities, unless they are founded on revolutionary slogans, with the obvious exception of a Jewish state in the Middle East.

Two, the designation of neoconservative thought and politics as Trotskyist does not exclude the possibility that they resemble other revolutionary ideologies. Ryn, for example, has stressed the parallels between neoconservative rhetoric and that of the radical wing of the French Revolution, the Jacobins, who planned the invasions of neighboring countries to spread the blessings of revolutionary France. The proposed fit is not hard to make, and not insignificantly, two years ago on a visit to France, our Secretary of State Condoleezza Rice, who often sounds like a neoconservative, praised the French government for having been established on a "universal revolutionary tradition" similar to ours. Like the Trotskyists, the admirers of the Jacobins try hard not to notice the butchery carried out in the name of the causes that they imagine are good for us. (The Jacobins executed more than one hundred thousand in their own country alone, including mothers and babies, as enemies of their "universal" values.)

Yet it seems to me that the Jacobins, like Woodrow Wilson, may have been a derivative influence for neoconservative thinking. More primal was their hero Trotsky, who incidentally saw the Jacobins as a model for Bolshevizing Russia and the rest of the world. The fact that neocons deviated from his plan for public ownership of productive forces does not mean that they gave up on the bigger picture. If "democratic capitalism," which means in effect the enforcement of cooperation between public administration and large corporations, can be used to penetrate and break down traditional societies, then it would serve the same modernizing end as the one that Marxists attached to full-blown socialism. English historian John Laughland has aptly summed up this neocon adaptation of Marxism as "using modified capitalism to attain revolutionary ends." An Australian scholar Philip Ayres begins a description of the neoconservative worldview for the Spring 2006 issue of the (Australian) *National Observer* with this perception:

> In fact they were not really conservative at all. They included a number of former Trotskyists (such as Irving Kristol and Christopher Hitchens) whose real loyalty in some cases was, and remained, to a strange form of utopianism that transformed their old Trotskyist notion of the 'permanent revolution' into an ongoing 'spreading of democracy and freedom,' the solution to the world's woes.

Ayres merits praise for noting the obvious, a practice that the captive American Right has still not picked up.

A Tale of Two Normans: Podhoretz and Finkelstein

Taki's Magazine

OCTOBER 28, 2007

U NLIKE SOME of my respondents, I am not surprised that Norman Podhoretz in his latest book, *World War IV: The Long Struggle Against Islamofascism* (2007), goes after the isolationist Right. For years Norman has been looking frenetically over his right shoulder, e.g., denouncing Taftites and representatives of the pre-neocon Right, a practice going back to *Commentary*'s spats with the Buchananites at the end of the Cold War and to its swipes at right-wingers who were perceived as being insufficiently supportive of the Israeli government. But even more interesting than the fact that the older generation of neoconservatives have always believed they were in a dog-fight with the hated "paleoconservatives" is the way the liberal establishment and the reconstructed conservative movement have kept us out of the public debate. The reviewers of Podhoretz's most recent book did not want to mention our guys, even if Podhoretz did; just as the anti-war leftist media continue to treat paleo opponents of the Iraq War as nonexistent or beneath contempt. If it were our partisans against theirs—that is, the neocons and their hacks—we might be able to hold our own.

Unfortunately it is the liberal side that helps to preserve the reputation of the neoconservatives as the only intelligent and relatively humane opposition to the Left. For those who seek more proof, look at the commentary "Saying the Unsayable" by British left-of-center journalist Andrew Stephen in the *New Statesman* (September 13, 2007). Although this commentary pretends to be about the Walt-Mearsheimer exposé of the American Jewish lobby, it quickly turns into a rant against the "far-right, libertarian congressman" Ron Paul. Supposedly, when Paul noted that the "neoconservatives" played a major role in getting the United States to invade Iraq, he was "saying the unsayable," by "resorting to coded language." Paul, who is apparently a bigot playing to "far rightists" was telling his audience that all of our problems in the Middle East have been "cooked up by the Jews." Walt and Mearsheimer, who say much more daring things in their book than Paul did in his debate response, are treated respectfully for obvious reasons. They are politically on the Left and identified with prestigious leftist academic institutions.

The reason I was struck by all of the errors and oversights in *The Long Struggle Against Islamofascism* that reviewers did not disclose is the inflated reputation that the media has created for the neoconservatives as the "brainy, cultured" Right. Although there is much I didn't like about the neoconservative sources that I consulted for my latest monograph on the conservative movement, the quotations from liberals about the high intelligence and learning of neoconservative journalists and fundraisers are not at all fabricated. I first learned about Podhoretz and his friends from reading *The New York Times* in the 1970s, and everything I saw there about him and his movement made me adore the neoconservatives. As late as the 1990s, the *Times Sunday Magazine* featured glossy pictures of Bill Kristol, Mr. and Mrs. David Frum, and other second-generation neocon dignitaries, with flattering commentaries typically prepared by neocon scribblers. *The Times* and *The Washington Post* give massive and usually favorable coverage to books published by such neoconservative authors as Gertrude Himmelfarb, David Brooks, and Dinesh D'Souza, and both of these national newspapers, as well as *Time* and *Newsweek* magazines, feature neocon columnists.

And well they might. It is they who helped manufacture this alternative opposition to a more genuine Right. Their exuberant support got others to buy into the kinder, gentler "Right" that the Left bestowed on this country. Opportunistic movement conservatives later ran to join those whom Clyde Wilson in the 1980s recognized as "interlopers." And certainly Zionist New Dealers and big-government corporate executives have thrown largesse in the direction of these "moderate conservatives."

But we got the neocons mostly because the Left wanted that kind of bogus opposition. My late friend Sam Francis knew whereof he spoke when he scorned the neocons as the "harmless persuasion." Sam meant that this group was innocuous to establishment liberals, who laid it on with a trowel when they described their "brilliant" neocon adversaries. But both groups were pure fury when it came to beating up on us.

Another related point is that Sam and I both became interested in studying certain Frankfurt School concepts, although neither of us was a "cultural Marxist," because they cast light on how the neocons took and exercised power. There is—it seemed to the two of us—a "hegemonic" leftist ideology, which among its defining traits is anti-anti-Semitic, anti-racist, anti-German, and generally anti-Southern white. This ideology also favors government social engineering and a welfare state but not necessarily a socialist economy. Most of the adherents of this ideology are not in fact Jews, although Jews may be disproportionately represented among its carriers. Indeed if its success depended on a two-percent Jewish minority in the United States, this hegemonic ideology could not have spread as well as it did. Its numerically preponderant supporters have been liberal Christians, who in recent years have been significantly supplemented by such Evangelicals as Michael Gerson, Cal Thomas, and George W. Bush.

There is a second layer to this hegemonic ideology—and here differences may be allowed in the United States but not in Western Europe, where the core ideology has progressed farther because of an extremely controlling public administration. The second layer centers on multiculturalism and special group rights for designated victims, such as gays and Muslims. In the face of an evolving core ideology, a mild opposition is allowed to function, as long as it challenges only certain implications of the belief or attitude system. And these "conservative" attacks are encouraged insofar as what is being attacked is only an advanced version of the core ideology but not the underlying sentiments and values. The "moderate conservative" critics of certain excrescences of the core ideology stress the legacy of the civil rights movement, as embodied by Martin Luther King, and the need to fight anti-Semitism with special zeal, a task that now apparently requires a new world war against "Islamofascism."

But the criticism here, to use another Frankfurt School term, remains "immanentist." It proceeds out of the same post-Christian, post-bourgeois hegemonic ideology as the Left that it pretends to resist. Since "democratic politics" requires some kind of organized debate, the neoconservatives and the liberals stage discussions within their own broad consensus—which obviously excludes "fascists" and "extremists," who challenge their shared understanding of progress and government-promoted equality or the need to exert force internationally in order to end gender disparities, homophobia, etc. Sam and I adopted another Frankfurt School term, "artificial negativity," to describe what went on when the hegemons blow off steam, mostly for show. Anyone who is looking for an illustration of "artificial negativity" should turn on *Hannity & Colmes* or listen to the discussions held between the two national parties that clog our TV and radio networks. Such spectacles typically combine utter triviality with the grunting and screaming that one might easily associate with professional wrestling.

A final point about the functioning of this mostly bogus opposition is that it reaches rightward in a way that affects the behavior of the Old Right. Earlier this week, I read on Frontpage, a neoconservative-financed website, a scathing article by the spirited Heather MacDonald on the "Jena Six" race-hustle, and the scapegoating in the national press of the whites in this Louisiana hamlet, for insisting that severe charges be brought against local blacks who had nearly killed a white high school student. I defy my paleo colleagues to publish anything as critical about American blacks as this lady did on a neocon website. The Old Right is terrified of the subject of race, and it is impossible even while reading its endless hymns to the Antebellum South to learn that what is being described is a slave society. Lest it be called racist, the Old Right tries to stay clear of pressing social issues that have to do with race. But neocons do not feel as constrained about the subject, perhaps because they are less likely to get attacked from the Left as racists. Nor are they as frightened of raising the question of significant behavioral differences among the races.

On the other hand, there is no philosophic consistency in how the neocons take on hot moral issues. Although sometimes, when it is useful, they may deplore gay marriage, they are also quite happy to back candidates who favor it. And when it helps their bellicose plans, they will bow and scrape before the gay lobby. For days now, I have been noticing the way neoconservative commentators are trying to enlist the gay movement against the government of Mahmoud Ahmadinejad. Apparently the failure of the Iranian regime to recognize gay rights now goes against conservative "values." Since these values, as I argue in my book, are whatever neocons say they are, neocons may be acting consistently on their own Hobbesian principle that *power determines meanings* as well as justice.

Someone who has dared to go beyond "decent" debate is former DePaul political science assistant professor Norman Finkelstein. This now-unemployed figure resigned from his post at DePaul University in September after having been denied tenure last spring. Although a self-described leftist and the son of Holocaust survivors from Poland, fifty-three-year-old Finkelstein leaned on the third rail once too often. By now, as I note in an article for the German weekly *Junge Freiheit*, this hapless truth-teller may have no other professional prospects left but to work in a shoe store. After all, he has published entire tomes exposing the pap of politically correct celebrities. Among Finkelstein's targets have been Alan Dershowitz's *The Case for Israel* (2003), a screed that Finkelstein shows was at least partly lifted from Joan Peterson's even longer botched work on how there were hardly any Palestinians in Palestine when the European Jews arrived, and Daniel Goldhagen's *Hitler's Willing Executioners* (1997). With incredible diligence, Finkelstein has dissected neocon-liberal fixations, about German history, the abuses of the Holocaust for propagandistic purposes, and the bullying tactics of AIPAC. Although never entirely in agreement with the solutions of this zealous pro-Palestinian advocate, I was astonished by his research and transparent courage. Two of the flawed books he focused on, by Goldhagen and Dershowitz, were so fetid and malicious, that I thought he may have been actually too kind to their factual errors and gratuitous gracelessness.

I was therefore not at all surprised that Dershowitz pressed the tenure committee and the president at DePaul to get rid of his critic. Nor was I appalled that he boasted of his accomplishment after Finkelstein was turned down for tenure—despite his voluminous accomplishments and advanced age. Nor was I horrified that the former president and current dean of the law school at Harvard took Dershowitz's side as a maligned scholar who had fallen into the hands of a bully. Note that the same institution had produced a plethora of endorsements for Goldhagen's sweeping indictment of the Germans as an "eliminationist anti-Semitic nation." As far as I know, no one at Harvard has bothered to acknowledge the fraudulent history that riddles Goldhagen's book. In passing I would note that Finkelstein's fate at a Catholic university paralleled my own at Catholic University of America in the late 1980s. Once some professional victimologist brings up the charge of nurturing "anti-Semitism," the timid administrators of such schools, often associated with easily intimidated Princes of the Church, cave in. Needless to say, it makes no difference if the would-be disseminator of "prejudice" happens to be Jewish. It serves me (and Finkelstein) right for challenging "enlightened" opinion in this most tolerant and caring-and-sharing of liberal democracies.

The Right Lesson

The American Conservative

NOVEMBER 17, 2008

B ARACK OBAMA'S victory has left the Republican Party and its allies reeling, groping frantically for a path back to power. Luckily, or not, the conservative establishment already has a handful of recently published critical works to guide its meditations. These include David Frum's *Comeback: Conservatism That Can Win Again* (2007) and Ross Douthat and Reihan Salam's *Grand New Party: How Republicans Can Win the Working Class and Save the American Dream* (2008), as well as columns by *The New York Times*' house conservative, David Brooks. All of these emphasize the need for a new social direction for the GOP and conservative movement.

These sources teach that Republicans have foundered because they have failed to move with the times. Whether it is Brooks asking us to treat homosexual marriage as an expression of "family values," Frum exhorting the GOP to ditch the Religious Right on abortion and gay rights—but obviously not on Zionism—or Douthat and Salam pushing for government subsidies for the working poor and "earned legalization programs" for undocumented aliens, the common theme is that the Right and the GOP should downplay, if not concede, contentious social issues and engage more purposefully in income manipulation. This move would supposedly help the Right get into sync with voters.

What is most striking here is that these authors are advocating more of the same. They are trying to push the conservative movement farther in the direction in which it has been going since the mid-1960s. Frum, Douthat, Salam, and Brooks would keep the GOP essentially in its present mold as a provider of social programs, a pale, albeit more militaristic, imitation of the Democratic Party. Yet this trend already belongs to the past. It took off more than forty years ago, after the crushing defeat of presidential candidate Barry Goldwater in 1964, a rout that dragged down many Republican congressmen and looked very much like the most recent election.

John McCain may hold the Senate seat that was once Goldwater's, but he is in no way his philosophical successor. The 2008 election was a contest between two varieties of the Left—between an actually left-wing candidate, Barack Obama, and a spurious, one might say "adjusted," right-winger, McCain. By contrast, 1964 was the real thing. As a critic of the New Deal and a passionate opponent of any attempt to expand it, Goldwater questioned the rationale for an American welfare state. Even more ominously, he combined his known desire to privatize Social Security, the TVA, and other federal projects with a strong Cold War posture. He not only spoke about the importance of defending the United States against communist aggression, he famously—or infamously—wished to support anti-communist insurgencies, and he hinted at the possibility of using nuclear weapons to end the incursions of North Vietnamese armies into the south. Only in his readiness to resort to force has McCain followed in Goldwater's footsteps.

The Republican candidate of 1964, significantly to the right of McCain, faced much greater vilification. He had the full power of the press and world opinion arrayed against him. Typical of this hostility was the remark by Martin Luther King, which was seconded by Governor Pat Brown of California, that "we see dangerous signs of Hitlerism in the Goldwater campaign. All we need to hear [at the Republican convention] is 'Heil Hitler.'" By fall 1964, when Johnson ran a television ad featuring a small girl picking flowers juxtaposed with images of a nuclear catastrophe caused by Goldwater's foreign policy, the election was already all but over.

But the movement conservative interpretation of the 1964 campaign, as found for example in Lee Edwards's *The Conservative Revolution* (1999), is that Goldwater's landslide defeat was in no way conclusive. Indeed, it became the prelude for much greater things. A Goldwater backer who broke into GOP politics because of his support for the Arizona senator, Ronald Reagan, went on to become president. And Reagan allegedly picked up where Goldwater left off, advancing the "conservative revolution" against the New Deal and achieving victory in the Cold War, which had been Goldwater's explicit aim. Such movement stalwarts as William F. Buckley Jr., Russell Kirk, F. Clifton White, and Milton Friedman moved from backing Goldwater to endorsing Reagan. Certainly some argument for continuity can be made here, even if one hesitates to go all the way with Edwards's proclamation of an unbroken tradition uniting Reagan and Goldwater to Robert Taft.

In point of fact, however, Goldwater's defeat did not lead to a "Reagan revolution." Instead, the fate of Goldwater and his movement in 1964 caused the American Right to move leftward over the next two decades and encouraged the GOP to fall back into its customary country-club avoidance of tough choices. After 1964, as Jonathan M. Schoenwald persuasively argues in *A Time for Choosing: The Rise of Modern American Conservatism* (2001), the conservative movement's leaders came up with a blander, more mainstream version of their beliefs and policies. Because of his leftist bias, Schoenwald presents this process in a positive way, stressing how the post-Goldwater conservatives "deflated their extremism," "cut off the extremist millstone," and "shifted from pure ideology to electoral pragmatism." Thus Reagan, when he became governor of California in 1966, did not make the rash budget cuts that some had expected, and he subsequently signed a very liberal abortion bill into law.

Schoenwald notices that after 1964 conservatives abandoned their opposition to the Civil Rights Act that had passed that year and stopped talking about getting rid of Social Security as opposed to "privatizing" a certain percentage of it. Harry Truman and FDR went from being conservative punching bags to being admired, even worshipped, figures in the ensuing twenty years. While the Right remained anti-communist, it gave up its earlier postwar anti-Soviet rhetoric and took over certain Cold War liberal themes. These included attacks on the Soviets' resistance to allowing Russian Jews to emigrate to Israel and long, drawn out comparisons between Soviet and fascist opposition to independent labor union movements.

Such a revamping of the conservative movement, Schoenwald suggests, came before the neoconservative ascendancy of the 1980s and in fact laid the groundwork for it. In 1968, *National Review* endorsed the centrist Republican Richard Nixon as a presidential candidate, someone who supposedly represented "the conservative mainstream." In June 1969, one of *National Review*'s senior editors, Jeffrey Hart, who this year supported Obama as a "Burkean conservative," responded in a commentary to both traditionalists and libertarians who had complained about the magazine's drift into the Nixon fold: "We have got in America what we have got. It is not what we would have but neither is it as bad as what we might have." When in July 1971 the editors "suspended support of the administration," their main reason was not that Nixon had embraced affirmative action and highly interventionist economic policies. Rather, they objected to Nixon's pursuit of détente with Soviet Russia. In the 1980s, neoconservatives could take the commanding heights in conservative institutions because the movement had already embraced a weaker form of their social-democratic domestic policies.

Steps in this direction were deftly hidden by referring to an unchanging conservative substance, in the form of "permanent things" or "values." Besides, even if the welfare state continued to grow under Republicans and Democrats alike, that would only remain the case—or so the faithful were assured—until conservatives obtained positions throughout the federal bureaucracy. Then right-wing bureaucrats would rescue taxpayers from all the other federal employees. Needless to say, this didn't happen. Instead, under Nixon and Reagan the rescuers grew fat feeding at the public trough.

According to Larry M. Schwab in *The Illusion of a Conservative Reagan Revolution* (1991), continuities between the Carter and Reagan administrations were far greater than either liberals or conservatives wished to admit. Reagan's military budget during his first year in office was only slightly higher than the one passed in the last year of the Carter administration. Far more important, however, Reagan did nothing significant to reduce the size of the welfare state or the entitlement programs that he had inherited from his predecessor.

Admittedly, Reagan achieved some good for the Right by upping the ante on the Soviets and hastening the collapse of the financially decrepit Evil Empire. He also appointed fewer left-leaning federal judges than a Democratic president would have selected, and he made modest cuts in the federal bureaucracy. But he did not reverse the New Deal or the Great Society, and he left us with neoconservatives cluttering the Department of Education and the State Department. And even more fatefully, his vice president and heir apparent, George H. W. Bush, endorsed the Americans with Disabilities Act and a new Civil Rights Act, which came replete with minority quotas and set-asides.

After Goldwater, the conservative movement made its peace with the New Deal and the leftward drift of the country. Despite their occasional moments of good sense, Douthat, Frum, and their friends would not change that direction. Indeed, they urge conservatives further and faster down that road. Not that they are entirely wrong when they claim to be offering the GOP a chance to survive. Republicans might benefit at least in the near term by adopting some of their policy suggestions, such as inflation-indexing the tax credits for children, wage subsidies for low-income families, awarding points to immigration applicants for learning English, and the creation of a national identity card. Frum, moreover, is to be congratulated for ridiculing the GOP's frenzied, sporadic attempts to reach out to black voters. He also notes that it would be counterproductive for Republicans to get behind amnesty for illegal immigrants, a policy that would turn red states blue.

Frum thinks the GOP should be working to hold on to—or recover—the broad middle class by structuring taxes and public benefits in their favor. Douthat looks to a different stratum as the mainstay for a reinvigorated Republican Party. His proposals are aimed mostly at the working poor, but he also wishes to expand exurbia into the "wide open spaces" of the country through government subsidies. Somehow, according to Douthat, moving populations away from urban cores will make them more communal and more likely to vote Republican. Frum's idea for scoring points among soccer moms and religiously liberal white Christians for the GOP is to adopt more liberal attitudes toward homosexuality and abortion. Republicans apparently don't need to worry about the Religious Right, whose younger members are moving left with their age cohort and whose older members may have no choice but to go on voting Republican.

There was nothing inevitable about the conservative movement's leftward swerve after Goldwater's defeat, however, and there may be alternatives to that course today. Possibilities might include real devolution of power from the federal administration to state and local bodies, abandoning the idea of the "living constitution," identifying national security with protecting our national borders rather than exporting democracy, and other proposals now coming almost exclusively from the ostracized paleo-Right.

The catalyst for changing course will not come from the compromised conservative movement. Getting rid of what now passes for movement conservatism, with its establishment journalists and DC bureaucrats and insiders, and replacing it with a genuine oppositional force would be necessary to reform the Right. There is a moral as well as a practical reason for such a housecleaning: respectable conservatives have been implicated up to their ears in our present politics and have never risen above the role of being shills for the GOP.

There are several signs in this year's election returns that the Right may be returning to the path abandoned after 1964. Much of the Right in my state of Pennsylvania rejected McCain. They found his saber-rattling and neocon boilerplate about a "league of democracies" to be unacceptable. The fifteen percent of Republican voters who went for Ron Paul in the primary did not, contrary to journalistic expectations, return to the fold. My culturally traditionalist, anti-war Mennonite neighbors voted in protest for Obama, other right-wing Pennsylvanians voted for one of the alternative candidates, while some chose not to vote at all. This anti-war and/or anti-neocon Right will not go away, even if establishment conservatives and liberals persist in pretending it doesn't exist.

This leads me to believe that there may be an opportunity to rebuild the American conservative movement and possibly even the GOP around a new strategy. But the first thing to be done is to abandon the failed precedent of the post-Goldwater epoch. The course the conservative movement pursued in alliance with the GOP after 1964 ended disastrously last week, in a spectacular victory for the radical, multicultural Left.

Derb's National Rebuke

Taki's Magazine

APRIL 10, 2012

U NLIKE RICH LOWRY's predictably PC response to John Derbyshire's controversial article on what parents should tell their
kids about race, I was less than "appalled" by it. John's judgments are not entirely mine, and unlike my good friend I probably would
stop (and I hope my grown-up children would stop) for a black person
stranded on a highway who didn't look quite like "one of the boyz from
the hood." But John's article was a response to numerous rants by black
celebrities in the wake of the Trayvon Martin shooting. These anti-white
invectives, proudly featured in *Time*, *The New York Times*, and other
establishment fixtures, were also directed toward the young and emphasized the persistence of white "prejudices." In one passage particularly
lacking in self-awareness, someone named Touré explained:

> Being black could turn an ordinary situation into a life-or-death
> moment even if you're doing nothing wrong.

Given the glaringly disproportionate number of violent crimes black
youth commit each year, most often against each other, Touré and his
editors should be medically treated for being delusional. What do they
think is the color of violent crime? I doubt that any of John's accusers
would dwell critically on black responsibility for black crime any more

than the editors of *National Review* would feel impelled to express indignation at the statements that occasioned John's rejoinder. A recent column by Rich Lowry affirming his agreement with Al Sharpton about the Trayvon Martin shooting would fit snugly into the obligatory liberal responses to this event.

I wonder whether the counter-instruction that John would bestow on his offspring would be an ultimately quixotic gesture. Most college students I encounter have had their heads so stuffed with misrepresentations of reality that mommy and daddy would have to use blowtorches to get the embedded nonsense off their brains. But these brain-damaged youths' parents seem to have been socialized in the same counterfactual way. This week I learned that throngs of people in nearby Lancaster and Harrisburg had put on hoods to express solidarity with Trayvon Martin, or perhaps with Reverends Jackson and Sharpton. These esteemed clerics with their media buddies are busily reminding us of the horrendous crime committed against a black youth by a nonblack Latino they're calling a "white Hispanic." The same celebrities also consistently underplay the most widespread source of violent crime. Perhaps the black thugs who in January 2007 raped, mutilated, and murdered a white couple in Knoxville were also wearing hoods. The gruesome Knoxville murders and numerous other violent crimes blacks commit against whites remain underreported. If these crimes were treated in the same way as Martin's shooting, *The Atlantic*, the *New York Daily News*, *The Guardian*, and all the other leftist publications denouncing my friend's "disgusting rant on race" would eagerly print his dispassionately presented conclusions.

Black hatemongers rarely provoke the public tongue-lashing that a scientifically literate English gentleman elicits by pointing out cognitive and social differences between races. Would any academic or journalist create the same brouhaha if a black "vocalist" called for "raping white bitches" or a professor of Black or Women's Studies grossly insulted white males? Not on your life. No disparagement of whites in favor of blacks, or of men in favor of feminists, or of straights in favor of gays would cause discomfort in our PC-drenched country or in any other Western nation in a comparable state of cultural disintegration. Not even sadistic black murders of defenseless whites can produce this effect. I am stating this as my fellow whites are still exhibiting ritualistic shock over a partly white male shooting a black teenager in circumstances that are still to be clarified.

I am impressed by the alacrity with which *The Guardian* and other leftist opinion sources close off discussions of non-approved subjects.

The editors presume to speak for the rest of us. It was no surprise that the pint-size Stalins who run our ideologically controlled opinions would try to bully John's employer into firing him for something posted on *Taki's Mag*. And this is only proper. Were maverick writers and thinkers allowed to publish things free of PC gatekeepers, there's no telling how far this exercise in intellectual freedom might go. *The Guardian* and likeminded publications are correct to insist that even the opposition should play by rules that favor them. This is not a double standard, since the Left always and everywhere is totalitarian. When it tries to suppress dissent, it is being most thoroughly itself.

I was not disappointed that Lowry and his fellow intellectual pygmies caved in and fired their most talented thinker and writer. But there was an amusing side to this outrage. Before the adolescent crew kicked John out, they raked him slowly over the coals. While groveling toward the Left as he was "parting ways" with John, Lowry complained about how Derb's piece "lurches from the politically incorrect to the nasty and indefensible." My thought at the time was that I'd like to see the clueless Lowry match wits with John by trying to prove that John's assertions were "indefensible." It would be like having a featherweight pick a fight with Mike Tyson during his prime.

I'd be delighted to see the utterly vapid *National Review* go down the tubes now that its editors have humiliated and fired a brilliant, principled subordinate. But I doubt that will happen. However worthless the magazine is likely to become (and even with John it wasn't very good), its neocon and GOP donors will probably continue to keep it afloat. At my age, I was hoping to see at least one pillar of the neocon agitprop empire collapse before I leave this vale of tears. Unfortunately, given its continued usefulness to its masters, this fate is not likely to befall *National Review*.

Throwing People Under the Bus to Stop a Runaway Vehicle

Taki's Magazine

APRIL 19, 2012

T HE RECENT pillorying of John Derbyshire and Bob Weissberg after being accused of making tactless remarks about race recalled a question that's been bothering me for decades. Why should we think that race is the only untouchable subject or the only issue that, to use George Will's misleading phrase, we as a society agreed to turn into a "stone, cold, dead, closed question"?

Yes, I know there used to be slavery and segregation, and then a civil rights movement came along that raised our spirits to new, hitherto uncharted levels of tolerance. Because of this experience we agreed, or someone agreed for us (I was never asked my opinion), not to discuss the forbidden subject in such a way that black spokesmen or their white liberal proxies in the media would find objectionable. I suppose this agreement was made in the same way as the one binding those who leave the state of nature and enter civil society in Hobbes's magisterial work *Leviathan* (1651). There the newcomers don't have to agree to anything explicitly, but by hanging around, they implicitly consent to the arrangements that someone else set down for them. In a similar manner I have agreed not to broach forbidden subjects by not leaving a country the mainstream media rules.

With the towering prohibition against expressing politically incorrect views about race, why would anyone be naive enough to believe that the demand for total consent will ever stop? The same bullying tactics that have been applied here have been extended to everything else that the Left and its obliging conservative-movement collaborators have tried to keep from being mentioned. The Left trots out the same victim narratives to shut us up about gender differences, our preference for heterosexual over homosexual family organization, or whatever else they deem unmentionable at a given moment. My friend, distinguished classicist Chris Kopff, says that at the university where he works it's Christianity, not racism, that gets singled out as the villain. Anyone linked to Christian belief has to answer for the Crusades, the Inquisition, the Holocaust, and many other iniquities that are traced back to Christianity's inherent intolerance.

Those whom Pat Buchanan describes as the "kennel-fed conservatives" are desperate to curry favor with the media and centrist Republicans. These survivors rail against that ole devil white racism, which appears to agonize them as much as it does the Left. This *Sturm und Drang* allows them to address other moral issues such as getting Mitt Romney elected president. These establishment conservatives may even occasionally suggest something that is indelicate about gender differences or declare their sympathy for heterosexual relations, and so far they have been able to pull this off without getting instantly zapped. These get-along types also get steamed up that others are noticing cognitive differences between racial groups. After all, can't we all do equally well in our propositional nation that was founded on the principle of equality?

My suggestion to those who wish to believe these statistically and historically questionable assumptions is to take up their argument with God or nature. This is not the way the world seems to operate, and those who wish to make counterarguments should be allowed to do their thing. The other side should be equally free to present a refutation on the basis of empirical evidence.

As PC demands get ratcheted up, I wonder whether those who are buying time (perhaps until they retire) understand the silliness of throwing people under the bus to stop a runaway vehicle. The Left is not going to be stopped in its tracks by signs of weakness. As the French say, *l'ap-*

pétit vient en mangeant. Either our side permits open discussion, especially discussion of what the Left doesn't want to have discussed, or we simply agree to capitulate every time the Left calls someone a racist, anti-Semite, anti-transsexual, or whatever. Although we should treat each other, including other races, with as much civility as circumstances permit, to me it is obscene that we should be kept from serious discussions of socially relevant empirical data because some media thugs may beat up someone who transgresses their no-nos.

I'm also not sure that noticing racial differences is less justified than observing other ones. We assume this priority because the media has usually come down harder on dissent here than they have with other verbal taboos. But that may be owing to the fact that other victim narratives have been piled on to the black and feminist ones, which gained momentum in the 1950s and 1960s. And in that period there was visible discrimination against blacks, particularly in Southern states, where they have always been most numerous. As Derbyshire and others have pointed out, this narrative should already be wearing thin. Other developments have overtaken it: desperate efforts by the government and private sector to provide blacks with compensatory justice, widespread violence among black youth, a conspicuously disintegrating black family structure, and increased restrictions on what members of other races are allowed to say about blacks. Then there are the publicized torrents of invectives against whites coming from black spokesmen and white liberals.

Given these problems, I'm not sure there is any moral or intellectual justification (if there ever was) for forbidding an honest discussion of innate racial differences as well as other group differences that may have genetic sources. It is not clear to me that these genetic disparities may be the most critical for understanding key behavioral differences, but it seems ridiculous to exclude them from public or scholarly discussion. The reason we do is our fear of suffering the wrath of the increasingly totalitarian Left.

In places such as Germany, the Left now unleashes collective violence on "fascist" targets rather than simply knocking them out of the public arena. It may reach that stage here no less than in Europe unless the Right is willing to stand up for intellectual freedom. By the "Right," I don't mean those "kennel-fed" publicists who are throwing people under the bus.

View from the Cocoon

American Greatness

APRIL 11, 2022

S OMETIMES ONE begins a book with such low expectations that one is delighted to find the printed material is not quite as bad as what one expected. This is precisely my impression of Matthew Continetti's much touted monograph, *The Right: The Hundred-Year War for American Conservatism* (2022). As someone who holds the honor of being Bill Kristol's son-in-law (and who holds his father-in-law's vacated place at Fox News), and a prominent Never Trumper to boot, Continetti is hardly an unbiased interpreter of conservatism. A revealing passage from his book tells us clearly where on the ideological divide he stands:

> The one hundred years war for the Right is to conceive of it as a battle between the forces of extremism and the conservatives who understood that mainstream acceptance of their ideas was the prerequisite for electoral success and lasting reform.

As the world's most notorious critic of misused political taxonomies, I shall allow myself to quibble about Continetti's eccentric use of the term "Right." For him and his well-connected friends, the designation mostly serves as a synonym for "Republican." There are two groups on his telling, both located in the GOP, that are fighting to be the true face of the Right, but only one passes muster as "non-extreme." This is where I start to part ways. Today, I would argue, the populist Right is the true American Right because it alone is fighting the cultural Left and its allies in the deep state, media, and educational establishment. I have no idea what makes its neocon and Republican establishment adversaries any kind of Right, since on most domestic social issues, and certainly on foreign policy, this group happily cooperates with leftist power elites.

In explaining how the current populist Right came along, Continetti stresses the divisive character of the Iraq War and the failure of the George W. Bush administration to carry along all self-identified conservatives. That prolonged struggle "delegitimized the conservative movement in the eyes of populist independents, conservative Democrats, and disaffected voters crucial to past GOP victories." This observation is entirely correct. Bush's invasion unleashed acrimonious debate at home, and a populist Right was able to consolidate itself by standing in opposition to a course of action heavily endorsed by neoconservative journalists and policy advisers. But cultural and moral issues, often intertwined with economic ones, soon became the sustaining themes of the populist revival, which has taken cultural wars and the plight of the working class more seriously than neocons and establishment Republicans have done.

There are two problems with Continetti's attempt to trace back present divisions to earlier events. One, he is mostly repeating what has already been said, perhaps *ad nauseam*. As the author of surveys on American conservatism, I found nothing in his book that indicated original insights or original research. Two, Continetti cannot seem to subdue his unbounded enthusiasm for one side of his divided Right, namely, the neocons and the conservative establishment they influenced. Therefore, those with sharply different views become the predictable fall guys. Continetti laces into Joe McCarthy and his defenders, but before he did, he might have read M. Stanton Evans's heavily documented account of the objects of McCarthy's investigation, *Blacklisted by History: The Untold Story of Senator Joe McCarthy and His Fight Against America's Enemies* (2007). Evans's work demonstrates that however deplorable his methods (and they were), many of McCarthy's targets merited investigation. Too often, Continetti simply repeats conventional views about subjects that he should have explored more deeply.

Although I think the late Senator Robert A. Taft sometimes went too far in his non-interventionism, he was not the cardboard-cutout isolationist Continetti depicts. In a Senate resolution of October 2000, Taft was named one of the seven greatest US senators of all time. He was first in his law class at Yale and a courageous dissenter, whom JFK (or his ghostwriter) properly celebrates in *Profiles in Courage* (1955). If Continetti had taken time to read James T. Patterson's comprehensive biography of Taft, published in 1972, he would have discovered that Taft's positions on American intervention in Europe before World War II and during the Cold War were far more nuanced than Continetti would have us believe. It pays to keep in mind that Taft and his father, who had been president from 1909 to 1913, were active interventionists during World War I, and like others of his generation, Robert believed that the American public had been gulled into a bloody European war that resulted in a harsh treaty against the defeated side. Rightly or wrongly, they carried that attitude with them into the period before the United States formally entered World War II. To his credit and unlike others in both parties, Taft had warned against chumminess with the Soviet government despite a shared interest in defeating Nazi Germany. Unfortunately, his admonitions went largely unheeded.

Finally, there is something painfully provincial in how Continetti treats the Southern Agrarians as a shabby foil to his neoconservative mentors. Norman Podhoretz's discovery in the 1970s that the Left was hostile to Jewish and Israeli interests was for Continetti an epiphany that led the conservative movement to its later glory. This neocon revelation paved the way for expanding the conservative pantheon to include, *inter alia*, Irving Kristol, Nathan Glazer, and, eventually, Continetti's father-in-law. By contrast, the Southern Agrarians, an association that Southern conservatives reveled in, are relegated to eternal perdition. Agrarian littérateurs were supposedly primitive bigots, who eventually "fell into sinkholes of nostalgia, pessimism, and fecklessness."

One has to wonder what kind of Beltway cocoon Continetti inhabits. You don't have to read Louis D. Rubin's multiple studies of the Agrarians to realize they were among America's leading literary figures for several generations. Their disciples taught not only at Vanderbilt and Sewanee but graced the English department at Yale, when I was there in the 1960s, and many other prestigious Northern universities. Robert Penn Warren, Cleanth Brooks, John Crowe Ransom, Allen Tate, Andrew Lytle, and Donald Davidson were all literary celebrities in postwar America, while Brooks and Ransom are generally admired as the founders of the New Criticism (along with William Wimsatt, a colleague of Brooks's at Yale) and were distinguished literary theorists with roots in the Southern Agrarian tradition.

The resounding manifesto, *I'll Take My Stand*, which Agrarian authors published in 1930, is a lament for the loss of rural America and a critique of an industrialized, urbanized society. It is not, *pace* Continetti, a defense of racism. Not all of those who have identified with that tradition, moreover, have been politically on the Right. Eugene Genovese praised the Agrarians while a Marxist, and both Brooks and Warren were outspoken opponents of racial segregation. Continetti may have belittled the Agrarians without knowing exactly who they were. All he may know in this regard is that prominent critics of the neocons (like the late M. E. Bradford) identified themselves as latter-day Agrarians, and so this group must therefore be unsavory.

On the plus side, this book is clearly and forcefully written and engages a topic that interests me profoundly.

CHAPTER ELEVEN

The Alternative Right

— ◆ ◆ ◆ —

The Revolution
and the Right

Taki's Magazine

FEBRUARY 18, 2008

This is the third installment in a four-part symposium on the Ron
Paul movement to be published in *Taki's Magazine*. John
Derbyshire and Justin Raimondo have made previous contributions.

A LTHOUGH IT might be premature to claim that Ron Paul's campaign is winding down, plainly the candidate has not done as well
as his supporters had expected and as his online fundraising might
have foretold. In the wake of disappointing showings in Florida, Michi-
gan, and South Carolina, Daniel Larison wrote a column in *The American
Conservative* (January 28, not online) in which he treats Paul's run as
pretty much over. Larison believes, nevertheless, that the "campaign has
the potential to be the start of a movement rather than an enthusiastic
fad" and that its "mix of constitutionalism and cultural conservatism
with hints of Jeffersonian populism is a powerful, appealing combination." Unfortunately Paul also has "some of the most unpopular ratings
of any Republican," and beyond "his relentless demonization in the
Republican media," he has also suffered from the sharp divide between
himself and "roughly two-thirds of the party" over the war in Iraq.

Larison raises sound points, but it is possible to sharpen his critical focus by noting Paul's other missed opportunities for attracting Republican votes. The Congressman did not really articulate a foreign policy, as opposed to telling Americans that the war in Iraq and almost all other wars the United States has engaged in during my lifetime have been "unconstitutional." His attempt to place the problem of Islamic terrorism entirely at the doorstep of our government, moreover, while based on valid concerns about American overreach, is also clearly an exaggeration. Islamic fundamentalism is a menace whether or not the neocons are trying to exploit it, and particularly given that the multicultural Europeans have allowed Muslim maniacs to get more than a foothold in their countries and that our own border controls have been incredibly lax. Even if Dubya had not launched his war of choice in Iraq, we would still be facing considerable foreign danger. This is a fact Paul should have acknowledged while presenting his own foreign policy and his own measures to insure domestic tranquility.

Paul's blaming of America for armed crackpots outside our borders has played disastrously among Republican voters, who are often wrongheaded but remain instinctive American nationalists. Paul's outbursts have also made him seem less than reflective about America's unavoidable position as a superpower and about the reality that there are groups in the world that mean to do us harm. This is, of course, different from arguing that Bush and his friends have done the opposite of what might have been advisable to deal with our present dangers, for instance, controlling our borders instead of fawning on Hispanic voters and not getting entangled in "democratic" nation-building in Iraq. Still, Paul was right to express his annoyance at mishandled problems, and he was at his best lambasting the neoconservatives as troublemakers.

On the other side of the ledger, the congressman struck me as a less than effective TV debater, and I found myself wondering why he alternated between ferocity and appearing to be removed from the ongoing discussion. When asked about his views on foreign policy, he would typically snarl at the moderator and then mutter something about this "unconstitutional war." But then when urged to pose his own questions to the other candidates, he would ask something so esoteric that I had no idea what he was talking about. (In one case, the target of his question, John McCain, looked as puzzled by his query as I was.) Paul is highly educated and never at a loss for words in conversation, but debating on TV is clearly not his forte.

Having been a Monday-morning quarterback, let me also stress that I'm not sure Paul would have done much better even if he had taken my advice. Even if he could have transformed himself into a silver-tongued orator with the yuppie looks of Mitt Romney, I don't think the outcome of the primaries would be significantly different. It is the content of Paul's old Republican message that is the sticking point, and this would be the case no matter how that message was presented. Unlike the party regulars, the TV pundits, and American (mis)educators, Paul calls for eliminating social programs instead of increasing them, and he disdains anti-discrimination laws and other forms of behavioral manipulation whether introduced by Congress or imposed extra-constitutionally through judicial decree. He is also serious in the matter of sending back illegal immigrants, unlike Hillary, Obama, and McCain, all media darlings, who seem to have never seen an illegal visitor whom they didn't want to bestow citizenship on. Moreover, Paul is really against nation-building abroad, unlike *The New York Times* and *The Washington Post*, which regularly showcase "pro-war conservatives." Indeed these may be the only "conservatives" whom the national press would care to call attention to. On social issues, what have leftist journalists to fear from Bill Kristol, David Frum, and David Brooks? As for wars to spread democracy, that bad idea spread from Clinton and Gore through the neocons to the Republicans. The *Times* was ecstatic about the vision of Bush and Michael Gerson when the Democrats tried to build a pluralistic, democratic Kosovo in 1999.

When Ron Paul at last caught hell for not giving back money donated by a "white supremacist" and then for not having kept out of his newsletter certain racist remarks that appeared there in 1998, I was not unduly critical of his conduct. What struck me was the feeding frenzy that these presumed slipups evoked among the liberal-neocon media and Beltway libertarians as opposed to the studied indifference that has greeted Barack Obama's membership in the Afrocentric Trinity United Church of Christ in Chicago. Obama's choice of membership in the congregation of Jeremiah Wright, a pastor whose sermons seemed to have been scripted for Louis Farrakhan (and may have been) and the fact that Obama, even according to his enthusiastic well-wishers at *The New York Post*, has the most leftist voting record of any US senator, have sparked less questioning of this "moderate" representative of racial conciliation than Paul's relatively innocent faux pas. The double standard, which has been outrageously characteristic of the entire political class, tells less about Paul's ineptitude or Obama's "moderateness" than it does about who is in power. And for those who haven't noticed, it's not Ron Paul's friends. Until our side can erect our own media infrastructure, the present tropism toward the Left and its candidates will continue to operate.

The bright spot in this situation is the likely presidential nomination of John McCain, to the joyous cheers of the neocon journalists, who seem to be faced with an embarrassment of riches, as Fred Barnes has been explaining on Fox and in *The Weekly Standard*. Poor Fred seems to adore McCain and Obama with equal intensity, and he may have to make a choice between his two superheroes on Election Day. In the best of all worlds, Fred and the rest of the Fox contributors would be able to have the "moderate" black Obama representing what they imagine to be the legacy of MLK at home, while McCain would be free to embroil us in military crusades abroad. In the last few months, Frum, Brooks, and the other paid "house conservatives" have been frantically warning "social conservatives" to get with the program and support what really counts, an aggressively internationalist foreign policy.

But the likely nomination of the "moderate conservative" McCain as the Republican presidential candidate has not thrilled certain usually dependable movement conservatives. Rush Limbaugh, Michelle Malkin, Ann Coulter, Glenn Beck, and the editors of *Human Events*, all of whom have usually cheered on the GOP, are now piling on McCain. And though they're strong enthusiasts for the war who have dutifully praised McCain as a war hero, they nonetheless consider him a sellout on immigration and other issues on which he has made common cause with liberal Democrats. For Southerners he is still remembered as someone who had insisted that South Carolinians desist from flying the Confederate flag on public buildings, a position that put McCain to the left of Mike Huckabee and Bill Clinton (at least during Clinton's 1996 presidential campaign). His upsurge of support among party regulars and the decision of the neoconservatives to throw their mouths behind him, in the absence of a thriving Giuliani candidacy, have ignited a war within the conservative movement. But at the present time, that war does not affect our side. It is a struggle going on among those groups that have excluded us from their debate.

Our interest here (to repeat a point that my friend Leon Hadar has already made) is in seeing this strife intensified, until it results, if I may use Obama's term, in "change." And this could occur if the fight over McCain's candidacy continues to divide the strictly neoconservative wing of the movement from those talk radio populists appealing to a predominantly heartland Republican base. Although this cleavage already became apparent during the summer over the immigration question, it has continued to widen as McCain has moved forward to lock up the nomination. If I were a mean-spirited right-wing extremist, I would be happy to see John McCain lose dismally in the forthcoming election. And it would be pleasing to have his defeat attributed to his close association with the neoconservatives.

Although the Democratic contenders are arguably more leftist than McCain, whether or not he is "reaching out" to them, either of these lefties might bring unintended benefits to the Right by getting elected. One possible advantage of getting Hillary or Obama is that inexorable push toward the social Left, generally promoted by the American government and the media since the 1960s, might reach a kind of culmination. If the voting patterns that Hillary and, even more, Obama have established in the Senate hold up and if Obama turns out to be even half the wacky, conflicted Afrocentrist-cum-post-racialist that his writings and church membership would suggest, we'll be in for interesting times. An old Russian proverb might apply to such a situation: "If you hold someone's head under water long enough, he may decide he doesn't like it." The problem here is that the human recipient of the water might also act like the yuppie, multicultural public in Europe who are handing over their countries to Muslims while punishing the "hateful" Christians who notice what is going on. That's the chance one takes when all hell breaks loose. But I suspect that we'll continue to move in the same direction more slowly with McCain, and especially if he embraces *The New York Post*'s counsel and puts Joe Lieberman on his ticket. Then we may suffer the fate of the lobster being slowly boiled until it suffocates. Of course, a reaction might also set in, if things become worse more quickly and if the neoconservatives are implicated in the defeat of a socially moderate, war-hawk Republican presidential candidate. In that case, the Right will likely grow larger and more vocal.

Ron Paul can aid this effort by staying in the race and by giving us someone to vote for, as a symbolic opposition. Any vote that the real Right bestows on a Democratic candidate would be interpreted by the media as a show of support for the sharp move leftward that the chattering class wishes to see. No one but a few scattered Old Right journalists would make the observation that disgusted conservatives voted for Hillary or Obama to underscore their disgust with the GOP. But a five percent vote for Paul running as a third-party candidate would make the point that we're opposing McCain as Taft Republicans rather than as advocates of more set-asides for minorities or friends of a European-style welfare state. That may be the final service that Congressman Paul could render his now badly disappointed followers.

A Paleo Epitaph

Taki's Magazine

APRIL 7, 2008

I N OCTOBER 2004, my longtime friend Sam Francis responded to a recent commentary by Franklin Foer in *The New York Times* about the paleoconservatives as a rising anti-war opposition to the neo-conservatives. Foer, a *New Republic* editor, believed that a defeat for Bush in the fall 2004 election might lead to a repudiation of his neoconservative advisers, and the return of the Old Right to favor. Sam and I had our doubts. In a letter printed in the *Times*, I noted that the imbalance of forces between the two sides was so overwhelming that no matter what occurred in the election, the paleos would not likely gain influence. Sam offered this interpretation: "A Bush victory would more likely mean their [the paleocons'] obliteration since neoconservative domination would be locked in. But even if Bush loses, it's dubious very many Republicans would leap on the paleo bandwagon." For Sam, this represented a glaring historical contradiction: despite the "bad press" the paleos received, he was convinced, "more rank and file conservatives agree with them than with the neocons." If they therefore "could learn to play more effectively, they could deal themselves a better hand in the future, even if it's outside the Republican Party."

With due regard for my now dead comrade, I don't think the biggest problem for the paleos has been their inability to play cards effectively. Their lack of resources in the face of a truly grim opposition is so great that I've no idea what arrangement of cards would work for them in the foreseeable future. Their aging, embittered leaders have spent so long fighting in the trenches that they've taken to turning on each other. The unending tirade against Protestants that some Catholic paleos now engage in is both silly and counterproductive. We are living in a predominantly Protestant country whose institutions (before they became corrupted) were tied to a recognizably Calvinist society. (For the record, Calvinists held a majority among Southerners and Yankees alike.) Rhapsodizing about the glories of the Catholic Middle Ages played well in early nineteenth-century France and the Rhineland, but by now such lyrical outbursts (together with expressed revulsion for the Reformation) are a bit out of place. What American traditionalists need to defend is a badly denatured liberal Protestant polity that is going quickly to seed. I've no idea how appeals to Mary Queen of Scots and Pius IX will save our political society, or the even more badly deteriorated Catholic regions of Western and Southern Europe.

Note this is not a commentary on European counterrevolutionary thought and certainly not on the totality of medieval philosophy. I am only speaking about the degree to which some paleos have descended into a caricature of what Peter and Brigitte Berger wrote about them in *Commentary* in 1986, in a description that, incidentally, was not true at the time it was written.[228]

According to the Bergers, the right-wing opponents of the neoconservatives were neo-medieval Catholic Romantics who had nothing positive to say about the modern world. Because of age and frustration, the paleoconservatives might be moving toward actually deserving this stereotype.

There was a time, however, roughly between the mid-1980s and the early 1990s, when the paleos looked like an insurgent force. In 1992, they found in Pat Buchanan a powerful presidential contender, and one who listened to their advice. The paleoconservatives and the paleolibertarians had patched up old disputes and come together in the John Randolph Club, a group whose meetings in Washington drew journalistic dignitaries, including but by no means limited to Buchanan. Although *National Review* by the early 1990s had thrown in its fortunes with the *Commentary* crowd, Buckley himself did continue to keep lines open to the other camp. *National Review* observers and the then-unknown David Frum came to Randolph Club meetings. A speech delivered by Murray Rothbard at one such gathering on January 18, 1992, has become legendary. In it he famously envisioned "repealing the twentieth century":

> With the inspiration of the death of the Soviet Union before us, we now know that it can be done. With Pat Buchanan as our leader, we shall break the clock of social democracy. We shall break the clock of the Great Society. We shall break the clock of the welfare state. We shall break the clock of the New Deal. We shall break the clock of Woodrow Wilson's New Freedom and perpetual war. We shall repeal the twentieth century.

Rothbard's bold rhetoric gained considerable attention throughout the country.

So did a remark by a leftist reporter Daniel Lazare in 1989, that "despite their backward-looking ideas, the traditionalists have all the vigor of youth, while the neocons after eight years of Reaganism and less than one year of Bush, are beginning to show their age." This was also the impression that John Judis had given in his essay on the "Conservative Wars," which had been published in *The New Republic* three years earlier.[229] Based on the research I had done for the second edition of *The Conservative Movement*, Pat Buchanan contemptuously observed in 1991, "neoconservatives are merely the fleas on the conservative dog," and assumed that they were a problem that would soon be removed.[230] Such an opinion did not seem out of the ordinary.

Although I thought Pat was overly optimistic, it seemed to me then that the paleos had wind in their sail. That was my conclusion in the second edition of *The Conservative Movement*, although anyone who consulted the chapters on neocon funding would have learned that our enemies had at their disposal more than a hundred times the annual funding we did. They also had their columnists plastered all over the liberal press; and they had their followers running commercial presses and ensconced in elite universities. Neocons were obviously part of the liberal establishment, while we would soon be what we then called our opponents, "interlopers on the Right."

It was an unpalatable journeyman, then writing for *National Review*, William McGurn, who stressed the real disparity between the opposing sides in his condescending remarks about Murray's speech at the Randolph Club. According to McGurn, the neocon panic, which came particularly from the president of the Heritage Foundation, was unnecessary. The paleos would go nowhere "once their presidential candidate had left." Their spokesmen had flair, and they took reactionary positions that attracted notice, particularly on immigration, but they had few of the available resources of their adversaries.

A comparison that comes to mind here is between, on the one side, Holland and Sweden and, on the other, France and England as world powers around 1650. Although the two smaller powers looked impressive in the early modern period because of some particular, temporary advantage, such as an efficient commercial navy or a well-trained infantry force, the differences between these regional powers and the more populous and wealthier European countries would eventually become decisive. The ultimately weaker side could be made to look more powerful than its opponent, but only for a brief period of time. In a similar way, the paleos once briefly looked more threatening to the ascending neocons than they really were, and that illusion could be sustained from the end of the Reagan administration through the first term of the elder George Bush.

The weaknesses of the paleo side eventually came to show: excruciatingly limited funding, exclusion from the national media, vilification as "racists" and "anti-Semites," and finally, strife within their own ranks. In retrospect, this was all predictable, although for me it was hard to grasp how totally the fall came when it did. An example of the disparity to which I'm referring is the differing fates that affected two recent books on American conservatism, one published by me, the other by David Frum. While my book has sold no more than seven hundred copies in English (although apparently it is doing better in Romanian translation), Frum's work has sold about one hundred times as many. It has also been widely reviewed in the national press, and has been slobbered over by liberal as well as neocon columnists, and most shamelessly by that predictable neocon sycophant E. J. Dionne in the (quasi-neocon) *Washington Post*. My own book has been hardly reviewed at all and the only ads for it I have seen are the ones I have paid for.

My publisher, Palgrave-Macmillan, suggests that there is little interest in my book among journalists, despite the noteworthy fact that it is simultaneously coming out in several foreign languages, including Russian. My ideas are clearly not acceptable to our national press, which has no interest in disseminating my "alternative interpretation" of what has happened on the American Right since the 1950s. (Apparently, convenient lies work better!) But my book is only an isolated example of a much larger problem for our side, namely the imbalance of resources that allows the liberals and neocons to blackout an entire political persuasion and the view of reality provided by those identified with it. Presumably if we had at our disposal the equivalent of Fox News, *The Wall Street Journal*, and about half the editorial space in the national press, our views would receive the same attention as those of David Frum.

Whatever the problems facing our side, however, it does not seem likely that the neoconservatives and their enablers will control "the American Right" forever. Like the paleos, but in a much more dramatic and successful way, the neocons are products of changing historical conditions, and as Carl Schmitt once wisely observed, "An historical truth is true only once." There is no reason to assume that those particular circumstances that aided the neoconservatives in their rise to total control over the establishment Right will continue to prevail indefinitely. That rise depended on time-bound conditions: the domination of the media by sympathetic patrons (many of whom were the children and grandchildren of Eastern European Jewish immigrants), the conclusion of a bizarre alliance between elements of this media elite and Dispensationalist Christians, the descent of the Republican Party and the postwar conservative movement into intellectual vacuity, and the fusion of the Right with Marxist and/or Jacobin revolutionary ideology. Therefore it is foolish to believe that the present power configuration will remain in place without change.

Even less likely is that the paleoconservatives will continue to play the role of the outnumbered, ridiculed opposition to the neocon-liberal establishment. This present Right opposition came into play when the neoconservative took over the conservative movement in the 1980s. Its achievement was to have gone on fighting against a formidable, world historical opponent, but it has not been able to make any headway in this confrontation. And even more certainly than its enemies, who are still drunk with the arrogance of power, the paleos will not be around forever.

Even now an alternative is coming into existence as a counterforce to neoconservative dominance. It consists mostly of younger (thirty-something) writers and political activists; and although they are still glaringly underfunded, this rising generation is building bridges on the Right. Their contacts are with disenchanted, onetime allies of the "conservative movement" and with those who would gladly jump ship if there were professional alternatives to serving neocon masters. The Evil Empire is spongier than it looks, and if its younger opponents had more serious resources, this empire would be under siege, no matter how loudly the liberal press rallied to its neocon talking partners. Daniel Lazare was right when he noticed twenty years ago the limited shelf-life of neoconservative ideology. Despite all of their resources, the neocons have had nothing of interest to say for at least three decades. On Fox, when the bleached blondes aren't on display, one is presented nonstop with the aging faces and tired voices of this neocon elite. In a less controlled society with more open discussion, these apparitions would have faded long ago.

The Ron Paul campaign was useful as a meeting point for a post-paleo Right that drew in younger activists. Paul's platform combined libertarian and traditionalist stands in a way that understandably upset the Republican regulars, that is, those who have presented us with the most decrepit exemplar of neocon ideology that one could have found for a presidential race. For these regulars and their neoconservative advisers, Ron Paul stood squarely against the policies of such unlikely "conservative" giants as Wilson, FDR, and Truman. This negative judgment is, of course, correct: Paul and his campaigners were harking back to the true American Right, identified with Taft Republicanism. And though Paul did not do as well as we had hoped, the contributions to his campaign and the millions of votes he picked up in elections suggest the beginnings of a new coalition on the Right. It will no longer be a paleo coalition, but it will attract younger right-wing activists who wish to be rid of the present neocon hegemony and who are willing to cooperate in an alliance that can bring this about. On a practical level, we white-haired paleos can do nothing more to advance our cause. We have done so much fighting that we have become radioactive even from the standpoint of those who sympathize with us. Our opportunities to express our views have become limited by the pugnacity we have shown in the past. Only younger warriors can carry on our fight.

This post-paleo Right will follow the paleos in breaking from the "conservative movement" as it now exists or as it has been reconstituted since the 1980s. It will seek to return to the constitutional liberal traditions of the anti–New Deal coalition. Decentralization, restriction on immigration as a source of social disorder and as an excuse for the expansion of the government's social engineering, and the total rejection of a global democratic foreign policy will likely be the pillars of the new political alignment. Most importantly, its advocates will have no "patriotic" illusions about our managerial regime. Unlike Bill Kristol and George Will, they will see the current American managerial state as a monstrous contrivance that must be dismantled. Judging by its direction, this youthful Right will be more libertarian than traditionalist. While no one would claim that this orientation has not influenced many paleoconservatives, among their successors it will become the focal point of their rebellious politics.

This younger generation exhibits nothing but contempt for the idea that one can make the regime better or more virtuous by trimming some of its excesses. Nor do they indulge those delusional or cynical "idealists" who exhort us to bring "democratic" values or institutions to non-Western societies. One can already recognize the mark of this younger generation in the call for punishing the Republicans by supporting Barack Obama in the presidential race. This identifiably Leninist tactic, summed up by the maxim "the worst is the better," may seem alien to most paleos; but it is the natural response of a younger, less inhibited generation of rightists to an intolerable political situation. Moreover, this new generation sees itself not as the latest phase of the post–World War II conservative movement but as a throwback to the interwar anti–New Deal Right. It has become contemptuous of the conservatism that arose in the 1950s under the auspices of *National Review*, because all it knows of this movement is the iron control of the neoconservative ruling class. Unlike the older generation, these younger rightists nurture no fond memories about the way things were before the 1980s or possibly before the 1970s. To underline my point: in no way do these activists identify with the movement that is the subject of my recent, neglected book. According to Jeffrey Hart, writing in *The American Conservative*, William F. Buckley before his death came to the conclusion that the movement he had founded was already ending. For the post-paleo Right, that movement has not yet even begun.

Responding to
My Respondents

Taki's Magazine

APRIL 15, 2008

M Y LAST full-length essay on *Taki's Magazine* evoked so many thoughtful comments, including essays by Daniel Larison and Richard Spencer (and a long opinion piece by Gerald Russello on the *American Conservative* website) that I am producing this detailed clarification. The critical thrust of the comments received was more or less the following: First of all, I have overstated the difference between the paleoconservatives and the younger generation of those who are attacking the neoconservatives from the Right. Both groups have said pretty much the same things about the evils of the welfare state, the folly of basing a foreign policy on Wilsonian rhetoric, and the leftist origins and cosmology of the neoconservative rulers of the "conservative move-ment." There is no significant distinction to be drawn among right-wingers based on generational differences. Where they differ, according to Russello, is that paleos show a deeper knowledge of philosophy and history than those who are coming after them. That difference indicates a greater intellectual reach on the part of the paleos, who have managed to be more than "journalists and activists."

While my respondents may not be aware of this fact, in 1986, the *Heritage Foundation's Policy Review* published a commissioned article from me on prominent second-generation paleoconservatives. Almost all of those qualities I now associate with the post-paleo Right are those that I then ascribed to the paleos, who were then mostly in their forties. But my judgments about how paleoconservatism would develop did not turn out to be accurate; one overriding reason for this miscalculation is that the times did not favor our side. Without *eutuxia* or Fortuna in one's camp, and particularly in the face of a grim, powerful enemy, a right-wing political movement is not likely to go anywhere in our age and society.

What separates the two rightist groups I discuss is more than a disparity in age or the whiteness of the hair of the older cohort. The paleos are for the most part rooted in the worldview and mentality of the postwar conservative movement, and except for their temporary alliances with the anti-war, libertarian maverick Murray Rothbard, they typically viewed the conservative movement as something that could be salvaged. The Cold War and the Republican Party had a formative influence on the paleoconservative mind. The predictability with which Pat Buchanan has always found a way of rallying at the eleventh hour to Republican presidential candidates, including W, and the praise that Pat, Paul Craig Roberts, Charley Reese, and other paleos of their generation lavish on Reagan and other Republican presidents reveals their political points of reference. My book on the conservative movement has not elicited any comment from this generation of paleoconservatives but it has received attention from the post-paleos. The reason may be that my attacks are aimed at the entire postwar conservative movement. Unlike my earlier treatments of the subject, my new book is not carefully confined to a few neoconservative targets. The post-paleos have no concern about discussing a work that is critical of a movement and a political party that they consider to be corrupt and archaic.

Post-paleos are also less inhibited about discussing topics that for the paleos have been clearly off the table since the death of Sam Francis, e.g., cognitive disparities among the races, the merit of causing the GOP to lose badly to its more frankly leftist opposition as a precondition for a realignment on the Right, and various Nietzschean critiques of Christianity. Although such openness to positions that would have offended the American conservative movement twenty-five years ago is not uniformly characteristic of all post-paleos, what is typical is their distance from the mindset of a movement to which they never belonged. In some ways they are also less bourgeois and more identifiably yuppie than the group they are destined to replace. But they are also more obviously aligned to an American Right that existed before the postwar conservative movement came along.

Note I am not providing a description that necessarily fits my tastes. Generationally I feel more aligned with the paleos, who by now may consider me a nuisance, than with those who are taking their place. I also share Gerald Russello's preference for theorists over activists, but here some qualifications may be in order. One, there is no indication that post-paleos do not think about their historical condition or that they have read less extensively than the founding generation of the postwar conservative movement. Nor are the young contributors to this site more militant activists than those who founded *National Review* in 1955. They are simply more alienated than those who preceded them from the "conservative movement" and its left-liberal support system. Two, what is essential to any political movement is activism. The problem with the kind of activism that those of my generation criticized was its mindless support of the GOP and its kowtowing to neoconservative foundation heads. If our side is to go anywhere, we will need pushy activists of our own. Otherwise we can resign ourselves to meeting in broom closets with shrinking dimensions. The reason Jonah Goldberg now lives on the *Glenn Beck* show, while its host has not shown any interest in me or the brilliant Mr. Russello, is that Mr. Goldberg has successful activists behind him. One can turn up one's nose at the publicity Goldberg bathes in, but the alternative is not to be widely noticed.

Finally, allow me to touch on the delicate question of religious controversy. While the Protestant Reformation contributed socially and economically to the early waves of European modernization, just as the Catholic world did in physics and cosmology, neither side in the religious schism of the sixteenth century contributed to our present problems in the contemporary West. Moreover, the idea that Catholics have somehow resisted current leftist trends more effectively than Protestants is palpably false. In the English-speaking world, Catholics have positioned themselves for the most part on the political and social Left; and such traditionally Catholic countries as Spain and Ireland are at least as disintegrated as their Protestant neighbors. The fact that Holland now has a Catholic majority has not resulted in that country moving toward the social or cultural Right. Although there are Catholic exceptions to the rule, particularly in Eastern Europe, one finds the same kinds of exceptions in Protestant countries that have been relatively untouched by the acids of late modernity. While the Flemish Vlaams Belang is largely Catholic, the Swiss conservatives led by Christoph Blocher are overwhelmingly Calvinist. Neither group of successful European anti-multiculturalists, however, is behaving like the anti-Catholic ranter James Hagee or like the more zealous anti-Protestants I have encountered on the American Right. European right-wing populists of all denominations show solidarity in defending their common civilization. The last thing the Right needs at this point is a return to the confessional strife of the sixteenth century.

I keep thinking in this matter about one particularly puzzling statement that I heard from a recent Catholic convert who told me that the United States would have been a "great country if only it were Catholic." My thought when I heard this is that my interlocutor had not been looking at the world for a very long time. Why does his supposed Catholic asset not apply to our Northern neighbor Quebec, a onetime agrarian region that now wallows in state-enforced, anti-Christian political correctness? Quebec's Catholic history, overwhelmingly Catholic population, and Bourbon fleur-de-lis flag have done nothing to prevent its descent into multicultural darkness. Indeed, Quebec managed to jettison its inherited political and cultural character in less than two generations. It went through the same flip-flop as onetime Calvinist Holland did in the same span of time. It is therefore unlikely that had the United States in 1790 been a Catholic country, it would have avoided the cultural depredations that ravaged the second half of the twentieth century, or that its Catholic citizens would have been any less further on the Left than many of them are at this time.

As for the neo-pagan critics of all Christians on the Right, I am astounded that such intellectuals think they have any workable solution to what ails our civilization. These critics usually propose a greatly sanitized, highly selective version of what the ancients actually believed; or else they act as if we can get people who have ceased believing in the biblical deity to build their lives around Wotan, Jupiter, or some other pre-Christian god. As Carl Schmitt correctly noted, "historical truths are true only once." Lapsed Christians are no more likely to embrace Graeco-Roman or Germanic deities than they are to bury deceased relatives in Egyptian pyramids. Although, of course, there are eccentric or bookish exceptions, I am speaking about the rule and not the isolated deviations from it.

The Rise of the Post-Paleos

Taki's Magazine

JUNE 24, 2008

I N VIEW of the numerous responses to my announcement of the death of paleoconservatism and my discussion of the transition from a paleo to a post-paleo opposition to the neoconservative-liberal media, there may be need for these further clarifications. One, the post-paleos' indifference to the post–World War II conservative movement is a decided advantage that they enjoy in relation to their elders. They are not mired in a past that can offer only very limited direction in charting a future course.

As Nietzsche wisely pointed out in *On the Advantage and Disadvantage of History for Life* (1874), there are some historical narratives that have ceased to advance human intelligence and creativity, and it is therefore a good idea that we try to move beyond them. It is even unwise to keep symbols around that may hide or falsify what is really going on. One might argue that such relics as the Swedish monarchy and various European national churches do harm by fostering the illusion of historical continuity in countries that have sunk into multicultural confusion and socialist behavior control.

Similar considerations would apply to magazines that now dispense neoconservative poisons that were once identified with the Taft Republican tradition or even at their fringes with European royalism. The continued operation of such publications as *Human Events* and *National Review* under radically different auspices from their original ones may be even more harmful for the real Right than such explicitly neoconservative organs as *The Weekly Standard* and *The New Criterion*. The semblance of continuity in publications that were formerly on the Right but have drifted into the neocon camp may promote the erroneous belief that these magazines still reflect the core values that had characterized them forty years ago.

Two, post-paleos do not intend to "take us back" to the "old movement," which is the fantasy of a golden age of American conservatism that never existed, or at least not in the stable form that the nostalgia-buffs believe it did. Since the 1950s the "conservative movement" has been in transition while exhibiting certain constant features. It has moved steadily leftward but has been micromanaged from the Northeast; and ever since the days of its construction, it has remained firmly in the hands of New York and Washington journalists. That this movement once pursued more traditional rightist politics and that it tolerated a higher degree of debate than it does now, are both indisputable facts.

But it is equally indisputable that the "movement" has steered since the 1950s in its current direction; and there is no reason for us to become nostalgic over the spilled milk left by this cobbled together, largely journalistic enterprise. The Conservative Movement should be viewed as a collection of resources that post-paleos should fight to take over or try to influence. Where such a possibility does not exist, the young Right should aim at destroying its enemies' assets.

Three, unlike many of their elders, the post-paleos have no need to cozy up to their enemies. They do not expect to be invited to a cocktail party sponsored by *The Nation* or *Commentary*, and if they happened to receive and then take such unlikely invitations, it would be to gather information they could deploy in their continuing war of attrition. This kind of hardheadedness is often lacking in those of an older generation who are constantly hoping to "crack the opposition" or to make belated careers as friends of the neocons or of the more radical Left. As Tom Piatak argued in a perceptive comment in *The American Conservative* [not available online], inflamed anti-Christian leftists like Sidney Blumenthal are not planning to befriend the traditionalist Right. Such ideologues are steaming at the neoconservatives for making even tactical alliances with those whom Blumenthal would like to sweep off the planet.

Recently I have developed the impression that at least some of those on the Right are attacking the war in Iraq partly in search of sympathy from the Left. Although this war is plainly unnecessary and being fought for questionable ideological reasons, it is not the unprecedented series of inhumanities that it is made to appear in some right-wing venues. It is probably the least vicious and the most restrained war launched by the United States in the last hundred years, give or take a few minor interventions such as the ones in Grenada. It is, moreover, possible to challenge the wisdom of the war, without descending into certain over-the-top practices, such as whitewashing the brutal mass murders of Saddam Hussein or bringing up the standard leftist charge of "fascist" when describing neoconservative military adventurers.

The invectives against the Bush administration as "fascist" and the focus on oil interests as the cause of the war are both tiresome leftist gestures that some paleos have begun to imitate. I would not be bothered by these outbursts if I did not believe that at least some of them look like pandering. Some of my comrades-in-arms may be more upset than I by the war and I respect their moral feelings. But other "anti-war conservatives," I have become convinced, appear to believe that by complaining about neocon "fascists," the Left might eventually start to applaud. Those who think so are living in a delusional world. In any event, the Right should not be hallucinating about the prospect of swilling martinis at a gathering at AEI or in the office of Victor Navasky.

Four, the post-paleos will have to pursue, and all the more vigorously as resources become available, the tasks of discrediting the neoconservatives and presenting themselves as the true Right. Post-paleos will have to get their hands dirty by continuing to go after their enemies and by doing so in a way that draws public notice. Dwelling on the images of Novalis's "Europa oder Christenheit?" (a subject taken up in my first book and in a very long German essay) may be an aesthetically gratifying act, but it will not have any effect in counteracting the marginal position to which our side has been relegated.

To break out of this encirclement, there is need for aggressive action; and I've no doubt the post-paleos will rise to this challenge. Their enemy will be the managerial therapeutic state and its liberal-neocon shock troops; and the doctrines under which this order will continue to be defended will likely remain the same as it has until now: namely, propositional nationhood, anti-racism, anti-homophobia, anti-anti-Semitism, and anti-fascism. All of the political class's campaigns of intimidation relate back to the same ideology of control; and what divides its members may be nothing more substantive than whether their hegemonic ideology is to be spread through war or by some other means.

The correct position for dealing with the dominant class is not the kind of ranting I have heard from the extreme Right against Jews, Masons, Skull and Bones, or whatever. An intelligent Right must make well-reasoned and thoroughly documented attacks on political correctness, global democracy, and other agents of managerial control.

Lastly, I trust the post-paleos will never hold back from flattening those who claim to be on the Right but who can't resist paying homage to leftist heroes. A young friend recently pounced on that onetime reliably conservative publication *Human Events*, for lying (as it now repeatedly does) about Martin Luther King. It is not coincidental that the same publication has begun to close itself off to the opinions of the non-neoconservative Right. The real Right should never lose an opportunity to accuse those who are blatantly catering to the Left of behaving indecently and mendaciously. Dissemblers who are playing to both sides are as much of a danger to us as such out-and-out foes as Sidney Blumenthal and Victor Navasky. And when these dissemblers get caught on their lies they look even worse.

The Decline and Rise of the Alternative Right

Taki's Magazine

DECEMBER 1, 2008

The following address was given at the H. L. Mencken Club's
Annual Meeting, November 21–23, 2008.

I F THE H. L. Mencken Club can achieve that for which it has been
formed, it should have an eventful and, for those who disagree with
us, profoundly disruptive future. We are part of an attempt to put
together an independent intellectual Right, one that exists without
movement establishment funding and one that our opponents would be
delighted not to have to deal with. Our group is also full of young
thinkers and activists, and if there is to be an independent Right, our
group will have to become its leaders.

For years I've belabored acquaintances with the observation by stating that the paleoconservatives, who had spent their lives butting their
heads against the American conservative movement, were becoming less
and less useful. Note that I do not excuse myself from this judgment
entirely, for what I'm describing is my own generation and those with
whom I've been associated. Paleoconservatives did an enormous service
in the 1980s when they kept the neoconservatives from swallowing up

the entire intellectual and political Right. They had performed something roughly analogous to what the Christians in Asturias and Old Castile had done in the eighth and ninth centuries, when they had whittled away at Muslim control of the Iberian Peninsula. But unlike the rulers of Castile and Aragon, the paleos never succeeded in getting the needed resources to win back lost ground. Unlike the medieval Spanish monarchs, they also didn't have the space of several centuries in which to realize their goals.

But equally significantly, the curmudgeonly personalities that had allowed the paleos to stand up to those from the Left who had occupied the Right prevented them from carrying their war further. Although spirited and highly intelligent, they were temperamentally unfit for a counterinsurgency. They quarreled to such a degree that they eventually fell out among themselves. Soon they were trying to throw each other out of the shaky lifeboat to which their endangered cause had been confined. Of course, considerable disparities in resources and contacts put these partisans into a weaker position than that of their enemies. But their breakdown into rival groups, led by competing heads, commenced early in the conservative wars, and (alas) it has been going on up until the present hour. The founding of our club came out of such a fissiparous event, of the kind that had occurred with some regularity on the Right during the preceding two decades.

Nor is it surprising that the same paleos who broke from the movement often imposed their own litmus tests. Or that their sectarianisms involved highly sectarian opinions over such questions as whether Elizabeth the First's defeat of the Spanish Armada or the later discomfiting of the Stuarts doomed Anglo-American societies to unspeakable moral and political corruption; or (supposedly even more relevant) whether the ethics of Irving Babbitt as selectively filtered through the aesthetics of Benedetto Croce can help save this country from anti-intellectualism or from the disciples of Leo Strauss. Or even more timely, whether being instructed in Babbitt's view of the Higher Will would have mitigated the misfortune of having the stock market plunge. Although there are other such paleo ruminations that can be cited, I shall be merciful and spare my audience the heavy burden of having to hear about them.

The late Sam Francis used to conjure up an ideal-type essay that sprang from the archaic conservative mentality. It was a fifty-page study by a now-deceased University of Georgia professor of English; and it dwelled on how Western society was going to rack and ruin because no one read Flannery O'Connor anymore in light of Eric Voegelin's *Order and History*. There was, indeed, such an essay, which was not entirely a product of Sam's fertile imagination and Menckenesque wit. And having read this literary-cultural exercise, I would have to agree that it typified a certain kind of paleo cultural commentary. It is moralizing aspiring to be scholarship. As a European intellectual historian, it seems to me that such tracts at their best strain to resemble something that might have been composed by a French counterrevolutionary two hundred years ago. But these reproductions operate at a higher level of abstraction without showing anything that strikes this reader as being historically relevant. While not all paleo polemics fit this description, many of them do—or at the very least, bear more than a vague resemblance to what is being caricatured.

And I've been struck by how often these jeremiads have been accompanied by either frantic endorsements of third- or fourth-party politicians or else mournful laments about how the barbarians are climbing in through our windows and how we should therefore prepare ourselves for pious deaths. The fact that I myself have sometimes written in this vein need not detract from my critical remark. My observation is arguably true even if I too am an aging paleo.

To put this into perspective: what is now called paleoconservatism did not grow out of resistance to the Reformation or French Revolution. It is the product of recent historical circumstances, and it assumed its current form about thirty years ago as a diffuse reaction to the neoconservative ascendancy. It was never unified philosophically, and its division between libertarians and traditionalists was only one of the many lines of demarcation separating those who began to call themselves "paleos" about twenty-five years ago. In 1986 I noted in an article for the Heritage Foundation's *Policy Review* that most paleo thinkers were Protestants or Jews. They were also preoccupied with sociobiology, a discipline or way of thinking that had influenced them deeply. Today the paleo camp looks markedly different as well as much older, and it shows little interest in the cognitive, hereditary preconditions for intellectual and cultural achievements. And the despair about American society among paleos may be pushing some of them toward the liberal immigrationist camp, providing they're not already there. Others of this group have become so terrified by those on their left that they pretend not to notice the stark fact of human cognitive disparities. This quest for innocuousness sometimes takes the form of seminars on educational problems centering on endless sermons about values and featuring rotating lists of edifying books. Presumably everyone would perform up to speed if he/she could avail himself/herself of the proper cultural tools. The fact that not everyone enjoys the same genetic precondition for learning is irrelevant for this politically motivated experiment in wishful thinking.

More recently we have been confronted by another problem on the Right, namely, groups that give little evidence of being what they claim to be. As far as I can tell, there is nothing intrinsically right-wing about denying the claims of family and society on the putatively autonomous individual. And the dream of living outside of the state in a society of self-actualizing individuals, opening themselves up to being physically displaced by the entire Third World, if its population chooses to settle on this continent, is not a rightist alternative to anything. It is a failed leftist utopia. It is one thing to deplore the modern welfare state as a vehicle of grotesque social change or for its violations of the US Constitution. It is another matter to believe that all authority structures can be reduced to insurance companies formed to protect the property and lives of anarcho-capitalists. Such a belief goes counter to everything we know about human nature, and even such an embattled anti-welfare-statist as H. L. Mencken never hoped to destroy all government. He loathed egalitarian democracy but not the traditional social and political authorities in which communal life had developed and which conforms to our intertwined social needs.

Having made these critical observations, I would also stress the possibility for positive change represented by this organization. We have youth and exuberance on our side, and a membership that is largely in its twenties and thirties. We have attracted besides old-timers like me, as I noted in my introductory paragraph, well-educated young professionals who consider themselves to be on the Right but not of the current conservative movement. These "post-paleos," to whom I have alluded in internet commentaries, are out in force here tonight. And they are radical in the sense in which William F. Buckley once defined a true Right, an oppositional force that tries to uncover the root causes of our political and cultural crises and then to address them.

And when I speak about the post-paleos, it goes without saying that I'm referring to a growing communion beyond this organization. It is one that now includes Takimag.com, VDARE.com, and other websites that are willing to engage sensitive, timely subjects.

A question that has been asked of me and of others in this room is why we don't try to join the official conservative movement. This movement controls hundreds of millions of dollars, TV networks, strings of newspapers and magazines, multitudinous foundations and institutes, and a bevy of real and bleached blondes on Fox News. This is not even to mention the movement's influence on the GOP, the leaders of which dutifully recite neoconservative slogans. To whatever extent the GOP still has something that can be described as a "mind," it is what neoconservative surgeons have implanted.

Why then don't the post-paleos ask to be admitted to this edifice of power? Even as the beneficiaries of second- or even third-rung posts, our younger members would be better off financially than they are in their present genteel, hand-to-mouth existences. It is easy to imagine that even the secretaries at AEI, Heritage, or *The Weekly Standard* earn more than many of those in this room. Movement conservatives certainly have the wind in their sails; and perhaps most of us have been tempted at one time or another to join them in order to benefit from their considerable wealth.

Allow me to suggest two reasons that most of us have not gone over to the Dark Side. One, that side will not have us; and it has treated us, in contrast to such worthies as black nationalists, radical feminists, and open-borders advocates, as being unfit for admittance into the political conversation. We are not viewed as honorable dissenters but depicted as subhuman infidels or ignored in the same way as one would a senile uncle who occasionally wanders into one's living room. This imperial ban has been extended even to brilliant social scientists and statisticians who are viewed as excessively intimate with the wrong people, that is, with those who stand outside the camp that the neocons occupy and now share with neo-liberals and the center-left. I suspect that most of us, including those who belong to my children's generation, would not be trusted even if we feigned admiration for Martin Luther King, Joe Lieberman, and Scoop Jackson, and even if we called for having open borders with Mexico and for attacking and occupying Iran. Even then a credibility gap would be cited to justify our further marginalization.

But there is another factor, besides necessity, that keeps us where we are. We are convinced that we are right in our historical and cultural observations while those who have quarantined us are wrong. This is indeed my position, and it is one that the officers of this organization fully share. But to move from theory to practice, there are two counsels that I would strenuously urge. First, we must try to do what is possible rather than what lies beyond our limited material resources. What we can hope to achieve in the near term as opposed to what we might be able to do in the fullness of time is to gain recognition as an intellectual Right—and one that is critical of the neoconservative-controlled conservative establishment. Although that establishment does permit some internal dissent and has even provided support for a handful of worthwhile scholars, it is at least as closed as were the communist parties of

Eastern Europe before the collapse of the Soviet Empire. But unlike that now-vanished domination, the neocon media empire is not particularly porous, and with the help of the Left, it is more than able to keep out of public view any serious challenge from the Right. It is precisely our goal to become such a challenge. And it is my hope that a younger generation will acquire the resources to do so and will know how to deploy them.

Second, if we wish to advance our cause, we must meditate on the successes of our most implacable enemies. The neocons marched non-stop through the institutions and treasuries of the Right and took them over almost without breaking a sweat. And they did so without themselves having to move to the right. In fact they converted the Right to the Left, by equating their mostly leftist politics with reasonable or non-extremist conservatism. They then pushed into near oblivion anyone on the Right who resisted their transformations. And as one of their victims, I certainly begrudge them these successes. But as much as I might rage over neocon mendacity and movement conservative gullibility and cowardice, I can also understand the magnitude of the domination achieved. And as painful as it may be for us, we must try to grasp that in Machiavelli's language, it was not just Fortuna but also *virtù* that was at work in making possible our enemies' spectacular achievements. Their opponents failed not only because they were obviously outgunned but also because we were less well organized, less able to network, and less capable of burying internal grievances.

A friend once noted my ambivalence when I describe my enemies. My repugnance for their shallow ideas and grubby personalities has always been mixed with deep admiration for how they stick together like a band of brothers. It is this side of neoconservative history that we must keep in mind and imitate if we intend to climb out of the oblivion into which they have cast us. Our enemies may be vulgar, but they are surely not fools. And their indubitable successes have much to teach anyone who hopes to supplant them, ultimately to do to them what they have done to us.

The Faileocons

Taki's Magazine

JUNE 18, 2009

W E ARE all entitled to our memories, but Charles Coulombe's reminiscences about the American conservative movement are very different from mine. Although his recollections are not incorrect, they are excessively selective. Charles is looking from the perspective of the late 1970s back to the 1950s and trying to freeze the postwar conservative movement at a point at which it would coincide with his traditionalist Catholic inclinations. But the 1950s constituted only a single decade in the conservative movement, and it was not a particularly typical one. My own memories reach back further since I am older than Charles; and I have also researched several books on the subject under discussion. The conservatism of the 1950s was heavily influenced and disproportionately populated by Irish Catholics and by Jews and Protestants who ran to embrace the Catholic Church. It was also shaped by militant anti-communism, and it featured European immigrants, who often combined Catholic beliefs with anti-communist enthusiasm. Patrick Allitt has produced an informative book, *Catholic Intellectuals and Conservative Politics in America, 1950–1985* (1993), on this theme.

In these characteristics, the conservative movement of the 1950s was a cultural and sociological anomaly. Catholic political influence in the next generation would be felt mostly on the political Left, as it had been

417

during the New Deal. The small-town, heartland Protestants who had dominated the American Right before the 1950s would not resume the cultural leadership they had enjoyed before. Instead there would be new power brokers taking over the movement, swaggering Machiavellian princes who espoused leftist views but wrapped them in American nationalist rhetoric. The neoconservatives would thereafter achieve such a formidable lock-hold on the respectable American Right that no other group would ever be in a position to challenge them.

Charles's favorite thinkers are better than those who are currently running the conservative movement but not exactly exponents of his Catholic monarchical stance. Pat Buchanan has made a reputation as an economic nationalist and as a (somewhat inconsistent) defender of the Republican Party and GOP presidential candidates. He is also surviving and flourishing in the present media environment, a fact that indicates that the conservative present may not be entirely distinct from the conservative past. And regarding Charles's other hero Russell Kirk, I can't possibly imagine that one would find much political theory or political direction from reading his works. On this point, although perhaps on nothing else, I agree with David Frum, that Kirk was first and always a literary figure; and as far as I could tell from having known him, he would not have defined himself in any other way.

I likewise agree with my colleague Wes McDonald, who has written an intellectual biography of his mentor—*Russell Kirk and the Age of Ideology* (2004)—that Kirk's Catholicism was always problematic. Indeed one could present this figure as a cultural Protestant or disciple of Irving Babbitt as easily as one could as a believing Catholic. But the essential point here is that Kirk was interested only very incidentally in political affairs; and although he contributed regularly to *National Review* in the 1950s and 1960s, his contributions consisted almost entirely of commentaries on American education.

I must also challenge Charles's distinctions between the old and new paleoconservatives, and I do so with considerable authority. Although his commentary does not mention me, I have acquired the reputation, at least in *The New York Times* and in ISI publications, of being America's leading paleoconservative thinker. I feel in no way slighted because Charles does not list me as such. There is no reason he should. Everyone who goes by this name has developed his own "paleoconservatism" and the meanings of the operative term do not necessarily overlap. Journalists, of course, knew what "paleoconservative" meant when I invented that designation twenty years ago. But things have changed since then. We now have two groups that claim the term "conservative": an establishment power structure dominated by neocon opinions and lubricated with neocon money; and those people on the Right who have been kept out of the country club but who also don't get along well with each other. Most of those who have been excluded and who are beyond a certain age have fought themselves into stupefaction, without gaining ground. Most of the younger people in this camp of the marginalized are therefore unimpressed by those who have preceded them, and they are searching for new ways to get their views noticed, while reassessing the inspired texts of the older generation.

In this contest of the generations, I stand entirely on the side of those with a future. My generation of rightists has wasted its chance for success. We can only point to humiliations, continued marginalization, and internecine strife as our war record. Nor have we provided much assistance to each other, unlike our enemies, who like the ancient Spartans as described by Xenophon, "suffer and rejoice together." Most of my generation of paleos has done little to establish a sense of community. The more fortunate ones have husbanded their resources while doing next to nothing for their allies.

That the young are still groping for a way out of the wilderness is to their credit. It is also the privilege of youth to be looking for new paths, and especially given the failures of their quarrelsome elders. Charles has noticed the obvious here, that the "new paleos" have little to feel happy about as they view their country and most of the Western world in the grasp of cultural gravediggers and a reckless political class. Does he dispute the justification for this pessimism or the justification for the young paleos' unwillingness to pretend that the solution for Obama is electing more GOP politicians? As for his censures about their sexual morals, which Charles may fear do not quite meet the standard of Trappist monks, I don't see the licentiousness here that he does. None of the young paleos, to my knowledge, is leading a life of wine and roses. For one thing, they don't have the disposable income for fun and games that their neoconservative enemies are being showered with. Moreover, compared to the philandering Catholic monarchist Charles Maurras, who spent most of his adult life tumbling from one mistress to the next, the "new paleos" seem to be models of Puritan sobriety.

Let me stir the pot further by drawing another distinction, between those who want to be political activists and those who do not. Many of the paleos I've listened to show an otherworldly side, when they're not bashing each other in geriatric rage. They glorify Catholic monastic ideals or invoke the memories of Christian crusades. They complain ceaselessly about modern life and insist that we return to scholastic precepts and medieval models of social organization. But such advice cannot possibly resonate in the current climate of debate, and it is foolish to castigate those young people who wish to have impact on the present age for not following someone else's nostalgic reveries.

What Charles's dirge seems to convey is that things were much better in the 1950s. He is urging us to look back to that decade for our conservative benchmark. But my book *Conservatism in America* (2007) suggests a far more critical view of movement conservatives sixty years ago. Most of the bad habits that establishment conservative leaders acquired, such as booting dissenters out of the conservative fold, began in the 1950s, and there is little in the way of nastiness that the neocons have practiced that was not already present in the movement that Buckley built.

Resurrecting
the Old Right

Chronicles

SEPTEMBER 2019

F OR THOSE who may have noticed, I've been absent from this venerable magazine for more than twelve years. Upon returning, I feel obliged to give an account of what I've learned in the intervening time. Aside from visiting my family and doing research for several monographs, I've been pondering the vicissitudes of the American Right.

That last activity leads me to this judgment: We need to bring back the Old Right. Without this rallying point, a credible Right will not be part of America's future. Neither our present conservative establishment nor white nationalism, nor that part of the Alt-Right dominated by white nationalists, will do for this purpose; and I shall try to explain why.

After years of observing the conservative establishment, I can safely state that most of its media stars won't exert themselves on behalf of unfashionable social issues. They may jolly up the Religious Right in order to keep that constituency Republican, but they tiptoe around gay marriage, feminism, and other divisive social matters. These "authorized" conservatives are typically reduced to defending onetime leftist positions that they pretend are conservative, such as second-wave feminism, gay marriage (other than protesting the penalties inflicted on

Christian bakers who won't bake for gay weddings), and the legitimacy of myriad genders (other than allowing transgendered male athletes to compete with biological women). That compromise is still to come. On the immigration question, the conservative media have compromised dramatically, from limiting the legal number of immigrants to holding down the influx of illegals.

Despite my advanced age, I remain astounded by how the conservative "movement" slides from one leftist social position into an even more radical one just shy of whatever extreme standard the established Left sets for a particular issue. Accordingly, we are introduced on Fox News and in conservative publications to "proud" conservative gays who are married to other gays and to Republican feminists and Republican feminist lesbians, who are outraged by the more progressive representatives of their anti-traditional lifestyle.

I've also noticed the absence of outrage among media conservatives when leftist state administrations began pulling down Confederate memorial statues. The editor-in-chief of *National Review*, Rich Lowry, urged the expeditious removal of Robert E. Lee's statues from all over the country. As if this truckling to the Left weren't sufficient, a recent commentary on the same magazine's website castigates Ronald Reagan for making a racially insensitive comment to Richard Nixon over the phone in 1969. Perhaps a respectable conservative just can't truckle enough these days, particularly in responding to a leftist friend at *The Atlantic*.

Such acts of homage toward the Left has not kept Conservatism Inc. from speaking for "permanent things" and "values," although the definitions of these elusive quiddities keep changing depending on the zeitgeist, the availability of sponsors, and—at least equally important—the possibility of triangulating a new compromise in the leftward-shifting "center." To all appearances, the movement's younger stars avoid doing anything that might limit their career opportunities. They crave invitations to participate on network programs like *Meet the Press* and to write for *The New York Times*, *The Washington Post*, and *The Atlantic*. Successful conservatives who play their hands right have achieved such career goals, for example: Rich Lowry, David French, Kevin Williamson, and Jonah Goldberg. And they have done this while holding on to their largely Republican base. Media conservatives also labor to accommodate their fat-cat donors, whether the Murdoch family, Sheldon Adelson, Paul Singer, the Koch brothers, or members of the very friendly defense industries. We are also not supposed to comment on the amount of Zionist funding going into the conservative infrastructure. And it's surely no secret that the Zionists who donate the most heavily to Conservatism Inc., like Murdoch, Singer, and Adelson, are supporters of left-leaning social causes.

Conservative power brokers have also worked to marginalize inconvenient or uncooperative voices on the Right. Whether anti-interventionists, Southern conservatives, or people like me who have been persistent nuisances, the conservative movement has both exiled and defamed those whom it deems problematic. In a grotesque overgeneralization, Jonah Goldberg, Sam Tanenhaus, and E. J. Dionne have maintained that those who suffered such a battering have been racists and anti-Semites. Such accusations were usually made once the assaults had begun, in order to bring the liberal media on board to deliver the *coup de grâce*. I provide a cross section of these victims in the concluding essay of a new anthology, *The Vanishing Tradition: Perspectives on American Conservatism* (2020), published by Cornell University Press.

The purges have taken place for varied reasons, one of which was to secure scarce academic resources. For example, the neoconservatives targeted Southern literary scholar M. E. Bradford in the hope of denying him a directorship at the National Endowment for the Humanities, a position that they wanted for themselves. Other times they were driven by the desire to punish those who weren't on board with the imperial military project, such as when the establishment turned against the John Birch Society in July 1965 because of their opposition to the war in Vietnam. Attacks on the Birchers as racist and anti-Semitic were used by William F. Buckley to justify a decision to support military intervention, which had nothing to do with these charges. The Bircher magazine at the time, *American Opinion*, had both Jewish and black contributors.

Recent charges leveled against me by the conservative establishment as a white nationalist may be more of the same—that is, a further justification for a process of blacklisting that I've endured since the 1980s, when I began protesting the neoconservative takeover of what had been the conservative movement. Already in 1987, neoconservatives and Straussians teamed up to keep me from a graduate professorship at Catholic University of America. The dean of humanities was reputedly informed that I was "not quite reliable on Israel." That turned out to be a deadly accusation that shattered my chances for teaching Aristotle's *Politics* and other putatively anti-Zionist texts like Polybius's *Histories*. Back then, I still leaned toward the Israeli Right—as if that made any difference to my accusers, who intended the post that I sought for one of their own.

On the other end of the conservative spectrum is another obstacle to a credible, authentic Right: white nationalism. Its adherents represent a moribund ideology that offers an imaginary antidote to a misdiagnosed pathology. Throughout the Western world today a cultural war has erupted in which non-radicals are fighting to hold their ground against the Left. As a professor for forty years I observed that the vast majority of my leftist colleagues were white. It was white academics who brought radicalized minorities into academia in order to further "diversity." A struggle for cultural and political dominance, moreover, goes on even in countries where nonwhites are politically insignificant. Indeed, the European Left has worked to improve their hand by importing Third World, non-Christian populations. After he left office, former British Prime Minister Tony Blair admitted to doing precisely this. The depiction of our cultural wars as based exclusively or primarily on race misrepresents what's happening. Our most numerous adversaries in the struggle for Western civilization are white, and often belong to an affluent white elite.

To make matters even worse, white nationalists are no further on the Right on social issues than the triangulating media conservatives. For the sake of white solidarity, white nationalists are willing to make massive concessions to the social Left. Their reasoning seems to be, "Who cares about social or sexual morality as long as we can stand together with other whites, against everyone else?" Unfortunately for white nationalists, this is not how the cultural battle lines are drawn, and those battle lines will not likely change in the near future.

There are, of course, white nationalists who are not only strategically misguided but also given to violent acts. Indeed, one such white nationalist went berserk in El Paso, Texas, on August 3, when he shot up a shopping mall and killed twenty-two people while wounding twenty-four others. But I'm not looking at crazed killers who identify themselves as white nationalists. Rather, I am looking at the so-called thought leaders among the white nationalists, who imagine they have come up with a strategy for fighting the Left.

Such militants believe they can break into the established media political conversation by being outrageous. They pride themselves on being "edgy," as if this quality all by itself would win them acceptance in the national debate. But there's only one way, as far as I can tell, that a political force can take off. It's the way neoconservatives moved up, by putting together a king's fortune, which they used to acquire media power. Unlike our isolated white nationalists, these political players had the advantage of holding conventional, almost left-of-center views, other than their extravagant Zionism and aggressive, missionary foreign policy. They also enjoyed support from the media and in government circles as they advanced themselves and their agenda. White nationalists aren't going to approximate this accomplishment merely by shocking us.

I would note in their partial defense that white nationalists are doing for whites what Jesse Jackson, Al Sharpton, Cory Booker, and other black political figures have been doing for blacks. They are trying to raise group self-esteem by portraying their own race as victimized by adversaries. They are also generally no worse in their expressions of bigotry than anti-white blacks, who are media darlings. In a revealing biography entitled *Sharpton: A Demagogue's Rise* (2015), Carl Horowitz shows that it would be hard to surpass the Reverend Al in crude race baiting and incitement to violence. Yet Sharpton is not only a god figure in the present Democratic Party but, as Horowitz documents, an honored guest on Fox News for almost a decade. Undoubtedly, a double standard operates here, to the disadvantage of white nationalists. But they should blame other whites for allowing this uneven standard to exist. Without the promotion of black nationalists by whites on the Left, this situation would not prevail. What has been loosely labeled the Alt-Right (yes, I helped to invent that term as well as "paleoconservative") is a more heterogeneous grouping than white nationalists, neoconservatives, or the homogenized media conservatives. A wide range of dissenters on the Right, from Breitbart, to immigration restrictionists, to race realists, and finally white nationalists have all been lumped together in the media. These Alt-Righters are mostly bloggers or website editors who have positioned themselves to the right of Conservatism Inc. but view paleoconservatives with a touch of scorn.

At their best, these critics sound very much like the paleoconservatives of the 1980s, when they were battling the neoconservatives. I for one have benefited from reading these miscellaneous independent Alt-Rightists on such subjects as the limits of pluralism, genetic influences on social behavior, and the folly of basing a conservative movement on such intrinsically leftist concepts as equality and human rights. It would be a mistake to confound these social and political critics with simple-minded, obsessive white nationalists.

But I would call attention to two problems that have affected my relations to the Alt-Right. First, as George Hawley argues in *Making Sense of the Alt-Right* (2019), his subjects have not been able to free themselves entirely from white nationalist and even neo-Nazi associations. This is something they'll definitely have to do if they wish to make themselves acceptable to larger numbers of people on the Right.

Second, although, as Hawley notes, my writings, particularly on neoconservatism and the European Right, profoundly influenced Alt-

Right authors, I continue to hold reservations about their positions. I am especially bothered by the reductionist argument about racial IQ made by some Alt-Righters. Like them, I recognize that high intelligence is useful to a society or civilization; and it's also possible that in some parts of the world this cognitive advantage may be lacking. But the "g factor," or general intelligence, is only one of many preconditions for sustaining human development. Too often, the view of the social good that I extract from Alt-Right authors is that of a society made up exclusively or predominantly of those eligible for MENSA membership. Let me stress once again that high native intelligence is a desirable trait. But in the United States, my major concern is not a paucity of Americans with above-average IQs. It is rather the social and cultural damage being wrought by the "high achievers," who seem determined to destroy the moral foundations of Western civilization.

An essay of mine on Charles Murray's 2012 book *Coming Apart* (which is in my anthology *Revisions and Dissents*) disputes an opinion argued by historian Niall Ferguson, that those high achievers whom Murray extols represent a "return to the republic's original foundations of family, vocation, community, and faith." What Murray describes are not present-day embodiments of Puritan culture but rather Congressman Jerry Nadler's voting base in Soho and Brooklyn Heights. These successful careerists, not incidentally, include those corporate executives in the high-tech sector who are conspiring to bring down all opposition to the cultural left. That such people score high on IQ tests is true enough. But I'd sooner trust our society to my rural Pennsylvania neighbors than to Mark Zuckerberg or Jeff Bezos.

This, by way of explaining why I haven't strayed far from where I began politically about fifty years ago. It also explains why a onetime follower of mine, Richard Spencer, was correct when he observed on Twitter in March 2018, "Paul Gottfried does not endorse race-conscious conservatism. He never has nor likely will." True enough! I've never stopped believing that the Old Right tradition, or paleoconservatism by any other name, is the only appropriate doctrine for the Right, to whatever extent the Right is still concerned with social morality, a sane non-interventionist foreign policy, and the taming of the egalitarian madness that is now subverting most Western societies.

In this protracted conflict, which is likely to go on for some time, we should stand for something that is worth standing for; and that something, I would argue, has to be different from virtue-signaling toward the Left, heaping undeserved praise on today's white race, or celebrating the IQ elite.

Endnotes

1   Joe Lancaster, "Industrial Policy Is Alive and Well at the Democratic National Convention," Reason, August 20, 2024, https://reason.com/2024/08/20/industrial-policy-is-alive-and-well-at-the-democratic-national-convention.

2   Holm Arno Leonhardt, "Von Alt-Links zu Neu-Links: Zur Transformation des Marxismus in die Woke-Bewegung," Jahrbuch der Wissenschaftsfreiheit 1 (2024): 154.

3   "Discours solennels au procès Papon," *L'Express*, November 26, 1997.

4   Jean-Robert Ragache and Gilles Ragache, *Des écrivains et des artistes sous l'occupation 1940–1944* (Paris: Hachette, 1988).

5   "La strage antifascista dopo la liberazione," *Corriere della Sera*, April 1995.

6   Horace Kallen and Herbert Croly, contributions to *New Republic*, 1920s.

7   John Patrick Diggins, *Mussolini and Fascism: The View from America* (Princeton, NJ: Princeton University Press, 1972).

8   Theodor W. Adorno, Else Frenkel-Brunswik, Daniel J. Levinson, and R. Nevitt Sanford, *The Authoritarian Personality* (New York: Harper & Brothers, 1950).

9   Richard Hofstadter, *The Paranoid Style in American Politics and Other Essays* (New York: Knopf, 1965).

10 Allan Bloom, *The Closing of the American Mind* (New York: Simon & Schuster, 1987).

11 Stanley Rothman and S. Robert Lichter, *Roots of Radicalism: Jews, Christians, and the New Left* (New York: Oxford University Press, 1982).

12 Paul Gottfried, "The F Word," Taki's Magazine, June 4, 2012, https://www.takimag.com/article/the_f_word_paul_gottfried/#axzz1x3LF97MM.

13 Austin Bramwell, "Goldberg's Trivial Pursuit," *American Conservative*, January 28, 2008, https://theamericanconservative.com/articles/goldbergs-trivial-pursuit.

14 William D. Gairdner, "Getting Used to the F-Word," *New Criterion*, October 2011, https://newcriterion.com/article/getting-used-to-the-f-word.

15   George Orwell, "What Is Fascism?," *Tribune*, 1946, reprinted in *The Collected Essays, Journalism and Letters of George Orwell*, ed. Sonia Orwell and Ian Angus, vol. 4 (London: Secker & Warburg, 1968), 111–14.

16   Jonah Goldberg, *Liberal Fascism: The Secret History of the American Left from Mussolini to the Politics of Meaning* (New York: Doubleday, 2007).

17   Zeev Sternhell, interview, *Haaretz*, August 2014.

18   Ezra Klein, "The Enemies of Liberalism Are Showing Us What It Really Means," *New York Times*, April 3, 2022, https://www.nytimes.com/2022/04/03/opinion/putin-ukraine-liberalism.html.

19   Jason Stanley, *How Fascism Works: The Politics of Us and Them* (New York: Random House, 2018); Mark Bray, *Antifa: The Anti-Fascist Handbook* (Brooklyn, NY: Melville House, 2017).

20   James Kirchick, "Fidel Castro's Horrific Record on Gay Rights," The Daily Beast, November 27, 2016, https://www.thedailybeast.com/fidel-castros-horrific-record-on-gay-rights.

21   Max Horkheimer and Theodor W. Adorno, *Dialectic of Enlightenment*, trans. John Cumming (New York: Herder and Herder, 1972).

22   Annie Kriegel, *The French Communists: Profile of a People*, trans. Elaine P. Halperin (Chicago: University of Chicago Press, 1972).

23   John Stuart Mill, *On Liberty* (London: John W. Parker and Son, 1859).

24   Willmoore Kendall, *The Conservative Affirmation* (Chicago: Henry Regnery Company, 1963).

25   Tony Woodlief, "The Fires Foretold: Willmoore Kendall and the Burning of America," *American Conservative*, June 8, 2020, https://www.theamericanconservative.com/the-fires-foretold-willmoore-kendall-and-the-burning-of-america.

26   Dan Proft, "It's Not a Race War. It's Something Much Bigger," American Greatness, April 21, 2021, https://amgreatness.com/2021/04/21/its-not-a-race-war-its-something-much-bigger.

27   Vera Lengsfeld, "Willkommen in der rechten Ecke!" *Reitschuster*, April 25, 2021, https://vera-lengsfeld.de/2021/04/25/willkommen-in-der-rechten-ecke-ein-offener-brief-an-jan-josef-liefers.

28   Victor Davis Hanson, "The New Antiracism Is the Old Racism," American Greatness, April 25, 2021, https://amgreatness.com/2021/04/25/the-new-antiracism-is-the-old-racism/.

29   "Bella Abzug," KeyWiki, accessed March 3, 2025, https://www.keywiki.org/Bella_Abzug.

30   Scott Johnson, "Walz Then and Now," *Power Line* (blog), January 2021, https://www.powerlineblog.com/archives/2021/01/walz-then-and-now.php.

31   Glenn Ellmers, "The 'New Normal' and the Assault on Reason," American Greatness, January 15, 2022, https://amgreatness.com/2022/01/15/the-new-normal-and-the-assault-on-reason.

32 John Stuart Mill, *On Liberty* (London: John W. Parker and Son, 1859).

33 Leo Strauss, *Natural Right and History* (Chicago: University of Chicago Press, 1953).

34 William A. Donahue, *The Politics of the American Civil Liberties Union* (New Brunswick, NJ: Transaction Publishers, 1985).

35 Yoram Hazony, *Conservatism: A Rediscovery* (Washington, DC: Regnery Gateway, 2022).

36 Franz Neumann, *Behemoth: The Structure and Practice of National Socialism* (London: Victor Gollancz, 1942).

37 Eliseo Vivas, *Contra Marcuse* (New Rochelle, NY: Arlington House, 1971).

38 Bloom, *The Closing of the American Mind.*

39 Christopher Lasch, *The True and Only Heaven: Progress and Its Critics* (New York: W. W. Norton, 1991).

40 Theodor W. Adorno, Else Frenkel-Brunswik, Daniel J. Levinson, and R. Nevitt Sanford, *The Authoritarian Personality* (New York: Harper & Brothers, 1950).

41 Simone Angela, "Angela Davis on Protest, 1968, and Her Old Teacher, Herbert Marcuse," Literary Hub, April 3, 2019, https://lithub.com/angela-davis-on-protest-1968-and-her-old-teacher-herbert-marcuse.

42 John P. Diggins, *Up from Communism: Conservative Odysseys in American Intellectual History* (New York: Harper & Row, 1975).

43 James Burnham, *The Machiavellians: Defenders of Freedom* (New York: John Day, 1943).

44 "Editorial," *Encounter*, May 1975.

45 James Burnham, *Suicide of the West: An Essay on the Meaning and Destiny of Liberalism* (New York: John Day, 1964).

46 Edmund Burke, *Reflections on the Revolution in France* (London: J. Dodsley, 1790).

47 Robert Nisbet, *The Quest for Community: A Study in the Ethics of Order and Freedom* (New York: Oxford University Press, 1953); Robert Nisbet, *The Sociological Tradition* (New York: Basic Books, 1966).

48 Russell Kirk, *The Conservative Mind: From Burke to Santayana* (Chicago: Henry Regnery Company, 1953).

49 Panajotis Kondylis, *Konservativismus: Geschichtlicher Gehalt und Untergang* (Stuttgart: Klett-Cotta, 1986).

50 Ibid., 51.

51 Panajotis Kondylis, "Marxismus, Kommunismus und die Geschichte des 20. Jahrhunderts," in *Der Marxismus in seinem Zeitalter* (Leipzig, 1994), 25, 33.

52 Letter from Kondylis dated February 14, 1997.

53 "Menschenrechte, begriffliche Verwirrung und politische Instrumentalisierung," *Frankfurter Rundschau*, August 18, 1996, 12.

54 Cf. George H. Nash, *The Conservative Intellectual Movement in America Since 1945*, revised edition (Wilmington, DE: Intercollegiate Studies Institute, 1996), 329–41; and Paul Gottfried, *The Conservative Movement*, second edition (New York: Twayne Publishers, 1993), 142–66.

55 Kondylis, "Marxismus, Kommunismus und die Geschichte des 20. Jahrhunderts," 25, 34.

56 For an expansive statement of this anti-American sentiment by Europe's most prominent New Right spokesman, see Alan de Benoist, *Il était une fois l'Amérique* (Paris, 1984); and Thomas Molnar, "American Culture: A Possible Threat," *World and I* (May 1987): 440–42.

57 See Kondylis, *Konservativismus: Geschichtlicher Gehalt und Untergang*, 387–447, 507.

58 See Panajotis Kondylis, *Der Niedergang der bürgerlichen Denk- und Lebensform: Die liberale Moderne und die massendemokratische Postmoderne* (Weinheim, 1991), especially 169–88.

59 Ibid., 208–26.

60 Ibid., 328–67.

61 Kondylis, "Marxismus, Kommunismus und die Geschichte des 20. Jahrhunderts," 15–16.

62 Ibid., 18–19.

63 Panajotis Kondylis, "Die Antiquiertheit der politischen Begriffe," *Frankfurter Allgemeine Zeitung*, October 5, 1991, 8.

64 Ibid.; see also Panajotis Kondylis, "Globalisierung, Politik, Verteilung," *Tagesanzeiger*, November 29, 1996, 8.

65 Kondylis, *Konservativismus*, 505.

66 References to Carl Schmitt abound in Kondylis's interview with the *Deutsche Zeitschrift für Philosophie* 4 (1994): 683–94; and in his work.

67 Kondylis, *Konservativismus*, 504.

68 See Kondylis's feature pieces "Globale Mobilmachung," in *Frankfurter Allgemeine Zeitung*, July 13, 1996, 7; "Blühende Geistesgeschäfte," *Frankfurter Allgemeine Zeitung*, December 28, 1995; "Was heisst schon westlich?," *Frankfurter Allgemeine Zeitung*, November 19, 1994; and *Planetarische Politik nach dem Kalten Krieg* (Berlin, 1992).

69 Samuel P. Huntington, "The Clash of Civilizations?" *Foreign Affairs* 72, no. 3 (Summer 1993): 22–49.

70 See "Globale Mobilmachung," in *Frankfurter Allgemeine* Zeitung, July 13, 1996, 7; and "Wege in die Ratlosigkeit," *Frankfurter Allgemeine Zeitung*, May 7, 1995. The latter article is particularly revealing of Kondylis's historical and moral outlook, inasmuch as it treats the "information revolution" dismissively and insists that the "logic of information will remain subordinate to interpersonal relations and ideological orientations."

71 Paul Gottfried, *Conservatism in America: Making Sense of the American Right* (New York: Palgrave-Macmillan, 2007).

72 "The John Birch Society and the Conservative Movement," *National Review*, July 13, 1965.

73 William F. Buckley Jr., *Up from Liberalism* (New York: McDowell, Obolensky, 1959).

74 Judith Thurman, "Dominique Venner's Final Solution," *New Yorker*, May 29, 2013.

75 Dominique Venner, *Histoire de l'Armée rouge*, 2 vols. (Paris: Éditions de la Table Ronde, 1984).

76 Dominique Venner, ed., *Enquête sur l'histoire* (Paris: various issues, 1990s); Dominique Venner, ed., *La Nouvelle Revue d'Histoire* (Paris: various issues, post-2000).

77 Eric Voegelin, *Political Religions*, trans. T. J. DiNapoli and E. S. Easterly III (Lewiston, NY: Edwin Mellen Press, 1986), first published in German in 1938 as *Die politischen Religionen*.

78 Eric Voegelin, *Order and History*, 5 vols. (Baton Rouge: Louisiana State University Press, 1956–1987).

79 Eric Voegelin, *The New Science of Politics: An Introduction* (Chicago: University of Chicago Press, 1952); Eric Voegelin, *Science, Politics and Gnosticism* (Chicago: Henry Regnery Company, 1968), first published in German in 1959 as *Wissenschaft, Politik und Gnosis*.

80 Eric Voegelin, "Schelling Essay," in *The Collected Works of Eric Voegelin*, vol. 7, *Published Essays, 1940–1952*, ed. Ellis Sandoz (Columbia: University of Missouri Press, 2000), 147–213.

81 Ellis Sandoz, *The Voegelinian Revolution: A Biographical Introduction* (Baton Rouge: Louisiana State University Press, 1981).

82 Eric Voegelin, *Hitler and the Germans*, trans. and ed. Detlev Clemens and Brendan Purcell (Columbia: University of Missouri Press, 1999).

83 George H. Nash, *The Conservative Intellectual Movement in America Since 1945* (New York: Basic Books, 1976).

84 Frank S. Meyer, *In Defense of Freedom: A Conservative Credo* (Chicago: Henry Regnery Company, 1962).

85 Frank S. Meyer, ed., *What Is Conservatism?* (New York: Holt, Rinehart, and Winston, 1964).

86 George H. Nash, *The Conservative Intellectual Movement in America Since 1945* (New York: Basic Books, 1976).

87 Aristotle, *Politics*, trans. H. Rackham (Cambridge, MA: Harvard University Press, 1932), Book III.

88 Plato, *Republic*, trans. G. M. A. Grube, rev. C. D. C. Reeve (Indianapolis: Hackett Publishing, 1992), Book IX.

89 Bertrand de Jouvenel, *The Pure Theory of Politics* (Cambridge: Cambridge University Press, 1963).

90   James Madison, *Federalist*, no. 51, in *The Federalist Papers*, ed. Clinton Rossiter (New York: New American Library, 1961).

91   Paul Edward Gottfried, *After Liberalism: Mass Democracy in the Managerial State* (Princeton, NJ: Princeton University Press, 1999).

92   Immanuel Kant, *To Perpetual Peace: A Philosophical Sketch*, trans. Ted Humphrey (Indianapolis: Hackett Publishing, 2003), first published in German in 1795 as *Zum Ewigen Frieden*.

93   Hermann Cohen, *Deutschtum und Judentum* (Giessen: Alfred Töpelmann, 1915).

94   Barry Alan Shain, "Defending the West: A Critique of Universalism," *Modern Age* 49, no. 3 (Summer 2007): 223–32.

95   Gottfried, *After Liberalism*.

96   John Stuart Mill, *On Liberty* (London: John W. Parker and Son, 1859).

97   Paul Gottfried, "Marx Was Not Woke," *Chronicles Magazine*, April 2023, https://chroniclesmagazine.org/view/marx-was-not-woke.

98   Hazony, *Conservatism*.

99   Douglas Blair, "Seeking Truth: Former Liberal James Lindsay Now Fights Critical Race Theory," The Daily Signal, February 23, 2022, https://www.dailysignal.com/2022/02/23/seeking-truth-former-liberal-james-lindsay-now-fights-critical-race-theory.

100   Gottfried, *After Liberalism*.

101   Bari Weiss, "Meet the Renegades of the Intellectual Dark Web," *New York Times*, May 8, 2018, https://www.nytimes.com/2018/05/08/opinion/intellectual-dark-web.html.

102   Helen Pluckrose and James Lindsay, *Cynical Theories: How Activist Scholarship Made Everything About Race, Gender, and Identity—and Why This Harms Everybody* (Durham, NC: Pitchstone Publishing, 2020).

103   Samuel P. Huntington, "Conservatism as an Ideology," *American Political Science Review* 51, no. 2 (June 1957): 454–73.

104   Russell Kirk, *The Conservative Mind: From Burke to Santayana* (Chicago: Henry Regnery Company, 1953).

105   Karl Mannheim, "Conservative Thought," in *Essays on Sociology and Social Psychology*, ed. and trans. Paul Kecskemeti (London: Routledge & Kegan Paul, 1953), 74–164.

106   Clinton Rossiter, *Conservatism in America: The Thankless Persuasion* (New York: Alfred A. Knopf, 1955).

107   Edmund Burke, *Reflections on the Revolution in France* (London: J. Dodsley, 1790).

108   Louis Hartz, *The Liberal Tradition in America: An Interpretation of American Political Thought Since the Revolution* (New York: Harcourt, Brace, 1955).

109   Alfred Cobban, *Edmund Burke and the Revolt Against the Eighteenth Century* (London: George Allen & Unwin, 1929).

110 Benjamin Disraeli, *Coningsby, or The New Generation* (London: Henry Colburn, 1844).

111 Rollin G. Osterweis, *Romanticism and Nationalism in the Old South* (New Haven, CT: Yale University Press, 1949).

112 Eugene D. Genovese, *Roll, Jordan, Roll: The World the Slaves Made* (New York: Pantheon Books, 1974).

113 Panajotis Kondylis, *Konservativismus: Geschichtlicher Gehalt und Untergang* (Stuttgart: Klett-Cotta, 1986).

114 James Burnham, *The Machiavellians: Defenders of Freedom* (New York: John Day, 1943).

115 E. Digby Baltzell, *Puritan Boston and Quaker Philadelphia: Two Protestant Ethics and the Spirit of Class Authority and Leadership* (New York: Free Press, 1979).

116 Barry Alan Shain, *The Myth of American Individualism: The Protestant Origins of American Political Thought* (Princeton, NJ: Princeton University Press, 1994); Willmoore Kendall and George W. Carey, *The Basic Symbols of the American Political Tradition* (Baton Rouge: Louisiana State University Press, 1970); Russell Kirk, *The Roots of American Order* (La Salle, IL: Open Court, 1974).

117 Paul Edward Gottfried, *Conservatism in America: Making Sense of the American Right* (New York: Palgrave Macmillan, 2007).

118 Gottfried, *After Liberalism*.

119 Paul Gottfried, "Of Opposite Minds: Maistre and Mill," *Chronicles Magazine*, November 2022, https://chroniclesmagazine.org/reviews/of-opposite-minds-maistre-and-mill.

120 Jeff Deist, "An Austrian Frame of Mind," *Chronicles Magazine*, January 2020, https://chroniclesmagazine.org/reviews/an-austrian-frame-of-mind.

121 Paul Gottfried, "What the Editors Are Reading: The *Politics*," *Chronicles Magazine*, November 23, 2020, https://chroniclesmagazine.org/web/what-the-editors-are-reading-the-politics.

122 Paul Gottfried, "Remembering Carl Schmitt," *Chronicles Magazine*, October 2023, https://chroniclesmagazine.org/remembering-the-right/remembering-carl-schmitt.

123 Edward Welsch, "The George Floyd Cover-Up," *Chronicles Magazine*, January 2024, https://chroniclesmagazine.org/editorials/the-george-floyd-cover-up.

124 Carl Schmitt, *The Nomos of the Earth in the International Law of the Jus Publicum Europaeum*, trans. G.L. Ulmen (New York: Telos Press, 2003), first published in German in 1950 as *Der Nomos der Erde im Völkerrecht des Jus Publicum Europaeum*.

125 Mark Lilla, "The Enemy of Liberalism," *New York Review of Books*, May 15, 1997.

126 Reinhard Mehring, *Carl Schmitt: Aufstieg und Fall* (Munich: C.H. Beck, 2009).

127 Carl Schmitt, *Dictatorship: From the Origin of the Modern Concept of Sovereignty to Proletarian Class Struggle*, trans. Michael Hoelzl and Graham Ward (Cambridge: Polity Press, 2014), first published in German in 1921 as *Die Diktatur. Von den Anfängen des modernen Souveränitätsgedankens bis zum proletarischen Klassenkampf*; Carl Schmitt, *Political Theology: Four Chapters on the Concept of Sovereignty*, trans. George Schwab (Chicago: University of Chicago Press, 2005), first published in German in 1922 as *Politische Theologie. Vier Kapitel zur Lehre von der Souveränität*; Carl Schmitt, *The Concept of the Political*, trans. George Schwab (Chicago: University of Chicago Press, 2007), first published in German in 1932 as *Der Begriff des Politischen*; Carl Schmitt, *Legality and Legitimacy*, trans. Jeffrey Seitzer (Durham, NC: Duke University Press, 2004), first published in German in 1932 as *Legalität und Legitimität*; and Carl Schmitt, *The Nomos of the Earth in the International Law of the Jus Publicum Europaeum*, trans. G.L. Ulmen (New York: Telos Press, 2003), first published in German in 1950 as *Der Nomos der Erde im Völkerrecht des Jus Publicum Europaeum*.

128 Walter Benjamin, "Critique of Violence," in *Reflections: Essays, Aphorisms, Autobiographical Writings*, ed. Peter Demetz, trans. Edmund Jephcott (New York: Harcourt Brace Jovanovich, 1978), 277–300.

129 Benjamin Disraeli, *Sybil, or The Two Nations* (London: Henry Colburn, 1845).

130 Emilio Gentile, *The Sacralization of Politics in Fascist Italy*, trans. Keith Botsford (Cambridge, MA: Harvard University Press, 1996).

131 Leszek Kołakowski, *Main Currents of Marxism: Its Rise, Growth, and Dissolution*, trans. P. S. Falla, 3 vols. (Oxford: Clarendon Press, 1978).

132 Carl Schmitt, *Political Theology: Four Chapters on the Concept of Sovereignty*, trans. George Schwab (Chicago: University of Chicago Press, 1985).

133 These "reflections" were dictated in the summer of 1973 and published as Eric Voegelin, *Autobiographical Reflections*, ed. Ellis Sandoz (Baton Rouge: Louisiana State University Press, 1989).

134 Carl Schmitt, *Political Theology II: The Myth of the Closure of Any Political Theology*, trans. Michael Hoelzl and Graham Ward (Cambridge: Polity Press, 2008).

135 Jack Trotter, "One Nation, Under Which God?," *Chronicles Magazine*, August 2021, https://chroniclesmagazine.org/view/one-nation-under-which-god/; Grant Havers, "The Flawed Attempt to Make a Religion for the Right," *Chronicles Magazine*, August 2021, https://chroniclesmagazine.org/view/the-flawed-attempt-to-make-a-religion-for-the-right.

136 Robert N. Bellah, "Civil Religion in America," *Daedalus* 96, no. 1 (Winter 1967): 1–21.

137 Walter A. McDougall, *Promised Land, Crusader State: The American Encounter with the World Since 1776* (Boston: Houghton Mifflin, 1997); Robert Nisbet, *The Quest for Community: A Study in the Ethics of Order and Freedom* (New York: Oxford University Press, 1953).

138 Mircea Eliade, *The Myth of the Eternal Return: Or, Cosmos and History*, trans. Willard R. Trask (Princeton, NJ: Princeton University Press, 1954).

139 Samuel Francis, "Our European Cousins," *Chronicles*, April 1991, https://chroniclesmagazine.org/reviews/our-european-cousins.

140 Srdja Trifkovic, "The Key to America's Pathologies," *Chronicles Magazine*, August 2021, https://chroniclesmagazine.org/columns/the-american-interest/the-key-to-americas-pathologies.

141 Carl Schmitt, *Political Romanticism*, trans. Guy Oakes (Cambridge, MA: MIT Press, 1986), first published in German in 1919 as *Politische Romantik*; Carl Schmitt, *Dictatorship: From the Origin of the Modern Concept of Sovereignty to Proletarian Class Struggle*, trans. Michael Hoelzl and Graham Ward (Cambridge: Polity Press, 2014), first published in German in 1921 as *Die Diktatur. Von den Anfängen des modernen Souveränitätsgedankens bis zum proletarischen Klassenkampf*; Carl Schmitt, *The Crisis of Parliamentary Democracy*, trans. Ellen Kennedy (Cambridge, MA: MIT Press, 1988), first published in German in 1923 as *Die geistesgeschichtliche Lage des heutigen Parlamentarismus*.

142 Carl Schmitt, *Political Theology: Four Chapters on the Concept of Sovereignty*, trans. George Schwab (Chicago: University of Chicago Press, 2005), first published in German in 1922 as *Politische Theologie. Vier Kapitel zur Lehre von der Souveränität*.

143 Carl Schmitt, *The Concept of the Political*, trans. George Schwab (Chicago: University of Chicago Press, 2007), first published in German in 1932 as *Der Begriff des Politischen*.

144 Carl Schmitt, *Legality and Legitimacy*, trans. Jeffrey Seitzer (Durham, NC: Duke University Press, 2004), first published in German in 1932 as *Legalität und Legitimität*.

145 Hugo von Hofmannsthal, *Jedermann: Das Spiel vom Sterben des reichen Mannes* (Berlin: S. Fischer, 1911).

146 Francis Fukuyama, "The End of History, 10 Years Later," *Wall Street Journal*, December 31, 1999.

147 Fred Siegel, "H. L. Mencken, Nietzsche's Disciple," *Weekly Standard*, January 30, 2002.

148 Arthur S. Link, *Wilson*, 5 vols. (Princeton, NJ: Princeton University Press, 1947–1965).

149 Richard M. Gamble, *The War for Righteousness: Progressive Christianity, the Great War, and the Rise of the Messianic Nation* (Wilmington, DE: ISI Books, 2003).

150 Bloom, *The Closing of the American Mind*.

151 Stéphane Giocanti, *Charles Maurras: Le chaos et l'ordre* (Paris: Flammarion, 2006).

152 Bloom, *The Closing of the American Mind*.

153 Charles Maurras, *Devant l'Allemagne éternelle, chronique d'une résistance* (Paris: Éditions de l'Homme Libre, 1937).

154 Charles Maurras, *L'Avenir de l'intelligence* (Paris: Nouvelle Librairie Nationale, 1905); Charles Maurras, *Dictionnaire politique et critique*, 5 vols. (Paris: Cité des Livres, 1931–1934); Charles Maurras, *Enquête sur la monarchie* (Paris: Nouvelle Librairie Nationale, 1900).

155   Patrick J. Buchanan, *Churchill, Hitler, and the "Unnecessary War": How Britain Lost Its Empire and the West Lost the World* (New York: Crown, 2008).

156   George F. Kennan, *American Diplomacy, 1900–1950* (Chicago: University of Chicago Press, 1951).

157   George F. Kennan, "The Resistance in Prussia," *New York Review of Books*, October 20, 1983.

158   "Was World War II 'The Good War'?," *American Conservative*, July 14, 2008.

159   Winston S. Churchill, *The Second World War*, 6 vols. (Boston: Houghton Mifflin, 1948–1953).

160   Fritz Stern, *The Politics of Cultural Despair: A Study in the Rise of the Germanic Ideology* (Berkeley: University of California Press, 1961).

161   Richard M. Gamble, *The War for Righteousness: Progressive Christianity, the Great War, and the Rise of the Messianic Nation* (Wilmington, DE: ISI Books, 2003).

162   Konrad Canis, *Der Weg in den Abgrund: Deutsche Außenpolitik 1902–1914* (Paderborn: Schöningh, 2011).

163   George F. Kennan, *The Fateful Alliance: France, Russia, and the Coming of the First World War* (New York: Pantheon Books, 1984); Sean McMeekin, *The Russian Origins of the First World War* (Cambridge, MA: Belknap Press, 2011).

164   Fritz Fischer, *Griff nach der Weltmacht: Die Kriegszielpolitik des kaiserlichen Deutschland 1914/18* (Düsseldorf: Droste, 1961), published in English as Fritz Fischer, *Germany's Aims in the First World War*, trans. C. A. Macartney (New York: W. W. Norton, 1967).

165   Niall Ferguson, *The Pity of War: Explaining World War I* (New York: Basic Books, 1999); Konrad Canis, *Der Weg in den Abgrund: Deutsche Außenpolitik 1902–1914* (Paderborn: Schöningh, 2011); Christopher Clark, *The Sleepwalkers: How Europe Went to War in 1914* (New York: Harper, 2013); Sean McMeekin, *The Russian Origins of the First World War* (Cambridge, MA: Belknap Press, 2013).

166   Klaus Hornung, *Alternativen zu Hitler: Wilhelm Groener* (Graz: Leopold Stocker Verlag, 2008).

167   Heinrich Brüning, *Memoiren 1918–1934* (Stuttgart: Deutsche Verlags-Anstalt, 1970).

168   Jennifer Popowycz, "Prelude to the Warsaw Uprising: Operation Tempest," National WWII Museum, August 23, 2021, https://www.nationalww2museum.org/war/articles/operation-tempest-eastern-front.

169   George H. Janczewski, "The Origin of the Lublin Government," *Slavonic and East European Review* 50, no. 120 (1972): 410–33, http://www.jstor.org/stable/4206573.

170   R. J. Rummel, "Statistics of Democide: Chapter 9," University of Hawaii, accessed March 3, 2025, https://hawaii.edu/powerkills/SOD.CHAP9.HTM.

171   John Lukacs, *The Hitler of History* (New York: Alfred A. Knopf, 1997).

172   A. J. P. Taylor, *The Course of German History: A Survey of the Development of Germany Since 1815* (London: Hamish Hamilton, 1945).

173 Rainer Zitelmann, *Hitler: Selbstverständnis eines Revolutionärs* (Stuttgart: Klett-Cotta, 1987).

174 Theodor W. Adorno, Else Frenkel-Brunswik, Daniel J. Levinson, and R. Nevitt Sanford, *The Authoritarian Personality* (New York: Harper & Brothers, 1950).

175 Brigitte Hamann, *Hitler's Vienna: A Portrait of the Tyrant as a Young Man*, trans. Thomas Thornton (New York: Oxford University Press, 1999), first published in German in 1996 as *Hitlers Wien. Lehrjahre eines Diktators*.

176 Ralf Georg Reuth, *Hitlers Judenhass: Klischee und Wirklichkeit* (Munich: Piper, 2009).

177 Joachim Fest, *Hitler*, trans. Richard and Clara Winston (New York: Harcourt Brace Jovanovich, 1974), first published in German in 1973 as *Hitler: Eine Biographie*.

178 Adolf Hitler, *Mein Kampf*, trans. Ralph Manheim (Boston: Houghton Mifflin, 1943).

179 Fritz Fischer, *Griff nach der Weltmacht: Die Kriegszielpolitik des kaiserlichen Deutschland 1914/18* (Düsseldorf: Droste, 1961), published in English as Fritz Fischer, *Germany's Aims in the First World War*, trans. C. A. Macartney (New York: W. W. Norton, 1967).

180 Niall Ferguson, *The Pity of War: Explaining World War I* (New York: Basic Books, 1999).

181 Klaus Grosse Kracht, "Fritz Fischer und seine Nachkriegskarriere," *Zeitschrift für Neuere Theologie-Geschichte* 10 (2003): 145–78.

182 Claus Nordbruch, *Der Verfassungsschutz. Organisation, Spitzel, Skandale* (Tübingen Hohenrain, 1999).

183 Claus Nordbruch, *Sind Gedanken noch frei? Zensur in Deutschland* (Munich: Universitas, 1999).

184 Ibid., dedicatory page.

185 Ibid., 152–53.

186 Josef Schüsslburner, *Demokratie-Sonderweg Bundesrepublik* (Fulda: Lindenblatt Media Verlag, 2004).

187 For evidence of Germany's parlous civil liberties situation, see Paul Gottfried, *Multikulturalismus. Unterwegs zum manipulativen Staat* (Graz: Ares Verlag, 2004), 67–69, 130–38.

188 See Friedbert Pflüger, *Weckruf für Europa* (Bonn: Bouvier Verlag, 2002).

189 *Die Zeit*, Sept. 12, 2004.

190 Tony Judt, *Postwar: A History of Europe Since 1945* (New York: Penguin Press, 2005).

191 Tony Judt, *A Grand Illusion: An Essay on Europe* (New York: Penguin Books, 1996). See also his essays for the *New York Review of Books*.

192 Caspar von Schrenck-Notzing, *Charakterwäsche: Die Reeducation der Deutschen und ihre bleibenden Auswirkungen*, enlarged ed. (Graz: Leopold Stocker Verlag, 2004).

193 Frank Bösch, *Die Adenauer-CDU. Gründung, Aufstieg und Krise einer Erfolgspartei, 1945–1969* (Munich: Deutsche Verlagsanstalt, 2001) may be the definitive study of this extraordinary statesman.

194 Franz Walter, *SPD: Vom Proletariat zur Neuen Mitte* (Berlin: Alexander Fest Verlag, 2002), 132.

195 Ralf Dahrendorf, *Die Krisen der Demokratie: Ein Gespräch Antonio mit Polito*, trans. Rita Seuss (Munich: C.H. Beck Verlag, 2002).

196 See Zachary Shore, "Can the West Win Muslim Hearts and Minds?," *Orbis* 49, no. 3 (Summer 2005): 475–90.

197 Gianfranco Miglio, *Una Repubblica migliore per gli italiani* (Milan: Giuffrè, 1983).

198 See Gianfranco Miglio, *Una costituzione per i prossimi trent'anni* (Laterza, 1990).

199 Marek Cichocki and Claus Leggewie, "Debate on European Memory," *Courrier International*, December 21, 2006.

200 Paul Gottfried, *The Strange Death of Marxism: The European Left in the New Millennium* (Columbia: University of Missouri Press, 2005).

201 Rolf Peter Sieferle, *Finis Germania* (Schnellroda: Antaios, 2017).

202 Martin Wagener, *Kulturkampf um das Volk: Der Verfassungsschutz und die nationale Identität der Deutschen* (Schnellroda: Antaios, 2021).

203 Antonia Grunenberg, *Antifaschismus: ein deutscher Mythos* (Reinbek: Rowohlt, 1993).

204 Jim Wallis, *The Great Awakening: Reviving Faith & Politics in a Post-Religious Right America*, foreword by Jimmy Carter (New York: HarperOne, 2008), ix–xii.

205 Perhaps the most explosive attack on neoconservative foreign policy from the Right is Claes G. Ryn's *America the Virtuous: The Crisis of Democracy and the Quest for Empire* (New York: Routledge, 2003). See also James Kurth's "The Neoconservatives Are History," *Orbis* 50 (Autumn 2006): 756–69; Paul Gottfried, "The Invincible Wilsonian Matrix" *Orbis* 51 (Spring 2007): 239–50; and more generally Andrew J. Bacevich, *The Limits of Power: The End of American Exceptionalism* (New York: Macmillan, 2008).

206 On the Anglosphere concept, see James C. Bennett, *The Anglosphere Challenge: Why the English-Speaking Nations Will Lead the Way in the Twenty-First Century* (Rowman & Littlefield, 2003); Andrew Roberts, *A History of the English-Speaking People Since 1900* (New York: Harper-Collins, 2007); and Robert Stove's blistering attack on Robert's prejudices and factual inaccuracies, "Bush Court Historian," *American Conservative*, September 22, 2008.

207 Paul Johnson, *Modern Times: The World from the Twenties to the Eighties* (New York: Harper and Row, 1983), 106; and Robert Kagan's equally empty salute to Fischer in *On the Origin of War and the Preservation of Peace* (New York: Doubleday, 1995), 169–73.

208 See Lee Congdon's *George Kennan: A Writing Life* (Wilmington, DE: ISI Books, 2008); Walter Isaacson and Evan Thomas, *The Wise Men: Six Friends and the World They Made* (New York: Simon and Schuster, 1986).

209 Among the works that offer this by now revisionist view of German and American involvement in the First World War are Thomas Fleming, *The Illusion of Victory: America in World War I* (New York: Basic Books, 2003); Walter Karp, *The Politics of War* (New York: Harper Collins, 1980); and the compilation of essays in H. W. Koch, ed., *The Origins of the First World War: Great Power Rivalries and German War Aims*, 2nd. ed. (London: Macmillan, 1984). See also the powerful essay by Ralph Raico, "World War One: Turning Point," in John V. Denson, ed., *The Costs of War: America's Pyrrhic Victories* (Brunswick, NJ: Transaction Publishers, 1999), 203–47; and Paul Gottfried, "Kriegsschuld im Ersten Weltkrieg Der letzte Kaiser im Wandel der Zeitgeschichte," *Neue Ordnung* (Fall 2009): 24–29.

210 Two books that deal with the costs of the war are Niall Ferguson, *The Pity of War: Explaining World War I* (New York: Basic Books, 1999); Hunt Tooley, *The Western Front: Battleground and Home Front in the First World War* (London: Palgrave Macmillan, 2003), especially 1–40.

211 On the sweeping nature of the British blockade and the use made of it even after hostilities had ended, see C. Paul Vincent, *The Politics of Hunger: The Allied Blockade of Germany, 1915–1919* (Athens: Ohio University Press, 1985).

212 Richard Gamble, *The War for Righteousness: Progressive Christianity, the Great War, and the Rise of the Messianic Nation* (Wilmington, DE: ISI Books, 2003), 111–208.

213 Heinz Gollwitzer, *Weltpolitik und deutsche Geschichte* (Vandenhoeck und Ruprecht, 2008), 286–301 and especially 327–31.

214 John Lukacs, *Outgrowing Democracy: A History of the United States in the Twentieth Century* (New York: Doubleday and Company, 1984), 223–27. The elitist character of the pro-British, interventionist side in World War I is famously highlighted in Henry F. May's well-known work *The End of American Innocence: A Study of the First Years of Our Own Time, 1912–1917* (New York: Alfred A Knopf, 1959), especially 390–97.

215 Eric P. Kaufmann, *The Rise and Fall of Anglo-America* (Harvard University Press, 2004).

216 Congressional Proceedings for the Senate Judiciary Committee convened to discuss the 1965 Immigration and Nationality Act Amendments. The author is grateful to independent researcher Lawrence Auster, who retrieved this quotation from stored documents in the New York Public Library, Main Branch, 42nd Street, New York, New York.

217 Justus D. Doenecke, *Storm on the Horizon: The Challenge to American Intervention, 1939–1941* (Rowman & Littlefield, 2003).

218 On the pro-interventionists and their backgrounds, see Mark Lincoln Chadwin, *The Hawks of World War II* (University of North Carolina Press, 1968); Stephen J. Sniegoski's unpublished dissertation "The Wellspring of American World War II Intervention," University of Maryland, 1977; and Sniegoski's summary of the argument of his dissertation "Decline and Renewal: American World War II Interventionists," *World and I*, February 1987.

219 Oswald Spengler, *The Hour of Decision* (New York: Alfred A. Knopf, 1934), 100–5.

220 Perry Miller, *Errand into the Wilderness* (Cambridge, MA: Harvard University Press, 1956), 10–15.

221 Dominique Bourel and Jacques Le Rider, eds., *De Sils-Maria à Jérusalem: Nietzsche et le judaïsme* (Paris: Cerf, 1991), 10–15.

222 Otto Weininger, *Sex and Character* (London: Heinemann, 1906), 300–5.

223 Paul Breines, *Tough Jews: Political Fantasies and the Moral Dilemma of American Jewry* (New York: Basic Books, 1990), 50–55.

224 Theodor W. Adorno, Else Frenkel-Brunswik, Daniel J. Levinson, and R. Nevitt Sanford, *The Authoritarian Personality* (New York: Harper & Brothers, 1950), 20–25.

225 Elmer Berger, *The Jewish Dilemma* (New York: Devin-Adair, 1945), 10–15.

226 Charles Norris Cochrane, *Thucydides and the Science of History* (Oxford: Oxford University Press, 1929), 5–10.

227 James Burnham, *The Managerial Revolution* (New York: John Day, 1941), 20–25.

228 Peter L. Berger and Brigitte Berger, "Our Conservatism and Theirs," *Commentary*, October 1986, 40–45.

229 John B. Judis, "The Conservative Wars," *New Republic*, August 11, 1986, 15–18.

230 Paul Gottfried and Thomas Fleming, *The Conservative Movement*, 2nd ed. (New York: Twayne Publishers, 1993), 100–5.

Index